GOVERNMENT GUARANTEES TO FOREIGN INVESTORS

Government Guarantees
to Foreign Investors

A. A. FATOUROS

New York and London 1962
Columbia University Press

Copyright 1962 Columbia University Press
Library of Congress Catalog Card Number: 62-12873
Manufactured in the United States of America

Foreword

THE problems arising from private foreign investment in sovereign countries have been the subject of a growing flood of legal literature in recent years. Much of it reflects the general outlook of the country or background with which the writer is associated. International lawyers from the highly industrialized and capital-exporting countries of the North American continent and Western Europe will generally argue in favor of the so-called "minimum standard" and of absolute protection of private property rights, while representatives of the less-developed and capital-importing countries will favor the "equality of treatment" principle and stress the sovereign power of government to interfere with foreign property rights in the national interest.

The political and economic background of this controversy—although immensely important—is generally neglected by lawyers arguing these problems in terms of analytical jurisprudence, or as special pleaders for one or the other point of view. This alone would make Mr. Fatouros's study a welcome departure from the usual approach, for the introductory part surveys the economic background and the conflicting outlook of underdeveloped and developed countries as a necessary prerequisite of a meaningful legal study.

The bulk of this monograph is, however, devoted to an analysis in depth of the problems arising from the increasingly frequent agreements made between governments (usually of less-developed countries) and foreign investors. This entire field, which until recently would have been regarded as outside the province of public international law proper, is now increasingly acknowledged to be a new and vitally important aspect of the widening scope of international law. Can state promises to foreign investors be characterized as contractual in nature? To what extent can legal commitments, on the part of sovereign governments, be reconciled with their powers and responsibilities as national legislators? Can the theory of contracts of public law, as developed especially in French jurisprudence, be usefully applied to this type of transaction? Apart from these more general questions, Mr. Fatouros undertakes an analysis of the various forms and modalities by which states enter into arrangements with foreign investors, and of such important collateral aspects, as exchange restrictions, employment of foreign personnel, and the like. No less important is the detailed treatment of the problem of compensation in the case of interference with foreign property interests, a matter usually neglected or dealt with in general and dogmatic propositions. The chapter that analyzes the respective merits of *ad hoc* agreements, bilateral treaties and multilateral conventions on the treatment of foreign investments, shows full awareness of the political and economic as well as the legal aspects of this approach to the protection of private investment.

I believe that this monograph, which has grown out of a Columbia doctoral thesis, is, not only in the scope of the analysis and in the use of comparative materials but also in the understanding of the wider non-legal aspects of this highly controversial field, and, last not least, in the scholarly detachment and balanced treatment of the subject matter, a major contribution to the science of international law. It is extremely important that the problem of state promises to foreign investors should be lifted out of the partisan contest which has characterized so much of the debate. This, Mr.

Fatouros has done. I am happy to present his study under the auspices of Columbia's International Legal Studies Program.

New York
February, 1962

WOLFGANG G. FRIEDMANN
Professor of Law, and
Director, International Legal Research
Columbia University School of Law

Preface

THE first draft of this study was written in 1956–1957, during my years of residence at Columbia University, and was submitted as a doctoral dissertation to the University's School of Law. Since then, it has been amended innumerable times and completely re-written twice, once in the years 1958 to 1960 during my stay in Athens, Greece, and then again in 1960–1961 in London, Canada. In its present form, it has been accepted by the School of Law of Columbia University in partial fulfillment of the requirements for the degree of Doctor in the Science of Law.

The book was continuously brought up to date in these successive drafts and even after it had gone to the publishers, who showed great patience on this as on many other points. It was not possible, however, to keep abreast of developments which, in the legislative as well as the scholarly field, have been rapid and numerous in the past few years. The literature on the subject has more than doubled since the first draft; it still was not possible to make use of some of the most recent studies, such as Dr. Gillian White's book on the nationalization of foreign property which reached the author only after the present book had gone to the printers. Whenever possible, reference to such recent material has been included in the footnotes and in the bibliography. Developments were equally (if not more) difficult to keep up with in the legislative field. Investment laws are being passed and repealed at a fast rate and information about them is usually slow in reaching academic libraries. I am therefore aware that some of the statutes referred to in this book are not any more in force and that new laws have been passed. This book is not intended, however, to provide last minute information on the laws in force; it describes trends and tendencies and only uses the provisions of investment laws as illustrations.

A related point, on which some explanation may be needed, is the absence of any detailed study of the actual economic effects of the guarantees here discussed. However, less than a decade has passed since most guarantees have come into effect and it is yet too early for any definite conclusions as to their success or failure. Despite the difficulties it involves, such a study is certainly necessary and it is to be hoped that it will be undertaken as soon as more data will be available.

I wish to express my deepest gratitude to Professor Wolfgang G. Friedmann, Director of International Legal Research at Columbia University. It is no mere figure of speech to state that without him this book would not have been written. He made the writing of it possible by his friendly interest, his encouragement and his assistance in academic as well as professional matters. He has read all three successive drafts of the book and has commented and advised in great detail. I have thus profited greatly from his broad knowledge and profound understanding of diverse legal systems and of international relations.

I should also like to express my gratitude to Professor Richard C. Pugh, of the Columbia University School of Law, who has read the entire second draft of this book and made many editorial and other suggestions, most of which have been embodied in the final draft, and to Professor John Koulis, of the Faculty of Law of the University of Athens, who read the draft of Part I and by his detailed commentary made possible the avoidance of many a mistake or half-truth on economic matters. I have also greatly profited from the comments of the other members of the Law School Committee on my dissertation, Professor (now Judge) Philip C. Jessup, Professor Oliver J. Lissitzyn, and Professor Robert Hamilton, as well as from the discussions and correspondence (not all directly related to this book) with Professors Harry W. Jones and Richard N. Gardner of Columbia University School of Law and Professor Kenneth S. Carlston of the University of Illinois College of Law. Many others, teachers, friends and students have assisted me, directly or indirectly, by their advice, suggestions, or comments. To all of them I owe my sincerest thanks. Needless to state that no one but myself is responsible for the book's failures.

And no expression of gratitude can repay the debt I owe to my teachers, the professors of law and economics at the universities of Athens and Columbia. It was they who first aroused and then developed my interest in the relationship between international law and international economics which lies at the foundation of the present study.

My two years at Columbia University were made possible by successive Ford Foundation fellowships in international law, under the University's International Legal Research program. This program also assisted materially in the expenses of publication of the present book.

A summary treatment of the problems here discussed has been published as chapter 41 of the symposium on *Legal Aspects of Foreign Investment*, edited by Professors W. G. Friedmann and R. C. Pugh. Parts of chapters 5 and 6 have been printed in the *University of Toronto Law Journal* and an enlarged version of chapter 3 in the University of Western Ontario's annual *Current Law and Social Problems*. The copyright holders have kindly permitted the reprinting of the material.

I also wish to thank Professors L. B. Sohn and R. R. Baxter and the President and Fellows of Harvard College for permission to reproduce parts of the latest Harvard Law School "Draft Convention on the International Responsibility of States for Injuries to Aliens" and Mr. H. Walker, Jr., and the *Minnesota Law Review* for permission to reproduce the outline on p. 95.

Without the unfailing help of the staffs of the libraries where I have worked this book could never have been written. I should like, therefore, to thank most sincerely the members of the staff of the International Law Library of the Columbia University School of Law in New York, the Hellenic Institute of International and Foreign Law in Athens, and the Law Library of the University of Western Ontario, in London, Canada. I also wish to thank the secretarial staff of the University of Western Ontario Faculty of Law for their patience and cooperation.

I have been very fortunate indeed in my publishers. The intelligent and helpful suggestions of their editorial staff have contributed greatly in eliminating obscurities and inconsistencies from the text. Their other departments have shown not only exceptional skill but also great patience and understanding. To all of them I wish to express my most sincere thanks.

My final acknowledgments and the expression of my gratitude go to those closest to me who have assisted and encouraged me through all the years before, during and after the writing of the present book: my parents, to whom this book is dedicated, my brother, and my wife. Above everything else, their love, kindness and patience have made this book possible.

A. A. F.

London, Canada
December, 1961

Contents

Note on Citations

THE method of citation used in this study is the one usually found in legal texts. The volume number of a periodical precedes the title; the number of the page where the article begins follows the title, omitting the sign "p." or "pp." The page number to which particular reference is intended follows the number of the first page, separated by a comma. E.g., 25 *Foreign Affairs* 612, 627 (1947) means: *Foreign Affairs*, vol. 25, the article beginning at p. 612, particular reference to p. 627.

Similar rules apply to references to books. E.g., 2 Hyde, *International Law* 1717, means C. C. Hyde, *International Law*, vol. 2, p. 1717.

Titles of periodicals or books which have in no way been abbreviated or where only a subtitle is omitted have not been included in the Key to Abbreviations.

Key to Abbreviations

Am. Bar Ass'n J.	*American Bar Association Journal*
Am. Econ. Rev.	*American Economic Review*
Am. Econ. Rev. Proc.	*American Economic Review. Papers and Proceedings* (Annual Supplement).
Am. J. Comp. L.	*American Journal of Comparative Law*
Am. J. Int'l L.	*American Journal of International Law*
Am. J. Int'l L. Sp. Supp.	*American Journal of International Law. Special Supplement.*
Am. J. Int'l L. Supp.	*American Journal of International Law. Supplement.*
Am. Soc. Int'l L. Proc.	*American Society of International Law. Proceedings.*
Annuaire Français Dr. Int'l.	*Annuaire Français de Droit International.*
Annual Digest	*Annual Digest and Reports of Public International Law Cases.*
Arbitr. J.	*Arbitration Journal*
Bauer and Yamey, *Economics*	P. T. Bauer and Basil S. Yamey, *The Economics of Underdeveloped Countries* (Cambridge, 1957).
Bogota Agreement	*Economic Agreement of Bogota* Pan American Union, Law and Treaty Series No. 25 (1948).
Boston U. L. Rev.	*Boston University Law Review*
Brand, *Struggle*	W. Brand, *The Struggle for a Higher Standard of Living—The Problem of the Underdeveloped Countries* (Glencoe, Ill. and The Hague, 1958).
Brit. Yb. Int'l L.	*British Yearbook of International Law*
Brooklyn L. Rev.	*Brooklyn Law Review*
Buchanan and Ellis, *Approaches*	Norman S. Buchanan and Howard S. Ellis, *Approaches to Economic Development* (New York, 1955).

Cambridge L. J.	*Cambridge Law Journal*
Can. Bar Rev.	*Canadian Bar Review*
Catholic U. L. Rev.	*Catholic University Law Review*
Cavaré, *Droits contractuels*	Louis Cavaré, *La protection des droits contractuels reconnus par les Etats à des étrangers à l'exception des emprunts* (Barcelona, 1956).
Colum. L. Rev.	*Columbia Law Review*
Cornell L. Qu.	*Cornell Law Quarterly*
Dep't State Bull.	[United States] *Department of State Bulletin*
Econ. Hist. Rev.	*Economic History Review*
Econ. J.	*Economic Journal*
Fed. Bar J.	*Federal Bar Journal*
Fordham L. Rev.	*Fordham Law Review*
Friedman, *Expropriation*	S. Friedman, *Expropriation in International Law* (London, 1953).
Georgetown L. J.	*Georgetown Law Journal*
Geo. Wash. L. Rev.	*George Washington Law Review*
Grotius Soc. Transactions	*Transactions of the Grotius Society*
Hackworth, *Digest*	Green Hackworth, *Digest of International Law* 7 vols. (Washington, D.C., 1940–1943).
Hague Recueil	Académie de Droit International (The Hague), *Recueil des Cours.*
Harv. L. Rev.	*Harvard Law Review.*
Havana Charter	Charter for an International Trade Organization, in United Nations Conference on Trade and Employment, *Final Act and Related Documents* (Havana, 1948).
Hyde, *International Law*	Charles Cheney Hyde, *International Law Chiefly as Interpreted and Applied by the United States* 3 vols. (2d rev. ed. Boston, 1945).
ICC Code	International Chamber of Commerce, *Fair Treatment for Foreign Investments. International Code* (I.C.C. Brochure 129, Paris, 1949).
I.C.J. Pleadings	International Court of Justice, *Pleadings, Oral Arguments, Documents.*
I.C.J. Reports	*Reports of Judgments, Advisory Opinions and Orders of the International Court of Justice.*
IMF Staff Papers	International Monetary Fund, *Staff Papers*

Int'l Affairs (Moscow)	*International Affairs* (Moscow, U.S.S.R.)
Int'l & Comp. L. Qu.	*International and Comparative Law Quarterly*
Int'l Conc.	*International Conciliation*
Int'l Development Rev.	*International Development Review.*
Int'l L. Qu.	*International Law Quarterly*
Int'l L. Rep.	*International Law Reports*
Int'l Organization	*International Organization*
Int'l Soc. Sc. Bull.	[UNESCO] *International Social Science Bulletin*
J. Bus. L.	*Journal of Business Law*
J. Droit Int'l (Clunet)	*Journal du Droit International* (Clunet).
J. Econ. History	*Journal of Economic History*
J. Econ. History Supp.	*Journal of Economic History Supplement*
Jewish Yb. Int'l L.	*Jewish Yearbook of International Law*
J. Farm Econ.	*Journal of Farm Economics*
J. Law & Econ.	*Journal of Law and Economics*
J. Legal Ed.	*Journal of Legal Education*
J. of Politics	*Journal of Politics*
J. Pol. Econ.	*Journal of Political Economy*
J. Pub. L.	*Journal of Public Law*
Katzarov, *Nationalisation*	Konst. Katzarov, *Théorie de la Nationalisation* (Neuchatel, 1960).
Law & Contemp. Problems	*Law and Contemporary Problems*
Legal Aspects	*Legal Aspects of Foreign Investment* (Wolfgang G. Friedmann and Richard C. Pugh. ed., Boston, 1959).
L. Qu. Rev.	*Law Quarterly Review.*
McGill L. J.	*McGill Law Journal*
Michigan L. Rev.	*Michigan Law Review*
Minn. L. Rev.	*Minnesota Law Review*
Mitchell, *Contracts*	J. D. B. Mitchell, *The Contracts of Public Authorities. A Comparative Study* (London, 1954).
Moore, *Digest*	John Bassett Moore, *A Digest of International Law* 8 vols. (Washington, 1906).
Moore, *International Arbitrations*	John Bassett Moore, *History and Digest of the International Arbitrations to which the United States has been a Party* 6 vols. (Washington, 1898).
Myrdal, *Economic Theory*	Gunnar Myrdal, *Economic Theory and Underdeveloped Regions* (London, 1957).

Ned. Tijdschrift voor Int. Recht	*Nederlands Tijdschrift voor International Recht*
New Zealand L. J.	*New Zealand Law Journal*
1959 Draft Convention	"Draft Convention on Investments Abroad," in 9 *J. Pub. L.* 116 (1960).
1957 Draft Convention	*International Convention for the Mutual Protection of Private Property Rights in Foreign Countries.* Draft Presented by the Gesellschaft zur Förderung des Schutzes von Auslandsinvestitionen e. V. (mimeo., Cologne, November 1957).
Nurkse, *Problems*	Ragnar Nurkse, *Problems of Capital Formation in Underdeveloped Countries* (Oxford, 1953).
Nw. U. L. Rev.	*Northwestern University Law Review*
N.Y.U. L. Qu. Rev.	*New York University Law Quarterly Review*
N.Y.U. L. Rev.	*New York University Law Review*
Ohio St. L. J.	*Ohio State Law Journal*
Oxford Econ. Papers	*Oxford Economic Papers*
P.C.I.J., Publ. Ser.	Permanent Court of International Justice, Publication Series. . . .
Pol. Qu.	*Political Quarterly*
Pol. Sc. Qu.	*Political Science Quarterly*
Qu. J. Econ.	*Quarterly Journal of Economics*
Record of N.Y.C. Bar Ass'n	*Record of the New York City Bar Association*
Recueil T.A.M.	*Recueil des décisions des Tribunaux Arbitraux Mixtes*
Rev. Critique Dr. Int. Privé	*Revue Critique de Droit International Privé*
Rev. Dr. Int. Legisl. Comp.	*Revue de Droit International et de Legislation Comparée*
Rev. Dr. Int'l Moyen-Orient	*Revue de Droit International pour le Moyen-Orient*
Rev. Droit Int'l	*Revue de Droit International* (A. LaPradelle).
Rev. Econ. & Stat.	*Review of Economics and Statistics*
Rev. Egypt. Droit Int'l	*Revue Egyptienne de Droit International*
Rev. Gén. Dr. Int'l Public	*Revue Générale de Droit International Public*
Rev. Hell. Dr. Int'l	*Revue Hellénique de Droit International*
Stanford L. Rev.	*Stanford Law Review*
Texas L. Rev.	*Texas Law Review*

T.I.A.S.	[United States] Treaties and Other International Agreements Series
U. Chicago L. Rev.	*University of Chicago Law Review*
U. Malaya L. Rev.	*University of Malaya Law Review*
U. Miami L. Rev.	*University of Miami Law Review*
UN *Flow 1956*	United Nations, Department of Economic and Social Affairs, *The International Flow of Private Capital 1956–1958* (New York, 1959).
UN *Flow 1946*	United Nations, Department of Economic Affairs, *The International Flow of Private Capital 1946–1952* (New York, 1954).
UN *Foreign Capital*	United Nations, Department of Economic and Social Affairs, *Foreign Capital in Latin America* (New York, 1955).
UN *Investment Laws*	United Nations, Department of Economic Affairs, *Foreign Investment Laws and Regulations of the Countries of Asia and the Far East* (New York, 1951).
UN *Measures*	United Nations, Department of Economic Affairs, *Measures for the Economic Development of Under-Developed Countries.* Report by a Group of Experts (New York, 1951).
UN *Processes*	United Nations, Department of Economic and Social Affairs, *Processes and Problems of Industrialization in Under-Developed Countries* (New York, 1955).
UN RIAA	United Nations Reports of International Arbitral Awards
U. Pa. L. Rev.	*University of Pennsylvania Law Review*
U.S.T.	United States Treaties series
Va. L. Rev.	*Virginia Law Review*
Wayne L. Rev.	*Wayne Law Review*
Whiteman, *Damages*	Marjorie M. Whiteman, *Damages in International Law* 3 vols. (Washington, 1937–1943).
Whitman, *The Guaranty Program*	Marina von Neumann Whitman, *The United States Investment Guaranty Program and Private Foreign Investment* (Princeton Studies in International Finance, No. 9, Princeton, 1959).

Wilson, *Treaties*

Robert R. Wilson, *United States Commercial Treaties and International Law* (New Orleans, 1960).

Wisconsin L. Rev.

Wisconsin Law Review

Wortley, *Expropriation*

B. A. Wortley, *Expropriation in Public International Law* (Cambridge, 1959)

Yale L. J.

Yale Law Journal

Yb. World Affairs

Yearbook of World Affairs

GOVERNMENT GUARANTEES
TO FOREIGN INVESTORS

I

Introduction

THE importance attributed to economic development is certainly
one of the major phenomena of our times. The term itself refers
to a process of economic change, as manifested in the increase of
a country's national income, a high degree of productivity, and a
general increase in the welfare of its inhabitants.[1] Within the frame
of reference of international relations, economic development, as
a relative term, denotes the existence today of two categories of
states. One consists of the so-called "developed" countries, which
are industrially advanced and have a high level of technology and
productivity and a high national income per capita; the other is
composed of the "underdeveloped" countries, which are primarily
agricultural and in which productivity, per capita national income,
and level of technical achievement are low.[2] Of the people living

[1] A country's national income per capita provides the handiest criterion of eco-
nomic development; cf. Leibenstein, *Economic Backwardness and Economic
Growth* 7-14 (1957); Brand, *The Struggle for a Higher Standard of Living* (here-
inafter cited Brand, *Struggle*) 18-25 (1958). But see, on its shortcomings, Viner,
International Trade and Economic Development 99 *et seq.* (1953); Bauer and
Yamey, *The Economics of Underdeveloped Countries* (hereinafter cited Bauer
and Yamey, *Economics*) 16 *et seq.* (1957). And cf. more generally, Buchanan and
Ellis, *Approaches to Economic Development* (hereinafter cited Buchanan and
Ellis, *Approaches*) 3-22 (1955); Meier and Baldwin, *Economic Development* 2
et seq. (1957); Higgins, *Economic Development* 3-24 (1959); Kuznets, *Six Lectures
on Economic Growth* 13-19 (1959).

[2] Several authors distinguish three, instead of two, categories of countries: developed, semideveloped, and underdeveloped; cf., e.g., Staley, *The Future of Underdeveloped Countries* 16-17 and *passim* (1954). To some extent, this is only a
matter of convenience in classification; though probably inadequate for advanced
economic analysis, the twofold distinction seems sufficient for the present limited

today on earth, more than two thirds are inhabitants of countries belonging to the second category. Since there is great diversity between countries in their degree and form of development, the position of certain countries in one or the other of these categories may be open to question. But there is little possibility for doubt or controversy in the great majority of cases. In 1955, the United States had an annual per capita national income of $1864, and Canada one of $1296, compared to $955 in Australia, $778 in the United Kingdom, $740 in Norway, $730 in France, and $508 in West Germany. That same year, Greece had an annual national income per capita of $204, Portugal $175, Egypt $122, Peru $115, India $64, and Burma $46.[3]

The existence of inequalities, on a national or international scale, is of course nothing new. Rich and poor countries have always existed in the world. The new element in the present situation is that the peoples in the underdeveloped countries of today have become acutely conscious of their condition and at the same time have acquired the political means to change it. Even the adoption by all concerned of the expression "underdeveloped countries," instead of the earlier one of "backward countries," implies, as has been aptly observed, a change in attitude, a desire for progress.[4]

On the part of the developed countries, this change of attitude should be attributed in part to economic considerations, since in

---

purposes. According to a particular theory of economic growth, however, the threefold classification corresponds to the three stages through which every developing economy must pass; cf. Rostow, "The Take-Off into Self-Sustained Growth," 66 *Econ. J.* 25 (1956) reprinted in *The Economics of Underdevelopment* 154 (Agarwala and Singh ed., 1958); Rostow, "The Stages of Economic Growth," 12 *Econ. Hist. Rev.* 1 (1959); and the more recent and detailed Rostow, *The Stages of Economic Growth: A Non-Communist Manifesto* (1960).

[3] Studenski, *The Income of Nations* 229–30 (table 16–3) (1958) (figures for 1955 or nearest year). Note, however, that Japan, with an annual per capita national income of $184, is usually included among the developed countries, while Greece, with $204, and Mexico, with $192, are as a rule considered underdeveloped.

[4] Myrdal, *Economic Theory and Underdeveloped Regions* (hereinafter cited Myrdal, *Economic Theory*) 7–8 (1957). This is the title of the English edition of a book published in the United States under the title *Rich Lands and Poor*. The English edition has been used throughout this study.

the long run they stand to gain from the backward countries' development. In the short run, however, this process involves certain hardships, and it makes necessary the sacrifice of existing economic advantage. Accordingly, the advanced countries' favorable attitude toward the development of the now underdeveloped areas should be attributed in large part to political reasons.[5] It is an indirect effect of the current attitude and position of the underdeveloped countries. Parallel with and in addition to political considerations, however, an unmistakable moral element is also apparent, whose importance should not be underestimated. The desire for economic development is itself an expression of Western ideals, and the Western countries cannot consistently ignore or fight it.[6]

As regards the underdeveloped countries, their drive toward economic development is closely related to their movement toward national political independence. These are different manifestations of the same force, and they cannot be properly understood unless viewed in conjunction.[7] At first glance, the latter movement seems considerably more advanced than the former, but the real difference is not as wide as it looks. The exaggerated impression is due to the formal character of the usual criteria of national political independence (declarations, recognition by other states, and the like). In measuring economic development, only substantive criteria are used. If the substance of the matter were considered in both cases,

[5] Cf., e.g., Stassen, "The Case for Private Investment Abroad," 32 *Foreign Affairs* 402 (1954); Viner, "America's Aims and the Progress of Underdeveloped Areas," in *The Progress of Underdeveloped Areas* 175 (Hoselitz ed., 1952); Elliot *et al.*, *The Political Economy of American Foreign Policy* 222 *et seq.* (1955); Committee for Economic Development, *Economic Development Abroad and the Role of American Foreign Investment* 3, 5–8 (1956); Mason, "Competitive Coexistence and Economic Development in Asia," in American Assembly, *International Stability and Progress* 59, 77–85 (1957); Thorp, "American Interest in Asian Development," in Kirk, Brown *et al.*, *The Changing Environment of International Relations* 117 (1956). And see also Myrdal, *An International Economy* 124 *et seq.* (1956); Myrdal, *Beyond the Welfare State* 263 *et seq.* (1960).

[6] See the studies cited in the preceding note and cf. Myrdal's thoughtful remarks in his *An International Economy* 158 *et seq.* (1956) and *Economic Theory* 125–27 (1957).

[7] Cf., e.g., Myrdal's treatment of the questions of national integration and economic development in his *An International Economy* 149–221 (1956).

the difference between the achievements of the two movements would be less marked.

Despite the adjective used, economic development cannot be understood as solely economic in character. It is "but one aspect of the general problem of social change" in modern society,[8] and, at its most basic, it is a matter of attitude.[9] The complex interplay of non-economic factors can by no means be ignored.[10] Underdevelopment itself is not a historical accident but the result of certain concrete social, cultural, and political as well as economic conditions.[11] For economic development to be possible, these conditions must change. It is true that strict adherence to the Western pattern of economic development is neither logically necessary nor historically possible. It is increasingly accepted that the underdeveloped countries of today will have to follow ways and methods of development importantly different from those followed by the Western countries.[12] Still, change is unavoidable as well as necessary. The existing

[8] Furtado, "Capital Formation and Economic Development," 4 *Int'l Econ. Papers* 124 (1954) reprinted in *The Economics of Underdevelopment* 308, 315 (Agarwala and Singh ed., 1958). See also Meier and Baldwin, *op. cit. supra* note 1, 118–24.

[9] "A strong and effectively expressed desire for change" is the basic element of economic development, according to Professor Galbraith, "Conditions for Economic Change in Underdeveloped Countries," 33 *J. Farm Econ.* 689, 694 (1951). Another contemporary scholar considers economic growth as "almost a spiritual problem"; McCord Wright, "Closing the Production Gap," in *Private Investment: The Key to International Industrial Development* 39, 43 (Daniel ed., 1957).

[10] Indeed, it has been held that, as long as the traditional distinction between economic and noneconomic factors is kept, no general theory of economic development is possible; Myrdal, *Economic Theory* 100 (1957).

[11] For some descriptions of these conditions, see Staley, *op. cit. supra* note 2, 201 *et seq.;* Buchanan and Ellis, *Approaches* 23–116 (1955); Bauer and Yamey, *Economics* 43–145 (1957); Baran, *The Political Economy of Growth* 134 *et seq.* (1957); Lacoste, *Les pays sous-développés* 5–92 (1959).

[12] See, among others, Myrdal, *An International Economy* 164 *et seq.* (1956); Myrdal, *Economic Theory* 98 *et seq.* (1957); Wallich, "Some Notes Towards a Theory of Derived Development," Paper presented at the Third Meeting of Central Bank Technicians of the American Continent (1952) reprinted in *The Economics of Underdevelopment* 189 (Agarwala and Singh ed., 1958); Singer, "Obstacles to Economic Development," 20 *Social Research* 19 (1953); Baster, "Development and the Free Economy—Some Typical Dilemmas," 7 *Kyklos* 1 (1954) and the subsequent comments, 9 *idem* 90, 94 (1956); Bonné, "Towards a Theory of Implanted Development in Underdeveloped Countries," 9 *idem* 1 (1956); Letiche, "The Relevance of Classical and Contemporary Theories of Growth to Economic Development," 49 *Am. Econ. Rev. Proc.* 473 (1959); Galbraith, "De-

social, political, and cultural patterns will have to be transformed. Values and attitudes will have to change, and the existing governmental and other institutions will have to assume new functions and forms. No fixed hierarchy, from the standpoint of absolute value or of time, can be set as between these changes. They are closely related to each other, so that a minimum level of all-round development is indispensable before further growth in any particular direction is possible.

Such a process of change, lasting for a period of time, necessarily involves general instability and uncertainty. These, in their turn, tend often to impede or delay national or international growth. They represent the growing pains that a world which has accepted the desirability and necessity of growth has to endure. They should not be allowed, however, to affect adversely the process of growth itself. Certain measures have therefore to be taken to assure the degree of certainty and stability necessary for a high rate of development. Such measures assume a variety of forms and relate to several particular objectives. On the international level, for instance, the international financial agencies and the International Monetary Fund, in particular, seek to preserve a certain degree of financial stability, while the United Nations attempts to assure some political stability.

The present study deals with one set of measures which tend to promote stability and which relate to the need for an increase of the capital invested in the now underdeveloped areas of the world.[13] The measures in question are the guarantees given, directly or indirectly, by states to foreign investors, assuring them of the safety of their investment, insofar as the latter is affected by state action. The fundamental purpose of these measures is to promote the economic development of the underdeveloped countries. The protection of foreign private investment is a means toward this end, not

veloped Economic Attitudes and the Underdeveloped Economy," 9 *Public Policy* 73 (1959). For a critical view, see Bauer, *Economic Analysis and Policy in Underdeveloped Countries* 14–25 (1957).

[13] See *infra* pp. 11 *et seq.*

the ultimate purpose of the guarantees. This is more than a mere difference in emphasis; it connotes the overriding importance of economic development in connection with all related issues. The same is true, of course, of all measures designed to promote stability. Their ultimate purpose should be to assist growth by eliminating some of the unfavorable consequences of instability. But to recognize the dangers of uncertainty and instability is not to consider stability as the principal aim.

The guarantees here studied are today highly important, and their importance will probably increase in the near future. It is prudent, however, to avoid exaggerating their importance or the extent to which they can affect economic development. Such guarantees relate only to a few of the factors affecting the international flow of private capital, namely, the factors generally included under the heading of "investment climate." [14] The problem of private international investment itself is but one of the problems relating to economic development today and probably not the most important.

In addition to the limitations of its subject matter, the present study is limited in other ways as well. It deals with the problems which such guarantees raise in public international law; it is therefore the international law aspects which are chiefly discussed and which receive the main emphasis, though, in several instances, these aspects may not be the most important from other standpoints. Legal problems relating to municipal law are not studied by and for themselves but only to the extent necessary in the context of international law. Private international law questions, in particular, which are of peculiar importance with respect to problems of private international investment, are almost totally ignored. This does not indicate lack of awareness of their significance; it is the result of a necessarily arbitrary choice imposed by the need for limiting the subject matter of the study. Even among problems of public international law, a certain choice had to be made. Only those problems

[14] See *infra* pp. 34 *et seq.*

are discussed which are directly relevant to state guarantees and, in a sense, peculiar to them. Therefore, no general treatment of the law of state responsibility for injuries to aliens is to be found in the present study. The problems relating to the taking of the property of aliens [15] are examined only incidentally, while some other important questions, such as those relating to espousal of claims of foreign shareholders in local companies, are totally ignored.

Since this is a legal study, it cannot be expected to deal with matters from an economic or sociological point of view. With regard, however, to problems such as those discussed here, no "strictly legal" study is possible. These problems are closely related to political, economic, social, and cultural questions, so that any "detached" legal scrutiny is both impossible and meaningless. To study these problems intelligently, one should be constantly aware of the non-legal factors involved. For this reason, it is also necessary, before tackling the problems themselves, to give a picture of their economic and political background, and of the concrete situations which make state guarantees necessary and which also create the problems regarding their implementation. This is the ground covered by Part I of this book. It is not intended, of course, as a complete survey of all related economic theories, discussions, and problems. It is only a necessarily over-simplified and summary description of the state of the factors and facts, chiefly economic, relating to the present study and a brief discussion of the main economic considerations involved in the grant of promises to foreign investors.

Part II is mainly descriptive in character. The forms under which guarantees are given to foreign investors are first discussed, and then their substantive provisions are dealt with in some detail. A theoretical investigation of the legal character of the guarantees concludes this Part. In Part III the legal effects of the guarantees are examined. Most of this Part is devoted to a discussion of a somewhat more general but closely related problem, that of the legal effects of com-

---

[15] As distinguished from the problems of state measures affecting the contractual rights of aliens, which are examined in greater detail. See *infra* Chapters 9 and 10.

mitments of states toward aliens, in the form of concessions, guarantees, or other state contracts. In this connection, some of the
questions arising with respect to compensation to persons contracting with a state for damages due to state action are studied. The
closing chapter contains the general conclusions of the study.

Part I

ECONOMIC DEVELOPMENT AND
PRIVATE FOREIGN INVESTMENT

2

Economic Development
and Foreign Capital

OF the factors affecting economic growth, the availability of capital is one of the most important. Economic development is achieved through the productive employment of labor and the full utilization of natural resources. Capital is needed for the realization of both these objectives. The productive employment of labor presupposes a raising of the general level of education and the acquisition of technical skills, the formation of a body of capable administrators and entrepreneurs, and provision of adequate tools and machinery, as well as the raising of the standard of living of the whole population through improved sanitation and medical care. For the exploitation of natural resources, on the other hand, a number of basic facilities are needed, such as roads, railways, and other means of transportation, and the harnessing of electrical power and other forms of energy. In most underdeveloped countries today, particular emphasis is laid on the development of manufacturing industry. This emphasis has ample justification from an economic standpoint and also from a political and social point of view.[1] On the other hand,

[1] For a compilation of the abundant literature on industrialization, see UN Headquarters Library, *Bibliography on Industrialization in Underdeveloped Countries* (1956). And cf. especially UN, Department of Economic and Social Affairs, *Processes and Problems of Industrialization in Underdeveloped Countries* (hereinafter cited UN, *Processes*) (1955); Datta, *The Economics of Industrialization* (1952); Buchanan and Ellis, *Approaches* 267–97 (1955); Brand, *Struggle* 71 *et seq.* (1958). For a critical review of the relevant arguments and policies, see Bauer

industrialization should not result in the total neglect of other sectors of the economy, especially agriculture.

It is evident that none of the objectives just noted can be achieved without substantial outlays of capital. In order to educate masses of people, to build roads, or to import machinery, one has to invest sizable amounts of capital. Of course, capital by itself is not sufficient. It has already been noted that several other factors are necessary.[2] Furthermore, the absence of certain basic facilities, the existence of "bottlenecks" in many important sectors of the economy, and the reluctance of local entrepreneurs to undertake long-range investments in new and unexplored fields render most underdeveloped countries' capacity to absorb capital very low. Thus, sometimes such countries are unable to find any immediate productive use for capital when it is offered. Despite such necessary qualifications, however, it remains true that no development is possible without capital.[3] And today capital is very scarce in the underdeveloped areas.

The Scarcity of Domestic Capital

This is valid with regard to domestic as well as to foreign capital. To begin with, the limits of domestic financing in underdeveloped countries are very restricted. Authors have spoken in this connection of a "vicious circle of poverty," of a "circular constellation

---

and Yamey, *Economics* 237 *et seq.* (1957); and, for a recent restatement of the need for industrial development, Prebisch, "Commercial Policy in the Under-developed Countries," 49 *Am. Econ. Rev. Proc.* 251 (1959).

[2] Indeed, capital may be considered as a secondary factor if the "desire for change" is accepted as the only basic determining factor. Cf. Galbraith, "Conditions for Economic Change in Underdeveloped Countries," 33 *J. Farm Econ.* 689, 694 (1951); and see also Bauer and Yamey, *Economics* 127 *et seq.* (1957); Hirschman, *The Strategy of Economic Development* 1–7 (1958); Nurkse, *Problems of Capital Formation in Underdeveloped Countries* (hereinafter cited Nurkse, *Problems*) 155–57 (1953).

[3] For recent discussions of the matter, see Kindleberger, *Economic Development* 35–55 (1958); Byé, "Le rôle du capital dans le développement économique," 11 *Economie Appliquée* 430 (1958), reprinted in English in *Economic Development for Latin America* 110 (Ellis and Wallich ed., 1961).

of forces tending to act and react upon one another in such a way as to keep a poor country in a state of poverty." [4]

In conjunction with this basic process, a conglomeration of particular factors affects both the volume and the direction of available savings.[5] Consumption is kept at a relatively high level, not only as a consequence of the low incomes of the majority of the population, but also because of prevailing habits of "conspicuous consumption," today strengthened by awareness and imitation of the consumption standards prevailing in the advanced countries.[6] The general climate of economic, and sometimes political, insecurity, on the other hand, encourages the non-productive use of whatever

[4] Nurkse, *Problems* 4 (1953). Myrdal, in his *Economic Theory* 12 and *passim* (1957), goes further and expounds the idea of a "circular causation of a cumulative process" resulting in increasing inequalities between countries or regions. See also Hilgerdt, "Uses and Limitations of International Trade in Overcoming Inequalities in World Distribution of Population and Resources," in 5 *Proceedings of the World Population Conference 1954* 47 (1955); Nurkse, *Patterns of Trade and Development* 17–18 (1959); Meier, "The Problem of Limited Economic Development," 6 *Economia Internazionale* 388 (1953) reprinted in *The Economics of Underdevelopment* 54, 60–64 (Agarwala and Singh ed., 1958); Meier and Baldwin, *Economic Development* 319–24 (1957). For a critical view, see Bauer, *Economic Analysis and Policy in Underdeveloped Countries* 63 (1957).

[5] For discussions of the related problems, see Nurkse, *Problems passim* (1953); Lewis, *The Theory of Economic Growth* 225–44 (1955); Buchanan and Ellis, *Approaches* 51–60, 301–3 (1955); Bauer and Yamey, *Economics* 131 *et seq.* (1957); Meier and Baldwin, *Economic Development* 303–10 (1957); Simonet, *La formation du capital dans les pays sous-développés et l'assistance financière étrangère* (1959). See also U.N., Department of Economic Affairs, *Methods of Financing Economic Development in Under-Developed Countries* (1949); idem, *Domestic Financing of Economic Development* (1950); idem, *Measures for the Economic Development of Under-Developed Countries*, Report by a Group of Experts (hereinafter cited UN *Measures*) 35–44 (1951).

[6] The late Professor Nurkse was the first to stress the importance of the "demonstration effect" in the international setting. Cf. his "Some International Aspects of the Problem of Economic Development," 42 *Am. Econ. Rev. Proc.* 571, 577–80 (1952) and Nurkse, *Problems* 58–77 (1953). He pointed out that "the presence or the mere knowledge of new goods and new methods of consumption tends to raise the general propensity to consume." Nurkse, *Problems* 62 (1953). Accordingly, consumption will tend to increase as fast as or faster than the general increase in the national income.

See also Furtado, "Capital Formation and Economic Development," in *The Economics of Underdevelopment* 308, 326–28 (Agarwala and Singh ed., 1958), the critique of Bauer and Yamey, *Economics* 137–42 (1957), Viner, "Stability and Progress: The Poorer Countries' Problem," in *Stability and Progress in the World Economy* 41, 55–56 (Hague ed., 1958), and Nurkse's comment on the latter, *idem* 69, 73–75.

capital is available—namely, hoarding, investment in luxury goods or real estate, and the pursuit of commercial and financial rather than industrial occupations, in view of their higher and faster profits.[7]

Therefore, though certain possibilities of improvement do exist, domestic financing of economic development in the underdeveloped countries is bound to be limited, assuming that no totalitarian methods are to be used. The methods of forced saving, or, more precisely, of increasing savings by compulsorily reducing consumption, which are available to the non-communist governments of underdeveloped countries seem to have little effect.[8] It is true that certain countries have managed to develop in the past through the exclusive use of domestic resources and without importing foreign capital to any significant degree. However, the social and political conditions [9] in England and in the countries of Western Europe in the beginning of the nineteenth century or in Japan some decades later were totally different from those now prevailing in the underdeveloped areas.[10] More recently, the communist states have been following

[7] Cf. UN *Measures* 35 *et seq.* (1951); Brand, *Struggle* 159 *et seq.* (1958); Baran, "On the Political Economy of Backwardness," 20 *The Manchester School of Economic and Social Studies* 66 (1952) reprinted in *The Economics of Underdevelopment* 75, 82–86 (Agarwala and Singh ed., 1958); Aubrey, "Investment Decisions in Underdeveloped Countries," in *Capital Formation and Economic Growth* 397, 404 *et seq.* (Abramovits ed., 1955); Levy, "Some Social Obstacles to 'Capital Formation' in 'Underdeveloped Countries,'" *idem* 441, 469 *et seq.*

[8] On the related problems of inflation and increased taxation, see, among many others, Brand, *Struggle* 212–51 (1958); Bauer and Yamey, *Economics* 190 *et seq.* (1957); Bernstein and Patel, "Inflation in Relation to Economic Development," 2 *IMF Staff Papers* 363 (1952); Buchanan and Ellis, *Approaches* 308–14 (1955); Campos, "Inflation and Balanced Growth," in *Economic Development for Latin America* 82 (Ellis and Wallich ed., 1961).

[9] Economic conditions, as well, were widely different. Western European countries were comparatively wealthy even during their preindustrial period. See Kuznets, "Under-developed Countries and the Pre-Industrial Phase in the Advanced Countries: An Attempt at Comparison," 5 *Proceedings of the World Population Conference 1954* 947 (1955) reprinted in *The Economics of Underdevelopment* 135 (Agarwala and Singh ed., 1958); Bauer, *op. cit. supra* note 4 at 45–49 (1957).

[10] To raise but one point, among several, Western European economic development is closely related to the rise in power of the middle classes, the *bourgeoisie* of traders and industrialists. For a variety of historical reasons, these classes are peculiarly weak in most of today's underdeveloped countries and cannot take the

their own road to economic development, founding their methods on strict state control and coercion.[11] Their achievements in the economic field cannot be contested,[12] even though these countries are still far from the point of total success. The choice between freedom and coercion, however, cannot be made on the sole basis of economic efficacy.[13] In some of the underdeveloped countries, it is true, other forms of totalitarian regimes, of a personal or tradi-

---

lead in their development. See Brand, *Struggle* 117–25 (1958); Baran, "On the Political Economy of Backwardness," *supra* note 7 at 77 *et seq.;* Lacoste, *Les pays sous-développés* 20, 51 *et seq.* (1959).

For a brief survey of sociocultural factors, see Buchanan and Ellis, *Approaches* 74 *et seq.* (1955); Higgins, *Economic Development* 249–61 (1959); Balandier, "Sociologie des régions sous-développés," in 1 *Traité de Sociologie* 332 (Gurvitch ed., 1958); and the reading list in Meier and Baldwin, *Economic Development* 545–48 (1957).

[11] It would be misleading, however, to assume that there exist no similarities between the Western and the Communist development process. The emphasis on low initial consumption levels, for instance, is common to both systems. Cf. Myrdal, *An International Economy* 162 (1956); 3 Perroux, *La coexistence pacifique* 588 *et seq.* (1958). But see also Rostow, *The Stages of Economic Growth* 93 *et seq.* (1960); Galbraith, "Developed Economic Attitudes and the Underdeveloped Economy," 9 *Public Policy* 73 (1959).

[12] Those of Communist China are perhaps the most interesting and relevant, in view of the initial conditions prevailing there. From the constantly increasing recent literature, see Malenbaum, "India and China: Development Contrasts," 64 *J. Pol. Econ.* 1 (1956); *idem,* "India and China: Contrasts in Development Performance," 49 *Am. Econ. Rev.* 284 (1959).

On a more general level, see Staley, *The Future of Underdeveloped Countries* 65–91 (1954); Watnick, "The Appeal of Communism to the Underdeveloped Peoples," in *The Progress of Underdeveloped Areas* 152 (Hoselitz ed., 1952); Heimann, "Marxism and Underdeveloped Countries," 19 *Social Research* 312 (1952); and, for the relevant Marxist views, Baran, *The Political Economy of Growth* 149 *et seq.* (1957); Rymalov, "An Important Problem" [Review of Junusov, *The Building of Socialism in Formerly Backward Countries* (1958)] 5 *Int'l Affairs* (Moscow) No. 7, 115 (1959); Kirsch, "The Soviet View of the Indian Economy," 9 *Public Policy* 207 (1959).

[13] Especially since there exists "no simple ideologic-economic relationship"; cf. Malenbaum and Stolper, "Political Ideology and Economic Progress: The Basic Question," 12 *World Politics* 412 (1960). The authors examine two pairs of ideologically opposed states (China and India, and East and West Germany), pointing out that while in the one case the totalitarian state seems to be developing at a faster pace than the democratic one, in the other case it is the democratic state which has advanced considerably more.

The force of a concrete example such as the above, though considerable, should not be overestimated. But the case stated in the text rests, it is believed, on solid philosophical grounds.

tional character, are still in power. Such regimes, however, are not generally of a type conducive to economic development.[14]

Foreign Investment in the Past

Importation of foreign capital is then necessary for a country's economic development. This is not a novel phenomenon. In the past, as well, especially during the nineteenth century, foreign capital contributed greatly to the economic development of several countries, particularly those in the "New Continents." The United States is a prime example. Today, however, conditions are radically different; and it is necessary, before proceeding further, to examine briefly these differences.

Foreign investment in the nineteenth century and the beginning of the twentieth [15] came from private sources. Governments took an active part in the process of investment, borrowing private capital in the domestic or in foreign markets, guaranteeing loans of private persons, or assisting in the realization of investment projects through subsidies, land grants, and so on.[16] There was no foreign public investment, however—that is, no investment of capital owned by a foreign government or public authority. Capital was in the main invested indirectly, through the buying of bonds or similar securities. Direct investment,[17] mostly in enterprises producing primary goods for export, played a part, but generally a minor one in relation to the total of foreign investments. In 1913 it constituted less than 20

[14] Cf. Galbraith, "Conditions for Economic Change in Underdeveloped Countries," *supra* note 2, at 694–96 (1951); Myrdal, *Economic Theory* 83 (1957); Deyrup, "Limits of Government Activity in Underdeveloped Countries," 24 *Social Research* 191, 193 (1957). But see also Theobald, *The Rich and the Poor* 52 *et seq.* (1961).

[15] The start of the First World War is generally considered as marking the effective end of the nineteenth century.

[16] Cf. the country studies in *The State and Economic Growth* (Aitken ed., 1959) and *infra* note 13 p. 35.

[17] "Direct" investment is investment in an enterprise controlled by the investor, while "portfolio" or "indirect" investment is investment in securities held by investors not exercising any managerial control. See Maffry, "Direct versus Portfolio Investment in the Balance of Payments," 44 *Am. Econ. Rev. Proc.* 614 (1954).

percent of total British foreign investment outstanding, while foreign railways and other public utilities bonds constituted about 45 percent and foreign governments bonds about 30 percent.[18] Capital was directed either to the European countries or toward the countries in the so-called "regions of recent settlement," [19] whose abundant resources were gradually but rapidly exploited by immigrants, mainly from Europe, with the aid of European capital.[20] Comparatively little investment took place in the densely populated areas of the underdeveloped countries of today, in the "Old Continents" of Asia and Africa.[21] Part of it was indirect, concentrated in public utility enterprises, chiefly the railways. Another part was invested directly and was mostly devoted to the production of raw materials for export.[22] In reviewing past conditions, one should also note the

[18] Cf. Nurkse, "International Investment To-Day in the Light of Nineteenth-Century Experience," 64 *Econ. J.* 744, 747 (1954); Brand, *Struggle* 262, 392 (1958); Cairncross, *Home and Foreign Investment 1870-1913* 183 *et seq.* (1953); Feis, *Europe the World's Banker 1870-1914* 22-24 (1930).

Note, however, that the bulk of the United States foreign investment of that period (concentrated in Latin America) was direct. In 1914, portfolio investment accounted for only 20 percent of total U.S. investment in Latin America; cf. UN, Department of Economic and Social Affairs, *Foreign Capital in Latin America* (hereinafter cited UN, *Foreign Capital*) 6, 154 (tables III and V) (1955).

[19] The term refers to the "empty" countries in the "New Continents" of America and Oceania and it includes Canada, the United States, Argentina, New Zealand, Australia, and probably one or two more countries. Cf. Hilgerdt, *The Network of World Trade* 76 (League of Nations, 1942); Nurkse, *supra* note 18, at 747-48; Nurkse, *Patterns of Trade and Development* 15-19 (1959).

[20] There was thus a close connection between the importation of capital and that of labor and there generally existed a high degree of cultural homogeneity between borrowers and lenders. Moreover, the social and political structures which made European economic development possible were present and powerful in the new countries. Cf. Nurkse, *supra* note 18, at 745-48; Baran, *The Political Economy of Growth* 137-41 (1957); Lacoste, *Les pays sous-développés* 52-56 (1959).

[21] In 1914, more than two thirds of British long-term foreign investment outstanding was in the regions of recent settlement and in Europe (the latter accounting for only 6 percent of the total). French and German investments were heavily concentrated in Europe; about two thirds of the former and half of the latter were in that region. Investment in today's underdeveloped countries never exceeded one third of the total; it usually amounted to much less. See UN, Department of Economic Affairs, *International Capital Movements During the Inter-War Period* 1-4 (1949) Nurkse, *supra* note 18, at 745; Kuznets, "International Differences in Capital Formation and Financing," Appendix, table II-5, in *Capital Formation and Economic Growth* 19, 74 (Abramovits ed., 1955).

[22] About 70 percent of total United States direct investment in Latin America in

extraordinary size of foreign investments. British annual foreign investment in the second half of the nineteenth century averaged about four percent of British annual national income. During the decade just before the First World War, it amounted to about seven percent,[23] and foreign holdings constituted about one fourth of total national wealth.[24]

The period between the First and the Second World Wars may be regarded, from the standpoint of international investment, as one of transition. Public capital movements acquired some importance, partly because of the large intergovernmental loans made during and immediately after the First World War.[25] Private capital, however, continued to dominate the field of foreign investment. During the 1920s, the bulk of the capital outflow from the creditor countries consisted of portfolio investments.[26] The 1929–32 international financial crisis caused the collapse of the market for foreign capital issues, and portfolio investment virtually disappeared during the 1930s. Direct investment, on the other hand, was of minor importance in the early 1920s, but showed a large increase in absolute as well as relative size by 1929. It came to dominate the field of foreign investment in the 1930s, though at greatly reduced annual rates.

Foreign investment during the interwar period remained concentrated in the developed countries and the by then developed or

---

1914 was in agriculture (plantations), mining and petroleum; about 20 percent was in public utilities and about 7 percent in manufacturing and distribution; UN, *Foreign Capital* 154 (table IV) (1955).

[23] Cf. Nurkse, *supra* note 18, at 744–45; Cairncross, *op. cit. supra* note 18, at 104–6, 180 (1953); Kuznets, *supra* note 21, at 70 (table II-4).

[24] Cf. Feis, *op. cit. supra* note 18, at 14.

[25] About 30 percent of total United States capital exports in 1919 and 1920 ($2 billion out of about $7 billion) consisted of government loans and advances to foreign governments; UN, Department of Economic Affairs, *International Capital Movements During the Inter-War Period* 19 (1949). The payment of war debts and reparations was one of the major financial issues of the whole interwar period.

[26] Such investment accounted for more than three fourths of the total capital outflow from the United States in the years 1924 to 1928; UN *idem*, 25–26; Lary and associates, *The United States in the World Economy* 89 *et seq.* (U.S. Department of Commerce, 1943).

semi-developed countries of the regions of recent settlement. In the years 1924–28, about 75 percent of average annual United States portfolio investment went to such countries, as well as 65 percent and 60 percent of average Dutch and British portfolio investment, respectively.[27] The direction of direct investments seems to have been more favorable to the underdeveloped countries. At the end of 1929, such countries accounted for about half the outstanding direct investments of both the United States and the United Kingdom. Most of such investment appears to have been concentrated in primary-producing industries and public utilities.[28]

The Present Situation of Foreign Investment

In the years since the Second World War, certain new trends have appeared while those first manifested in the interwar period have acquired full force.

A first new factor of major importance is the extraordinary part played by public investment. Though not unknown in the more distant past, interstate loans had virtually disappeared during the nineteenth century and had come to be regarded as a feature of war economies. Since the last war, however, public capital, in the form of inter-government lending as well as in other forms, has dominated the international financial scene.[29] The chief creditor government is that of the United States, either directly or through a number of special financial agencies, such as the Export-Import Bank of Washington and the Development Loan Fund.[30] In recent

[27] UN, *op. cit. supra* note 25, at 26 (table 4).
[28] Cf. UN *idem* 32–33; Lary and associates, *op. cit. supra* note 26, at 102–3.
[29] Cf. Malenbaum, "International Public Financing," 1955 *Int'l Conciliation* 315; Weiner and Dalla Chiesa, "International Movements of Public Long-Term Capital and Grants, 1946–50," 4 *IMF Staff Papers* 113 (1954); Barnerias, "International Movements of Public Long-Term Capital and Grants, 1951–52," 5 *idem* 108 (1956); Avramovic, *Debt Servicing Capacity and Postwar Growth in International Indebtedness* 3–18, 159–61 (1958); United Nations, Department of Economic and Social Affairs, *International Economic Assistance to the Less Developed Countries* (1961).
[30] Cf. Lewis, *The United States and Foreign Investment Problems* 190–219 (1948);

years several other states, including the Soviet Union,[31] have begun to offer long-term loans.[32] Public capital [33] is also provided by international financial agencies, such as the International Bank for Reconstruction and Development (IBRD or World Bank), the International Finance Corporation (IFC), and the newly established International Development Association (IDA).[34]

Another new form of public financing which today plays an important role is "economic aid," namely, capital in any form granted to foreign states without any obligation of repayment or payment of interest.[35] At present, most funds of this type are

---

Cutler, "U.S. Government as a Source of Capital for Private Investment Abroad," in Southwestern Legal Foundation, *Proceedings of the 1959 Institute on Private Investment Abroad* 209 (1959); U.S. Congress, House of Representatives, Committee on Foreign Affairs, *Staff Memorandum on International Lending Agencies* 22–34, 163–75 (1960); Asher, *Grants, Loans and Local Currencies—Their Role in Foreign Aid* (1961).

[31] Cf. Berliner, *Soviet Economic Aid* (1958); 3 Perroux, *La coexistence pacifique* 433 *et seq.* (1958); Aubrey, *Coexistence—Economic Challenge and Response* (1961). For recent expressions of the Soviet point of view, see Rymalov, "Soviet Assistance to Underdeveloped Countries," 5 *Int'l Affairs* (Moscow) No. 9, 23 (1959); Skorov and Stepanov, "Two Worlds-Two Types of Aid," 5 *idem* No. 12, 43 (1959); Demidov, "Disinterested Aid," 6 *idem* No. 1, 34 (1960).

[32] For a comprehensive survey of recent international public capital movements, by country of origin, see United Nations, Department of Economic and Social Affairs, *op. cit. supra* note 29, at 21–40.

[33] This term is not altogether exact when used in connection with international financial agencies, since much of their capital today is private in origin. For a discussion of the related problems, see Pazos, "Private versus Public Foreign Investment in Under-Developed Countries," in *Economic Development for Latin America* 201 (Ellis and Wallich ed., 1961).

[34] For an excellent recent survey, see Delaume, "International Machinery for Financing Economic Development," 28 *Geo. Wash. L. Rev.* 533 (1960). On the particular agencies, see International Bank for Reconstruction and Development, *The World Bank. Policies and Operations* (1957); Matecki, *Establishment of the International Finance Corporation and United States Policy* (1957); Jackson, *The Case for an International Development Authority* (1959); United States Senate, Committee on Banking and Currency, *International Development Association Hearings* (1958); Metzger, "The New International Development Association," 49 *Georgetown L.J.* 23 (1960). Brief surveys of the role and operations of the international financial agencies are to be found in most of the textbooks on economic development already cited. See also, U.S. Congress, *Staff Memorandum, supra* note 30, at 1–21, 35–162.

[35] For a discussion of its role, see Perroux, "The Gift: Its Economic Meaning in Contemporary Capitalism," *Diogenes* No. 6, 1 (1954). In the fiscal year ending in 1959, grants constituted 65 percent ($1,578 million out of $2,440 million) of the net economic assistance (loans plus grants minus repayments) provided to under-

provided by individual states, especially the United States.[36] A limited number of grants is also provided by some international agencies in connection with technical assistance projects or relief operations.[37] Despite the efforts of the representatives of under-developed countries in the United Nations, no international agency dealing with grants-in-aid has been established as yet.[38]

During the first postwar years, public capital accounted for almost all international capital movements. In the seven-year period 1946–52, the total net export of public capital from the United States amounted to over $34 billion, while net private capital exports did not exceed $8 billion.[39] Since that time, the role of public capital has somewhat diminished, both in absolute amounts [40] and in relation to private capital movements.[41] On the other hand, significant

---

developed countries on a bilateral basis; United Nations, Department of Economic and Social Affairs, *op. cit. supra* note 29, at 14 (table 2).

[36] The United States is and has been since the war the main supplier of economic aid; cf. Brown and Opie, *American Economic Assistance* (1953), and the studies cited *supra* note 29. In the fiscal year ending in 1959, the United States contributed over 70 percent of the total grants given to underdeveloped countries on a bilateral basis ($1,132 million out of $1,578 million); United Nations, Department of Economic and Social Affairs, *op. cit. supra* note 29, at 14 (table 2).

[37] In the fiscal year ending in 1959, international agencies provided a total of $101 million in grants to underdeveloped countries; *ibid.*

[38] Cf. UN Document A/2906 (1955), the "Scheyven Report" on a Special United Nations Fund for Economic Development, and see also Myrdal, *An International Economy* 123 et seq. (1956); Brand, *Struggle* 323-27 (1958). The United Nations Special Fund recently set up is not a financing agency; the few grants it is authorized to make are closely related to technical assistance projects; cf. Hoffman, *One Hundred Countries One and One Quarter Billion People* 39-43 (1960). But see also *The Emerging Nations—Their Growth and United States Policy* 128-31 (Millikan and Blackmer ed., 1961).

[39] Cf. Barnerias, *supra* note 29, at 110 (table 2); UN, Department of Economic Affairs, *The International Flow of Private Capital 1946-1952* (hereinafter cited UN *Flow 1946*) 3 (1954). And cf. Avramovic, *op. cit. supra* note 29, at 3-18.

[40] The gross amount of public funds transferred internationally between 1946 and 1950 exceeded the $61 billion: they averaged more than $12 billion per year; cf. Weiner and Dalla Chiesa, *supra* note 29, at 114. In 1952, only about $7.2 billion of such funds were transferred; Barnerias, *supra* note 29, at 109. A further decline in amount has been noted since then.

[41] In 1951, United States Government credits and grants for non-military purposes amounted to about $3.3 billion, while United States private foreign investment that year barely exceeded $1.7 billion; cf. UN Document E/2901, 21 June 1956, 20 (table 1), 44 (table 13). In 1957, the net private capital exports of the United States amounted to about $2.6 billion, while the outflow of public funds

changes, favorable to the underdeveloped countries, have occurred in the geographical distribution of public funds.[42] Public capital is of principal importance in the present-day international scene, especially with regard to the underdeveloped areas.[43]

Apart from the growth of public international investment, several other important changes have occurred with regard to foreign investment.[44] To begin with, if past and present levels of national income, world production, and international trade are taken into account, an important relative decrease will be noted in the private capital invested abroad during the postwar years, as compared with investments during the late nineteenth century.[45] Up to 1955, the average annual volume of private international investment did not exceed $2 billion.[46] Since then, a significant increase has been noted. The average annual outflow of long-term capital in the years 1955–58 has exceeded $4 billion.[47] The peak was reached in 1957, with a gross outflow of $5.7 billion; [48] despite their drop in 1958,[49] capital exports remain at a consistently high level. In 1958 and 1959 they

---

was about $2 billion; cf. UN, Department of Economic and Social Affairs, *The International Flow of Private Capital 1956–1958* (hereinafter cited UN *Flow 1956*) 19 (table 2), 81 (table A of Annex II) (1959).

[42] Cf. *infra* p. 27.   [43] Cf. *infra* pp. 27–28, 59–60.

[44] The postwar situation and developments have been thoroughly covered by successive United Nations reports; cf. UN *Flow 1946* (1954), UN *Flow 1956* (1959), and the annual reports of the Secretary-General, UN Documents E/2901, 21 June 1956; E/3021, 21 June 1957; E/3128, 4 June 1958; E/3369, 13 May 1960; and E/3513, 14 June 1961.

[45] If public capital is also taken into account, however, the relative size of total international investment in recent years closely approaches that of the nineteenth century; cf. Nurkse, *Patterns of Trade and Development* 29–30 (1959). For a comparison with the 1920's, see Avramovic, *op. cit. supra* note 29, at 16–18.

[46] Cf. UN Document E/2901, 21 June 1956, 7.

[47] Cf. UN *Flow 1956* 9 (1959).

[48] The increase was chiefly due to a small number of exceptionally large transactions in the petroleum field, the most important of which was the acquisition of new concessions in Venezuela by United States concerns, resulting eventually in investments of over $1 billion; see UN *Flow 1956* 29 (1959); Pizer and Cutler, *U.S. Business Investments in Foreign Countries* 21 (U.S. Department of Commerce, 1960). For a glimpse at the political background of these transactions, see Porter and Alexander, *The Struggle for Democracy in Latin America* 118 (1961).

[49] The relative decrease in direct investment in that year was partly offset by an increase in portfolio investment. Cf. UN *Flow 1956* 9–10 (1959); Pizer and Cutler, "Capital Flow to Foreign Countries Slackens," 39 *Survey of Current Business* No. 8, 25 (U.S. Department of Commerce, 1959).

averaged over $5 billion per year.[50] The chief creditor country is the United States; during the postwar years, it has accounted for from 60 to 100 percent of the annual long-term capital outflow.[51] The second most important creditor country is the United Kingdom, supplying regularly over 10 percent of the annual capital outflow. Then come France, Switzerland, The Netherlands, and, starting quite recently but with increasing importance, the Federal Republic of Germany.

Even at its present levels, private foreign investment falls short of the needs of the underdeveloped countries, not only because of its inadequate amount but also because of its form and direction. It has been noted that in the nineteenth century private capital went mainly to the underdeveloped countries of the regions of recent settlement, was mainly indirect in form, and was heavily concentrated in transportation and other public utilities. Today, direct investment clearly prevails over indirect. In the period from 1946 to 1952, United States direct investment amounted annually to about five times the total of portfolio investment.[52] Recently, the position of portfolio investment has considerably improved. While in the six years 1950–55 there was a net increase of $800 million in United States portfolio investment, in the three subsequent years 1956–58 the net increase amounted to more than $1 billion.[53] Nonetheless, portfolio investment is still below past levels. According to a recent estimate, during the period 1953–57 United States direct investments abroad have been about ten times as large as the net outflow of portfolio capital.[54] At the end of 1959, however, total United States indirect investment amounted to over $11 billion, as compared to about $30 billion of total direct investment.[55]

[50] UN Document E/3513, 14 June 1961, at p. 10.
[51] For these and the following figures, see UN *Flow 1956* 19 (table 2) (1959).
[52] Cf. Buchanan and Ellis, *Approaches* 346 (1955); Buchanan, "International Investment," in 2 *Survey of Contemporary Economics* 307, 342–343 (Haley ed., 1952). The situation in the United Kingdom seems to have been similar, though slightly more favorable to portfolio investment; cf. UN *Flow 1946* 16 et seq. (1954); UN *Flow 1956* 56 et seq. (1959).
[53] Cf. UN *Flow 1956* 50–51 (1959).   [54] *Idem* 25.
[55] Cf. "United States Foreign Investments: Measures of Growth and Economic

The predominance of direct investment in the postwar period is in part due to the lack of confidence generated by the defaults and currency devaluations of the 1930s.[56] It is also attributable to changes in the domestic economic conditions in the creditor countries [57] and to the increased needs for some primary products. Direct investment is not necessarily safer than portfolio investment, but it is undertaken by entrepreneurs, "professional risk-bearers," [58] and it generally offers higher profits. The shift from portfolio to direct investment may be considered as one of the main causes of the increase in public foreign investment, since the latter tends to cover the activities which in the past were financed through portfolio investment.[59]

Direct foreign investment is heavily concentrated in industries producing primary goods for export. Petroleum production is the most important single industry. Investment in the petroleum industry has accounted for over 45 percent of the average annual increase in United States direct foreign investment in the years 1946–51.[60] After a slight drop, it reached another peak in the years 1955–58, when it accounted for over 50 percent of annual United States direct investment.[61] At the end of 1959, investment in the petroleum industry amounted to about 35 percent of the value of total United States direct investment abroad.[62] Manufacturing ac-

---

Effects," 40 *Survey of Current Business* No. 9, 15, at 24 (U.S. Department of Commerce, 1960).

[56] Note, however, that only 15 percent of the bonds issued by underdeveloped countries in the Nineteen Twenties have remained in default; cf. *Report to the President on Foreign Economic Policies* (Gray Report) 62 (1950).

[57] Chiefly the presence of profitable domestic investment opportunities and the increasing importance of institutional investors, such as banks, insurance companies, etc., whose charters or policies preclude investment in foreign bonds. Cf. Buchanan and Ellis, *Approaches* 345 (1955); Brand, *Struggle* 269 (1958).

[58] Buchanan and Ellis, *Approaches* 346 (1955).

[59] Cf. also *infra* p. 60.   [60] Cf. UN *Flow 1946* 12, 33 (1954).

[61] The peak year was 1957, when petroleum investment accounted for over 55 percent of the total outflow of U.S. direct investment capital ($1696 million out of $3089 million); cf. UN *Flow 1956* 27 (table 7) (1959). And see *supra* note 48.

[62] See Pizer and Cutler, *U.S. Business Investments in Foreign Countries* 89 (table 1) (U.S. Department of Commerce, 1960).

counts for another large part of direct foreign investments. It has accounted for about 30 percent of average annual United States direct investment abroad since 1946,[63] and at the end of 1959 it constituted over 30 percent of total United States foreign direct investment.[64] Investment in mining and smelting amounts to about 10 percent of total United States direct investment, while public utilities account for about 8 percent.

The form of private foreign investment and its distribution among industries become particularly important when its direction—that is to say, its geographical distribution—is taken into consideration. The bulk of foreign capital continues to flow to the now highly developed countries of the regions of recent settlement and goes only in relatively low proportion to the underdeveloped countries of the "Old Continents." [65] At the end of 1959, investments in Canada and Western Europe constituted more than 50 percent of total United States private investment abroad.[66] The proportion holds true of other capital-exporting countries as well. Only about 40 percent of total West German and about 20 percent of Swiss private foreign investment abroad have gone to underdeveloped areas.[67] The United Kingdom and France, chiefly because of their status as colonial powers, seem to be exceptions to this rule. The United Kingdom's investments in the underdeveloped countries in the sterling area, between 1954 and 1957, constituted about 70 percent of its total private investments,[68] while French foreign investments, private as well as public, are concentrated in the French overseas territories.[69] According to recent estimates, the inflow of

[63] See UN *Flow 1946* 13 (table 3) (1954); UN *Flow 1956* 27 (table 7) (1959); Pizer and Cutler, *op. cit. supra* note 62, at 19–21, 96 (table 8).

[64] For details on these and the following figures, see Pizer and Cutler, *op. cit. supra* note 62, at 89 (table 1).

[65] In discussing the geographical distribution of investments, we include among the developed countries the Western European states, Canada, the United States, Argentina, Japan, the Union of South Africa, New Zealand and Australia (the last five only when available data are sufficiently detailed).

[66] See Pizer and Cutler, *op. cit. supra* note 62, at 89 (table 1).

[67] Cf. UN *Flow 1956* 23 (1959).   [68] *Idem* 18, 20–21.

[69] *Idem* 21–22, 40–42.

private long-term capital to the underdeveloped countries in the years 1958 and 1959 averaged over $2 billion a year (the total average annual outflow of capital being more than $5 billion).[70]

The preference for developed countries is more marked in the case of portfolio investment. Canadian and Western European securities accounted for over 70 percent of the total United States private foreign portfolio at the end of 1959.[71] The geographical distribution of direct investments is a little more favorable to the underdeveloped countries. Still, almost 60 percent of total United States direct investment is in developed countries.[72] Of special importance in this connection is the distribution of capital among industries as well as countries. Direct investment in underdeveloped areas is today heavily concentrated in extractive industries, while manufacturing and public utilities are comparatively neglected. At the end of 1958, United States total direct investment in underdeveloped countries amounted to about $11.5 billion, out of which $5.3 billion (or over 45 percent) constituted investments in the petroleum industry and about $1.6 billion (or over 13 percent) constituted investments in mining and smelting.[73] Manufacturing accounted for 13 percent (or about $1.6 billion) and public utilities for 10 percent (or about $1.2 billion). However, there has been a steady increase of United States investment in manufacturing in the underdeveloped countries (especially in Latin America),[74] though its share of total investment has remained more or less the same, owing to the simultaneous increase of other investments, particularly in petroleum production. On the other hand, there has

[70] Cf. UN Document E/3513, 14 June 1961, at 9, 10, 19.

[71] Cf. "United States Foreign Investments: Measures of Growth and Economic Effects," 40 *Survey of Current Business* No. 9, 15, at 24 (U.S. Department of Commerce, 1960). For analyses of recent developments, see UN *Flow 1956* 51 *et seq.* (1959); UN Document E/3513, 14 June 1961, 48 *et seq.*

[72] Cf. Pizer and Cutler, *op. cit. supra* note 62, at 89 (table 1). Investment in such countries constituted over 60 percent of the outflow of United States direct capital investment in 1959; *idem* at 136 (table 48).

[73] These and the following figures are based on table 1, *idem* at 89.

[74] A large part of such investment, from 60 to 100 percent, has consisted of reinvested profits; cf. UN *Flow 1946* 12–14 (1954); UN *Flow 1956* 27 (table 7), 30 *et seq.* (1959).

been a decline in the relative position of investment in public utilities.[75]

The unequal distribution of foreign private capital, with respect both to geographical areas and to industries, is to some extent counterbalanced by the effects of public capital. A high proportion of public capital is directed today to the underdeveloped areas. The situation was not the same in the first postwar years. Net total exports of public capital by the United States in the five-year period 1946–50 amounted to about $28 billion, out of which less than $2 billion went to underdeveloped countries.[76] By 1954, however, the underdeveloped countries received more than 50 percent of United States government grants and credits; [77] since then their proportion has steadily increased.[78] Total world movements of public capital follow similar lines,[79] and the same trend may be noted in the direction of the World Bank's loans. In the late 1940s a high proportion of such loans was given to developed countries, for purposes of reconstruction.[80] By June 1959, about 60 percent of total World Bank loans were given to countries in the underdeveloped areas.[81] From the point of view of the underdeveloped countries, this trend

---

[75] Compare its present position to that in 1954, when it accounted for about 15 percent of total U.S. direct investment in underdeveloped areas; cf. UN Document E/2901, 21 June 1956, 27 (table 5) and compare the earlier situation, as found in UN *Flow 1946* 13 (table 3) and 14 (table 4) (1954).

[76] Cf. Weiner and Dalla Chiesa, "International Movements of Public Long-Term Capital and Grants, 1946–50," 4 *IMF Staff Papers* 113, 116 (table 1) (1954). Note that the underdeveloped countries' net receipts of public funds during these five years, totalling about $3 billion, were equal to their total net receipts over the next two years. Cf. *idem* 117–118; Barnerias, "International Movements of Public Long-Term Capital and Grants, 1951–52," 5 *IMF Staff Papers* 108, 110, 114–115 (1956).

[77] Cf. UN Document E/2901, 21 June 1956, 44 (table 13).

[78] Cf. Kerber, "Foreign Grants and Credits in 1958," 39 *Survey of Current Business* No. 4, 17, 19–20 (U.S. Department of Commerce, 1959); "Economic Aid Steady under Foreign Programs," 40 *idem* No. 5, 11 (1960). And see the excellent analysis of the overall distribution of United States foreign aid in Asher, *Grants, Loans, and Local Currencies—Their Role in Foreign Aid* 59–66 (1961).

[79] Cf. Avramovic, *Debt Servicing Capacity and Postwar Growth in International Indebtedness* 6, 159–161 (1958).

[80] More than 70 percent of the effective loans granted by the IBRD, up to June 30, 1950, went to European countries only; cf. IBRD, *Fifth Annual Report 1949–1950* 50–51 (Appendix C) (1950).

[81] Cf. IBRD, *Fourteenth Annual Report 1958–1959* 39 (Appendix E) (1959).

more than offsets the general decrease in the amount of public capital movements.[82] According to recent United Nations estimates, the flow of grants and long-term loans to the underdeveloped areas increased by more than two fifths in the last four years.[83] Both grants and net loans have increased in amount, but the amount of net loans has increased more than that of grants.[84]

[82] See *supra* p. 21.

[83] United Nations, Department of Economic and Social Affairs, *International Economic Assistance to the Less Developed Countries* 43 (1961).

[84] *Ibid.* In 1953–54 and 1955–56, grants accounted for 72.7 percent of the total amount of public economic assistance to underdeveloped areas and loans for 27.3 percent. In 1957–58 and 1958–59, their respective shares were 63.4 and 36.6 percent. *Idem* at 44.

3

Obstacles to Private Foreign Investment

A REVIEW of international investment conditions today leads then to the conclusion that the underdeveloped countries receive less private foreign capital than they need.[1] It is difficult to provide a complete list or a comprehensive classification of the causes for this shortage.[2] The countries involved differ widely from each other in culture, in present stage or future possibilities of development, and in many other respects.[3] The factors limiting private foreign

[1] It has been estimated that these countries will need in the next few years an additional sum of $3 to 4 billion yearly in order to achieve a minimum rate of growth. The major part of this amount will have to consist of public capital. See the summary of calculations from several sources in Asher, *Grants, Loans, and Local Currencies—Their Role in Foreign Aid* 116-18 (1961). See also, Rosenstein-Rodan, "International Aid for Underdeveloped Countries," 43 *Rev. Econ. & Stat.* 107 (1961). For a more elaborate discussion of the problems studied in this Chapter, see Fatouros, "Obstacles to Private Foreign Investment in Underdeveloped Countries," 2 *Current Law and Social Problems* 194 (1961).

[2] For descriptions and discussions, see League of Nations, Special Joint Committee on Private Foreign Investment, *Conditions of Private Foreign Investment* (1946); Lewis, *The United States and Foreign Investment Problems* 141-67 (1948); Comment, "Point Four: A Re-examination of Ends and Means," 59 *Yale L.J.* 1277, 1286-92 (1950); Brandon, "Legal Deterrents and Incentives to Private Foreign Investments," 43 *Grotius Soc. Transactions* 39 (1957); Higgins, *Economic Development* 572-78 (1959). See also the major surveys in this field, National Industrial Conference Board, *Obstacles to Direct Foreign Investment* (Gaston ed., 1951); United States Department of Commerce, *Factors Limiting U.S. Investment Abroad*, Part 1: Survey of Factors in Foreign Countries (1953), Part 2: Business Views on the U.S. Government's Role (1954); [Canadian] Advisory Committee on Overseas Investment, *Report* (1951).

[3] For an interesting classification of "types of underdeveloped countries," see Lacoste, *Les pays sous-développés* 77-92 (1959).

investment in these countries are of diverse character, economic, legal, social, and psychological. They follow no fixed hierarchy of importance and they are largely cumulative in their effects. The total or partial elimination of a number of these limiting factors may or may not improve the rate of the flow of private capital; the remaining obstacles in each case may be sufficient to keep the flow at its present level. Elimination of one or more impediments is therefore a necessary but not a sufficient condition for the increase of private foreign investment. This is particularly important for us to note, since the present study is devoted to only a few of the deterrents in question—namely, those that can be removed through legal reform, or, more particularly, by means of state guarantees. Their removal will render an increase of private foreign investment in the underdeveloped areas more probable but cannot make it certain.

The Economic Background

One very important obstacle to private foreign investment in underdeveloped countries is the presence of competing opportunities for highly profitable investments in the already developed countries. This has been considered by some authorities as the most important single cause of the shortage in private international investment in underdeveloped areas.[4] During the postwar period, with the exception of relatively short and rare deflationary periods, the profit rates in most developed countries have been consistently high. While the rates of return of foreign investment have generally been, equally consistently, higher,[5] the relative lack of response on the

[4] Cf., e.g., Higgins, *Economic Development* 571–72, 579–82 (1959); Diamond, "Economic Problems of Foreign Trade and Investment in Underdeveloped Countries," 17 *Ohio State L.J.* 254, 256 (1956). See also Nurkse, "International Investment To-day in the Light of Nineteenth-Century Experience," 64 *Econ. J.* 744, 753–54 (1954); Buchanan and Ellis, *Approaches* 345 (1955); Myrdal, *An International Economy* 110 (1956).

[5] The average annual rate of return for American direct foreign investment from 1946 to 1953 was 15 percent of book value, compared to about 10.5 percent

part of businessmen indicates that, with the notable exception of petroleum enterprises,[6] the existing difference between rates of return was not considered as sufficiently high.

Another important factor, which limits the amount of capital invested in underdeveloped areas and determines the particular form of the investment is the absence of sizable markets in such areas.[7] The effect on the size of foreign investment is evident. Prospective foreign investors will not attempt to invest in any industry producing for the local market, if the latter is too small to permit a reasonably sized industry as well as future expansion. Another equally important consequence is the trend toward investment in industries producing for the export market.

A third serious impediment to private foreign investment in underdeveloped countries is the lack of certain basic facilities, such as railways, roads, or electric power.[8] This is the cause of major bottlenecks in their economies. Another group of major bottlenecks relates to the lack of some categories of personnel whose direct or indirect cooperation is essential for the effective operation of the foreign investor's enterprise. There is a general scarcity of skilled native labor and there are few trained persons who can be used in higher managerial positions,[9] while the use of aliens, even apart

---

for domestic investments. Axilrod, "Yield on U.S. Foreign Investment, 1920–1953," 38 *Rev. Econ. & Stat.* 331, 333 (table 2) (1956). Similar figures, for the periods 1946–55 and 1950–55, respectively, are given by Adler, Statement in U.S. Congress, Joint Committee on the Economic Report (84th Cong., 1st sess.), *Hearings before the Subcommittee on Foreign Economic Policy* 456, 458–59 (1955) and Mikesell, *Promoting United States Private Investment Abroad* 21–22 (1957). Cf. also Rippy, *Globe and Hemisphere: Latin America's Place in the Postwar Foreign Relations of the United States* 73–77 (1958).

[6] The yield on petroleum investments abroad was, in 1951, over 24 percent of the investments' value, while that on domestic petroleum investments was about 11.5 percent. Cf. Axilrod, *supra* note 5, at 333 (table 3).

[7] For a masterful analysis of this factor, see Nurkse, *Problems* 6 *et seq.* and *passim* (1953). See also Diamond, *supra* note 4, at 257–59; Meier and Baldwin, *Economic Development* 316–18 (1957).

[8] Cf. the data and observations in Bhatt, "Employment and Capital Formation in Underdeveloped Economies," 11 *Economia Internazionale* 121, 124–26 (1958).

[9] For some good surveys of the question, see Harbison, "Entrepreneurial Organization as a Factor in Economic Development," 70 *Qu. J. Econ.* 364 (1956); Harbison and Myers, *Management in the Industrial World. An International*

from possible legal difficulties, is not always possible or appropriate. The state of public administration, on whose smooth and efficient functioning depends the development of both the private and the public sectors of the economy, is also in most cases far from satisfactory. Banking and credit facilities are often inadequate, too, and the related institutions are not always adequately developed.

Political instability is another impediment of major importance.[10] The political situation of poverty-ridden countries in South-East Asia, Latin America, or the Middle East is a function of their economic and social condition. Several of these countries have only recently acquired their independence. Others, while nominally independent for a longer period, have until recently been ruled by totalitarian factions, often subservient to foreign interests. Their politics are governed by a reaction to their previous condition. But they have not yet found the form and substance of their political regimes and their peoples have yet to learn the techniques and limitations of self-government. Their emergence as political units coincided with the deep division of the world into opposed "blocs"; the "cold war" has contributed to the political difficulties and confusion already existing in these states. As a consequence, the political climate in underdeveloped countries is today stormy and unpredictable. Not only governments and parties but political regimes as well are rapidly changing, with consequent effects on the legal regulation of the economic affairs of these countries. Economic underdevelopment greatly contributes to the persistence of political instability though it is not the sole factor affecting it.

Analysis (1959); Vakil and Brahmanand, "Technical Knowledge and Managerial Capacity as Limiting Factors on Industrial Expansion in Underdeveloped Countries," 6 *Int'l Soc. Sc. Bull.* 212 (1954); Lewis, *The Theory of Economic Growth* 177–82 (1955); UN, Economic Commission for Asia and the Far East, "Fields of Economic Development Handicapped by Lack of Trained Personnel in ECAFE Countries," 1 *Economic Bulletin for Asia and the Far East* 40 (1950); UN, Department of Economic and Social Affairs, *Management of Industrial Enterprises in Under-Developed Countries* (1958).

[10] Cf. the recent study of Spengler, "Economic Development: Political Preconditions and Political Consequences," 22 *J. of Politics* 387 (1960). For a recent general survey and interpretation, see *The Politics of the Developing Areas* (Almond and Coleman ed., 1960).

Closely related to their political instability and partly due to the same causes is the economic and financial instability of the underdeveloped countries. It is chiefly a consequence of their underdevelopment, of their political situation, and of world economic and financial conditions.[11] Its importance as a deterrent to foreign investment is evident. Financial instability in the capital-importing countries is the main reason for the predominance of direct investment, because of the dependence of portfolio investment on stable financial conditions.

One can do little more than enumerate these obstacles. Their main common characteristic is that they do not relate specifically to private foreign investment. They affect it to the same extent, more or less, to which they influence other manifestations of the economic and political life in the underdeveloped countries. Generally, they are not due to direct governmental action. They are manifestations of the conditions prevailing there and of the very fact of economic underdevelopment.

It is difficult to propose any concrete measures for the elimination of these obstacles. The average foreign investor can affect them only slightly. He may adapt his products and techniques to local conditions when possible; he may provide himself the necessary basic facilities for the operation of his enterprise if his investment is important or profitable enough. Governments, especially those of the capital-importing countries, can be more effective. They can offer tax exemptions or other arrangements, thus effectively raising the investment's profit rate; they can improve their own administrative services and provide training for skilled workers and technicians;

[11] Especially their dependence on the export of primary products, whose prices are subject to wide fluctuations. Cf. Viner, "Stability and Progress: The Poorer Countries' Problem," in *Stability and Progress in the World Economy* 41, 59 *et seq.* (Hague ed., 1958); Diamond, *supra* note 4, at 262; Blough, "The Role of Government in Promoting Economic Stability," in *The State of the Social Sciences* 353, 360–61 (White ed., 1956). See also the United Nations Department of Economic Affairs studies, *Relative Prices of Exports and Imports of Underdeveloped Countries* (1949); *Instability in Export Markets of Underdeveloped Countries* (1952); *Commodity Trade and Economic Development* (1954) and *World Economic Survey 1958* 17–176 (1959). But see the critical comments of May, "Folklore and Fact about Underdeveloped Areas," 33 *Foreign Affairs* 212 (1955).

and they can affect, through their fiscal policies, their countries' financial situation, though not to the point of total control. In most cases, economic development itself constitutes the only really effective solution. We are thus confronted with another vicious circle, or rather with a group of vicious circles. Any one of them may be broken by government or other action. How to break all of them at the same time, as is necessary, constitutes the main problem not only of foreign private investment but of economic development itself.

The Investment Climate in Underdeveloped Countries

A second category of obstacles to private foreign investment in the underdeveloped countries consists of those sometimes classified under the general heading of "investment climate." [12] For present purposes, this term should be understood as referring to the general attitude in a given country toward foreign investment, chiefly as expressed in the relevant legal regulations. Many elements, of diverse character, contribute to the formation of a country's investment climate. The use of a single term is more than a matter of convenience, however; it suggests the underlying unity in the origin and functions of these various elements.

A country's investment climate depends closely, though not solely, on positive or negative action on the part of its government. Government interference in a country's economy is not a new idea, nor is it a practice confined to underdeveloped areas. In fact, the question of state interference is one of degree only. It is true, nonetheless, that, in the noncommunist world, there is a stronger tendency toward extensive interference by the state in the underdeveloped countries than in most of the developed countries. This should be attributed to the very fact of their underdevelopment. Economic

[12] The term is commonly employed in a number of related meanings, differing from each other in their inclusiveness. The meaning here adopted includes all factors affecting foreign investors chiefly in a legal form and neither purely economic nor purely psychological in character. For similar use of the term, see Diamond, *supra* note 4, at 263; Brandon, "Legal Deterrents and Incentives to Private Foreign Investments," 43 *Grotius Soc. Transactions* 39, 41 and *passim* (1957).

history is instructive in this connection. In all the now developed countries, governments had to intervene extensively in the economy during the initial stages of the economic development in order to make such development possible.[13]

Thus, the conditions today prevailing in the underdeveloped countries make it necessary for their governments to undertake a wide range of functions. They have to provide the basic facilities that are lacking, to substitute for reluctant or missing entrepreneurs in founding new industries,[14] and to protect the weaker classes from exploitation. In the developed countries, some of the corresponding functions belong to the private sector, while others are exercised by the government through indirect measures, which cannot be very effective in less developed economies.

The ultimate synthesis of all state measures of interference in a given country is the national plan, which provides a classification of particular measures and specific objectives. That the underdeveloped countries must plan can hardly be disputed, but the precise content of particular plans as well as the degree and manner of state interference are highly controversial issues.

State measures affecting private foreign investment are taken in response to a number of causes which will be examined in more detail when each of the varieties of measures is studied by itself.

[13] For a theoretical statement of the wider issues involved, see Stone, "The Myths of Planning and Laissez-Faire: A Re-orientation," 18 *Geo. Wash. L. Rev.* 1 (1949). See also the historical and theoretical studies in *The State and Economic Growth* (Aitken ed., 1959). And cf. Brebner, "Laissez Faire and State Intervention in Nineteenth-Century Britain," 8 *J. Econ. History Supp.* 59 (1948); Aubrey, "The Role of the State in Economic Development," 41 *Am. Econ. Rev. Proc.* 266, 266–69 (1951); Gerschenkron, "Economic Backwardness in Historical Perspective," in *The Progress of Underdeveloped Areas* 3 (Hoselitz ed., 1952); Easterbrook, "State Control and Free Enterprise in Their Impact on Economic Growth," *idem* 60; Baster, "Development and the Free Economy—Some Typical Dilemmas," 7 *Kyklos* 1 (1954); Spengler, *supra* note 10.

[14] The weakness of the private sector in many underdeveloped economies is one of the chief reasons for the high degree of state intervention. Cf. Baster, *supra* note 13; Krivine, "Private Enterprise in an Underdeveloped Economy," 30 *Political Qu.* 379 (1959); Bhambri, "Myth and Reality about Private Enterprise in India," 12 *World Politics* 186 (1960); and cf. *contra* Bauer and Yamey, *Economics* 82–112 (1957). For an interesting description of the conditions prevailing in some underdeveloped areas, see Tax, *Penny Capitalism* (Smithsonian Institution Publ., 1953).

At this point two general categories of such measures may be distinguished on the basis of the relation of their objectives to foreign investment. The first consists of measures relating specifically to foreign investors whose activities they are intended to control or regulate—screening requirements, for example, or restrictions on the ownership of enterprises, or measures which are directly discriminatory against the foreign investor. The second category is composed of measures whose objectives are general in the sense that they relate to both foreign and domestic investors but which either affect foreign investors more than domestic ones (for example, exchange restrictions) or affect both to the same extent but are of vital importance to all investors (for example, expropriation or taxation measures).

It does not seem likely that state interference by itself is the chief cause of unfavorable investment climates. State interference works both ways, and few investors have ever been heard to complain about interference favorable to their interests. It is rather the particular quality of state interference today that prospective foreign investors find objectionable. The chief cause for this quality lies in the general attitude of the peoples in underdeveloped countries toward foreign interference in their political and economic affairs. Their attitude is governed by a desire for liberation from foreign influences and the assertion of national autonomy in the economic, political, and even cultural spheres. One should be careful not to confuse such "nationalism" with that of European states in the nineteenth century. The contemporary brand of nationalism is much more openly economic in its origin and manifestations than its Western counterpart. Moreover, it expresses a strong feeling of resentment; it is a reaction to earlier situations and conditions. Such nationalism is not solely, not even chiefly, a negative attitude. It is the strongest of the integrating forces today operative in the underdeveloped countries. The success of their development policies depends upon it as much as the success of their liberation struggles did. Nationalist feelings may thus provide some of the incentives and other conditions for economic development which are inadequate or lacking today in the underdeveloped countries.[15]

With specific regard to private foreign investment, nationalism is generally expressed by a distrust of foreign investors. Foreign investment has often been associated in the past with political and economic control of the capital-importing state.[16] However changed the situation might be today, past experience cannot easily be forgotten or ignored. Even under present-day conditions, the size and power of some of the internationally operating modern corporations, as well as the open support afforded to them by their governments, strengthen the distrust and suspicion felt by the people and the governments of the underdeveloped countries.

A final note before entering into the discussion of particular elements of a country's investment climate. The conditions here studied constitute, for the foreign investors, "non-business risks"— that is to say, risks far beyond those which the average businessman regards as normal. This qualification does not add anything to our picture of the factors themselves. It provides, however, an insight into the prospective investors' mentality. The investors' criteria are generally the habits and conventions of their own economies. Extensive interference and an unfriendly public attitude are risks which the investors are not willing to undertake without added

[15] This idea has been stated in a variety of ways by several writers, but it has yet to receive an appropriately thorough and extensive treatment. See, e.g., Wallich, "Some Notes towards a Theory of Derived Development," Paper presented at the Third Meeting of Central Bank Technicians of the American Continent (1952), reprinted in *The Economics of Underdevelopment* 189, 191 (Agarwala and Singh ed., 1958); Singer, "Obstacles to Economic Development," 20 *Social Research* 19, 22 (1953); Myint, "An Interpretation of Economic Backwardness," 7 *Oxford Econ. Papers* 132 (1954), reprinted in *The Economics of Underdevelopment* 93, 131–32 (Agarwala and Singh ed., 1958); Levy, "Some Social Obstacles to 'Capital Formation' in 'Underdeveloped Areas,'" in *Capital Formation and Economic Growth* 441, 483–84 (Abramovits ed., 1955); Bonné, "Towards a Theory of Implanted Development in Underdeveloped Countries," 9 *Kyklos* 1, 17 (1956); Bendix, "A Study of Managerial Ideologies," 5 *Economic Development and Cultural Change* 118, 128 (1957); Nicholls, "Accommodating Economic Change in Underdeveloped Countries," 49 *Am. Econ. Rev. Proc.* 156, 156–58 (1959). And cf. Myrdal, *Beyond the Welfare State* 200–225 (1960).

[16] For a survey of past and present conditions, see Nichols, "Hazards of American Private Investment in Underdeveloped Countries," 4 *Orbis* 174 (1960).

inducement. However correct or realistic, this is a point of view which should be kept in mind when discussing the investors' opinions on their own interests and on the problems of foreign investment.

The "Screening" of Foreign Investment

One of the situations sometimes cited as constituting an obstacle to private foreign investment in underdeveloped countries is the imposition by these countries of restrictions or conditions on the entry of foreign capital. Typically, such restrictions take the form of "screening": [17] in order to import his capital, the prospective investor needs prior approval of the competent government body to which he submits his plans and which reaches its decision on the basis of considerations of general economic policy. Lately, this practice has assumed in many countries a slightly different form, closely related to the granting of legal guarantees to foreign investors. In these countries the importation of foreign capital is left nominally free and no approval of the government of the capital-receiving state is mandatory. On the other hand, if such approval is granted, certain legal guarantees or privileges, or both, regarding such matters as taxation and exchange restrictions are granted along with it. Thus, the approval of the capital-importing state becomes necessary in substance, even if not in form.

The requirement of approval, in whatever form, is founded on a number of considerations of economic policy. Perhaps the most important and, in any case, the most widely found consideration, is the concern over the condition of the capital-importing country's balance-of-payments.[18] A second objective of screening relates to the avoidance of excessive concentration of foreign investment in a

[17] For a recent survey of screening procedures and criteria, see UN Document A/AC. 97/5/Rev. 1, 27 December 1960, pp. 52–60.
[18] Balance-of-payments difficulties also account in large part for another important obstacle to private foreign investment, namely, exchange control, on which see *infra* pp. 47 *et seq*.

few fields. Such concentration of productive capital, within a poor and capital-hungry economy, might well create difficult long-range problems.[19] More generally, control over the entry and direction of capital is an indispensable condition for the operation of national economic planning. Finally, screening may be used in order to exclude foreign investors from certain fields of the economy,[20] to avoid the possible inflationary effects of foreign investment, or to pursue any other objectives deemed appropriate by the government of the capital-importing country. The desirability of such objectives cannot, of course, be evaluated in the abstract, since it depends on the conditions obtaining in each particular country.

The practice of screening has sometimes been blamed by prospective investors for contributing seriously to the shortage of private international investment. Its removal has been advocated as a necessary precondition for the increase of such investments.[21] The extent, however, to which screening affects the volume of foreign capital invested in underdeveloped areas is open to grave doubts. It is true that in some cases the criteria in effect express not only excessive nationalistic attitudes but also a desire to protect existing uneconomic or privileged domestic industries. Furthermore, screening sometimes results in the establishment of a governmental bureaucracy which may be to some extent antagonistic to foreign investors. The latter complain that screening authorities are generally rigid and sometimes arbitrary in their application of the relevant regulations; their inquiries into the projected enterprises' plans and prospects are detailed to the point of absurdity and their

[19] Cf. Singer, "The Distribution of Gains between Investing and Borrowing Countries," 40 *Am. Econ. Rev. Proc.* 473 (1950). See also Nurkse, *Problems* 24–31 (1953); Myrdal, *An International Economy* 99 et seq. (1956); Baran, *The Political Economy of Growth* 178 et seq. (1957). The matter is in dispute; cf. *contra* Collado, "Private U.S. Direct Investment Abroad," in *International Banking and Foreign Trade* 180, 183 et seq. (1956); and, by direct implication, Pizer and Cutler, *U.S. Investments in the Latin American Economy* 3–26 and *passim* (U.S. Dep't. of Commerce, 1957).

[20] Cf. *infra* pp. 40 et seq.

[21] Cf., e.g., International Chamber of Commerce, *Fair Treatment for International Investments: International Code*, Appendix, 19 (I.C.C. Brochure No. 129, 1949); Collado, *supra* note 19, at 191; Brandon, *supra* note 12 at 51.

standards of valuation of such capital assets as machinery and patents are arbitrary and detrimental to the investors' interests. Such charges may in several instances be justified, but they indicate the need for improving rather than for totally eliminating the practice of screening. From a legal point of view, the lawfulness of the practice in international law cannot be contested.[22] Furthermore, when adequately administered, screening seems to have little adverse effect on the individual investor's interests. Before its admission into a country, foreign capital is not committed in any way; once it is admitted, it generally ceases to be affected by the conditions regarding its entry.[23] There is then considerable substance to the argument that screening is "probably desirable from the standpoint of the foreign investor," since it carries with it the assurance that the investor has successfully met the capital-importing country's public policy requirements as well as certain safeguards and possibly privileges.[24]

Restrictions on the Entry of Foreign Capital

The practice of screening is as a rule closely related to the imposition of restrictions on the entry of foreign capital, either into certain specified fields of the economy or into the country as a whole. Such restrictions are usually imposed by legislation, but they sometimes result indirectly from the consistent policies of screening authorities. Some of these restrictions are imposed for reasons of national security and have little to do with foreign investment. For instance, in

[22] Screening may be considered as coming under the general rules allowing states to impose any restrictions they see fit on the entry and residence of aliens; cf. 1 Hyde, *International Law* 216–18 (rev. ed., 1945); and cf. also Brandon, *supra* note 12, at 51. Roth, *The Minimum Standard of International Law Applied to Aliens* 46 (1949), holds that "excessive use of the discretionary power of a state in this matter" would constitute an "act against international comity," but he does not indicate what the specific legal effects would be.

[23] Screening may, however, be harmful to the investors when it relates to the entry of additional capital to be invested in an already established enterprise. Denial of entry in such a case may be highly damaging to the enterprise. This is a special case, and special provision can be made about it in the relevant regulations.

[24] Mikesell, *Promoting United States Private Investment Abroad* 45 (1957).

many states the acquisition of real property near the state's borders or coasts is forbidden to aliens. This restriction affects foreign investors only if they are exploiting or intend to exploit natural resources located in such territories. Such restrictions hardly affect the country's investment climate.

In most underdeveloped countries, however (as well as in most developed ones, though we are not dealing with them here), there exist today certain additional restrictions which are directed specifically against foreign investment. In large part such restrictions express the deep distrust of foreign investors which, as has been noted, prevails in many such countries. Control over a country's key industries entails a significant measure of influence over the operations of its whole economy. It is understandable that this may be found inadmissible by governments which, while valuing highly their country's independence, still feel rather insecure about it.

Such restrictions, however, often seek to achieve not the total exclusion of aliens but the increased participation of local capital in foreign-financed enterprises. Such participation is highly useful to the capital-importing country, for it tends to "facilitate the integration of such enterprises in the economic system of the country and promote the development of domestic capital and skills." [25]

The lawfulness of restrictions of this type under international law is well-settled.[26] It is well accepted in international law that a state has exclusive competence to regulate all matters pertaining to the acquisition and transfer of property within its territory as well as to determine the conditions for the exercise in it of the economic activities of natural or legal persons. It is not unlawful for it to require that no foreign-owned enterprises operate in certain industries or that certain pursuits be open to its nationals only. A fortiori, it may require that local nationals own a part of such enterprises.

[25] League of Nations, Special Joint Committee on Private Foreign Investment, *Conditions of Private Foreign Investment* 14 (1946). A thorough survey of measures requiring or encouraging such participation is found in UN Document A/AC. 97/5/Rev. 1, 27 December 1960, pp. 76–95. And cf. *infra*, note 36.
[26] Cf., e.g., 1 Hyde, *International Law* 650 *et seq.* (rev. ed., 1945); 3 Hackworth, *Digest of International Law* 612–19 (1942); Brandon, *supra note* 12, at 51.

In most instances, the ownership of a minority share by local nationals is accepted as sufficient to permit the establishment of a foreign-financed enterprise. In India, where a 1948 government policy statement provides that, with respect to all industrial undertakings, "as a rule, the major interest in ownership and effective control should always be in Indian hands," it is further provided that "power will be taken to deal with exceptional cases in a manner calculated to serve the national interest." [27] In fact, several enterprises in which aliens own a majority share have been allowed to operate.[28] Government policies favoring the participation of local nationals in the ownership of foreign-controlled enterprises have resulted in the creation of jointly-owned undertakings in several other countries, such as Burma and Turkey.[29]

Whether or not there are general requirements on participation of nationals in the ownership of local enterprises, most countries place restrictions on the entry of aliens and foreign capital in a number of fields, mainly, in mining, petroleum extraction,[30] transportation, public utilities, banking, and insurance.[31] In Colombia, for instance, aliens may have only a minority share in the ownership of enterprises engaged in air transport or coastal shipping.[32] In several countries, certain fields are state controlled and the entry of private investors, domestic as well as foreign, in them is severely limited.[33]

[27] Government of India Resolution on Industrial Policy, of April 6, 1948; cf. UN, Department of Economic Affairs, *Foreign Investment Laws and Regulations of the Countries of Asia and the Far East* (hereinafter cited UN, *Investment Laws*) 15 (1951); U.S. Department of Commerce, *Investment in India* 107 (1953); Narayanan, "India" in *Legal Aspects of Foreign Investment* (hereinafter cited *Legal Aspects*) 249, 256–57 (Friedmann and Pugh ed., 1959).

[28] Cf. *Joint International Business Ventures* 194, 197–98 (Friedmann and Kalmanoff ed., 1961).

[29] Cf. *idem* 194–96.

[30] For a thorough survey and analysis of restrictions in these fields, see United Nations, Office of Legal Affairs, *Survey of Mining Legislation with Special Reference to Asia and the Far East* (1957).

[31] For a general discussion and description of such measures, see UN Document A/AC. 97/5/Rev. 1, 27 December 1960, pp. 150 *et seq.*

[32] See UN, *Foreign Capital* 71 (1955); U.S. Department of Commerce, *Investment in Colombia* 13 (1953); Kalmanoff and Bernal Salamanca, "Colombia" in *Legal Aspects* 169, 174–75.

[33] For a survey, see UN Document A/AC. 97/5/Rev. 1, 27 December 1960, pp. 161–66.

In several of the Latin American states, for instance, there exist state petroleum monopolies of varying strictness.[34] In India, shipbuilding, banking, mining, petroleum extraction, coastal shipping, and several other industries are under government control, though private investors, domestic or foreign, may be admitted under certain conditions.[35]

It is now possible to assess more clearly the importance of restrictions on the ownership of enterprises by aliens as a deterrent to private foreign investment. Provisions of this sort may affect unfavorably the interests of foreign investors when they require majority participation or effective control of the enterprise by local nationals. Even in such cases, several foreign investors have found it profitable to operate in underdeveloped countries, relying either on the continuing need for the services they provide or on a number of legal arrangements, such as management contracts, which permit them to retain effective control over the operation of the enterprise. As has been noted, however, majority participation of nationals is not often required in fact; when it is, special arrangements and individual exceptions are often allowed.

Requirements for minority participation are more common but it is hardly possible to regard them as major deterrents to foreign investment. Their main disadvantages seem to be the sharing of profits, on the one hand, and the possibility of friction between the "partners," on the other. But they also offer distinct advantages to the foreign investor. Collaboration with local businessmen assures a knowledge of local conditions, economic as well as political or cultural. It also assists in increasing good will in countries which are preeminently nationalistic and, often enough, it makes possible the use of local "connections" to promote the interests of the enterprise. The usefulness of such association is then undeniable [36] and

[34] Cf., e.g., Aramayo, "Chile" in *Legal Aspects* 135, at 150; Nattier, "Brazil" *idem*, 77, at 82; Hidalgo, "Mexico" *idem*, 355, at 356–57; UN, *Foreign Capital* 19 (1955).

[35] Cf. Government of India Resolution on Industrial Policy, of April 6, 1948, and Statement of the Prime Minister on the participation of foreign capital in industry, of April 6, 1949, *supra* note 27.

[36] For a thorough discussion of the related legal and economic problems, see *Joint International Business Ventures* (Friedmann and Kalmanoff ed., 1961).

it has been recognized even by conservative spokesmen for prospective investors.[37]

Restrictions on the Employment of Aliens

Similar problems arise with regard to the requirements found in the labor legislation of several states concerning the obligatory employment of their nationals by all enterprises operating therein. Under such legislation, a certain proportion of the personnel of all enterprises must be nationals of the country in which they are operating. An additional or alternative requirement is sometimes imposed to the effect that a minimum percentage of the payroll of an enterprise must be paid to local nationals. The fixed proportions vary from 50 to 90 percent. Limitations of this type may also be imposed indirectly by means of administrative regulations concerning the entry, residence, and work permits of aliens.

Limitations on the employment of aliens are a direct consequence of the labor situation in underdeveloped countries.[38] They are calculated to contribute to the raising of the general level of employment and to reduce the existing shortage of native skilled labor.[39]

[37] "[I]t is frequently desirable that local capital participate with foreign capital in enterprises established at the initiative of foreign investors. . . ." National Association of Manufacturers, International Relations Committee, *The Bold New Plan—A Program for Underdeveloped Areas*, Annex A, Statement of Principles Prerequisite to the Free Flow of Foreign Investment Capital, 2 (1949, mimeo.).

[38] These limitations, and, more generally, the state of labor law in many underdeveloped countries today, may serve as a vivid illustration of the basic contradiction in their present situation, namely, that between a backward economy and the modern demands for nationalism, democracy, and social welfare.

In attempting to establish certain standards of "social justice," labor legislation in these countries tends to add new elements of rigidity to those already present in underdeveloped economies. Nonetheless, such legislation is perhaps more needed (in terms of immediate human welfare) in such countries than in the developed ones. No doubt, it is necessary for these countries to keep "welfare" legislation at a "minimum" level; cf., e.g., Spengler, "Economic Development: Political Preconditions and Political Consequences," 22 *J. of Politics* 387, 414 (1960); Myrdal, *Economic Theory* 82 (1957). Even a "minimum" level, however, will certainly have to be far above that of, say, the European equivalent in the beginning of the industrial revolution.

[39] This is of particular importance with respect to managerial personnel, whose training largely depends on practical experience; cf. Lewis, *The Theory of Economic Growth* 258 (1955).

Their legality in international law is unquestionable, since they rest on the uncontested right of every state to control the entry of aliens in its territory and to regulate their economic activities therein.[40]

With respect to unskilled labor, no serious problem seems to arise, since in the great majority of cases there exist obvious economic reasons in favor of the employment of local labor. It is true that in a few cases the importation of foreign cheap labor might be practically possible and economically profitable to the individual investor. But the social, political and economic consequences of such a practice to the capital-importing country as a whole are as a rule such that its limitation is generally indicated.

More serious problems are raised by the limitations on the employment of skilled personnel in technical or managerial capacities. Foreign investors tend to emphasize the complications and inefficiency likely to arise because of the presence of inexperienced and unqualified persons among the higher-level personnel. They stress their need for having the freedom to employ foreign technical and managerial personnel in order to ensure the efficient operation of their enterprises. Such fears and demands are to some extent justified, but the needs of the capital-importing state's economy cannot but take precedence over the mere convenience of foreign investors.

On the other hand, there is no doubt that such legislation should be elastic enough to admit of exceptions whenever the employment of foreign personnel is essential for the efficient operation of the enterprise. The relevant legislation in most underdeveloped countries makes special provision for such exceptions, though wide variations exist between states. In some cases, special proportions are determined with respect to high-level or trained personnel, differing from the proportions applicable with regard to unskilled labor. In

[40] Such limitations may, however, be illegal according to the municipal law of a particular country. Such is the case in the United States, where it has been held that the right of aliens "to work for a living in the common occupations of the community" is protected from state interference by the Fourteenth Amendment to the U.S. Constitution; Truax et al. v. Raich, 239 U.S. 33 (1915). Cf. 3 Hackworth, *Digest of International Law* 612–14 (1942); *The Constitution of the U.S.A. Analysis and Interpretation* 1157–58 (Corwin ed., 1953); Wilson, *U.S. Commercial Treaties and International Law* 60–66 (1960).

Burma only 25 percent of skilled personnel must consist of Burmese nationals,[41] while in Pakistan [42] the required proportion is 50 percent. The labor legislation in several other states admits exceptions to the general rules requiring set proportions of nationals in the personnel of an enterprise in cases where the aliens involved are specially qualified and no local persons correspondingly qualified are available.[43] Such provisions are, of course, interpreted and applied with varying degrees of strictness.[44]

Requirements of this sort are sometimes also imposed with respect to the members of the boards of directors or equivalent bodies of domestic corporations. In the United Arab Republic, for instance, the majority of the members of any company's board of directors must be citizens of the Republic.[45] In most instances, such provisions require that company directors be residents, and not necessarily citizens, of the country. Thus, in Iran, all members of a corporation's board of directors must be permanent residents.[46] In Mexico a similar legislative provision is construed as applying to managing directors only.[47] Several capital-importing countries do not impose such requirements,[48] but in some cases similar demands are made as a matter of policy rather than statute, on the basis of the consistent practice of the competent administrative authorities.

Such requirements do not in fact relate to employment of aliens or to labor legislation but rather to ownership of enterprises and company law. They are an effective indirect (though fairly obvious)

[41] Cf. UN *Investment Laws* 2–3 (1951).
[42] With respect to certain industries only and with a gradual increase in the proportion of nationals employed; cf. *idem* 57–58; U.S. Department of Commerce, *Investment in Pakistan* 54, 187 (1954).
[43] This is, for instance, the case in Brazil, Chile, Mexico, and Uruguay; cf. UN *Foreign Capital* 56, 65, 115, 141 (1955). Also in Ceylon and India; cf. UN *Investment Laws* 8, 14 (1951); Narayanan, "India" in *Legal Aspects* 249, 261.
[44] An important related problem is that of the effect of exchange restrictions on the remittances of foreign personnel, on which see *infra* pp. 49, 162.
[45] Decree of August 12, 1958; cf. Habachy, "United Arab Republic" in *Legal Aspects* 562, 572.
[46] Cf. Nasr, "Iran" *idem* 280, 285.
[47] Cf. Hidalgo, "Mexico" *idem* 355, 365–66.
[48] Cf., e.g., Kalmanoff and Bernal Salamanca, "Colombia" *idem* 169, 175; Koh, "Korea" *idem* 334, 345; Gibbons, "Venezuela" *idem* 647, 652.

means for achieving participation of local nationals in the ownership and control of enterprises established by foreign investors.[49] As such, they are subject to the considerations advanced in the previous section.

Exchange Control and Restrictions

Foreign exchange control has a long history but, like other mercantilist policies, it had disappeared from the peacetime practice of states in the nineteenth and early twentieth centuries. It made its appearance again in the interwar period and has been extensively used since the end of World War Two. In recent years, its dominance has begun to decrease,[50] but it still incontestably constitutes an all-important feature of the international financial scene.

In its typical form, exchange control involves a monopoly of all foreign exchange by a central agency which handles all imports and exports of foreign currencies and allocates the available foreign exchange. Exchange restrictions may also involve the use of multiple exchange rates, that is to say, different currency rates for different categories of transactions.

The basic purpose of exchange control is the protection of a country's balance-of-payments position through the limitation of effective demand for foreign exchange and the full utilization of available foreign currency. Its original objective, in the early 'thirties, was the limitation of outward movements of capital in times of financial crisis. Such control involves restrictions on capital outflows only, without any limitation on current transactions.[51] This

[49] Cf. *Joint International Business Ventures* 199–202 (Friedmann and Kalmanoff ed., 1961).

[50] The most significant manifestation of this trend has been the adoption of convertibility by several European countries at the end of 1958. For a statement of its importance, see Jacobsson, "Toward More Stable Money," 37 *Foreign Affairs* 378 (1959) and cf. International Monetary Fund, *Tenth Annual Report on Exchange Restrictions 1959* 1–9; Goldstein, "Progress in Currency Convertibility and Its Significance for Trade and Investment," in Southwestern Legal Foundation, *Proceedings of the 1959 Institute on Private Investments Abroad* 165 (1959).

[51] Transfers and payments for "current transactions" are defined in the IMF

form of control is still permitted, under the provisions of the International Monetary Fund Agreement.[52] However, in view of the continuing national and international financial difficulties, of the necessities of its operation and of its suitability as a tool of economic policy, exchange control soon spread over all international transactions. It also came to serve a variety of subsidiary purposes: protecting currency parities, providing public revenue, or supporting domestic industries.

Foreign exchange control is of particular importance to the underdeveloped countries. The fluctuations in the prices of primary products, which are these countries' principal exports, constitute a constant source of balance-of-payments instability.[53] The effort to industrialize places great strains on their balances-of-payments.[54] Furthermore, such countries are vulnerable to the adverse effects of capital movements, particularly in view of the latter's tendency to occur in times of financial difficulties. Besides being needed to protect a country's balance-of-payments position, exchange control constitutes today one of the main tools of the underdeveloped countries' economic development policies.[55]

Originally set up by municipal legislation, exchange control led necessarily to the conclusion of numerous bilateral arrangements

---

Agreement, Article XIX (i), as payments due in connection with foreign trade and other current business, normal short-term banking and credit facilities, interest and amortization on loans, net income from and depreciation on direct investments and remittances for family living expenses. The list is not exhaustive; the term includes all "payments which are not for the purpose of transferring capital."

[52] IMF Agreement, Article VI(3).

[53] See UN, Department of Economic Affairs, *Instability in Export Markets of Under-Developed Countries* (1952); Mikesell, *Foreign Exchange in the Postwar World* 441-44 (1954); Jacobsson, "Toward More Stable Money," 37 *Foreign Affairs* 378, 382-83 (1959). And cf. the studies cited *supra* note 11.

[54] Developing countries need foreign exchange to buy the capital equipment for the establishment of new industries and the raw materials necessary for their operation. Their other expenditures before and during such operation will also be probably used in part, directly or indirectly, for imports. For a survey of balance-of-payments problems of industrialization, see UN *Processes* 58 et seq. (1955).

[55] See the survey of related policies in UN *Processes* 60-65 (1955), and the critique in Mikesell, *op. cit. supra* note 53, at 444-49.

between countries ("payment agreements"). Later, certain multilateral conventions were also concluded, the most general and most
important of which is that instituting the International Monetary
Fund.[56] The Fund's members undertook not to impose exchange
restrictions on current transactions, to furnish certain information
to the Fund regarding their financial conditions, and to abide by its
decisions or suggestions. At the same time, the Fund disposes of
reserves which its members may use to weather temporary difficulties.

Despite the development of treaty law on the matter, customary
international law seems to have evolved no special rules regarding
exchange control. The general principle applicable is that a state has
exclusive competence to regulate monetary matters. Consequently,
the imposition of exchange control and restrictions is in no way unlawful in international law.[57]

The existence, or possibility of future imposition, of exchange
control constitutes a major obstacle to foreign private investment.[58]
Foreign investors have, at best, to submit to various requirements,
formalities and delays, whenever they wish to transfer their earnings or their capital outside the country of investment. At worst,
they may not be allowed to take such funds out of the country, or
they may be permitted to take out only a fraction. Exchange control also affects foreign enterprises in that it renders difficult the
employment of foreign technical or managerial personnel, in view
of the limitations on the transfer of their salaries abroad.

The problem is not an easy one to solve. Under present conditions,

[56] Cf. Mann, *The Legal Aspects of Money* 339-40, 378-87 (2d ed., 1953); Nussbaum, *Money in the Law, National and International* 513-46 (2d ed., 1950).

[57] Cf. 1 Hyde, *International Law* 690-92 (rev. ed., 1945); Mann, *op. cit. supra*
note 56, at 419-23.

[58] According to a 1951 survey, measures of exchange control were the most frequently mentioned of the conditions regarded by American businessmen as constituting obstacles to private investment abroad; cf. National Industrial Conference
Board, *Obstacles to Direct Foreign Investment* 8 (Gaston ed., 1951). A Canadian
survey around the same time reached similar conclusions, though with certain
important differences in emphasis; cf. [Canadian] Advisory Committee on Overseas Investment, *Report* 42-44, 64-65, 69, 73 (1951).

the underdeveloped countries cannot be expected to eliminate all measures of exchange control or to guarantee that none will be imposed in the future. And foreign investors are justified in preferring to invest their capital in stable advanced countries or in industries less affected by exchange control.[59] Any improvement in the investment climate of capital-importing countries will then have to be a compromise between the two extreme positions. The measures to be taken fall mostly within the competence of the governments of the capital-importing countries, which should limit the effects of exchange control on foreign investment even if they do not eliminate it altogether.

The Fear of Expropriation

The strongest possible measure against an investor's interests is the taking of his property without compensation or with inadequate compensation. Accordingly, the fear of expropriation constitutes a serious deterrent to private foreign investment in underdeveloped countries.

The problem of expropriation is in itself but one aspect of the more general question of the status of private property in the present national and international social setting. It is not possible to deal adequately with such a problem in the present context. In broad terms, it is correct to state that the right of private property has never been an absolute one, in the sense that it has always been determined, and thereby limited, by law. In the last century, especial emphasis was placed on the rights of property owners rather than on their corresponding obligations. In our times, the emphasis has changed. The limitations imposed on private property by the laws in effect in the various states have greatly increased in scope

[59] The presence of exchange restrictions is an additional cause for the predominance of foreign investment in primary-goods industries producing for export. Since their receipts are usually in foreign currency, it is easier to have them transferred to the investors' own currency, despite certain possible limitations and other difficulties.

as well as number. The "social function" of property and the consequent duties of property owners are now stressed.[60] The extent, however, to which this trend has affected the law in every state varies greatly. There is no well-established general consensus on the matter, as there was during the latter half of the nineteenth century.

State action often affects private property indirectly, through measures regulating the exercise of property rights. But direct state action, resulting in the deprivation of individuals of their property, is also possible. The state's right to expropriate the property of its subjects has been well-established for a long time, both in positive law and in legal theory.[61] However, the manner in which this right is exercised and, ultimately, the whole conception of expropriation, have changed radically in our days. During the nineteenth century, expropriations were generally rare and their legality depended on certain strict conditions: private property was not to be taken except for a public purpose and against payment of adequate compensation. Since the end of the First World War,[62] the picture has changed completely. A great number of expropriations have occurred in a great number of states.[63] Today, expropriations are generally as-

[60] For some descriptions and comments, see Friedmann, *Law in a Changing Society* 65–89 (1959); Pound, *Jurisprudence* vol. III, 135–40, vol. V, 123–25 (1959). A survey of developments from the socialist viewpoint is found in Katzarov, *Théorie de la nationalisation* (hereinafter cited Katzarov, *Nationalisation*) 153–95 (1960).

[61] See the excellent historical survey in Mann, "Outlines of a History of Expropriation," 75 *L. Qu. Rev.* 188 (1959). The learned writer seems, however, to minimize unduly the effects of twentieth-century developments.

[62] For a discussion of certain earlier manifestations, indicative of present trends, see Katzarov, *Nationalisation* 27–32.

[63] The most systematic survey seems to be Katzarov's, *Nationalisation* 32–131. See also Friedman, *Expropriation in International Law* (hereinafter cited Friedman, *Expropriation*) 12–66 (1953); Foighel, *Nationalization* 56–69 (1957). Several detailed studies have been published, covering particular countries (especially the Western European ones). Cf., e.g., on France, 1 *Les nationalisations en France et à l'étranger: Les nationalisations en France* (Julliot de la Morandière and Byé ed., 1948); Einaudi, Byé, and Rossi, *Nationalization in France and Italy* (1955); on the United Kingdom, *Problems of Nationalized Industry* (Robson ed., 1952); and more generally, 2 *Les nationalisations en France et à l'étranger: Les nationalisations à l'étranger* (Puget ed., 1958).

sociated with social, political and economic reforms. They are large-scale operations and they assume a variety of forms, the most important of which is "nationalization," that is, the taking over by the state of the ownership and operation of whole sectors of the economy.[64] The requirements for their validity in the various states have also changed. But there is today little uniformity in the matter from which general rules could be deduced.[65]

The effect of these radical changes upon international law has yet to be ascertained with any precision. The "classical" theory of international law was largely founded on the nineteenth century Western European conception of private property. There is wide disagreement today, among states as well as among scholars, as to the extent to which modern conceptions of private property have been adopted in international law.[66] The same is true with respect to questions of expropriation or nationalization. Despite several recent attempts to formulate the law on the matter,[67] there are relatively few points which may be considered as settled.

Questions with respect to expropriations arise in international law chiefly when a state expropriates the property of aliens within its territory. Certain particular aspects of the problem, namely, those relating to the effect of state measures affecting the contractual rights

[64] For a discussion of the meaning of "nationalization," see Foighel, *Nationalization* 14–23 (1957). See also Katzarov, *Nationalisation* 21–27, 125–28.

[65] The constitutional and legislative provisions with respect to expropriation which are in effect in the various states are reviewed in detail in UN Document A/AC. 97/5/Rev. 1, 27 December 1960, pp. 125–50.

[66] The main difficulty, of course, is that conceptions vary widely between the states of the world community. For a perceptive early statement of the problem, see Dunn, "International Law and Private Property Rights," 28 *Columbia L. Rev.* 166 (1928). A more recent discussion, from the socialist (though not orthodox Marxist) viewpoint, is found in Katzarov, *Nationalisation* 372–91, for an English version of which see his "Private Property and Public International Law," 84 *J. Droit Int'l* (Clunet) 6 (1957). Indications of a natural law approach to this issue may be found in Wortley, *Expropriation in Public International Law* (hereinafter cited Wortley, *Expropriation*) 12 *et seq.* (1959).

[67] In addition to a considerable number of articles on the problem, five recent books have dealt with it; Friedman, *Expropriation* (1953); Foighel, *Nationalization* (1957); Wortley, *Expropriation* (1959); Katzarov, *Nationalisation* 392–483 (1960); and White, *Nationalisation of Foreign Property* (1961).

of aliens, will be dealt with at a later stage.[68] It is generally accepted that expropriations in violation of international commitments of the state are internationally unlawful. Normally, a direct consequence of any expropriation of alien property is the expropriating state's obligation to grant fair compensation to the aliens affected. Whether as a condition for the expropriation's legality or as an obligation arising out of the act of expropriation,[69] the payment of compensation is well-established in modern state practice as well as in theory and judicial practice.[70]

The main field of controversy is the manner and the extent to which, in the absence of discrimination or violation of international commitments, a state may protect its national whose property has been taken by another state without compensation or with inadequate compensation. No general answer to the above question is possible at this stage because the law on the matter is still developing and therefore uncertain.

The expropriation of foreign owned property has a special appeal to the peoples of underdeveloped countries, which can be explained on several grounds. From a strictly economic point of view, there may be serious profit to a country's economy from the confiscation of foreign holdings.[71] This profit is often bound to be limited, however, in view of the possible reactions of the states affected by such measures and the present conditions in most underdeveloped countries.[72] Psychological considerations are also important: the widely felt fear and resentment of the Western powers account in part for

---

[68] See *infra* Chapter 9, p. 232.   [69] See *infra* Chapter 10, pp. 314 *et seq.*

[70] See *infra* Chapter 10, pp. 302 *et seq.*

[71] See particularly, Bronfenbrenner, "The Appeal of Confiscation in Economic Development," 3 *Economic Development and Cultural Change* 201 (1955), reprinted in *The Economics of Underdevelopment* 472 (Agarwala and Singh ed., 1958). The learned author's concluding suggestion of a "neoisolationist" policy seems, however, much less convincing than his main argument.

[72] Thus, in view of the shortage of skilled technical personnel, it may not be possible to operate the nationalized industries. The measure of control exercised by the major capital-exporting states over the distribution of several primary products should also be taken into account, in view of their possible reaction to nationalizations.

the incidence of expropriations of the property of their nationals.[73] Finally, in some of the underdeveloped countries, private property never had the "sacrosanct" character it had in nineteenth century England or the United States, while, at the same time, the powers of the state in most such countries are, either traditionally or because of their present condition, much wider than they are in Western countries.

It is easy enough to understand how the fear of expropriation operates as a deterrent to private foreign investment. It may be that its importance is sometimes overemphasized, at least as far as outright expropriation [74] is concerned. Existing surveys certainly do not indicate that businessmen consider expropriation one of the principal deterrents,[75] though recent events may have affected their attitude on this point. Whatever its exact rank, the fear of expropriation is a serious obstacle to foreign investment. The existence of an obligation to compensate on the part of the expropriating state may not be always sufficient assurance to the investors, if they fear that such compensation may be inadequate or may be granted only after a long time.

Problems of Taxation

Taxation is the last of the elements of a country's investment climate to be discussed. Compared to the other elements which have been examined, it presents certain peculiarities of its own. In the

[73] Cf. Myrdal, *Beyond the Welfare State* 214–15, 259–60 (1960).

[74] In contradistinction to the so-called "creeping expropriation," that is, the gradual taking over of an enterprise through increasing economic controls, taxation, and other government measures, which may actually be more feared by foreign investors. For a discussion of the process of "creeping expropriation," see Rubin, *Private Foreign Investment* 37–43 (1956).

[75] In the 1951 National Industrial Conference Board survey, *supra* note 58, the fear of expropriation ranked thirteenth among twenty-two possible obstacles to private foreign investment. Its rank was eighth with respect to investment in Europe (memory of the postwar nationalizations was still fresh), fourteenth with respect to investment in Asia and Latin America, and nineteenth with regard to investment in Africa. The Canadian survey's conclusions were largely similar; cf. its *Report, supra* note 58, at 40–41, 60.

first place, the capital-exporting countries' policies and measures are in this connection as important as those of the capital-importing ones. In the second place, taxation is usually considered as a normal business risk. It is only under exceptional conditions that it becomes a non-business risk. In the third place, taxation is the sole element of the investment climate which affects directly a basic economic factor, namely, the investment's rate of return. From the investor's point of view, any increase or decrease in the taxes which he would normally have to pay corresponds to a change in the profit rate of his investment. Taxation, therefore, constitutes not only a possible deterrent but also a possible incentive to private foreign investment. Because of its peculiarities, the extent of its domain, and the variety of possible measures and policies, the subject of taxation constitutes by itself a topic of separate study.[76] It can only be treated summarily in the present context.

Taxation is an obstacle to foreign investment chiefly in two ways. On the one hand, the foreign investor's income may be taxed both in his state of residence (that is, the capital-exporting state) and in the state of investment (that is, the capital-importing state). Though lawful under international law,[77] "double taxation" is resented by the investors and seems undesirable from the point of view of the development of international trade and investment. Under certain conditions, its partial elimination may be achieved by unilateral action on the part of individual states.[78] It may be more effectively achieved by joint action on the part of capital-exporting and capital-

---

[76] Cf. the work of the Harvard Law School International Program in Taxation and, especially, Barlow and Wender, *United States Tax Incentives to Direct Private Foreign Investment* (1954); Barlow and Wender, *Foreign Investment and Taxation* (1955). And see now, Bittker and Ebb, *Taxation of Foreign Income* (1960).

[77] Cf. 1 Hyde, *International Law* 673–76 (1945); Allix, "La condition des étrangers au point de vue fiscal," 61 *Hague Recueil* 541, 616 *et seq.* (1937); Chrétien, *À la recherche du droit international fiscal commun* 208–12 (1955).

[78] This is the case with the United States, whose income tax legislation provides for "foreign tax credit" and "tax deferral" on income earned abroad by American corporations, whether or not international agreements to that effect have been concluded. See Surrey, "Current Issues in the Taxation of Corporate Foreign Investment," 56 *Columbia L. Rev.* 815, 817–38 (1956); Surrey, "The United States Taxation of Foreign Income," 1 *J. Law & Econ.* 72, 73–77, 84–85 (1958); and the studies cited *supra* note 76.

importing states. A great number of related international agreements have been concluded to regulate interstate problems of taxation.[79]

A second manner in which tax measures affect unfavorably foreign investment relates to possible discrimination against aliens, to excessive taxation and, especially, to the imperfect functioning of the capital-importing country's tax system and the consequent uncertainty and instability. Discrimination or excessive taxation should be avoided in view of their obvious adverse effect on prospective foreign investors. They cannot, however, be considered as unlawful in international law,[80] except perhaps in so far as they become in fact confiscatory.[81] The achievement of a degree of stability and certainty in taxation, on the other hand, should be considered as a *conditio sine qua non* not only of foreign investment but of economic development itself.[82] As long as they can make fairly accurate predictions concerning its impact, businessmen all over the world are used to coping with taxation.

Taxation can play an important role as an incentive to foreign investment. Generally speaking, and apart from the question of double taxation, tax considerations favor investment in the underdeveloped countries, for the investor's tax burden there is, as a rule, less heavy than in the developed countries. Additional measures may also be taken, by capital-exporting as well as capital-importing countries, to render such investment more attractive to investors. Foreign investors may be exempted from some taxes or they may be granted

[79] See the UN Department of Economic and Social Affairs series *International Tax Agreements,* especially vol. VIII, *World Guide to International Tax Agreements* (1958), and the publications of the International Bureau of Fiscal Documentation. On the related legal problems, see the earlier studies of Niboyet, "Les doubles impositions au point de vue juridique," 31 *Hague Recueil* 5 (1930) and Bühler, "Les accords internationaux concernant la double imposition et l'évasion fiscale," 55 *idem* 433 (1936).

[80] Cf. Chrétien, *A la recherche du droit international fiscal commun* 215–19 (1955); Grizioti, "L'imposition fiscale des étrangers," 13 *Hague Recueil* 4, 64–67 (1926); Allix, "La condition des étrangers au point de vue fiscal," 61 *idem* 541, 601, 603 (1937).

[81] Cf. 1 Hyde, *International Law* 664 (1945); Albrecht, "Taxation of Aliens under International Law," 29 *Brit. Yb. Int'l L.* 145, 170–71 (1952).

[82] Cf. Surrey, "Tax Administration in Underdeveloped Countries," 12 *U. Miami L. Rev.* 158 (1958).

special facilities. It is not possible to enumerate or study here the tax incentives which may be offered.[83] Nor can we deal with the fundamental question of whether and to what extent tax incentives are in fact an effective tool for the promotion of a country's economic development.[84] All one can do at this point is glance at the policy background of the measures in question.

On the part of capital-exporting states, the willingness to offer tax incentives, to the detriment of their public revenue, should be chiefly attributed to their general economic and political interest in the development of the underdeveloped areas. Certain more immediate economic considerations, such as the need for raw materials and the necessity to utilize their potentially excessive domestic savings,[85] are other strong arguments for the expansion of foreign investment. State revenue from the taxation of such investment, moreover, is of relatively minor importance. The extent, therefore, to which tax relief may be granted in such states to enterprises investing abroad will chiefly depend on considerations of domestic and international policy as well as on the prevailing views as to the effectiveness of such relief as a means of increasing private foreign investment. Serious doubts have been expressed on this last point.[86]

The underdeveloped countries' economic interest in attracting foreign investors is certainly more immediate. Their offer of tax incentives represents the sacrifice of possible future revenue for the sake not only of the country's development but also of the increase

[83] For a recent survey of such incentives, see Ross, "Foreign Governments' Tax Incentives for Investment," in Southwestern Legal Foundation, *Proceedings of the 1959 Institute on Private Investments Abroad* 285 (1959). See also *infra* Chapter 6, pp. 173–80.

[84] Note, however, that in view of the differences in needs and in taxation structures between developed and underdeveloped countries, different considerations may apply to each category of countries. Cf., on this point, Surrey, "The United States Taxation of Foreign Income," 1 *J. Law & Econ.* 72, 90, note 26 (1958).

[85] The latter consideration, it is true, may not be operative at all times; it has been of relatively minor importance in the postwar years. It does constitute, however, a significant factor which should not be left out of consideration.

[86] Cf., e.g., Surrey, "Current Issues in the Taxation of Foreign Corporate Investment," 56 *Columbia L. Rev.* 815, 838–57; Surrey, *supra* note 84, at 80 *et seq.*; Gordon, "Some Aspects of United States Policy in the Taxation of Foreign Income," in *Legal Problems of International Trade* 222, 225–28 (Proehl ed., 1959).

of public revenue which is a necessary consequence of such development. Their chief criterion in granting tax relief will be the usefulness of the particular investment and its effect on the country's economy. It cannot be denied that, even if all private foreign investment benefits the country in which it is made, certain kinds of investment are of more (or more immediate) benefit to it. A capital-importing country may then, with justification, grant tax exemptions or other privileges to some investors only and not to all of them. Moreover, the offer of tax concessions may be limited in time, as well. Exemptions or reductions may be granted for a specified number of years only (usually five to ten). In this manner, the foreign-owned enterprise is materially assisted during its critical first years in the country of investment, while the latter retains its right to tax it at the regular rates after the end of the prescribed period.

It should never be forgotten, on the other hand, that underdeveloped countries are not always able to act in pursuit of their long-run aims. Their revenue from the taxation of some large foreign enterprises may sometimes be of such immediate importance that they cannot afford to sacrifice it. With respect to taxation, as with respect to many other economic considerations, they have to effect a compromise between their long-range interests and their immediate needs.

Finally, important problems arise with respect to the coordination of the tax policies of capital-importing and capital-exporting states. The "tax sparing" issue may serve as an illustration of the needs and difficulties in this field.[87]

[87] For some discussions of the problem, see Surrey, *supra* note 86, at 849–50, 854–57; Surrey, *supra* note 84, at 84–90; Surrey, Statement in *Private Foreign Investment Hearings before the Subcommittee on Foreign Trade Policy of the House Committee on Ways and Means,* 85th Cong., 2d sess. 377, 381–83, 389–91 (1958); Gordon, *supra* note 86, at 230–32; Kust, "United States Tax Concessions for American Private Enterprise Abroad," in Southwestern Legal Foundation, *Proceedings of the 1959 Institute on Private Investments Abroad* 145, 148–52 (1959); *Joint International Business Ventures* 232 *et seq.* (Friedmann and Kalmanoff ed., 1961).

4

Necessity for State Guarantees

IT IS hoped that even so elementary a study has shown that the conditions responsible for the present shortage in private foreign investment in underdeveloped countries are not accidental phenomena, nor are they due to the immorality and malevolence of either the foreign investors or the governments of the capital-importing countries. There exist certain objective causes for the shortage which are, in part, outside the control of individual foreign investors and of the governments of particular countries.

The Role of Private Foreign Investment

Apart from the shortage of private foreign investment, there exist certain limitations on its role with respect to the underdeveloped countries. The chief limitation stems from the demand for an accelerated rate of economic development. Private foreign investment can certainly assist and probably, in the long run, assure a country's development, but it cannot do so within the short limits of time imposed by the contemporary "revolution of rising expectations." The underdeveloped countries' need for basic industries, such as public utilities and transportation, which do not, under present conditions, attract foreign investors is another limitation of great importance which reinforces the effects of the first.

Out of this situation arises the need for public capital. Its use entails certain definite advantages to the underdeveloped countries.

In the first place, public capital can be used to provide the basic facilities which are scarce or lacking and which cannot be provided by private investors. Secondly, public capital is strictly controlled by the country's government and may thus be used in accordance with an overall plan to cover in a balanced manner the multiple needs of the economy.

The extensive employment of public capital is not devoid of problems and difficulties.[1] Prevailing political conditions may often affect adversely its effective use. Furthermore, the condition of government administration in many underdeveloped countries is hardly promising of a rational and economic use of available capital and resources. Overall plans are often lacking or they are the product of wishful thinking or of the influence of special interests rather than of objective study. Under such conditions, the available public capital might well be wasted in whole or in part, contributing little to the country's economic development.[2]

Problems also arise when the sources of public capital are considered. The poverty which prevails in the underdeveloped countries strictly limits, in the great majority of cases,[3] the amount of public capital which can be raised locally. Foreign public capital is then indispensable. Such capital may be provided in the form of loans or grants, by individual states or through international financial organizations. Political rather than economic considerations determine the choice of form and the allocation of capital between recipient countries.

Acceptance of the need for public capital does not imply any dis-

---

[1] Cf. Deyrup, "Limits of Government Activity in Underdeveloped Countries," 24 *Social Research* 191 (1957); and, for a rather extreme view, limiting government activity to measures concerning education and public health, cf. Schultz, "The Role of Government in Promoting Economic Growth," in *The State of the Social Sciences* 372 (White ed., 1956). And cf. *supra* Chapter 2, note 16.

[2] These observations should not be understood as implying the condemnation of all experimentation, even though it may result in the wasteful use of public funds. Within reasonable limits, such experimentation is unavoidable and necessary.

[3] The exceptional cases are those of a few petroleum-producing countries, where, despite the general poverty of the inhabitants, governments dispose of important amounts of money received as royalties for the oil extracted by foreign companies.

regard of the importance of private investment, domestic or foreign. Under present conditions, these two forms of financing are not exclusive of each other but complementary. Ideological as well as practical considerations may be adduced to support this view.

The practical considerations operative in noncommunist underdeveloped countries may be summarized in the observation that, with respect to foreign capital, they hardly have any choice in the matter. The actual or potential capital-exporting countries today, such as the United States, the United Kingdom, or the Federal Republic of Germany,[4] are all, in their domestic as well as foreign economic policies, committed to the support of private enterprise. Their attitudes will not change overnight even though their governments will certainly better appreciate in the near future the importance of providing public capital to the underdeveloped areas.

Private capital, in general, and private foreign investment, in particular, has then a highly important role to play in the economic growth of the underdeveloped countries. Its importance will be probably greater in the countries which have already set the foundations for their economy, the semideveloped countries, such as Brazil or India today, rather than in the still wholly undeveloped areas of the world. Private capital can assist chiefly by establishing new industries in certain fields; it may establish manufacturing and other consumption-oriented industries or it may deal in primary goods for export or set up enterprises of "heavy industry," processsing local raw materials or producing capital goods for the local market. Its contribution is twofold. In the first place, it provides the capital necessary for the establishment of the industries. In the second place, private foreign investment brings with it the technical and managerial experience which is scarce and needed in capital-importing countries, thus making possible both the operation of the industry and the training of local nationals. Such experience is at least as important to the underdeveloped country as capital itself.

[4] The Soviet Union does not belong, of course, to the same category of countries. Its past performance, however, makes voluntary exclusive dependence of any country outside the Soviet bloc on its aid alone highly unlikely.

The development of new industries is certainly to the benefit of the underdeveloped country, especially since, under present conditions, it does not have to be coupled with control of the economy by the foreign investors. The host country's government is today in a position to exercise direct or indirect control over the distribution of foreign investment among the sectors of the economy. It may also ensure that foreign investors do not interfere in local politics, as they have sometimes done in the past. It is up to the government of the capital-importing country to provide efficient administrative machinery, capable of exercising effectively, but without undue burden on the investor, such control and supervision. If this machinery cannot be made to operate well, as is sometimes argued by the proponents of the exclusive use of public capital, one wonders how or why public investment would fare better, since the same administrative machinery would be handling it.

The Need for State Guarantees

If there is to be any permanent increase in the amount of private foreign capital invested in underdeveloped countries, some or all of the obstacles to its investment must be removed. Government action can affect most of these obstacles to various extents; it can be particularly effective with respect to the obstacles discussed under the general heading of "investment climate." One particular characteristic of such obstacles is of importance in this connection. A country's investment climate must be understood as referring not only to the present but also to the future. By investing his capital in a foreign country, an alien subjects it to local conditions for an indefinite period of time. Accordingly, the existing situation with respect to foreign investments, no doubt important enough by itself, is to him even more important as an indication of the situation which will probably exist in the future.

Any change, therefore, in the legal conditions existing in a state at a particular time is not by itself sufficient to attract foreign investors, or, more generally, to render favorable a formerly unfavorable investment climate. In some cases, it is true, investors may be willing to take the risk of a future worsening of investment conditions, especially when they are reasonably confident of their ability to defend effectively their own interests or when the expected profits are high enough to warrant taking the risk. Both these considerations have been operative in the case of postwar petroleum investments. But in other cases, and in particular with respect to those industries whose establishment is sought by capital-importing states (for example, heavy industries or export-substituting industries), some assurance as to the future is needed. The investor must be made to believe that there is little or no possibility that an unfavorable legal situation will be created at a later date. The investor gains some such assurance when a favorable legal situation has existed for a sufficiently long time, or when the country's economic and political structure is so stable that there is little probability of any radical change in the immediate future. In the case of most underdeveloped countries today, however, it is impossible to predict with confidence that conditions of stability and security will exist during the period of dynamic change ahead. Thus arises the need for legal guarantees,[5] to be given by the state or states concerned to foreign investors. The guaranteeing states have to commit themselves as to the future, to promise that certain measures are not going to be taken, that certain others will continue to be taken, or that the investor will be compensated for any loss due to changes in such measures. Foreign investors have to be assured that they will receive, both today and in the future, a definite legal treatment, specified in the relevant legal instruments, and that consequently they need not fear any major changes in local legal or political conditions that would be unfavorable to their interests.

State guarantees of this sort differ in certain important respects

[5] The terms "guarantee" and "promise" are used here interchangeably in the general sense of commitment to do or not to do certain things, regardless of the enforceability of such a commitment. The use of these terms does not then prejudge the outcome of our study of their legal effects.

from private insurance schemes.[6] To begin with, they cover different kinds of risks. Private guarantees, on the basis of past experience as expressed in terms of probabilities, cover commercial risks, while public guarantees apply to risks which cannot be measured quantitatively. Moreover, private guarantees are not, in the main, intended to protect the investor from the risk itself; they only provide compensation for any eventual loss. Government guarantees, in addition to their compensatory function, have a definite effect on the risks themselves, making the investor's loss less probable. This function of public guarantees is obvious in the case of guarantees founded on an international treaty between two or more states.

Legal guarantees to foreign investors are in all cases issued by states,[7] but the party to whom the guarantees are directly addressed is not always the same. It may be a single state, several states, a category of private persons or a single private person. From the standpoint of form, one may distinguish two main categories of guarantees according to the law on which they were originally founded. Guarantees may be granted by international instruments and thus be founded on international law, or they may originate in provisions of municipal law and instruments issued in accordance with them. The real importance of this distinction, however, is limited, since international law guarantees have important municipal law aspects and municipal law guarantees have definite effects in public international law; but it does provide a handy criterion for classification. It would be much too difficult to make any clear distinctions in content. The type of guarantee to be granted in each case will depend on a variety of factors, including the political and economic situation, international and domestic, of the capital-im-

[6] Cf. Nurkse, *Internationale Kapitalbewegungen* 24 *et seq.* (1935); Shenkman, *Insurance against Credit Risks* 169 *et seq.* (1935); and the condensed treatment of the question by von Neumann Whitman, *The United States Investment Guaranty Program and Private Foreign Investment* 18–19 (1959).

[7] This general statement is apparently not applicable to the system proposed by the then Vice-President Nixon in 1957; he suggested at that time the creation of a privately operated guarantee fund. Cf. *infra* Chapter 5, note 185. It is evident that in the present context, the terms "state guarantees" and "government guarantees" are synonymous.

porting state involved and the particular obstacles to foreign investment prevalent there at a given time. Even though certain types
of guarantees are usually granted by one sort of legal instrument
and others by another, the differences in content among guarantees
do not necessarily correspond to differences in form.

Part II

FORM AND CONTENT OF

STATE PROMISES

5

Form of State Promises

BEFORE considering the precise content of state guarantees to foreign investors, it is necessary to examine in some detail the particular forms which such guarantees may take. States may offer protection to foreign investors by concluding international agreements regarding foreign investment. Capital-exporting and capital-importing states may come together in pairs and conclude several bilateral agreements, or all states concerned may conclude a single multilateral convention, embodying a "code" regarding the treatment of foreign investment. On the other hand, each state by itself may guarantee the security of investments of foreigners in the state or of investments by the state's nationals abroad, by means of general promises or of specific instruments addressed to each particular investor.

Investment Codes and Their Problems

The idea of an international code of state practice with regard to foreign investors is relatively recent.[1] During the interwar period some League of Nations agencies made a few uncertain and generally fruitless attempts in this direction.[2] After the Second World

[1] Gustav Lippert's attempt to provide a code of International Financial Law is partly related in scope but differs widely in its motives and objectives; cf. his *Rechtbuch des internationalen Finanzrechtes* (1935).

[2] Cf., e.g., the Draft Convention on the Treatment of Foreigners of 1929, League of Nations Document C.174.M.53.1928.II.14, on which, see Cutler, "The Treat-

War, increased consciousness of international economic problems along with widespread optimism as to the possibilities of international organization led to the formation of a fairly strong movement for the general adoption of such a code. This movement found support among scholars [3] as well as businessmen [4] and was favorably discussed by governments and international agencies, but without any concrete result. After some years of comparative neglect, the idea was recently revived with considerable force.

The chief official attempt at a general multilateral treaty embodying an elementary code for foreign investment was the Charter of the International Trade Organization (ITO),[5] signed at Havana, Cuba, on March 24, 1948, which never became effective. The Charter dealt in part with economic development and, in connection with it, laid down certain general rules regarding the treatment and position of foreign investment in the signatory states.[6] The relevant provisions had been included in the Charter at the insistence of influential American business groups, but in their final formulation they bore the imprint of the underdeveloped countries' point of view.

---

ment of Foreigners in Relation to the Draft Convention and Conference of 1929," 27 *Am. J. Int'l L.* 224 (1933). See also League of Nations, Committee for the Study of International Loan Contracts, *Report* (1939); League of Nations, Special Joint Committee on Private Foreign Investment, *Conditions of Private Foreign Investment* (1946).

[3] Cf. Viner, "Conflicts of Principle in Drafting a Trade Charter," 25 *Foreign Affairs* 612, 627 (1947); Bidwell and Diebold, "The United States and the International Trade Organization," 1949 *Int'l Conc.* No. 449, 183, 212.

[4] Cf. e.g., International Chamber of Commerce, *Fair Treatment for Foreign Investments. International Code* (I.C.C. Brochure No. 129, 1949); National Foreign Trade Council, *Position of the National Foreign Trade Council with Respect to the Havana Charter for an International Trade Organization* 53-54 (1950).

[5] Cf. United Nations Conference on Trade and Employment, *Final Act and Related Documents* (1948) (hereinafter cited as *Havana Charter*).

[6] *Id.* Chapter III, especially article 12 on "International Investment for Economic Development and Reconstruction." From among the numerous accounts and commentaries, see Wilcox, *A Charter for World Trade* 145-48 (1949); Bidwell and Diebold, *supra* note 3, at 208-12; Bronz, "The International Trade Organization Charter," 62 *Harv. L. Rev.* 1089, 1110-12 (1949); Fawcett, "The Havana Charter," 5 *Yb. World Affairs* 269, 272-73 (1951); Gardner, *Sterling-Dollar Diplomacy* 365-66 (1956).

The Charter recognized the value of international investment, private as well as public, and the need for allowing opportunities for private investments and for assuring their security.[7] Capital-import-ing countries undertook in the Charter to avoid "unreasonable or unjustifiable action" injurious to the foreign investors' interests,[8] to "provide reasonable opportunities for investments acceptable to them and adequate security for existing and future investments," [9] to "give due regard to the desirability of avoiding discrimination as between foreign investments," [10] and to enter into consultation or negotiations with other governments with the object of con-cluding bilateral or multilateral agreements relating to such matters.[11] On the other hand, the Charter expressly recognized the right of capital-receiving countries to interfere with foreign investments through screening, restrictions on the ownership of enterprises, and any "other reasonable requirements." [12]

The Charter's provisions on international investment were in-adequate. Every positive statement was closely circumscribed by qualifications and exceptions whose extent could not be determined with any precision. The determination of the rights and obligations of the parties depended for the major part on the interpretation of such indefinite terms as "reasonable," "appropriate" or "unjustified." The right of capital-importing states to interfere with private for-eign investments was stated much more clearly than their corre-sponding obligation to give fair treatment.[13] These provisions of the Charter came under strong attack on the part of American business circles and this was largely responsible for the Charter's ultimate non-ratification by the United States and the other signatory states.[14] The Organization of Trade Cooperation, which was pro-

---

[7] *Havana Charter*, article 12(1)(a) and (b).   [8] *Idem* article 11(1)(b).
[9] *Idem* article 12(2)(a)(i).   [10] *Idem* article 12(2)(a)(ii).
[11] *Idem* article 12(2)(b).   [12] *Idem* article 12(1)(c).
[13] Cf. Gardner, *op. cit., supra* note 6, at 366; Bidwell and Diebold, *supra* note 3, at 211.
[14] See, in particular: National Foreign Trade Council, *op. cit. supra* note 4, at 5–6, 53–60; National Association of Manufacturers, *The Havana Charter for an*

posed later to replace the ITO had a much more limited jurisdiction and function. In the agreement instituting it [15] there were no provisions relating to economic development, international investment, and like matters.[16]

Another multilateral international instrument dealing in part with the protection of private international investment is the Economic Agreement of Bogota, signed at the Ninth International Conference of American States on May 2, 1948.[17] The relevant provisions, which constitute Chapter IV of the Agreement (articles 22–27), are similar to those in the Havana Charter, though more elaborate and positive. The importance of foreign investment is again emphasized and a general guarantee of "equitable treatment," especially non-discrimination, is given.[18] The desirability of employing foreign skilled personnel is recognized, the signatory states undertaking not to hinder such employment unduly.[19] They also undertake to lighten the tax burden, when excessive,[20] and to "impose no unjustifiable restrictions" on the transfer of earnings and capital outside the capital-receiving state.[21] Expropriation of property, when effected in accordance with local legislation and when non-discriminatory, is authorized; it is unequivocally stated, however, that "any expropriation shall be accompanied by payment of fair compensation in a prompt, adequate and effective manner." [22] These provisions

International Trade Organization 3, 10–11 (1949); Committee for Economic Development, _The International Trade Organization and the Reconstruction of World Trade_ 30–32, 37–38 (1949). See also the excellent account of business opposition to the ITO in Diebold, _The End of the ITO_ 11–24 (1952).

[15] Text in 32 _Dep't State Bull._ 579 (1953); cf. Bronz, "An International Trade Organization: The Second Attempt," 69 _Harv. L. Rev._ 440 (1956).

[16] The proponents of American participation in OTC have laid particular emphasis on this point; cf. _Hearings Before the House Committee on Ways and Means_, 84th Cong. 2d sess., 7–8, 41 (Statement of Secretary of State Dulles), 397, 407–8 (Statement of Mr. S. Rubin), 791 (Statement of Professor R. Blough) (1956).

[17] _Economic Agreement of Bogota_, Pan American Union, Law and Treaty Series No. 25 (1948) (hereinafter cited as _Bogota Agreement_). Cf. Fenwick, "The Ninth International Conference of American States," 42 _Am. J. Int'l L._ 553, 561–62 (1948).

[18] _Bogota Agreement_ article 22.   [19] _Idem_ article 23(3).
[20] _Idem_ article 27.   [21] _Idem_ article 22(4).
[22] _Idem_ article 25.

lose much of their importance through the constant use of indefinite terms such as "appropriate," "unjustifiable," "just" or "equitable." Furthermore, several states attached at the time of signature express reservations on the scope and effects of the relevant articles, especially the article dealing with expropriation. The Bogota Agreement, like the ITO Charter, has never become legally effective.[23]

Since that time, no other multilateral conventions dealing with the protection of international investment have been concluded. The subject has been brought up within some international bodies, but the related discussions either were inconclusive, or resulted in general recommendations on state policies leading to the improvement of the investment climate in underdeveloped countries.

In 1947, the Economic and Employment Commission of the Economic and Social Council of the United Nations instructed its Sub-Commission on Economic Development:

To commence a study . . . with the view to making recommendations regarding the need for an international code relating to foreign investment which will cover among other things the protection of economic and social interests of the countries in which investments are to

---

[23] Subsequent multilateral instruments concluded by the American states place less emphasis on the protection of private foreign investment. In the Economic Declaration of Buenos Aires of September 2, 1957, it is stated that the governments of American states should take measures to promote international trade and investment and should intensify their efforts "to expand the flow of public capital to the countries of the American continent . . . and to encourage private investment therein. . . ." 37 *Dep't State Bull.* 540, 541 (1957). The recent Charter of Punta del Este of August 17, 1961, deals almost exclusively with government measures and expenditure of public capital to promote economic development in the general framework of economies with important private sectors. See, on this last point, the Declaration to the Peoples of America, 45 *idem* 562 (1961), where the stimulation of "private enterprise in order to encourage the development of Latin American countries" is stated to be one of the goals of the signatory countries. See also the related statement of the United States Secretary of the Treasury Dillon, *idem* 441, at 443. But, whereas the measures for the development of the public sector are spelled out in concrete terms, those relating to the private sector are referred to in rather general terms. The only direct reference to private foreign investment is found in a statement to the effect that "national development programs should incorporate self-help efforts directed to: . . . the promotion through appropriate measures, including the signing of agreements for the purpose of reducing or eliminating double taxation, of conditions that will encourage the flow of foreign investments. . . ." *Idem* 463, at 465.

be made, as well as the protection of investors, both public and private. . . .[24]

The topic was discussed in the Council's next session [25] and was mentioned occasionally in the meetings of the Commission and Sub-Commission during the next few months.[26] It was dropped altogether after the signature of the Havana Charter.

A few years later, the United Nations General Assembly adopted in its 1954 session a resolution concerning the encouragement of foreign private investment.[27] The Assembly recognized the useful role of private foreign investment in the development of under-developed countries and, noting its present shortage, made various recommendations to capital-importing and capital-exporting states. To the former it recommended, *inter alia*, the avoidance of discrimination and the facilitation of the importation of capital goods and of the transfer abroad of the investors' earnings.[28] It also recommended to both categories of states the conclusion of agreements for the encouragement of private foreign investments.[29]

The question was again raised in a speech of the Prime Minister of the Federation of Malaya before the 14th session of the Economic Commission for Africa and the Far East.[30] The investment charter

[24] UN Document E/255, 5 February 1947, 12–13.
[25] Cf. UN Economic and Social Council, *Official Records* 2d year, 4th session, 56th to 59th meetings (6–7 March 1947), 33–34, 41, 46, 49–50, 54, 55–56.
[26] Cf. the following UN Documents: E/CN. 1/47, 18 December 1947, at 9, 20–21; E/CN. 1/61, 1 July 1948, at 20; E/CN. 1/Sub. 3/4, 14 November 1947, *passim*.
[27] U.N. General Assembly Resolution 824 (IX) of December 11, 1954, *1954 Yearbook of the United Nations* 135 (1955).
[28] Note, however, that, around the same time, certain discussions on the principle of self-determination of states resulted in the adoption of resolutions and other texts stressing the absolute character of the "right of peoples freely to use and exploit their natural wealth and resources." Cf. UN General Assembly Resolution 626 (VII) of December 21, 1952. That this emphasis was chiefly directed against the "exploitation" by foreign investors is brought out forcefully in Hyde, "Permanent Sovereignty over Natural Wealth and Resources," 50 *Am. J. Int'l L.* 854 (1956).
[29] Similar resolutions were taken by the Tenth International Conference of American States, in 1954 (Resolutions LXX and LXXI), and the Contracting Parties to the General Agreement on Trade and Tariffs (Resolution of March 4, 1955).
[30] Cf. UN, Economic Commission for Asia and the Far East, *Official Records,* 14th sess. (March 1958), UN Document E/CN. 11/483, 3 June 1958, 29. And see

he suggested would provide for the equitable treatment of foreign investors and for the protection of their legal rights while at the same time assuring the respect for the sovereignty and national interest of the capital-importing country. The matter came before the UN General Assembly and its Second Committee in their 1958 session. The resolution finally adopted, however, while stressing the need for an improvement of the investment climate of the underdeveloped countries, did not refer directly to the possible formulation of an investment code.[31] It only requested the Secretary-General to consult "qualified persons" concerning the fields of activity where foreign private investment "is needed and sought by underdeveloped countries," its appropriate form and volume, and the types of projects in which foreign investors might be interested.

The Secretary-General's report, submitted early in 1960,[32] followed closely the lines laid down by the resolution. It reviewed the fields of investment in underdeveloped countries and the government policies affecting them and then went on to examine the various forms of investment. It dealt in detail with incentive measures taken by capital-importing as well as capital-exporting countries, such as the provision of basic facilities and of development capital and the national and international measures relating to taxation and exchange control. In dealing with measures for the protection of private foreign investment, the report examines briefly the particular forms which they may take. It is in this connection that the question of an international investment code is discussed. A survey of some of the related proposals is followed by a brief commentary which stresses the difficulties and dangers inherent in the attempt to formulate such a code. The report as a whole is highly informative, but it can by no means be considered as promoting the cause of an international investment code.

Larson, "Recipients' Rights Under an International Investment Code," 9 *J. Pub. L.* 172, 172–73 (1960).

[31] UN General Assembly Resolution 1318 (XIII), of December 12, 1958, *1958 Yearbook of the United Nations* 145 (1959).

[32] "The Promotion of the International Flow of Private Capital," Progress Report by the Secretary-General, UN Document E/3325, 26 February 1960.

Of greater importance, though of dubious effectiveness as yet, are the discussions within the Consultative Assembly of the Council of Europe. A 1957 report of a study group, dealing with the problems of the cooperation between European and African states for the latter's economic development, mentioned the possibility of preparing an Investment Statute "defining the rights and duties of investors and borrowers" and providing for certain other matters.[33] The idea was adopted by the Assembly's Economic Committee [34] and by the Consultative Assembly itself, which recommended to the Committee of Ministers the convocation of a conference of European and African states to deal with these questions.[35] The Committee of Ministers having deferred its action, the Assembly instructed its Economic Committee to present detailed proposals.[36] The resulting report [37] did not contain a draft text but dealt in some detail with the problems and possible content of an investment code. In its subsequent recommendation,[38] the Assembly admits the possibility that it might be some time before an Investment Statute is adopted. Considering the subject as one eminently suitable for joint European-African discussion, it insists on the convocation of a conference [39] and requests the governments of the Council of

[33] Report of the Study Group for the Development of Africa, Consultative Assembly Document 701, 26 September 1957. For an analysis, see Gaitskell, "Europe and the Economic Development of Africa," 6 *European Yearbook 1958* 29, 44-49 (1959).

[34] Draft recommendation (with Explanatory Memorandum) submitted by the Economic Committee, Cons. Ass. Doc. 798, 1 April 1958.

[35] Consultative Assembly Recommendation 159 (1958) on the Development of Africa. The Committee of Ministers, composed of the Foreign Ministers of the member states, is the Council of Europe's chief executive organ, in effect the only one with the power to decide and act. The Assembly's competence, as indicated by its name, is of a purely advisory character. Cf. Robertson, *European Institutions* 61 *et seq.* (1959).

[36] Consultative Assembly Order 124, 10 October 1958.

[37] Report on an Investment Statute and a Guarantee Fund against Political Risks, Cons. Ass. Doc. 1027, 8 September 1959.

[38] Consultative Assembly Recommendation 211 (1959) on the Development of Africa.

[39] See also the subsequent Consultative Assembly Recommendation 223 (1960) on the same subject, where the Assembly's point of view is restated in answer to the Committee of Ministers' reservations with respect to the proposed conference.

Europe's member states to prepare drafts for the proposed Statute, on the lines set out in the aforementioned report.

According to this report, the proposed Investment Statute should assume the form of an international convention among a "large enough number" of European and African states. It should lay down general rules, leaving detailed provisions to be worked out in the specific contracts between states and private investors. It should provide for the rights and duties of capital-importing states as well as foreign investors. Its Preamble would consist chiefly of a basic statement of principles, including an affirmation of the state's extensive rights with respect to the admission and regulation of foreign investment, a statement on the investors' duties toward the host state,[40] and a stipulation on the part of the contracting states to treat foreign investors equitably, protect them from the effects of future state action, and carry out in good faith their obligations under the convention. The Statute in question would apply to future long-term investments, direct as well as portfolio.[41] It would provide for non-discrimination toward foreign investors, for national treatment with respect to taxation and to civil and legal rights, for freedom of transfer of the foreign investors' earnings,[42] and for due process and fair compensation in the case of any expropriation of property. An annexed Protocol would provide for compulsory arbitration in case of dispute; not only the contracting states but the nationals concerned, as well, would be able to take advantage of the arbitration procedure. Especial emphasis is placed, throughout the report, on the duty of the capital-importing state not to alter its own system of regulations affecting foreign investments, when such in-

---

[40] It would be made clear that foreign investors have the obligation "to respect national laws and customs, abstain from political interference, integrate activities in the domestic economy, collaborate with the nationals of the country concerned and co-operate in the technical field." Cons. Ass. Doc. 1027, *supra* note 37, at 11.

[41] With respect to past investments, equitable treatment would be provided and, perhaps, freedom of transfer of earnings and fair compensation in case of dispossession. *Idem* 12–13.

[42] Limitations on such transfers might be imposed under exceptional conditions. With respect to repatriation of capital, reasonable limitations would be allowed. *Idem* 17–18.

vestments have been undertaken because of the system's existence.[43] The report's realistic approach is evident in the proposed provisions for compensation (instead of restitution) in cases of infringement of the convention and for *ad hoc* consultation of the contracting states with respect to each eventual case where the imposition of sanctions is deemed necessary.

The Organization for European Economic Cooperation (OEEC) has also been studying in recent years the problems involved in the proposals for an international investment code. Two draft conventions were submitted to it in 1958, one by the German and one by the Swiss government, and they have been under consideration by the Organization's Committee for Invisible Transactions. The two proposals differ in some important respects and they can be said to complement each other. Neither of them, however, deals with the obligations of foreign investors toward the states of investment. The German proposal is the latest reformulation of a privately proposed draft convention, which will be discussed at a later point.[44] The Swiss proposal is a draft international convention concerning guarantees for the investment of foreign capital. It is relatively brief, consisting of seven articles, and it places special emphasis on the elimination of exchange restrictions. It provides for free transfer of all earnings as well as of amortization payments and of the original capital invested. Requirements with respect to expropriation are limited to the payment of adequate compensation, which the investor would be allowed to repatriate freely. Provisions regarding the establishment of an Arbitration Tribunal, competent to deal with any disputes arising out of the application or interpretation of the Convention are also included.

Rather more important, though still of doubtful practical significance up to now, are the proposals of influential private groups,

---

[43] This duty would be mentioned both in the Preamble and in the main body of the convention. In the Preamble, the contracting states would undertake "to afford future investments reasonable protection against worsening of the conditions prevailing at the time the investment is made, when those conditions are laid down by the law and administrative or other regulations and when the deteriorating situation is such as to jeopardize the investment." *Idem* 11 and see also *idem* 16.

[44] Cf. *infra* pp. 80 *et seq.*

representative of the prospective investors' points of view. In 1949, the International Chamber of Commerce published a draft International Code of Fair Treatment for Foreign Investors, to be embodied eventually in a multilateral international instrument.[45] The code strongly condemns discrimination against foreign investors and prohibits all restrictions on the ownership and personnel of private enterprises, allowing an exception only in the case of "enterprises directly concerned with national defense." [46] Foreign investors are to be granted full freedom in the transfer of their profits, capital, and any other related funds outside the capital-importing state; [47] and they are to be fully compensated in the event of their property's expropriation.[48] The code also contains provisions on the adjudication of disputes arising over its application before a proposed International Court of Arbitration.[49] Though first proposed more than ten years ago and repeatedly mentioned by the successive ICC Congresses since then,[50] the Code of Fair Treatment has received no official support or recognition as yet.

The recent revival of interest in investment codes is due in major part to the activities of a single private group, namely, the German Society to Advance the Protection of Foreign Investments, to whose initiative should be attributed several of the recent drafts and proposals.[51] In December 1958, a private group of an international character was set up, the International Association for the Promotion and Protection of Private Foreign Investment (APPI), composed

[45] International Chamber of Commerce, *Fair Treatment for Foreign Investments. International Code* (I.C.C. Brochure 129, 1949) (hereinafter cited as *ICC Code*). The code was based on the proposals of the Committee on the Flow of Capital of the United States Associates of the I.C.C.; cf. its *Report* (1946). For commentaries, see Wortley, "Examination of Draft of International Chamber of Commerce Code of Fair Treatment for Foreign Investments," Int'l Bar Association, *Third Int'l Conference of the Legal Profession* 241 (1952); Folsom, "The Code of Fair Treatment for Foreign Investors," in Am. Soc. Int'l L., *1958 Investment Law Conference* (mimeo.)

[46] *ICC Code* articles 3 to 7.

[47] *Idem* articles 9, 10 and 11(c) and (d). Cf. *infra* p. 153.

[48] *Idem* article 11. Cf. *infra* p. 174.

[49] *Idem* articles 13 and 14. Cf. *infra* p. 181.

[50] Cf. the resolutions of the 16th Congress of the International Chamber of Commerce, May 1954, ICC Brochure 193.

[51] Compare notes 55, 66, and 79 *infra*.

of a number of well-known European lawyers and representatives of "a considerable number of industrial, banking and other concerns having international relations and interests in the development of foreign trade and investment." [52] This Association seems to have supplanted the German Society, on the international scene.

The German Society's first major move was its proposal for the adoption of a "Magna Charta" of foreign investment, made at the International Industrial Development Conference held in San Francisco in 1957.[53] The proposal had a favorable reception in business circles and received considerable publicity.[54] Although the original text of a draft convention, as proposed in 1957,[55] has been amended on many important points subsequently, it is still worthy of further study, as a clear and able statement of the views of a considerable segment of prospective foreign investors.

The Draft Convention's chief objective is to provide to foreign investors the most extensive protection possible. Aliens are guaranteed "national treatment" and freedom from any restriction on the acquisition and utilization of property rights with the exception of activities in a few specified fields.[56] The convention limits very strictly the capital-importing state's right to expropriate the aliens' holdings and describes with precision the form and extent of the compensation to be awarded.[57]

[52] Brandon, "Recent Measures to Improve the International Investment Climate," 9 *J. Pub. L.* 125 (1960). Mr. Brandon is Geneva Secretary of APPI.

[53] See Abs, "The Safety of Capital," in *Private Investment: The Key to International Industrial Development* 69, 76–77 (Daniel ed., 1958). See also, Abs, "The Protection of Duly Acquired Rights in International Dealings as a European Duty," in Society to Advance the Protection of Foreign Investment, *Foundation and Purpose* 51 (n.d., [1956]).

[54] On the proposal's extensive press coverage, see Miller, "Protection of Private Foreign Investment by Multilateral Convention," 53 *Am. J. Int'l L.* 371, 375, note 25 (1959).

[55] Society to Advance the Protection of Foreign Investment, *International Convention for the Mutual Protection of Private Property Rights in Foreign Countries* (with Introduction and Comments in English translation, Cologne 1957) (hereinafter cited as *1957 Draft Convention*). For a summary and comments, see Miller, *supra* note 54.

[56] *1957 Draft Convention*, articles IV and V. The fields mentioned are public utilities, public transport, utilization of nuclear energy, and production of war material. Cf. *infra* p. 146.

[57] *Idem* articles VI and VII. Cf. *infra* pp. 165–66.

Two of the Convention's provisions are of special interest at this point. Not only the states party to the convention but their nationals as well are to be directly entitled to the rights thereunder. The convention's stipulations are to be directly binding on the courts and other government instrumentalities of the party states and they will prevail over national legislation in these states.[58] The investors therefore do not depend on their state's espousal of their claims in order to enforce their rights. The draft convention gives also a list of possible sanctions against states violating its provisions [59] and provides for the creation of an International Court of Claims.[60] The second interesting novelty is a provision that the states party to the convention "undertake to apply the stipulations of the Convention mutatis mutandis in the case of unlawful measures adopted against the property, rights and interests of nationals of the High Contracting Parties by States which are not parties to the Convention." [61] This provision may in all fairness be understood as proposing the formation of a coalition of capital-exporting states with the object of keeping in line the capital-importing states.

Early in 1958, a group of European jurists, under the chairmanship of Lord Shawcross, prepared another draft convention,[62] said to be based on the provisions of the United States FCN treaties.[63] The draft convention provided for the equitable treatment of aliens, and the strict limitation of the states' rights to expropriate foreign property.[64] It also included provisions on the adjudication of any related disputes.[65]

[58] *Idem* article IX.   [59] *Idem* article XI(5)(3) and appendix.
[60] *Idem* articles X and XI. Cf. *infra* p. 182.   [61] *Idem* article XII.
[62] For a detailed summary, see Brandon, "An International Investment Code: Current Plans," 1959 *J. Business L.* 7, 12–15.

[63] See *infra* pp. 92 *et seq.* Note, however, that the corresponding provisions in the U.S. treaties are far more restricted in applicability; cf. the relevant comments on a later draft by Metzger, "Multilateral Conventions for the Protection of Private Foreign Investment," 9 *J. Pub. L.* 133, 139–43 (1960).

[64] The limitations apply to direct or indirect takings of alien property. Such takings are possible only for a public purpose, in the absence of discrimination or of specific engagements toward the aliens, in accordance with due process of law and after provision for full compensation in transferable form and without undue delay; Brandon, *supra* note 62, at 13.

[65] Disputes were to be submitted to the International Court of Justice. It was

The above draft convention and the one proposed by the German Society to Advance the Protection of Foreign Investment were ultimately combined in a new draft which, after repeated amendments, reached its present form in May 1959.[66] This draft is now under consideration by the Organization for European Economic Cooperation [67] and has been extensively discussed among jurists.[68] The proposed convention would provide for the equitable treatment of the property of aliens [69] and for the obligation of states to observe strictly "any undertakings which [they] may have given in relation to investments made by nationals of any other Party." [70] Expropriation of foreign property is to be allowed only under certain conditions.[71] Disputes relating to the convention are to be submitted to an Arbitration Tribunal,[72] to which nationals of the states party to it may also have access.[73] The draft convention provides for measures to be taken by states, individually or collectively, in cases of breach of the convention [74] or of noncompliance with the

---

also provided that states would be entitled to take measures to give effect to the Court's judgments, if the other state failed to comply with it; Brandon, *supra* note 62, at 14, 15.

[66] The text of this draft (hereinafter cited as *1959 Draft Convention*) with a comment by its authors is printed in 9 *J. Pub. L.* 116 (1960).

[67] Now the Organization for Economic Cooperation and Development (OECD). And cf. *supra* p. 78.

[68] Cf. especially, Shawcross, "The Promotion of International Investment," 8 *NATO Letter* No. 2, 19 (1960); Metzger, *supra* note 63; Schwarzenberger, "The Abs-Shawcross Draft Convention on Investments Abroad: A Critical Commentary," 9 *J. Pub. L.* 147 (1960).

[69] *1959 Draft Convention* article I.

[70] *Idem* article II. This provision is meant to cover the cases of contractual commitments of states to aliens; cf. the Comment by the draft convention's authors, 9 *J. Pub. L.* 119, 120–21 (1960).

[71] *1959 Draft Convention* article III. The conditions are roughly the same with those mentioned in the first Shawcross draft, *supra* note 64, with the exception of the requirement of "public interest" which is not mentioned in the later draft.

[72] *Idem* article VII(1). An Annex attached to the convention provides for the composition and operation of the Arbitration Tribunal. If the parties to a dispute do not agree to submit it to arbitration, the dispute may be brought to the International Court of Justice.

[73] *Idem* article VII(2). Such access will depend on an express declaration to that effect which may be made by any state party to the convention.

[74] *Idem* article IV. The parties to the convention undertake not to "recognize or enforce within their territories any measures conflicting with the principles of this Convention. . . ."

Tribunal's award.[75] It is to be noted that the 1957 Draft Convention's provision on measures to be taken against states not party to the convention [76] has been dropped. The new draft's authors, however, seem still to favor the initial adoption of the convention by a limited number of (chiefly capital-exporting) states, probably those of Western Europe.[77]

This last point of view is expressed openly in a slightly earlier study by another European group, the European League for Economic Cooperation,[78] prepared on the initiative of the group's German National Committee.[79] Without presenting any draft text, this study goes further than any other proposal in upholding measures intended to "protect" foreign investors to the utmost extent. Its central proposal is the formulation and implementation by the six European Common Market countries of a common policy with respect to private foreign investments. It is suggested that a "Solidarity Convention" should be concluded among these countries, binding them to concerted action with respect to foreign investments. This proposal might be construed as an effort to achieve European unity in an additional field of economic policy, were it not for the study's emphasis on the extension of the Convention "as soon as possible to include all the great net capital-exporting countries and even, if feasible, the great international financial organisations" (for example, the World Bank and the IFC).[80] It is frankly

[75] *Idem* article VIII. States "shall be entitled . . . to take such measures as are strictly required to give effect to" the award. Note that they are not bound to that effect.

[76] Cf. *supra* p. 81, note 61.

[77] The draft convention's submission to the O.E.E.C. is indicative of such a point of view; see also Shawcross, *supra* note 68, at 22. Needless to stress the fact that Western European states are economically developed and that most of them are capital-exporting.

[78] European League for Economic Cooperation, *Common Protection for Private International Investments* (1958). The E.L.E.C. is one of the private groups associated with the European Movement and seems to represent the views of industrial and banking circles.

[79] The original suggestion came from Dr. Hermann Abs, Chairman of the League's German Committee and President of the Society to Advance the Protection of Foreign Investment.

[80] European League for Economic Cooperation, *op. cit. supra* note 78, at 17, and cf. *idem* 27.

stated that this Convention "should first and foremost be an instrument of pressure for inducing third countries" to accept a Charter of Fair Treatment for Foreign Investments.[81] Such a Charter would provide for the national treatment of foreign investors, full indemnification in case of expropriation,[82] freedom of transfer for earnings and part of capital, virtual exemption from any requirements for the employment of local nationals,[83] and a high degree of respect for existing concessions.[84] Provision for an arbitration procedure to be followed in cases of disputes is to be made by a Special Protocol annexed to the Charter.[85]

The report is remarkable for the detailed exposition of possible methods to be used in assuring the Charter's implementation. The states party to the Solidarity Convention will undertake to act in concert against any state not acting in accordance with the Convention, whether or not itself a party to the Convention or the Charter.[86] The measures to be taken may be official, such as the refusal to accord loans to the state at fault or to give commercial or investment guarantees to new investments in that state.[87] But meas-

[81] *Idem* at 17.

[82] "This indemnity must cover the principal, appreciation and outstanding dividends and interest. It must be made payable in a transferable currency, with a gold clause, and be remitted to the investor within a fixed period." *Idem* 19.

[83] The business concerns involved "would never be refused permission to import (at least temporarily) the technicians they required." *Ibid.* But see also *infra* note 91.

[84] The state of investment should not make any change in the act of concession or in the state regulations under which a foreign enterprise is operating (e.g., with respect to wage or price determination) "without authorising corresponding alterations in the schedule of charges for the products or services provided by the concern, so that its profit-making capacity would not be compromised." *Idem* 19.

[85] *Idem* 16, 20, 25–26.

[86] It is even assumed in the study that in most cases the state "at fault" will not be a party to these instruments. Note, e.g., the language used in this connection: the members of the Solidarity Convention will undertake to take measures against "any country which is at fault, even if that country is itself a signatory of the Solidarity Convention." *Idem* 16.

[87] *Idem* 25. These measures are to be taken in the case of nonexecution of an arbitral award; it is not clear whether they could be taken in the case of a refusal to submit to arbitration. It is, however, expressly stated that collective action of some sort, on the part of the states signatory to the Solidarity Convention, will be taken against any country violating the principles of the Charter, "whether that country has adhered to the Charter or not." *Idem* 16.

ures may be taken by private persons, as well, namely, foreign investors who would be induced to conclude contracts with their governments "not to invest in a country black-listed for interfering with foreign capital after the entry in force of the Solidarity Convention." [88] The ways in which investors may be induced to enter into such contracts are also examined. They may consist in the offering of protection under the Convention or in persuading banks "to sign a gentlemen's agreement whereby they would make it more difficult to obtain credit for operations based on an investment made in violation of the rules it is hoped to lay down." [89]

The European League's study favors the conclusion of special agreements between foreign investors and the government of the country of investment, if only in order to make evident any future violation of certain standard provisions which would be included in such agreements.[90] It also admits, with certain qualifications, the desirability of associating local interests with the investment, through their participation in ownership or management. The investor's obligations to respect the local laws and to contribute to the development of the host country are also mentioned, though placed on a moral rather than a legal basis.[91]

A few other private groups have also been considering the problem of an international investment code. In the United Kingdom, a group of Members of Parliament prepared a detailed report on the matter.[92] The report favors the conclusion of an international convention which would lay down certain "objectives and procedures," without providing a strict "Code of rules." [93] Particular emphasis is laid on the necessity of a wide membership and the participation

[88] *Idem* 22–23. In cases of special need, the Government of the capital-exporting state might grant to individual investors exemption from this prohibition.
[89] *Idem* 23, and cf. *idem* 25.
[90] *Idem* 22. The study also suggests, however, that the investor may undertake not to repatriate his investment for a specified number of years. *Idem* 23.
[91] *Idem* 13–14.
[92] Parliamentary Group for World Government, *A World Investment Convention?* Report of an All-Party Commission on a World Investment Code (1959). No draft text is proposed in this report.
[93] *Idem* 14–15.

of underdeveloped countries. In fact, the report envisages the creation of a special international agency, possibly connected with one
of the international organizations now in existence,[94] and disposing
of a Governing Body and a permanent Secretariat.[95] The report
stresses the need for including in any international convention of
this sort provisions concerning the rights, as well as the duties, of
capital-importing countries.[96] The foreign investors' views are not
accepted in their entirety. Thus, the report disapproves of requirements for majority participation of nationals in the ownership of
enterprises, but it strongly favors requirements for minority participation.[97] Exchange restrictions or requirements for the employment
of local nationals are treated in the same vein. The possibility of
the conclusion of special agreements between foreign investors and
the governments of capital-importing states is generally favored.
It is stated in this connection that such agreements should be respected or "fair compensation should be paid if they are revoked." [98]
The report further provides for the establishment of an Arbitration
Tribunal, but it does not favor the provision of sanctions to be
applied in the case of non-compliance with the award.[99] Though
undoubtedly too brief and therefore lacking in precision with respect to concrete arrangements, the report in question constitutes
one of the few balanced and unbiased contributions in this field.

A number of international private groups have expressed in general terms their support of the adoption of an international investment code, stating, on occasion, certain general principles whose
inclusion in the code they favor. Such support is expressed in a
resolution proposed at the 1958 Conference of the International Bar
Association,[100] a resolution adopted by the 1958 Conference of the

[94] The World Bank is considered as the most appropriate of the United Nations
agencies in this connection; *idem* 16.
[95] *Idem* 6, 17–19. The agency's permanent seat would be in one of the underdeveloped areas. The Governing Body may include representatives not only of
governments but also of public and private interests.
[96] Cf. *idem* 10–12, 15.   [97] *Idem* 13.   [98] *Idem* 12.
[99] Cf. *idem* 18–20.
[100] International Bar Association, *Seventh Conference Report* 484 (1958). In its

Inter-Parliamentary Union,[101] and the first resolution of the International Association for the Promotion and Protection of Private Foreign Investments.[102] The idea has also found support in the statements of several jurists, both in Europe and in the United States.[103] The reports and studies on the international law of state responsibility by the Harvard Law School [104] and by the International Law Commission [105] should also be mentioned here, for they are relevant, even though they are not directly related to the question of an investment code of the type here discussed.

The problems relating to the formulation and adoption of an international investment code have received a good deal of attention lately. It is only possible to indicate the outlines of the related arguments here.

The proponents of an investment code point out that it is the simplest as well as the most effective means to assure the protection of private foreign investment. They generally admit the difficulties involved in assuring that states will comply with the provisions of the code, but they tend to assume that the existence of the code, in the form of a multilateral international convention, will in most cases be sufficient to prevent any breach of its provisions. In some proposals, an effort has been made to provide sanctions for non-compliance, through direct or indirect action of the states concerned. The effectiveness of such sanctions depends on the capital-

---

1960 session, the Association dealt chiefly with the possible creation of an international tribunal for private claimants.

[101] As reported by Brandon, "An International Investment Code: Current Plans," 1959 *J. Business L.* 7, 16–17.

[102] Cf. Brandon, "Recent Measures to Improve the International Investment Climate," 9 *J. Pub. L.* 125, 126 (1960).

[103] Cf., e.g., Mr. C. S. Rhyne's address, cited by Brandon, "An International Investment Code: Current Plans," *supra* note 101, at 15; Mr. L. Hjerner's remarks in International Law Association, *Report of the Forty-Eighth Conference* 167–70 (1958); Haight, "Activities of the International Chamber of Commerce and Other Business Groups," 54 *Am. Soc. Int'l L. Proc.* 200, 203–5 (1960).

[104] Cf. the Draft Convention on International Responsibility of States for Injuries to Aliens, 55 *Am. J. Int'l L.* 548 (1961).

[105] Cf. the successive reports of the Commission's Special Rapporteur, Dr. Garcia Amador, in 1956-II *Yearbook of the International Law Commission* 173 (1957), 1957-II *idem* 104 (1958), 1958-II *idem* 47 (1958) and 1959-II *idem* 1 (1960).

importing countries' continuing need for foreign capital and on the possibility of concerted action on the part of capital-exporting states.

The idea of an investment code is partly founded on the assumption that the commercial and financial interests of capital-exporting and capital-importing countries are largely identical.[106] Though an ultimate identity of interests, in the long run, may perhaps be presumed, it is certainly not true that there are no divergences in the immediate interests of the various countries. Such divergences are manifested not only in the commercial policies of developed and underdeveloped countries [107] but also in their conception of international relations and even of certain issues in international law. Matters regarding the taking of private property owned by aliens are well-known illustrations of such issues. It is difficult to see how the underdeveloped countries can be induced to accept the views of the capital-exporting countries with respect to these questions. Their undeniable need for capital is not likely to constitute sufficient inducement by itself, particularly when the present world political situation is taken into account. Underdeveloped countries depend only in part on private direct foreign investment, and the lack of an investment code does not necessarily affect the other existing sources of capital. The exercise of direct or indirect pressure on the part of capital-exporting states, by means, for instance, of the refusal to give public loans or grants or the imposition of restrictions on export credits, seems improbable, under present conditions. Capital-exporting countries are not at present prepared to jeopardize the political allegiance of underdeveloped countries in order to achieve their reluctant adherence to a charter of doubtful effectiveness.[108]

[106] For a critique of this assumption, see Miller, "Protection of Private Foreign Investment by Multilateral Convention," 53 *Am. J. Int'l L.* 371, 375–76 (1959). And see also Proehl, "Private Investments Abroad," 9 *J. Pub. L.* 362 (1960); Porter, "Multilateral Protection of Foreign Investment," 3 *Int'l Development Rev.* 23 (1961).

[107] Cf., e.g., Myrdal, *An International Economy* 222 et seq. (1956) and see *supra* p. 33, note 11.

[108] Such considerations are especially operative with respect to the proposals

Apart from considerations of this order, the general adoption of an effective investment code appears unlikely for several reasons. A code's provisions, if they are to afford some protection to foreign investors, would have to limit the sovereignty of all states participating in it. It seems certain that many states, including several capital-exporting ones, would not be prepared to undertake far-reaching commitments in this connection.[109] Their reluctance should in part be attributed to a desire not to commit themselves on matters of domestic economic policy. In some cases, a state's federal system of government may make difficult the acceptance of such commitments. More generally, capital-exporting as well as capital-importing states usually prefer to retain a high degree of freedom of movement in their domestic and international policies. They tend, therefore, to favor specific and limited commitments rather than general and extensive undertakings. There is, then, no real inconsistency in the willingness of capital-importing states to grant to individual foreign investors certain rights or privileges which they refuse to give to investors as a whole.

Certain additional considerations obtain in the particular case of capital-importing countries. First, capital-exporting states cannot give any assurance that substantial amounts of new foreign private capital will be invested, since their governments have limited control over the disposition of the funds of private citizens. Even if legal obstacles are removed, economic reasons may well prevent foreign investments in some or all underdeveloped countries. Thus, capital-importing states would have to accept certain definite obligations

---

involving the creation of a coalition of capital-exporting states, attempting to impose a charter of fair treatment on the capital-importing ones. Cf. *supra* pp. 81, 83. It is interesting to note that a good deal of agitation for an international investment code comes from the Federal Republic of Germany, whose international political responsibilities at this moment can hardly be compared to those of the United States or the United Kingdom.

[109] On the probable attitude of the United States and other states in this respect, see Rubin, *Private Foreign Investment* 20, 81 (1956); Fulton, Address in 52 *Am. Soc. Int'l L. Proc.* 200, 204 (1958); Metzger, "Multilateral Conventions for the Protection of Private Foreign Investment," 9 *J. Pub. L.* 133, 138, 145 (1960).

without any corresponding obligations on the part of the capital-exporting states.[110] It may be argued at this point that, if no investment is made, the obligations of the capital-importing countries would remain without object and, therefore, ineffective. There exists, however, a variety of possible levels and forms of investment. A capital-importing country would adhere to an investment code only in order to assure itself of a high level of foreign investment. It would object to having to apply its obligations under the code to a limited number of foreign investors, perhaps in fields that are not important to its economic development.

Most of the proposed draft codes are one-sided in another way, too. They provide for the protection of the investors' interests, without attempting to safeguard the host state's interests. There is no convincing justification for this bias. It is sometimes said that nowadays it is the foreign investor rather than the host state that is in need of protection.[111] The accuracy of this contention is doubtful, to start with, but, even if it were true, it does not follow that provisions on the investors' duties toward the host state as well as the duties of capital-exporting countries toward capital-importing countries should not be included in a comprehensive investment code. If such duties are well-determined and there is no possible dispute about them, certainly their inclusion in the code would do no harm. If, on the other hand, they are not well-settled, they evidently should be examined and better determined in the interests of both the investors and the capital-importing states. Though ultimately intended to provide assurance to foreign investors, an investment code should not be a one-sided instrument. It should attempt to regulate comprehensively the whole relationship between

---

[110] See *contra* Shawcross, "The Promotion of International Investment," 8 *NATO Letter* No. 2, 19, at 21 (1960): he argues that "the *quid pro quo* for the borrowing States' undertakings is in fact, in the English vernacular, the provision of the 'quids,' that the capital importing countries, in return for agreeing to abide by the generally recognized procedure of International Law, will receive more private investment . . . than would otherwise be the case." But is this really certain?

[111] Cf., e.g., *ICC Code*, Introductory Report, para. 19; Hyde, Book Review, 66 *Yale L.J.* 813, 816 (1957).

host state and foreign investors.[112] Otherwise, such a code might be construed as limiting the powers of the host state without restricting the freedom of action of foreign investors.

It is true that, in spite of the difficulties we have mentioned, the formulation and adoption of an investment code might still be possible. In view of present day conditions, however, it is highly improbable that such a code, if adopted, would be significantly effective. The multilateral convention is a difficult kind of instrument when one is dealing with matters where particular situations and exceptional cases are of importance. An international investment convention would have to be couched in general terms, since many states with various political and economic structures, and innumerable kinds of investment would be involved. Qualifications and exceptions would have to be added, each one of them quite necessary to the state or states immediately concerned. The end result is bound to be a cumbersome and vague instrument which would be open to a variety of interpretations. The precedents of the Havana Charter and the Bogota Economic Agreement are instructive in this connection. And it should be noted that the political power of underdeveloped countries as a whole has greatly increased since the first postwar years, while the capital-exporting countries are in no way in a stronger position than they were then.

As long as there exists a divergence in the interests of capital-exporting and capital-importing states, the positive contribution of an investment code is bound to be very limited. But its negative impact may be far more serious. The preliminary negotiations and discussions and the international conference which would presumably follow would tend to intensify rather than reduce the existing differences of opinion and might lead to the adoption of extreme and rigid positions.[113] Capital-importing countries might then be

---

[112] For a strong statement in support of this view, see Larson, "Recipients' Rights Under an International Investment Code," 9 *J. Pub. L.* 172 (1960). Note that some of the proposed codes discussed *supra* have attempted to do this, with varying degrees of success. And see also Shawcross, *supra* note 110, at 21.

[113] Cf., in agreement, Fulton, *supra* note 109, at 202; Gardner, "International

unwilling to grant exemptions or privileges to individual foreign investors, for they would fear that such action might be used as an argument against their official position.

An alternative course might perhaps still be open. It has been suggested recently [114] that the staff of one of the international financial agencies dealing with international investment could draft a set of principles laying down the obligations as well as the rights of foreign investors in underdeveloped countries. Compliance with this charter would be required of all firms and governments seeking the agency's aid. In this manner, the disadvantages of negotiations between government representatives might in part be eliminated. The difficulties, however, which are inherent in the formulation of a widely acceptable set of principles would still persist. The advantage of this scheme lies in its institutional setting, which makes possible the application of such principles in a flexible and sophisticated manner and provides a number of ways for the settlement of disputes. From this standpoint, the proposal presents certain similarities with some other suggestions which stress the institutions charged with applying the charter rather than the charter itself.[115]

Bilateral Investment Treaties

The realization of the difficulties involved in the creation of an investment code is one of the main reasons for the present orientation of the major capital-exporting states toward the conclusion of bilateral agreements on the protection of private foreign investments.[116] This is a relatively new phenomenon. It is true that in the

---

Measures for the Promotion and Protection of Foreign Investment," 53 *Am. Soc. Int'l L. Proc.* 255, 259–62 (1959); Metzger, *supra* note 109, 145–46.

[114] See Gardner, *supra* note 113, 265–66; Gardner, "New Directions in U.S. Foreign Economic Policy," 1959 *Headline Series* No. 133, at 42.

[115] Cf., e.g., the proposals of the Parliamentary Group for World Government, *supra* p. 86. And see Carlston, *Law and Structures of Social Action* 168 (1956).

[116] This does not preclude their being at the same time interested in the formulation of an investment code. Western Germany, which is today the chief proponent of the code approach, has also concluded a number of investment treaties; cf. *infra* note 121. The United States' emphasis is still on the bilateral approach, but it has apparently been giving some consideration to code proposals, too; cf. Smith,

past, as well, provisions concerning the protection of foreign merchants and investors had been included in the commercial treaties concluded by the capital-exporting states. However, in the treaties concluded before the end of the Second World War, attention was focused on the trader and merchant rather than on the industrial investor.[117] The emphasis was justified under the conditions then prevailing, for, at that time, the main form of economic activity of aliens in foreign states was commerce rather than industry.

After the war of 1939-45, treaty provisions dealing with investments and investors began to increase in number and relative importance. The United States first inaugurated a series of treaties dealing chiefly with investment problems.[118] The United Kingdom did not follow its example until recently; for several years it continued to include occasional provisions, dealing in a rather general manner with foreign investments, in its treaties with underdeveloped countries.[119] In 1959, however, it concluded a treaty with Iran [120] which, though not modeled exactly on the United States pattern, should still be considered as an "investment treaty." Since 1957, the Federal Republic of Germany has also concluded a number of investment treaties, which follow closely the United States model.[121]

Statement before the Subcommittee on Foreign Trade Policy of the House Committee on Ways and Means, 39 *Dep't State Bull.* 1060, 1062-63 (1958). But cf. *supra,* note 109.

[117] On United States practice on this point, see Foster, "Some Aspects of the Commercial Treaty Program of the United States—Past and Present," 11 *Law & Contemp. Problems* 647 (1946); Walker, "Modern Treaties of Friendship, Commerce and Navigation," 42 *Minn. L. Rev.* 805, 806-8 (1958); Walker, "The Post-War Commercial Treaty Program of the United States," 73 *Pol. Sc. Qu.* 57, 58 (1958).

[118] These treaties have been thoroughly studied by Professor Wilson in several articles and, more recently, in his *United States Commercial Treaties and International Law* (1960), which includes a detailed bibliography.

[119] Cf., e.g., Exchange of Notes of October 17, 1947, with Burma, annexed to the treaty regarding the recognition of Burmese independence, 1948 [U.K.] *Treaty Series* No. 16, Cmd. 7360; and the treaties with Nepal, 1951 *idem* No. 46, Cmd. 8271, and with Muscat and Oman, 1952 *idem* No. 44, Cmd. 8633.

[120] Treaty of Commerce, Establishment and Navigation, of March 11, 1959, Cmd. 698.

[121] Cf., e.g., the treaty of Friendship, Commerce and Navigation of December 23, 1957, with the Dominican Republic, 1959 *Bundesgesetzblatt* (II) 1468. Similar treaties have been concluded with Italy, France, and other states.

The United States program of investment treaties remains the most important one, both because of the position of the United States as the chief capital-exporting country and because of the number of treaties already concluded and their focus on investment problems. This emphasis on investment is already apparent in some of the early postwar commercial treaties of the United States,[122] but the program really came into its own, with the initiation of the "Point Four" Program in 1949. It was referred to both in President Truman's Inaugural Address of January 20, 1949 [123] and in his subsequent Message to Congress on "Point Four Legislation" (June 23, 1949).[124] Since that time, the conclusion of bilateral treaties for the protection and encouragement of American private investment abroad has consistently been a major objective of American foreign economic policy.[125] The program has found strong approval among influential American business circles.[126]

[122] Cf. Agreement of Friendship and Commerce with Yemen of May 4, 1946, *T.I.A.S.* No. 1535; Treaty of Friendship, Commerce and Navigation with China of November 4, 1946, *T.I.A.S.* No. 1871; Treaty of Friendship, Commerce and Navigation with Italy of February 2, 1948, *T.I.A.S.* No. 1965. For a survey, see Wilson, "Postwar Commercial Treaties of the United States," 43 *Am. J. Int'l L.* 262 (1949).

[123] Cf. the excerpts quoted in United States Dep't of State, *Point Four* (U.S. Dep't of State Publ. 3719) Appendix A, 95–96 (1950).

[124] In this message, it was stated in part: "All countries concerned with the program should work together to bring about conditions favorable to the flow of private capital. To this end we are negotiating agreements with other countries to protect the American investor from unwarranted or discriminatory treatment under the laws of the country in which he makes his investment." *Idem*, Appendix B, 97, 101 (1950). The three other main means to this end were the provision of guarantees and Export-Import Bank loans to the investors and that of technical assistance to the underdeveloped countries. *Ibid.*

[125] Cf. Thibodeaux, "United States Government Assistance to American Business Abroad," 34 *Dep't State Bull.* 22, 23–24 (1956); U.S. Dep't of State, *Commercial Treaty Program of the United States,* (Dep't of State Publ. 6565, 1958); Dillon, Statement before the Subcommittee on Foreign Trade Policy of the House Committee on Ways and Means, 39 *Dep't State Bull.* 1056, 1058 (1958).

[126] Cf. e.g., National Association of Manufacturers, *The Bold New Plan. A Program for Underdeveloped Areas* 10 (1949); National Planning Association, *The United States and the Lesser Developed Countries of the World: A Statement of Principles . . .* 10 (1951); United States Dep't of Commerce, *Factors Limiting U.S. Investment Abroad.* Part 2: Business Views on the U.S. Government's Role 16 (1954). Cf. also the statements and declarations cited by Walker, "The Post-War Commercial Treaty Program of the United States," 73 *Pol. Sc. Qu.* 57, 60, note 7 (1958).

The particular form which the agreements take is not new in itself. The provisions on investment have been included in treaties of Friendship, Commerce and Navigation (FCN treaties) which constitute the traditional instrument for the regulation of United States commercial relations with foreign nations. The whole structure of the instrument had to be altered to suit the modern emphasis on investment problems.[127] Still, the FCN treaties do not deal solely with such problems but with several other questions as well; nor is it always possible to determine which provisions deal directly with investment and which only indirectly. The general features of FCN treaties can be better seen in the following "synoptical outline of normal content," provided by a scholar who has thoroughly studied the subject:

Preamble, general purposes.
Entry, movement and residence of individuals.
Liberty of conscience and communication.
Protection of persons from molestation and police malpractice.
Protection of acquired property.
Standing in the courts.
Right to establish and operate businesses.
Formation and management of corporations.
Non-profit activities.
Acquisition and tenure of property.
Tax treatment.
Administration and exchange controls.
Rules on international trade and customs administration.
Rules governing the state in business.
Treatment of ships and shipping.
Transit of goods and persons.
Reservations, definitions and general provisions.
Settlement of disputes.
Procedural clauses.
Protocol, an appendix of varying length, containing material construing

---

[127] This was in part made possible by the use of other forms of instruments for the regulation of most trade matters; cf. Walker, "Modern Treaties of Friendship, Commerce and Navigation," 42 *Minn. L. Rev.* 805, 806–7 (1958).

and clarifying the treaty text, and making accommodations to take account of individual situations.[128]

It is characteristic in this regard that all FCN treaties of the type discussed here, with one exception,[129] mention in their Preambles, among the general purposes of the treaty, the "encouragement" of "mutually beneficial investments," [130] of the "flow of investment capital," [131] or use other equivalent expressions.[132]

Since 1949, a considerable number of such treaties have been concluded by the United States,[133] though less than half of them with countries which may be considered economically underdeveloped.[134] It should be noted, in this connection, that when the countries involved are at an extremely low level of administrative and economic development, the whole pattern of the instrument undergoes important changes.[135] The treaties are shorter, less detailed in their provisions and deal with certain additional matters (for example, consular rights). More significantly, the standard of "national treatment" of foreign investors is given less prominence than in the other treaties while the "most-favored-nation" standard receives greater emphasis.

The FCN treaties involve, like all treaties, the undertaking of reciprocal obligations by the party states. The real meaning and

---

[128] Walker, *ibid.* 808.   [129] That of the treaty with Ireland.
[130] Cf. e.g., the treaties with Ethiopia, Israel, Japan, Denmark, Germany, Haiti, Iran, Nicaragua, Korea, France, and the Netherlands.
[131] Cf. the treaty with Greece.
[132] Cf., e.g., the treaties with Uruguay and with Muscat and Oman.
[133] Cf. Table 1, p. 97.
[134] Of the treaties presently in effect, only those with Ethiopia, Greece, Iran, Korea, Muscat and Oman, Nicaragua, and Pakistan can be included in this category. Three other treaties, with Colombia, Haiti, and Uruguay, have been signed but they will probably never become effective; cf. notes a, e, and i in Table 1, p. 97.
[135] Cf. Department of State Statement in *Commercial Treaty Hearing Before the Subcommittee of the Senate Committee on Foreign Relations*, 83d Cong. 1st sess., 6 (1953). On a formal level, the change is manifested by the use of a slightly different treaty title, instead of the usual one of "Treaty of Friendship, Commerce and Navigation." The treaties with Iran and Muscat and Oman are treaties "of Amity, Economic Relations and Consular Rights," while that with Ethiopia is "of Amity and Economic Relations."

Table 1. FCN Treaties of the United States signed since 1949

State	Date of signature	Date of entry in force	T.I.A.S.
Belgium	Feb. 21, 1961		
Colombia	Apr. 26, 1951 [a]		
Denmark	Oct. 1, 1951 [b]		
Ethiopia [c]	Sept. 7, 1951	Oct. 8, 1953	2864
France [d]	Nov. 25, 1959	Dec. 21, 1960	4625
Germany, Fed. Rep.	Oct. 29, 1954	July 14, 1956	3593
Greece	Aug. 3, 1951	Oct. 13, 1954	3057
Haiti	March 3, 1955 [e]		
Iran [f]	Aug. 15, 1955	June 16, 1957	3853
Ireland	Jan. 21, 1950	Sept. 14, 1950	2155
Israel	Aug. 23, 1951	Apr. 3, 1954	2948
Italy [g]	Sept. 26, 1951	March 2, 1961	
Japan	Apr. 2, 1953	Oct. 30, 1953	2863
Korea	Nov. 28, 1956	Nov. 7, 1957	3947
Muscat and Oman [f]	Dec. 20, 1958	June 11, 1960	4530
The Netherlands	March 27, 1956	Dec. 5, 1957	3942
Nicaragua	Jan. 21, 1956	May 24, 1958	4024
Pakistan	Nov. 12, 1959	Feb. 12, 1961	
Uruguay [h]	Nov. 23, 1949 [i]		

Sources: United States *Treaties and Other International Acts Series* (T.I.A.S.); United States *Department of State Bulletin;* and three letters by Vernon G. Setser, Chief, Commercial Treaties Branch, Commercial Policy and Treaties Division, Department of State, dated April 7, 1956, August 20, 1957, and March 14, 1961. The instruments listed are Treaties of Friendship, Commerce and Navigation, unless otherwise indicated in the Notes.

[a] Withdrawn from U.S. Senate, on June 30, 1953. A public controversy regarding the provisions on religious activities having arisen in Colombia, the Colombian Government declared its inability to ratify the treaty.

[b] Approved by U.S. Senate, July 21, 1953. Presented to Danish Folketing, December 9, 1960. The delay was attributed by the Danish Foreign Minister to a desire to ratify the treaty after settlement of the Danish shipowners' claims for the use of their ships during the war and after clarification of the situation as to the European market arrangements.

[c] Treaty of Amity and Economic Relations.

[d] Convention of Establishment.

[e] Approved by Haitian National Assembly, June 27, 1955. Withdrawn from U.S. Senate for further consideration, July 1957. Decision to withdraw attributed to (1) its having been before the Senate for over two years without action, owing to the opposition of certain Protestant organizations (the treaty does not contain provisions on freedom of religious activities), and (2) the fact "the Haitian Government that agreed to the treaty had been forced out of office and there has subsequently been no regularly constituted government in that country whose views regarding the treaty could be taken into consideration." (Setser Letter, of August 20, 1957).

[f] Treaty of Amity, Economic Relations and Consular Rights.

[g] Agreement Supplementing the Treaty of Friendship, Commerce and Navigation of February 2, 1948.

[h] Treaty of Friendship, Commerce and Economic Development.

[i] Approved by U.S. Senate, August 9, 1950. Still under consideration before the Uruguayan National Assembly.

extent of such reciprocity are determined by the existing conditions. The United States does not have to give assurances of fair treatment to prospective foreign investors. Its economy is relatively stable, much more so than that of any underdeveloped country. Even though restrictions on the economic activities of aliens do exist, they are less extensive than those prevailing in most capital-importing states. Moreover, it has no need to import foreign capital. For political as well as economic reasons, it is interested in furthering the exportation of the capital of its nationals, and to this end it endeavors to assure their fair treatment in foreign countries. In fact, therefore, FCN treaties are in the main instruments through which capital-receiving states guarantee that American investors will be fairly treated. Reciprocity becomes an issue only with regard to a few provisions, chiefly those covering matters with respect to which the aliens' activities are restricted in the United States.[136] Thus, in the case of the navigation provisions of the treaties, the granting of fully "national treatment" to foreign-owned vessels might raise difficult problems for the United States, whose shipping policies involve the subsidizing and the preferential treatment of domestic shipowners.[137] More directly connected with investment are the restrictions on the activities of aliens in certain fields, such as air transport,[138] the exercise of a number of professions,[139] the owner-

[136] On reciprocity in connection with FCN treaties, see Wilson, *op. cit. supra* note 118, at 14, 133–35; Walker, *supra* note 127, *passim*. For a general survey of the problems of foreign enterprises in the United States, see Thompson, "Foreign Businesses Operating in the United States," in *Legal Problems of International Trade* 282 (Proehl ed., 1959).

[137] For a description of discriminatory U.S. policies, see Gorter, *United States Shipping Policy* 78–82 (subsidies to vessel operators), 106–17 (cargo preferences), 131–39 (cabotage restrictions) (1956). The navigation provisions of the FCN treaties are discussed in some detail in Hawkins, *Commercial Treaties and Agreements* 34–44 (1951) and Walker, *supra* note 127, at 816–17.

In two recent FCN treaties, with Pakistan and France, no navigation provisions were included. For the reasons for this omission, see Martin, Statement to the U.S. Senate Foreign Relations Committee, 43 *Dep't State Bull.* 56 (1960).

[138] Cf. the United States Civil Aeronautics Act, 49 U.S.C.A. § 1401(b) (1960).

[139] The related provisions of state statutes in the United States have generally been upheld by the courts as a "justifiable and necessary exercise" of the states' police power; cf. 3 Hackworth, *Digest* 618–19 (1942). And see Hunt, "International Law: Reservations to Commercial Treaties Dealing with Aliens' Right to

ship of real property,[140] and the exploitation of the country's natural resources,[141] as well as the discriminatory treatment of aliens in matters of taxation.[142] Such restrictions exist today in most states.[143] Consequently, these fields are usually excepted from the national treatment generally granted to foreign investors.

A related problem, peculiar to the United States, arises out of the federal structure of its government. American states keep a high degree of competence with regard to certain matters.[144] The Federal Government, which negotiates the FCN treaties, cannot undertake any commitments with respect to such matters. Special formulae have been developed to take care of such cases. The treatment accorded to American investors in the foreign country is made to depend on the specific treatment accorded to aliens in the investors' home states.[145]

Bilateral investment treaties present definite advantages over multilateral arrangements, such as the proposed investment code. Generally speaking, multilateral conventions are more difficult to conclude than bilateral ones, if only because of the need to reconcile a greater number of points of view and special interests. Bilateral treaties are also, as a rule, more flexible. Though largely following

---

Engage in the Professions," 52 *Michigan L. Rev.* 1184 (1954); Wilson, *op. cit. supra* note 118, at 58–94.

[140] See Hackworth, *op. cit. supra* note 139, at 678–83, and Wilson, *op. cit. supra* note 118, at 135–37.

[141] Cf., e.g., the statutory provisions on mining, 30 U.S.C.A. § 22(1960) and those of the Federal Power Act, 16 U.S.C.A. § 797 (e) (1960). For a detailed study, see Wilson, *op. cit. supra* note 118, at 126–55, and for some related cases, 3 Hackworth, *Digest* 678 (1942).

[142] Cf. Singer, "Some American Discriminations against Foreign Enterprises," 11 *Law & Contemp. Problems* 776 (1946); Wilson, *op. cit. supra* note 118, at 156–81.

[143] An exhaustive survey of national and international regulatory measures relating to the exploitation of natural resources in the various countries, has been prepared recently by the United Nations Secretariat Staff; see "The Status of Permanent Sovereignty over Natural Wealth and Resources," UN Document A/AC. 97/5/Rev. 1, 27 December 1960.

[144] Such as ownership of real property, *supra* note 140, the exercise of certain professions, *supra* note 139.

[145] Cf. Wilson, *op. cit. supra* note 118, at 10–16; Walker, *supra* note 127, at 821–22; Walker, "Treaties for the Encouragement and Protection of Foreign Investment: Present United States Practice," 5 *Am. J. Comp. L.* 229, 237 (1956).

a common pattern, the United States FCN treaties have adjusted to an important extent to the particular conditions prevailing in each country. Sometimes their whole form is altered, as in the case of the treaties with Ethiopia, Iran or Muscat and Oman. In other cases, they have adjusted by omitting some types of provisions, for example, those on navigation in the recent treaties with France and Pakistan. In the majority of cases, the variations have been more subtle, but no less real. Compare, for instance, the regulation of exchange control problems in the treaty with Germany with that in the treaty with Greece.

The bilateral approach, however, also has its limitations. Most of the difficulties mentioned in connection with investment codes also obtain, to various extents, in the case of treaties between two states. The fundamental problem is again the difference in the interests and points of view of developed and underdeveloped countries. Because of this great difference, the effectiveness of any international instrument attempting to regulate fully the economic relations between the two is bound to be limited. Such instruments are by no means useless; but no single legal formula can be expected to resolve by itself the underlying economic, political, or cultural problems.

Some of the other observations made in connection with investment codes are also applicable, *mutatis mutandis,* to bilateral treaties.[146] States may be unwilling to commit themselves under international law with respect to matters of domestic economic policy. A treaty's language will have to be general and it will probably be subject to more than one interpretation. The protection afforded to investors is also limited by the fact that the treaty is going to apply to all investments, regardless of type or size. A capital-importing state may be prepared to offer more extensive protection to certain individual investments or certain kinds of investment, but rarely will it be willing to extend it to any and all investments.

The recent history of the United States FCN treaties brings out

[146] Cf. *supra* pp. 87 *et seq.*

clearly the limitations of the medium. Despite its efforts for over a decade, the United States has not been able to conclude more than half a dozen such treaties with underdeveloped countries. It is characteristic that the only three of the FCN treaties which were signed but never became effective are all treaties with underdeveloped countries.[147] Most of the writers who have dealt with the United States FCN treaties take pains to point out that such treaties cannot be expected to solve by themselves the existing problems of private foreign investment. They tend to consider them as making manifest, but not creating, a preexisting atmosphere favorable to private foreign investment in a particular country.[148]

Before leaving the subject of bilateral investment treaties, another development should be noted. In recent years, a number of bilateral agreements dealing with investments have been concluded between underdeveloped countries, or between underdeveloped and semi-developed countries, that is, countries which, though economically developed to some degree, are still far behind the highly developed economies of the United States, the United Kingdom, or Germany. Thus, India has concluded treaties with Afghanistan, Iran, and Japan; Burma has concluded economic cooperation agreements with Israel and Japan.[149] This is a new development which warrants special attention; it may indicate a potentially important field of study to those interested in the problems of international investment.

Guarantees by Capital-Exporting States

In view of the difficulties and limitations of international arrangements, bilateral or multilateral, the need for legal guarantees to foreign investors is chiefly met through municipal state action.

[147] Cf. *supra* note 134 and Table 1.

[148] Cf. Brown, "Treaty, Guaranty and Tax Inducements for Foreign Investment," 40 *Am. Econ. Rev. Proc.* 486, 492 (1950); United States Commission on Foreign Economic Policy (Randall Commission), *Staff Papers Presented to the Commission* 95 (1954); Walker, *supra* note 145, at 247.

[149] For a list of bilateral agreements dealing with trade and investments, see UN Document A/AC.97/5/Rev. 1, 27 December 1960, pp. 192–95.

Since it is the capital-importing states that are in need of foreign capital, it is usually they that offer legal guarantees to prospective investors. Nevertheless, in accordance with their general policy of encouraging foreign investment, certain capital-exporting states, as well, offer guarantees to those of their nationals who invest abroad. Guarantees of this type are, in the main, a modern development, though they were not totally unknown in the past. In the period before the Second World War, a number of loans to underdeveloped or developing countries were guaranteed by individual capital-exporting countries or by several such countries jointly.[150] Closely related to investment guarantees are also the export credit guarantee programs instituted in several capital-exporting countries both before and after the Second World War.[151] Today, investment guarantee programs operate in at least three major capital-exporting states. The earliest and most important program is that of the United States. In recent years, both West Germany and Japan have expanded their export credit guarantee programs, already in operation, to include guarantees to foreign investments.

The United States investment guarantee program has been in operation since 1948. Together with the investment treaty program, it is a by-product of the Marshall Plan and of "Point Four" legislation.[152] Its initial scope was strictly limited. Insurance was available

[150] Cf. Lewis, *The United States and Foreign Investment Problems* 232–37 (1948); Williams, "L'entre-aide financière internationale," 5 *Hague Recueil* 109 (1924).
[151] On the prewar experience, see Shenkman, *Insurance Against Credit Risks* 177 *et seq.* (1935); von Neumann Whitman, *The United States Investment Guaranty Program and Private Foreign Investment* (hereinafter cited Whitman, *The Guaranty Program*) 17–18 (Princeton Studies in International Finance No. 9, 1959). On the programs today in operation, see UN *Flow 1956* 69–76 (1959); UN Document E/3369, 13 May 1960, ch. IV. A European multilateral export credit guarantee system has been recently proposed, within the framework of the reorganization of the O.E.E.C.; cf. O.E.E.C., *A Remodelled Economic Organization*, A Report by the Group of Four 26 (para. 61) (1960), and for more details, Zolotas, *A Proposal for the Establishment of an International Export Credit Guarantee Unit* (mimeo., 1960).
[152] Cf. *supra* notes 123, 124. The program was set up by the Foreign Assistance Act of 1948, 62 Stat. 143 (1948); it is now governed by Section 413(b)(4) of the Mutual Security Act of 1954, as amended by the Mutual Security Acts of 1956, 1958 and 1959, 22 U.S.C.A. § 1933(b)(4) (1960). Note that certain other U.S. Government agencies, such as the Export-Import Bank of Washington and the De-

to new investment projects in the Marshall Plan countries and against the sole risk of inconvertibility of currency. Gradually, its scope has broadened in all respects and it has acquired an emphasis on the underdeveloped countries.[153] Today, eligible investments may be in the form of equity, loan, or licensing agreements and investment contributions may be made in cash, in equipment or materials, in patents or processes, or in services. Eligible investments include accumulated profits or other additions to existing investments. Insurance is available against the risks of expropriation of property and war losses as well as inconvertibility of currency and it covers investments in more than forty states.[154] The guarantees cover only nonbusiness risks and not those normally associated with business ventures, such as devaluation of a foreign currency or inability to make a profit.

The program appears at first glance to be operating on the lines of a private insurance agency. On closer scrutiny, however, it becomes evident that it is intimately related to and governed by considerations of public policy. Guarantees are available only to United States citizens or to corporations which are created under the law of one of the United States and in which substantial beneficial ownership is held by United States citizens.[155] Eligible investments must be new, and though this requirement is now understood in a rather broad sense, it still excludes any investment which has been firmly committed before the filing of an application for insurance and the issuance of a guarantee.[156] Only investments made in countries which

---

velopment Loan Fund, are also competent to issue guarantees to private investors; cf. Whitman, *The Guaranty Program* 30-31, 45 (1959).

[153] For a summary of the related legislative and administrative developments, see Whitman, *The Guaranty Program* 20-45 (1959). The description that follows is chiefly based on International Cooperation Administration, *Investment Guaranty Handbook* (1960 ed.).

[154] See Table 2, p. 104, for a list of these states.

[155] Mutual Security Act of 1954, as amended, s. 413(b)(4)(H)(i), 22 U.S.C.A. § 1933(b)(4)(H)(i) (1960); ICA, *op. cit. supra* note 153, at 5.

[156] *Idem* 2, 11. After an application is filed and before the issuance of the guarantee, it is possible for an investor to request an ICA "waiver letter," providing that he may proceed with his investment plans or make commitments without prejudice to his application. *Idem* 11-12.

have concluded special agreements with the United States [157] are eligible for insurance.

The international agreements in question are usually made in the form of an exchange of notes between the two governments and follow a largely common pattern. They do not mention specifically

Table 2. Countries where United States investment guarantees are available as of January, 1961

Convertibility	*Expropriation*	*War risk*
Afghanistan	Afghanistan	Afghanistan
Argentina [a]		
Austria [b]	Austria [b]	
Belgium [c]	Belgium [c]	
Bolivia	Bolivia	
China (Taiwan)	China (Taiwan)	China (Taiwan)
Colombia [a]		
Costa Rica	Costa Rica	
Cuba [d]	Cuba [d]	
Denmark [c]	Denmark [c]	
Ecuador	Ecuador	
El Salvador	El Salvador	
Finland [b]	Finland [b]	
France [c]	France [c]	
Germany, Fed. Rep. [b]	Germany, Fed. Rep. [b]	
Ghana	Ghana	
Greece	Greece	
Guatemala [a]	Guatemala [a]	
Haiti	Haiti	
Honduras	Honduras	
India	India	
Iran	Iran	
Ireland [b]	Ireland [b]	
Israel	Israel	Israel
Italy [b]	Italy [b]	Italy [b]
Japan [b]	Japan [b]	
Jordan	Jordan	Jordan
Korea	Korea	Korea
Liberia	Liberia	Liberia
Luxembourg [b]	Luxembourg [b]	
Malaya, Fed.	Malaya, Fed.	
Nepal	Nepal	Nepal
Netherlands [c]	Netherlands [c]	
Nicaragua	Nicaragua	Nicaragua
Norway [c]	Norway [c]	

[157] Cf. Table 2, above. The description that follows is based on the study of several such agreements and the draft note quoted in Whitman, *The Guaranty Program* 89–91 (1959).

Table 2 (continued)

Convertibility	Expropriation	War risk
Pakistan	Pakistan	
Panama ^a	Panama ^a	Panama ^a
Paraguay	Paraguay	
Peru		
Philippines	Philippines	
Portugal	Portugal	
Spain	Spain	
Sudan	Sudan	Sudan
Thailand	Thailand	Thailand
Tunisia	Tunisia	Tunisia
Turkey	Turkey	
United Kingdom ^c		
Viet Nam	Viet Nam	Viet Nam
Yugoslavia	Yugoslavia	

Source: International Cooperation Administration, Investment Guaranties Division.

^a Not yet ratified.

^b Agreement in effect but inoperative after January 1, 1960, due to amendment of Mutual Security Act providing for issuance of guaranties for underdeveloped areas only.

^c Agreement in effect but, due to above stated reason, operative only as to underdeveloped overseas dependencies.

^d Agreement in effect but inoperative due to the conditions existing in that country.

the risks covered by the guarantees,[158] referring instead to the relevant United States legislation. They provide for consultation between the two governments regarding the investments proposed for guarantee. The state contracting with the United States agrees that in the event an investor is paid by the United States pursuant to a guarantee approved by the state in question, the latter will recognize the subrogation of the United States to his claims or rights in connection with the guaranteed investment. It also agrees to treat the local currency thus acquired by the United States in no less favorable a manner than corresponding private funds and to make such currency available for administrative expenses of the United States Government within the state in question. In most cases, the agreement includes the express undertaking on the part of the United States not to issue a guarantee on any project not

[158] With the exception of war risks, which are expressly mentioned though not defined.

previously approved by the contracting state. Another quite common clause provides for direct negotiations between the two governments with respect to any claim under the agreement and for arbitration by a sole arbitrator if no agreement is reached in the negotiations. Guarantee agreements do not generally provide for special treatment of the guaranteed investments. With regard to war risk guarantees, however, the agreements provide that the investors concerned will receive national and most-favored-nation treatment with respect to compensation or any other payment for losses by reason of war.[159]

An investment project may be insured only if it has been formally approved by both the International Cooperation Administration (ICA), as agent of the United States Government, and the host country's government.[160] Until 1959, ICA approval indicated nothing more than that the investment was considered as furthering the purposes of Mutual Security legislation.[161] These purposes were understood quite broadly, in a way which would cover most normal investment projects.[162] Since the Mutual Security Act of 1959, however, approval of a project depends on its "furthering the development of the economic resources and productive capacities of economically underdeveloped areas." [163] The exact interpretation of the last term has not yet been determined. Though it will be probably understood in a wide sense, the Western European countries will still not be included.[164] The necessity for government

[159] ICA, *op. cit. supra* note 153, at 3-4. Cf., e.g., para. 3(c) of the agreement with Sudan of March 17, 1959, *T.I.A.S.* 4201.

[160] Mutual Security Act of 1954, as amended, s. 413(b)(4)(A), 22 U.S.C.A. § 1933(b)(4)(A) (1960).

[161] Mutual Security Act of 1954, 22 U.S.C.A. § 1933(b)(4)(A) (1952 ed., Supp. V, 1958).

[162] Cf. ICA, *Investment Guaranty Handbook* 2-3 (1957 ed.)

[163] Mutual Security Act of 1959 (Public Law 86-108, July 24, 1959) s. 413(b)(4) (A), 73 Stat. 251. And cf. ICA, *Investment Guaranty Handbook* 2-3 (1960 ed.). See also Table 2, p. 104.

[164] Cf. Whitman, *The Guaranty Program* 34-35 (1959). The amendment in question should be attributed to the Congress' belief that, after the complete recovery of Western Europe, no added inducement was necessary for investments in that region. Cf. *ibid.* and Table 2, p. 104.

approval makes it possible for the ICA to exercise regulatory supervision over United States investment abroad. It appears, however,
that this power has been exercised sparingly if at all.

The approval of the capital-receiving country's government is
additional to any other particular approvals or permissions which
the local law may require of an investor. It indicates the host government's agreement to the inclusion of the specific investment
project under the guarantee program. Should a claim arise in the
future, such approval is useful to the United States in establishing
that the investment involved was, beyond any dispute, within the
scope of the guarantee agreement concluded with the host state.
The host state has wide discretion in determining which investments
it will accept or favor. The investment guarantee program thus
acquires an international character, since its continuous operation
depends on the continuing cooperation between the governments
involved.

If an application meets the aforementioned requirements, the investor is invited to sign a contract whose provisions will thenceforth
govern his relationship with the United States Government. The
second party to the contract, the one issuing the guarantees, is at
this stage the Export-Import Bank of Washington, as agent for the
ICA.[165] The various guarantee contracts are, as a rule, quite similar
to each other, though specific provisions dealing with particular
situations may be included after the necessary negotiations between
the Bank and the investor.[166] The United States Government,
through its agents, guarantees the investor against any or all of
the following: (a) the inconvertibility of foreign currency received

[165] ICA, *op. cit. supra* note 163, at 2. The ICA administers the program as a
whole and develops the contracts, while the Export-Import Bank acts as its agent
in the administration and execution of the contracts. On certain efforts to transfer
the responsibility for the whole program to the Export-Import Bank, see Whitman, *The Guaranty Program* 25–26 (1959).

[166] Cf. ICA, *op. cit. supra* note 163, at 1, 12; Note, "United States Agencies and
International Organizations Which Foster Private American Investment Abroad,"
71 *Harv. L. Rev.* 1102, 1120 (1958). The developments that follow are chiefly
based on a study of specimen contracts kindly furnished by the ICA Investment
Guaranties Staff.

by him as profits or interest on his investment, (b) the loss of his property because of expropriation by the host government, or (c) the loss of his property by reason of war. The terms "convertibility," "expropriation," and "losses by reason of war" are defined neither in the relevant legislation nor in the intergovernmental guarantee agreements. The Export-Import Bank retains, therefore, a wide discretion in determining what particular actions constitute expropriation or render a currency inconvertible. It is bound, however, by its own contracts with the investors where the terms in question are defined in some detail.

Thus, under the convertibility guarantee, the Bank guarantees the transfer into United States dollars of foreign local currency received by the investor as profits or interest which he either is prevented from transferring through the operation of exchange restrictions (which were not in existence at the time the guarantee contract was signed) or is able to transfer only at an unfavorable rate. A "reference rate" is established, which is as a rule the rate officially recognized by the United States Treasury for customs purposes at the time of transfer, and the investor is guaranteed transfer of his foreign holdings at 95 percent of this rate.[167] Detailed provisions in the contracts deal with the question of multiple exchange rates and other special matters.

The guarantee against expropriation covers any action of the host government by which the investor is prevented from exercising control over the operation of his enterprise or the disposition of its property and stock.[168] This guarantee does not cover losses by reason of war or civil disorder or losses due to regulatory action of the host government or to violations of laws or provocation on

---

[167] The difference of 5 percent represents allowance for minor fluctuations and for expenses in connection with the contract or the transfer; ICA, *op. cit. supra* note 163, at 13–14.

[168] The above apply to equity investments. In the case of loans, a somewhat more limited coverage is provided. For an interesting discussion of this issue, see Tidd, "The Investment Guaranty Program and the Problem of Expropriation," 26 *Geo. Wash. L. Rev.* 710, 718–21 (1958). Few portfolio investments have been guaranteed as yet; cf. Whitman, *The Guaranty Program* 2 (1959).

the part of the investor, except when the host government's measures are taken with the primary object of divesting the investor of his property. The guarantee contract also provides for the manner in which the investor's loss will be computed.

The guarantee against losses by reason of war is the most recent. The guarantee covers only losses resulting from direct damage caused by interstate war and not consequential damage or damage caused by civil war or revolution. Part of the loss, at least 10 percent of it, is to be borne by the investor.[169]

On his part, the investor undertakes to pay an annual fee, amounting today to one half of one percent of the face value of the contract for each type of risk.[170] He further undertakes to disclose to the ICA all requested information pertinent to the contract, under penalty of its termination. He finally undertakes to cooperate closely with the United States Government in the preservation of any judicial or other remedies and the preservation and prosecution of any eventual claims. The guarantee contracts also provide for the various procedures to be followed for invocation of a claim under the contract and for the contract's modification and termination.

The legal issues arising in connection with the United States Government guarantee program are numerous and varied. Since no formal claim for payment under a guarantee has been presented as yet,[171] there has been no occasion to observe how the program operates under stress. A major question is the determination of the particular actions and situations which justify invocation of the guarantees, that is, of the actions and situations covered by the

---

[169] Cf. ICA, *op. cit. supra* note 163, at 21–23.

[170] The relevant legislation provides that the annual fee may not exceed one percent in the case of convertibility guarantees and four percent in the two other cases; Mutual Security Act of 1954, as amended, s. 413(b)(4)(E), 22 U.S.C.A. § 1933(b)(4)(E). The fees were considerably higher in the early days of the program; cf. Whitman, *The Guaranty Program* 30, 69 (1959). The establishment of a combined-risks contract at a lower total fee seems to have been considered by the ICA staff; cf. Note, *supra* note 166, at 1114, note 124.

[171] A single case arose early in the operation of the program but it seems to have been dropped after a practical arrangement, without any clear-cut solution. On a number of recent possible cases, see Whitman, *The Guaranty Program* 44, note 70 (1959).

guarantees. Despite the detailed contractual provisions, the Export-Import Bank retains a considerable amount of discretion in this respect.[172] Moreover, since neither the intergovernmental guarantee agreements nor the United States legislation to which they refer determine with any precision the risks covered by the guarantees, another possibility arises. The United States Government might in certain instances be liable to the investor under the guarantee contract while at the same time being unable to assert its claims under the intergovernmental agreement. The capital-receiving state might not recognize the particular situation as warranting application of the guarantee agreement, and might even base its position on treaty provisions or on general international law. In the case of an "indirect expropriation," for instance, when the measures involved are nominally regulatory or punitive, the Export-Import Bank might admit the investor's claim, deeming that the measures in question were taken with the primary purpose of divesting him of his property. The host government would probably reject such a construction and might well refuse to recognize the subrogation of the United States Government to the investor's rights and require the exhaustion of local remedies before entering into negotiations with the United States.[173]

The presence of such a possibility is by no means due to inadvertence or excessive optimism. It rather indicates official recognition of the fact that an agreement appropriately covering the points noted above and assuring the acceptance of any eventual American claims by the capital-receiving state would be very difficult to prepare [174] and probably unacceptable to many capital-receiving states. The lack of precision of legislative texts and international agreements should then be understood as a calculated risk assumed by the United States Government in order to further its foreign policy objectives. To the extent, therefore, that investment guarantees cover risks

---

[172] Cf. Note, "Government Guaranties of Foreign Investment," 66 *Harv. L. Rev.* 514, 517–18 (1953); Note, *supra* note 166, at 1120–21.

[173] This question has been thoroughly studied in Tidd, *supra* note 168, at 721–29.

[174] Cf. Wu, "Government Guarantees and Private Foreign Investment," 40 *Am. Econ. Rev.* 61, 68 (1950).

which are not covered in the related intergovernmental agreements, they should be considered as indirect and conditional subsidies to American private persons investing abroad. They can be successfully upheld as such on the basis of foreign policy considerations.[175]

The United States investment guarantee program has been in operation for more than ten years. During the greater part of this period, little use was made of its facilities. Recently, however, a significant increase of interest in the program has been noted. While the total guarantees issued up to the end of 1957 amounted to about $187.5 million, less than two years later, on June 30, 1959, they amounted to $448.2 million.[176] On the same date, pending applications for guarantees amounted to $877.4 million.[177] The geographical distribution of guarantees has also changed significantly. About 20 percent of the guarantees issued by the end of 1957 involved projects located in the underdeveloped areas. Their share had increased to over 35 percent by June 30, 1959,[178] while they constituted over 55 percent of the applications pending at that date.[179] These changes cannot be attributed to the increase in the number of countries participating in the program or to the issue of war risk guarantees.[180] They are due partly to the general increase in private foreign investment since 1956 and chiefly to an increased awareness of the program and its possibilities and advantages on the part of American investors.

A similar system of investment guarantees has been established in Japan since 1956, as an extension of its export credit guarantee program which has been in operation since 1950.[181] Eligible invest-

---

[175] Cf. Tidd, *supra* note 168, at 728–29.

[176] Cf. Whitman, *The Guaranty Program* 51 (table VI) (1959).

[177] *Idem* 51 (table VII).

[178] *Idem* 51 (table VI). Note that more than half of the guarantees issued during the peak year of 1958 were directed to underdeveloped areas (about $113.3 million out of a total of $212 million). *Ibid.*

[179] *Idem* 51 (table VII).

[180] Note that the total of issued guarantees and the bulk of pending applications ($784.9 million out of a total of $877.4 million) relate to the two other insurable risks. *Idem* 50.

[181] Cf. UN Document E/3325, 26 February 1960, 66 (para. 179). The description that follows is based on the information provided in this document, para. 179–86.

ment projects must be approved by the Japanese Government. No limitations are imposed as to the countries of investment: they may be developed as well as underdeveloped and there is no necessity for a related special intergovernmental agreement. The guarantees cover risks of expropriation, war and insurrection, and nonconvertibility of investment earnings. The investor is required to bear at least 25 percent of the loss himself. The same lack of enthusiasm on the part of investors which has been noted until recently with respect to the United States investment guarantees has also been noted in the case of the Japanese guarantees.

The most recent investment guarantee program is that established by the Federal Republic of Germany in 1959.[182] This program is closely related to the export credits guarantee program which has been operating for several years through two state-owned corporations, the Hermes Kreditversicherungs A. G. and the Deutsche Revisions- und Treuhand-A. G.[183] These companies are now responsible for the operation of the investment guarantee program, which follows in its general lines the American model, though offering more extensive protection and greater flexibility.

The guarantees are available to all firms established in Germany which invest abroad, and especially to those investing in developing countries. The investments in question have to be "worthy of promotion" and to contribute to the strengthening of Germany's economic relations with the developing countries. The investors' applications are examined by a committee composed of the representatives of the Federal Ministries of Economic Affairs, Finance and Foreign Affairs, which decides in each particular case whether to grant a guarantee. There is no formal requirement of specific

---

[182] Cf. the Federal Budget Law of 1959, section 18 (1), 1959 *Bundesgesetzblatt* (II) 793, 797. The description that follows is chiefly based on this provision, the Regulations issued in accordance with it by the Federal Minister of Economic Affairs, printed in *Bundesanzeiger* No. 194, October 9, 1959, and an "Information Sheet" on the same subject (*Merkblatt für die Übernahme von Bundesgarantien für Kapitalanlagen im Ausland*). See also UN *Flow 1956* 100 (1959); UN Document E/3325, 26 February 1960, 66–69 (para. 179–86).

[183] Cf. *supra* note 151.

approval by the government of the country of investment, as in the case of the United States guarantees. But the investor is expected to have obtained all necessary permits prior to the grant of the guarantee and to observe all relevant regulations, both in the country of investment and in the Federal Republic of Germany.

As a rule, guarantees are available only to investments made in countries which have concluded related agreements with the German Federal Republic. The relevant provisions, however, are very flexible, much more so than the corresponding United States ones. Guarantees may be granted even in the absence of such an agreement, if the "legal order" of the country of investment, or any other means (such as, apparently, concession contracts) afford sufficient protection to foreign investments. When agreements have to be concluded, they do not have to be of a special type; presumably, a general treaty of friendship and commerce may be deemed sufficient. A particular type of treaty, dealing with the "Promotion and Protection of Investments," seems, however, to be envisaged. Such a treaty was concluded in 1959 with Pakistan, and negotiations have been going on for the conclusion of similar treaties with other states. In contradistinction to the corresponding United States agreements, the treaty with Pakistan is fairly elaborate. In addition to provisions on the subrogation of the Federal Republic of Germany to the claims of German investors who have received payment by virtue of a guarantee contract and those dealing with the settlement of any related disputes through negotiation or arbitration or by bringing them before the International Court of Justice, the treaty in question also contains certain substantive clauses. It provides for nondiscrimination, for payment of adequate compensation in case of expropriation in the public benefit, and for facilities for the repatriation of profits and capital. Treaties of this type seem to be a cross between the United States investment guarantee agreements and its FCN treaties.

The risk-coverage of the German investment guarantee program is also more extensive than that of the United States. The guar-

antees are designed to afford protection against all "political risks";
under this heading are included not only the risks of expropriation,[184]
nonconvertibility, and war, but also those of any other armed conflict, including civil war or insurrection, and of monetary devaluation when occurring in conjunction with the imposition of exchange
restrictions.

The German investment guarantees are chiefly intended to protect direct investment, though they also may cover loans issued in
connection with such investments. They are to be issued for a period
not exceeding ten years, as a rule, or fifteen years, in certain special
cases. The annual fee to be paid by the investor varies from 1.0
to 1.5 percent of the investment according to the duration of the
coverage. This fee is payable only after the investment is completed.
Certain other relatively minor fees are also to be paid, such as a fee
for consideration of the application and an annual fee for the period
after the grant of the guarantee and before the completion of the
investment.

In addition to the national programs already in operation, the
establishment of multinational guarantee programs has been suggested. In an address before the 1957 International Industrial Development Conference, the then Vice-President of the United States
suggested the initiation of studies "which would examine the feasibility of setting up a privately operated international investment
guarantee fund. Its object would be to protect both present and
future investments from the hazards of expropriation, devaluation,
blocked currencies, and similar risks." [185] The suggestion does not
seem to have been carried any further. More recently, the Directing
Committee of the International Association for the Promotion and
Protection of Private Foreign Investment (APPI) has been con-

---

[184] In the Regulations and the "Information Sheet" cited *supra* note 182 it is made
clear that any state measure amounting in effect to expropriation (i.e., indirect or
"creeping" expropriation) is to be included under this general heading.

[185] Cf. Nixon, "Private Investment and the Economic Challenge," 37 *Dep't State
Bull.* 703, 706 (1957), reprinted as "A Call to Americans" in *Private Investment:
the Key to International Industrial Development* 105 (Daniel ed., 1958).

sidering an investment guarantee fund, presumably to be privately operated.[186]

A more ambitious proposal, involving the creation of an international public corporation jointly owned by governments and private persons has been set out in a paper submitted to a Subcommittee of the United States House of Representatives; it was suggested that an International Business Insurance Corporation be established, which would be registered as an "international corporation" [187] and would operate through subsidiaries in each state participating in it. The subsidiaries' shares would be owned by business firms, trade associations, and governments. The Corporation would insure foreign investors against losses arising out of unilateral breach of contract. Any claims which would arise would be paid by the local subsidiary and, only if the subsidiary did not have sufficient funds available, by the international corporation itself. The proposal provides several additional details on the operation and function of the proposed corporation. Its activities would be related to the operation of an International Court of Business Law whose establishment is also proposed.[188]

More recently, the Consultative Assembly of the Council of Europe discussed the possibility of the creation of an investment guarantee fund in connection with the cooperation among European and African states for the development of Africa.[189] The related report of the Assembly's Economic Committee [190] stressed the inter-

[186] Cf. a summary report of the Committee's October 28, 1960 meeting in 1961 *J. Business L.* 98. On the APPI in general, see *supra* pp. 79–80.

[187] Cf. Robinson, "A Program for International Business," in *Private Foreign Investment*, Hearings before the Subcommittee on Foreign Trade Policy of the Committee on Ways and Means, U.S. House of Representatives, 85th Cong., 2d sess., December 1958, 543, at 554 (1958). The creation of "international corporations" chartered and regulated by the World Bank or the International Monetary Fund, is another of the paper's proposals. Such corporations would have to be owned by citizens of several countries and would have to be operating internationally. Cf. *idem* 575–76.

[188] *Idem* 554–55.

[189] The relevant documents and recommendations deal also with the problems of the formulation of an Investment Statute; see *supra* p. 76 and notes 33–39.

[190] Report on an Investment Statute and a Guarantee Fund Against Political Risks, Consultative Assembly Document 1027, 8 September 1959, at 20 *et seq.*

national character of the proposed Fund: it should be established by an international convention, binding upon all participating states, and operated as an international venture by these states, on a footing of equality. The system would not operate on an automatic basis: guarantees would have to be requested and the agreement of the host country would be necessary. The premiums to be imposed would be uniform in all participating states. The Fund would guarantee direct as well as portfolio investments [191] against "political risks." There would be no guarantee against normal business risks or the risk of natural catastrophe. The coverage to be provided would in fact be similar to, though rather more extensive than, that provided by the United States guarantee program. Freedom of transfer for current payments would be guaranteed, as well as a limited freedom of capital movements; but the investor would be expected to bear a part of the risk: only about 80 to 90 percent of the investment would be insured. The expropriation guarantee would be broader than its American equivalent, for it would provide for compensation in the case of government measures resulting indirectly in the investors' dispossession, such as measures "partially or wholly preventing the investor from operating in the conditions originally prevailing" (for example, price regulation, taxation, denial of import licenses) or measures "preventing the investor from managing his affairs and interests." [192] Investors would also be insured against losses caused by wars, riots, or civil strife, but not when the investor's home state is a party to the war. After paying on a guarantee, the Fund would be subrogated to the investors' rights.

In its recommendation subsequent to the aforementioned report, the Consultative Assembly suggested the immediate establishment of the Guarantee Fund, even prior to the adoption of an Investment Statute, and it invited the members of the Council of Europe to submit their related proposals.[193]

[191] *Idem* 23. It could also guarantee public loans of African states; *idem* 30–31. The Fund would be jointly financed by the participating states; cf. *idem* 28–30.
[192] *Idem* 26.
[193] Consultative Assembly Recommendation 211 (1959) on the Development of Africa.

The possibility of a "European Guarantee Agency" has also been considered in the report of the European League for Economic Cooperation on common protection of private foreign investments.[194] After a brief discussion of the qualities and disadvantages of investment guarantees, the report accepts with some reservations their usefulness. A guarantee system is then proposed, against the sole risks of nonconvertibility and loss of investment "caused by arbitrary government action." The system would be closely linked to the Solidarity Convention and the Charter of Fair Treatment proposed elsewhere in the report. It would operate on a national basis, each of the cooperating states having its own guarantee agency. An over-all "European Guarantee Agency" might also be set up to insure multinational European investments and to reinsure the national agencies. The report seems less concerned with the precise mechanics of the scheme and more interested in preventing any competition (or "outbidding") among European foreign investors, a situation which might make more difficult the imposition of strict rules of conduct on capital-importing countries.

The most important of the investment guarantee programs operating today is the United States program. It is also the only one which has operated long enough to permit certain general conclusions. Since its earliest days, the program has been criticized on a variety of grounds.[195] From the investors' viewpoint, it has been argued that such guarantees shift the burden of fulfilling the capital-importing states' obligations to the capital-exporting states and, by failing to punish the former states' unfair treatment of foreign investors, tend to encourage them in the wrong direction. Moreover, the risk normally associated with any economic venture is now

[194] European League for Economic Cooperation, *Common Protection for Private International Investments* 28–33 (1958). Cf. *supra.* p. 83, notes 78 *et seq.*

[195] The chief study of the related problems is now von Neumann Whitman's *The United States Investment Guaranty Program and Private Foreign Investment* (1959). See also: Comment, "Point Four: A Re-examination of Ends and Means," 59 *Yale L.J.* 1277, 1312–15 (1950); Miller, "The ECA Guaranties and the Protection and Stimulation of Private Foreign Investment," 39 *Georgetown L.J.* 1 (1950); Brown, "Treaty, Guaranty and Tax Inducements for Foreign Investment," 40 *Am. Econ. Rev. Proc.* 486 (1950) and the studies cited in previous notes to this section.

borne by the American taxpayers and not by the investors. Among business circles, there was also some resentment against the possibilities for government interference inherent in the provisions on approval of investments and a general reluctance to disclose the requested information on the policies and operations of the enterprises concerned. Finally, the eligibility of new investments only for such guarantees was criticized as an unwarranted discrimination between old and new investments.

The operation of the program has done much to dispel many of these fears and objections.[196] Capital-importing countries have not taken undue advantage of the guarantees, both because of their supposed willingness to fulfill their commitments and because of their continuing need for American private and public capital. The American taxpayers have not yet had to pay for any investor's losses, while the agencies administering the program have shown considerable restraint and discretion in their requests for information and their interference with the investors' policies. And, though the existence of the guarantee does constitute a factor favoring new, as opposed to earlier, investments, the host countries seem to have treated guaranteed and nonguaranteed investments in the same manner. Generally speaking, the attitude of business circles toward investment guarantees seems to have greatly improved since the first days of the program.[197]

The investment guarantee program has been criticized on different grounds from the point of view of the capital-receiving countries. Several of these countries have been reluctant to conclude guarantee agreements because they regard the provisions on immediate direct negotiations and the consequent by-passing of requirements for local redress as a possible infringement of their sovereignty. The guarantee arrangements imply, moreover, that the United States, and in particular the Export-Import Bank of Washington, will be the sole judge of the fair or unfair character of the government

[196] Cf. Whitman, *The Guaranty Program* 61–64 (1959).
[197] Cf. *idem* 63–64; UN Document E/3325, 26 February 1960, 69 (para. 185).

policies in the capital-importing countries, determining by itself whether certain measures constitute expropriation and whether they render a currency nonconvertible. Such implications might well be resented in capital-receiving countries. Even these objections, however, though of a psychological character and therefore largely not susceptible of proof, have been dispelled in great part by the program's smooth operation. The recent conclusion of a guarantee agreement with India [198] may be considered as evidence of a change of attitude on the part of some of the underdeveloped countries.[199]

From a more general point of view, the criticisms seem to miss the main characteristics of the United States investment guarantee program, as well as of the other national programs modeled on it. These are national projects, not international ones. Their object is the encouragement of private foreign investment in accordance with the foreign policy objectives of the particular states. Their international law aspects are therefore subordinated to municipal law considerations. In the final analysis, investment guarantees cannot by themselves induce an important increase in foreign investment. Within their limitations, they are useful tools of foreign policy and they are certainly of great assistance to investors by relieving them of some risks.[200] But it is illusory to expect that they will provide by themselves a solution to the numerous problems relating to the legal security of foreign investments.

[198] Exchange of Notes of September 19, 1957, *T.I.A.S.* 3900, 8 U.S.T. 1442 (1957) (convertibility guarantee) supplemented by an Exchange of Notes of December 7, 1959, *T.I.A.S.* 4368 (expropriation guarantee).

[199] Cf. also Whitman, *The Guaranty Program* 68, 69 (1959). Note that of the 49 states which had concluded convertibility guarantee agreements by the end of 1960, only about 13 could be considered economically developed; see Table 2, p. 104.

[200] There is much to be said for an extension of the United States guarantees' functional coverage; see the thoughtful observations in Whitman, *The Guaranty Program* 65-67 (1959). The coverage of the German program and that suggested for the proposed Euro-African Guarantee Fund provide perhaps useful examples of possible extension.

Guarantees by Capital-Importing States

The most widely found type of state guarantees today consists of guarantees given to foreign investors by the governments of capital-importing countries. The exact manner in which such guarantees are offered varies in several respects. In recent years, the use of "investment laws," that is, statutes specifically designed to provide protection and encouragement to foreign investors, has been increasingly favored.[201] Such statutes often bear indicative titles, such as "Law Regarding the Investment and Protection of Foreign Capital" [202] or "Law for the Protection of Foreign Capital Investment." [203] However, guarantees of various kinds are still given in several other ways, as well: through general constitutional provisions,[204] by means of special provisions in statutes of general application,[205] through government policy directives assuring consistent practice on the part of administrative bodies, or by means of various combinations of these and other methods. In several cases, the governments of underdeveloped countries have issued formal statements of policy, indicating their general attitude toward foreign investment and laying down the particular policies to be pursued by administrative or legislative action.[206]

[201] For a collection of several texts of investment statutes, with a brief but interesting general introduction, see Baade, *Gesetzgebung zur Förderung ausländischer Kapitalanlagen* (1957). A complete list of recent investment laws is provided in UN Document E/3369, 13 May 1960, Appendix.

[202] Greece, Legislative Decree 2687 of October 22, 1953; text in 7 *Rev. Hell. Dr. Int'l* 351 (1954).

[203] Turkey, Law No. 6224 of January 18, 1954; text in U.S. Department of Commerce, *Investment in Turkey* 173 (1956) and in Cenani, *Foreign Capital Investments in Turkey* (rev. ed., 1958).

[204] E.g., provisions on protection of private property are contained in most modern constitutions; see the review of relevant constitutional provisions in Friedman, *Expropriation* 7–12 (1953) and in UN Document A/AC. 97/5/Rev. 1, 27 December 1960, pp. 125–32.

[205] E.g., provisions on foreign companies are often found in Companies Acts; cf., for instance, Wahn, "Canada" in *Legal Aspects* 116, 117 and *passim*. Also provisions on tax exemptions and arrangements are often found in Tax Codes or Acts.

[206] Cf., e.g., Burma, Statement of principles relating to investments of June 8, 1955; Ceylon, Statement of 1958 on government policy towards foreign private invest-

These variations in the manner in which guarantees are offered are of relative importance. The choice among them is dictated by considerations of national policy or domestic politics, by the peculiarities of each country's legal system, and by purely psychological considerations. Generally speaking investment statutes are more effective than any of the other means.[207] They are bound to be clearer and less subject to changes at short notice; they may even possess increased formal validity, so that they can be altered only through special procedures.[208] On the other hand, investment statutes may represent merely the point of view of the party in power or they may be issued in the form of decree laws or other semiexecutive instruments.[209] Instead of providing for a number of well-determined guarantees to foreign investors, they may only establish a committee or other administrative agency with wide discretionary powers, thus increasing rather than eliminating the existing elements of uncertainty. And statements of policy, while theoretically easily revocable and less dependable than special statutes, may in some cases be of more real value to the investors, when, for instance, they represent the definite views of a popular government.

Another distinction in the manner in which legal guarantees are given is of particular importance. The "guarantees" given by capital-importing states are often quite general in character. They consist of general statements concerning the treatment of all foreign

---

ment in Ceylon; India, Government resolution on industrial policy of April 6, 1948, Prime Minister's statement on the participation of foreign capital in industry of April 6, 1949, Industrial Policy Resolution of April 30, 1956.

[207] For a discussion of the usefulness of investment statutes, see Littell, "Encouragement and Obstruction to Foreign Investment in Foreign Investment Laws," 52 *Am. Soc. Int'l L. Proc.* 209, 211 (1958).

[208] This is, for instance, true in the case of the Greek investment law, Legislative Decree No. 2687 of October 22, 1953, which by virtue of article 112 of the Greek Constitution cannot be altered except by means of a constitutional amendment. See also Lambadarios, "Greece," in *Legal Aspects* 233, 244–45.

[209] In many modern states, the Executive has the power to issue administrative decrees having the force of statutes ("decree-laws") under certain conditions and in accordance with certain procedures of varying strictness. See, for instance, the description of French practice in von Mehren, *The Civil Law System* 174–85 (1957). In countries under dictatorial regimes, this practice results in the virtual elimination of the distinction between legislative and administrative acts.

investors and providing assurances of fair treatment, nondiscrimination and the like. It is often difficult, in fact, to distinguish such general "guarantees" from ordinary regulatory provisions. Their nonspecific content, as well as their unilateral character—for they are usually contained in constitutional or statutory provisions or in policy statements—diminish greatly their practical importance for the foreign investor. The main significance of such provisions lies in their representing formal expressions of an attitude favorable to private foreign investment and in their constituting a suitable background for more specific measures.[210]

State guarantees to foreign investors, however, may also be specific in character, designed to serve the needs of particular investments. The basic investment laws or other instruments often provide for special procedures through which specific guarantees, which refer to each individual investor, may be granted. A wide variety of provisions determine the procedures through which such guarantees are granted.[211] In the typical procedure, the prospective investor must apply to the competent state agency, designated and quite often created [212] by the basic investment law, in order to have his investment approved or "registered." [213] The agency investigates the nature and the qualities of the proposed investment, particularly with regard to certain general requirements usually set out in the original investment law.[214] On the basis of this investigation, it

---

[210] Their importance also depends on the character of the political regime in power in each particular state. In some cases, such general guarantees or assurances may constitute mere "window-dressing," while in others they may represent well-settled principles, accepted by, and determining the actions of, public authorities.

[211] See in this connection the procedures described in the country studies in *Legal Aspects.*

[212] Cf., e.g., Greece, L.D. No. 2687 of October 22, 1953, article III (1). Israel, Law No. 30 of 5710–1950, sections 1, 27–34; cf. Sher, "Israel," in *Legal Aspects* 292, 298. Japan, Law No. 163 of 1950, articles 19-(2), 19-(3); cf. Ishii, "Japan," *idem* 318, 331. Turkey, Law No. 6224 of January 18, 1954, article 8; cf. Ansay "Turkey," *idem* 543, 559; Cenani *op. cit. supra* note 203, at 58–60.

[213] Registration is often in such cases a covert form of state approval, for instance, in connection with the grant of facilities regarding exchange control. Cf., e.g., Nattier, "Brazil," in *Legal Aspects* 77, 90; Kalmanoff and Bernal Salamanca, "Colombia," *idem* 169, 181–82.

[214] These requirements relate chiefly to the existing needs in the economy and

approves or rejects the investor's application. It may also ask the investor to modify the application in accordance with its own suggestions. The final instrument of approval is very often the product of extensive negotiations. By that instrument, the state grants to the investor some or all of the assurances and privileges provided for in the original investment law, while the investor undertakes certain obligations with respect to the form, amount, and other elements of the investment.[215] The precise form of the instrument varies in the different countries. It is usually an act of the executive branch of government: an administrative decree,[216] a decision of the cabinet or of certain ministers,[217] or some other administrative act.

Instruments of approval were originally purely administrative acts. We still may find such instruments indicating nothing more than that the investor has complied with the procedure provided by law. This type of instrument is used, for instance, in connection with exchange control regulations in many states. In recent years, however, as a result of developments in the technique of investment laws, instruments of approval often assume a new function and a new significance. They are often preceded, as has been noted, by

---

in the particular fields of investment, to the probable effect of the investment on the country's balance-of-payments position, and to other similar considerations. For brief accounts of such conditions and the reasons for them, see Organization for European Economic Co-operation, *Private United States Investment in Europe and the Overseas Territories* 32–34, 36–39 (1954); UN Document E/2901, 21 June 1956, 49 *et seq.;* UN Document ECAFE/L. 122, 12 March 1957, 9 *et seq.* Cf. also Littell, *supra* note 207, at 211–15. And see *supra* p. 38 and *infra* pp. 134–35.

[215] The term "instrument of approval" is used in the present study in the sense here indicated, namely, of an instrument issued by virtue of an investment law and granting to a foreign investor, along with the formal approval of the importation of his capital, certain legal guarantees regarding the treatment of his investment. The term is commonly used both in this sense and in the broader sense of any instrument expressing the approval of administrative authorities. See also *infra* pp. 125–26.

[216] This is, e.g., the case in Chile, both under Decree-Law No. 437 of February 2, 1954, now repealed, and under Decree-Law No. 258 of March 30, 1960; also partly, in Greece, under L.D. No. 2687 of October 22, 1953, article III(2) and under the recent Law No. 4171 of 1961.

[217] Cf., e.g., Afghanistan, Law of April 19, 1954, article 13. Greece (partly), L.D. No. 2687 of October 22, 1953, article III(2). Israel, Law No. 30 of 5710–1950, section 28. Japan, Law No. 163 of 1950, article 10. Mexico, Law of January 4, 1955, articles 1(2) and (3), 12(3). Turkey, Law No. 6224 of January 18, 1954, article 1.

official or semiofficial negotiations and constitute, in fact and in spite of their form, a kind of agreement between the state and the investor, providing for the granting of guarantees to the latter and for his corresponding obligations.[218]

An interesting example of such an instrument is the one issued in May 1956, by the Greek Government concerning the importation of capital for the exploitation of Greek asbestos by an American corporation.[219] It is in the form of a Royal Decree, which, in accordance with the statute by virtue of which it was issued, is irrevocable and cannot be modified except with the investor's consent.[220] The decree starts with a statement of approval of the importation of capital up to the sum of $8,350,000, to be used by the investing company for exploration, research and mining for asbestos, and for its production and sale. The use of the capital for the purposes specified in the initial statement is an essential condition of the continued validity of the whole instrument. The capital is to be imported in the form of machinery and foreign exchange, in equal parts, over a period of slightly more than four years. The implementation of these provisions is to be ascertained, if any need should arise, by the Ministry of Industry. A special committee, composed of representatives of two other ministries and of the investor, may review the Ministry of Industry's original report if the investor contests its accuracy. The investing corporation is allowed to transfer abroad, without limitation, the capital imported and its profits. Its products may be exported abroad without restrictions, except for a proportion of ten percent yearly which must be disposed of in the local market, if the latter can absorb it. The corporation undertakes to sell its products at their current prices abroad; the same prices, minus transportation costs, should be ap-

---

[218] The legal character of such instruments is discussed at length *infra* Chapter 7.

[219] Royal Decree of May 30/June 23, 1956, concerning the approval of the importation of capital from abroad, by virtue of Legislative Decree No. 2687/1953, by the Kennecott Copper Corporation, 1956 *Ephimeris tis Kyverniseos* [Official Journal], Fasc. 1, No. 144, pp. 1427–30.

[220] L.D. No. 2687 of October 22, 1953, article III(3).

plicable to its sales within Greece. Certain other details regarding the company's pricing of its products are also contained in the instrument. The investing corporation is granted exemptions from import duties and other charges on the machinery imported by it during the initial period of ten years. During the same period, it is also exempted from all city and other local taxes and charges. The employment of foreign personnel up to the number of twenty-five person is permitted, and such personnel are allowed to export part of their salaries. Finally, the instrument contains detailed provisions for arbitration in case of dispute.

The instrument just described is fairly typical of the instruments of approval issued under the Greek investment law [221] and of this type of guarantee-granting instrument in general. There exist, however, two other types of instruments which serve similar functions and present several problems in common with instruments of approval, though they are significantly different from them in form, and sometimes in content. In a discussion of state guarantees to foreign investors, it is necessary to include an examination of these types of instruments, namely, concession agreements and special contracts of guarantee.

A "concession agreement" is an instrument concluded between a state and a private person and providing for the grant by the state to the individual of certain rights or powers which normally would belong to and be exercised by the state.[222] Typical examples of concession agreements are those relating to mineral and other natural resources or to the operation of enterprises of public utility. By "guarantee contract," on the other hand, is understood the instrument by which a state gives to an investor,[223] under certain

---

[221] *Supra* note 202. There exist, of course, several variations as between the particular provisions of each instrument. For a brief list of other provisions, see Fatouros, "Legal Security for International Investment," in *Legal Aspects* 699, 714–15.

[222] This is but a "working definition," admittedly incomplete and somewhat vague. The legal character of concession agreements and other instruments here described is discussed more fully *infra*, Chapter 7.

[223] The investor, in this case, as well as in that of a concession, may be either

conditions, certain guarantees or privileges, in the absence of a special statute regulating the granting of such guarantees.

Despite their similarities, the three types of instruments we are dealing with are not identical. They often differ in form: instruments of approval usually take the form of administrative acts, while concessions and guarantee contracts often assume the form of legislation. They also differ in content: concession agreements cover a wider range of issues of a legal, economic, and political character than either guarantee contracts or instruments of approval. These two last types of instruments cover the same general range of issues; they deal with questions of taxation, exchange control, and the like. They differ chiefly in that the content of instruments of approval is generally predetermined by the investment laws by virtue of which they are issued. No such limitation obtains in the case of guarantee contracts. Concession agreements and guarantee contracts are thus more individual in character; they are designed solely to fit the specific investment involved. Instruments of approval usually follow certain predetermined formulae.

The differences in scope between these legal instruments can be better perceived when we compare the instrument of approval previously described with examples of the two other types of instruments.

A most important recent concession agreement is the one between the so-called Iranian Oil Consortium (consisting of eight foreign oil companies) and the Government of Iran.[224] The agreement generally provides for the exploitation of Iranian oil through the cooperation of the two parties. Its provisions are numerous and complicated. Two operating companies are set up, one for the exploration and production, and the other for the refining, of pe-

---

a national of the country of investment or an alien. We are here concerned with the latter case only.

[224] The text is printed in 2 Hurewitz, *Diplomacy in the Near and Middle East* 348 (1956). For comments and analyses, see Farmanfarma, "The Oil Agreement Between Iran and the International Oil Consortium: The Law Controlling," 34 *Texas L. Rev.* 259 (1955); Carlston, "International Role of Concession Agreements," 52 *Nw. U.L. Rev.* 618, 637–39 (1957).

troleum; trading companies are also created which are in charge of the marketing end of the enterprise. The agreement describes in great detail, though not always with clarity, the organization of the operating companies, their duties and rights and their relations with the Government of Iran. The companies undertake, *inter alia*, to train Iranian personnel and "to be always mindful in the conduct of their operations of the rights and interests of Iran." An important section of the agreement is devoted to the financial arrangements between Iran and the Consortium. The latter undertakes to pay a "stated payment" of one eighth of the gross income (calculated to be about one fourth of the net income) per year. It also has to pay an income tax, at rates frozen at the time of the conclusion of the agreement, which go up to 50 percent of net income. Stated payments, however, and other payments "of a similar nature" are deducted from the tax due. In fact, therefore, this is basically a fifty-fifty arrangement [225] in complicated form.[226] Certain legal guarantees are also contained in the Consortium agreement. There exist strict provisions for arbitration in case of dispute, and also a clause stating the obligation of the Iranian Government not to interfere, by legislation or otherwise, with the operation of the arrangements described in the agreement.[227]

An agreement of a different sort is the one between the Indian Government and the Standard-Vacuum Oil Company concerning the establishment of oil refineries in India.[228] This may be considered as a typical guarantee contract, a common enough form of agree-

[225] For analyses of the function of fifty-fifty arrangements, see Carlston, *supra* note 224, at 640–41; Fanning, *Foreign Oil and the Free World* 71–122 (1954). For a survey of related legislation, see UN, Office of Legal Affairs, *Survey of Mining Legislation* 61 *et seq.*, especially 74–78 (1957).

[226] For the probable reason for these complications, see Farmanfarma, *supra* note 224, at 266–67.

[227] It should be noted that a similar clause was contained in the predecessor of this agreement, the 1933 Convention between the Anglo-Persian Oil Company and the Government of Iran (then Persia); text in Hurewitz, *op. cit. supra* note 224, at 188. Its existence did not prevent the nationalization of the oil industry in Iran, but the clause did figure prominently in the related legal discussions. See *infra* pp. 340 *et seq.*

[228] The text is printed in: Government of India, Ministry of Production, *Establishment of Oil Refineries in India: Text of Agreements with the Oil Companies* 1–12 (New Delhi, 1953). This booklet also contains two agreements with other

ment, in use in several Middle-Eastern and Latin-American states. It is now less common than in the past, because it is being increasingly replaced by instruments of approval, issued pursuant to an investment law. The agreement we are discussing was concluded in the form of an "exchange of notes"; that is, the investing company set forth in a letter all its proposals to the Indian Government and the latter replied accepting them en bloc. Thus, after stating briefly its projects regarding the formation of an Indian corporation to construct and operate a refinery of specified size, the company solicited from the Government certain "assurances," which the latter by its letter of acceptance consented to give. These assurances dealt with many matters. The Government agreed not to expropriate the refinery for at least twenty-five years, and to pay "reasonable compensation" for any expropriation thereafter. It also agreed that foreign exchange would be made available to the company to be formed for all expenses abroad, for the purchase of construction materials and equipment and of crude oil, and for remittance of profits and interest. The subject of taxation occupied a prominent place in the agreement. Certain points with regard to income taxation were determined, and exemptions from certain local taxes were granted. Tariff protection and special arrangements with respect to import duties and certain other taxes were agreed upon. Finally, the Government assured the company that it would use its "good offices" to secure for the company necessary lands, dock and harbor facilities, and supplies of water and electricity, and that it would use its "best efforts" to secure supplies for construction and adequate railway transportation. The investing company, in its turn, gave certain assurances regarding the prompt construction of the refinery, arrangements for the "training of an adequate number of Indian personnel," expenditure of certain sums to provide housing facilities for its employees, and the availability of its by-products at reasonable prices.

companies on the same subject which are similar in form and content to the one described in the text.

6

Content of State Promises

DESPITE the variety of actual and possible forms of state promises, there are close similarities between them from the standpoint of content. They all refer more or less to the same elements of a country's investment climate and they have largely common objectives. Certain variations in content do exist, of course. They are due to the particular qualities of each form of guarantee, to special needs arising in particular situations, and to shifts in emphasis between different states and governments.

The Recipients of State Promises

One particular point, with respect to which there exist important differences between guarantees, relates to the persons to whom the guarantees are addressed, the recipients of the guarantees. Treaty guarantees are generally addressed to states. In bilateral agreements, two states bind one another to observe particular treaty provisions regarding the treatment of foreign investors. The promises are addressed to prospective foreign investors only indirectly, insofar as the latter are nationals of one of the contracting states. In no case are they individual in character, in the sense of referring to the particular conditions of a single investor.

The investors protected under the terms of the United States FCN treaties may be either individuals [1] or companies. The latter

[1] Referred to in the treaties by the term "nationals," in contradistinction to "com-

term is defined as including "corporations, partnerships, companies and other associations, whether or not with limited liability and whether or not for pecuniary profit." [2] The treaties regulate the activities of both nationals and companies, though they do differentiate between them. Some provisions apply to "nationals of either Party," while others apply to "nationals and companies of either Party." [3] The same is true of the investment treaties recently concluded by the United Kingdom [4] and by the Federal Republic of Germany.[5]

The same considerations are generally applicable in the case of the proposed multilateral investment codes. Each signatory state would be bound toward the other states party to the convention to observe its provisions. Foreign investors would be indirect recipients of such promises. There exist, however, certain variations between the proposed codes. Several of them do not deal in any detail with the recipients of the guarantees, for example, the ITO Charter and the Bogota Economic Agreement. The ICC Code of Fair Treatment hardly refers to investors, as such. It favors the use of the more impersonal term of "investments." The otherwise dissimilar reports

---

panies." The former term is defined in one of the most recent treaties as meaning "natural persons having the nationality of a High Contracting Party"; U.S. treaty with France, article XIV(3). The other U.S. treaties do not define the term. See also article 2(2) of the U.K. treaty with Iran.

[2] Treaty with Japan, article XXII(3). Identical or closely similar provisions are found in all other U.S. FCN treaties.

[3] The recent FCN treaties of the United States are notable for their thorough coverage of the position, rights, and duties of companies. Cf., on this point, Walker, "Provisions on Companies in United States Commercial Treaties," 50 *Am. J. Int'l L.* 372 (1956), reprinted with additions in Wilson, *United States Commercial Treaties and International Law* (hereinafter cited as Wilson, *Treaties*) 182–208 (1960); Walker, "The Post-War Commercial Treaty Program of the United States," 73 *Pol. Sc. Qu.* 57, 66–69 (1958).

[4] U.K. treaty with Iran, article 2(4): "The term 'companies': (a) means all legal persons except physical persons; (b) in relation to a High Contracting Party means all companies which derive their status as such from the law in force in any territory of that High Contracting Party to which the present Treaty applies; (c) in relation to a country means all companies which derive their status as such from the law in force in that country."

[5] Cf., e.g., 1957 Treaty between Germany and Italy, article 33; 1957 treaty between Germany and the Dominican Republic, article 21(3).

of the European League for Economic Cooperation and the British Parliamentary Group for World Government also do not discuss in any detail the question of the guarantee's recipients.[6]

The 1957 Draft Convention for the Mutual Protection of Private Property Rights in Foreign Countries is far more explicit on the matter. The term "national of a state," which is meant to include both natural persons and companies, is given a detailed definition.[7] Both categories are broadly defined. In the case of natural persons of more than one nationality, it is provided that "all nationalities count."[8] This position is not in accord with the generally accepted rules of public international law on the matter[9] and would result in conferring to such persons extensive privileges. They would be able to enjoy the advantages of all their nationalities, while being in a position to avoid the corresponding obligations of one nationality by invoking the other. The convention's stand is supported on the grounds that otherwise "a state, by conferring its own nationality upon a non-national, might deprive the latter of protection under the Convention."[10] The possible abuses of the provision are left completely out of account. It should be noted, moreover, that the rare instances of imposition by a state of its nationality on an alien can be taken care of satisfactorily enough under existing rules of international law.[11] With respect to companies, the 1957 Draft Convention provides that their nationality is to be determined on the basis of any of three tests, namely, establishment under a state's laws, establishment of the company's seat within a state's territory,

---

[6] Both stress, however, the need for access of private persons to the tribunal which would adjudicate the disputes relating to the proposed international convention. Cf. *infra* pp. 181, 184.

[7] *1957 Draft Convention*, article II.   [8] *Idem*, article II(1).

[9] Cf., e.g., 1 Guggenheim, *Traité de droit international public* 312–13 (1953); Weis, *Nationality and Statelessness in International Law* 195–96 (1956); Parry, *Nationality and Citizenship Laws of the Commonwealth and of the Republic of Ireland* 13–14, 25–26 (1957); 3 Hackworth, *Digest* 354 (1942).

[10] *1957 Draft Convention* 45.

[11] Cf., e.g., Guggenheim, *op. cit. supra* note 9, at 314–17; Weis, *op. cit. supra* note 9, at 104 *et seq.*; Parry, *op. cit. supra* note 9, at 8–11; 5 Hackworth, *Digest* 813–14 (1943).

and holding of control or of a dominant interest by a state's nationals.[12]

The definition of natural persons has been dropped from the 1959 Draft Convention. Presumably, the proposed treaty's protection will extend to persons of plural nationalities only insofar as provided by the rules of customary international law. The definition of companies has also changed; the convention provides that

"nationals" in relation to a Party includes (i) companies which under the municipal law of that Party are considered national companies of that Party and (ii) companies in which nationals of that Party have directly or indirectly a controlling interest. "Companies" includes both juridical persons recognised as such by the law of a Party and associations even if they do not possess legal personality.[13]

Other proposals provide for a broad definition of the term "nationals" [14] or for a definition of the persons to be protected based on the principle of residence rather than that of nationality.[15]

The promises contained in the investment guarantees issued by the United States are quite different in this respect. The relevant legislative texts, which determine the extent and character of the guarantees, are addressed to all prospective American investors in general, though not to investors of any other nationality. Under the terms of the Mutual Security legislation, the persons to whom guarantees are issued have to be citizens of the United States or corporations or other associations "created under the law of the United States or of any State or territory and substantially beneficially owned by citizens of the United States." [16] They also have to comply with the procedures and meet the conditions described in the previous chapter.[17] Nevertheless, the promises themselves, when given, are addressed to each particular investor. The recipient of

---

[12] *1957 Draft Convention*, article II(b) and (c).

[13] *1959 Draft Convention*, article IX.

[14] Council of Europe Consultative Assembly Document 1027, 8 September 1959, at 12.

[15] Cf., e.g., the draft convention proposed to the OEEC by the Swiss Government.

[16] 22 U.S.C.A. § 1933(b)(4)(H)(i) (1960).   [17] Cf. *supra* pp. 106–9.

the promises is a single person, individual or corporation; and the guarantee contracts, while following a common pattern, admit of variations in their provisions "to meet the particular circumstances of the investment and the needs of the investor." [18]

The German investment guarantees are addressed to enterprises established within the territory of the Federal Republic which have met the conditions stated in the relevant regulations.[19] It is expressly noted that the grant of guarantees lies within the discretion of the competent state authorities and no claim can be raised with respect to such grant.[20] The individual guarantee contracts will presumably be adapted to the particular conditions of each investor.

The case of promises made by the investment laws of capital-importing countries is rather similar to that of investment guarantees by capital-exporting states, though not without certain peculiarities of its own. As we have noted, such laws are generally directed to foreign investors as a whole, giving certain details as to their treatment in the capital-receiving country. But they often provide, as well, for the issuance of special instruments by means of which the details of the treatment accorded to each particular investor are determined. In the great majority of cases, therefore, the final recipients of the promises are the particular investors, each by himself.

The various investment laws provide in detail for the categories of investors to whom the promises are addressed and the types of investments to which they are applicable. In some cases, such promises are addressed only to persons of an alien nationality, investing capital in the country.[21] In other instances, nationals residing abroad as well as aliens are promised special treatment for their investments.[22]

[18] ICA, *Investment Guaranty Handbook* 12 (1960 ed.).
[19] "Richtlinien für die Übernahme von Garantien für Kapitalanlagen im Ausland," *Bundesanzeiger* No. 194, 9 October 1959. Cf. *supra* pp. 112–14.
[20] *Ibid.*
[21] Cf., e.g., Chile, Decree No. 427 of May 3, 1954, article 2; cf. Aramayo, "Chile," in *Legal Aspects* 135. Iran, Law of November 28, 1955, article 1; cf. Nasr "Iran," in *Legal Aspects* 280, 288.
[22] Cf., e.g., Japan, Law No. 163 of 1950, as amended, article 3(1). Italy, Law of February 7, 1956, article 1; cf. Nobili "Italy," in *Legal Aspects* 303, 313.

In most cases, the promises are addressed to investors of "foreign capital," that is, capital imported from abroad, the special treatment being granted to the investment itself, regardless of the investor's nationality.[23] Lastly, promises are in some cases addressed to persons investing their capital in certain fields of the capital-importing country's economy, mainly in industrial activities, regardless of the investor's nationality or the capital's origin.[24]

The granting of state promises also depends on the character of the particular investment involved. The special agency which is competent to approve foreign investments, in judging whether a new investment should be approved and which promises shall be made to the investor, applies certain criteria, usually determined in the relevant legislation.[25] Such criteria are often expressed in broad terms, thus leaving considerable discretionary power to the approving agency; certain specific criteria may nevertheless be laid down, in accordance with the needs of the particular country and the views of the legislative body. One criterion is common to almost all investment laws, namely, that approved investment must further the economic development of the capital-importing country.[26] Par-

[23] Cf., e.g., Argentina, Law No. 14780 of December 22, 1958, as reported by de la Vega "Argentina," in *Legal Aspects* 3, 9. Greece, Legislative Decree No. 2687 of October 22, 1953, article 1; cf. Lambadarios, "Greece," *idem* 233, 244–45. Israel, Law No. 30 of 5710–1950, as amended, article 1; cf. Sher, "Israel," *idem* 292, 299. Turkey, Law No. 6224 of January 18, 1954, article 1; cf. Ansay "Turkey," *idem* 543, 559. United Arab Republic, Law of April 2, 1953, article 1(a)(b)(d); cf. Habachy, "United Arab Republic," *idem* 562.

[24] Cf., e.g., Ecuador, Industrial Encouragement Law of June 21, 1957. The Philippines, Tax Exemption Law (Republic Act No. 901); cf. Monzon, "Philippines," in *Legal Aspects* 414, 418–20. Thailand, Industrial Investment Promotion Act of 1960, and cf. Koh "Thailand," *idem* 526, 528. Mexico, Law for the Development of New and Necessary Industries of January 4, 1955. Puerto Rico, Industrial Tax Exemption Act, 1948, 13 *Laws of Puerto Rico Annotated* s. 221–338, and Industrial Incentive Act of 1954, *idem* s. 241–51. See also Friedmann and Pugh, "Comparative Analysis," in *Legal Aspects* 734, 744, note 19.

[25] Cf. Friedmann and Pugh, "Comparative Analysis," in *Legal Aspects* 734, 743; Baade, *Gesetzgebung zur Förderung ausländischer Kapitalanlagen* 27–28 (1957); Littell, "Encouragement and Obstruction to Private Investment in Foreign Investment Laws," 52 *Am. Soc. Int'l L. Proc.* 209, 212–15 (1958).

[26] Cf., e.g., Afghanistan, Law of April 19, 1954, articles 2 and 3. Chile, Decree-Law No. 258 of March 30, 1960, article 1; and cf. Aramayo, "Chile," in *Legal Aspects* 135, 136. Iran, Law of July 13, 1953, article 1. Israel, Law No. 30 of 5710-1950,

ticular emphasis is usually laid on industrial development.[27] Another frequent criterion is the investment's effect on the country's balance-of-payments position.[28] Specific requirements contained in investment laws include the absence of monopoly or special privileges,[29] the "development of low-cost housing including housing facilities for working people drawing fixed incomes," [30] and the furthering of a "rational distribution of the population throughout the area of the country." [31]

Standards of Treatment of Foreign Investors

In order to provide for the treatment of foreign investors, state guarantees have to determine certain legal standards by reference to which the lawfulness of any particular state measure is to be judged. Such standards have been classified under the two general headings of contingent and noncontingent standards.[32] The contingent standards are those which determine the treatment to be accorded investors in relative terms, by reference to municipal legislation or international treaties effective at the time the relevant

---

section 1; cf. Sher, "Israel," *idem* 292, 298. Japan, Law No. 163 of 1950, as amended, article 1. Greece, L.D. No. 2687 of October 22, 1953, article 1(2); cf. Lambadarios, "Greece," *idem* 233, 246. Libya, Foreign Capital Investment Law of 1958, article 1(a). Turkey, Law No. 6224 of January 18, 1954, article 1(a); cf. Ansay, "Turkey," *idem* 543, 559. United Arab Republic, Law of April 2, 1953, article 1.

[27] Cf., e.g., Guatemala, Industrial Development Law, Decree No. 1317 of October 23, 1959; Jordan, Law No. 27, 1955, sec. 2; Costa Rica, Law of Industrial Protection and Development, of September 3, 1959, article 3.

[28] Cf. Japan, Law No. 163 of 1950, article 1. Israel, Law No. 30 of 5710-1950, as amended, section 1(b); cf. Sher, "Israel," in *Legal Aspects* 292, 299; Ecuador, Law of June 21, 1957, article 7b.

[29] Turkey, Law No. 6224 of January 18, 1954, article 1(c); Costa Rica, Law of September 3, 1959, article 2.

[30] Greece, L.D. No. 2687 of October 22, 1953, article 1(2).

[31] Israel, Law No. 30 of 5710-1950, as amended, section 1(c); cf. Sher, "Israel," in *Legal Aspects* 292, 299.

[32] For a discussion of contingent and noncontingent standards in connection with the United States FCN treaties, see Walker, "Modern Treaties of Friendship, Commerce and Navigation," 42 *Minn. L. Rev.* 805, 810-12 (1958). And cf. Wilson, *Treaties* 6-9. For a more elaborate discussion of standards in international law, see 1 Schwarzenberger, *International Law* 231 et seq., 239 et seq. (3 ed., 1957).

issues arise. The noncontingent standards are those which use absolute terms and refer to certain more or less specific legal rules which are to be applied whenever the need arises.

Of the contingent standards, two are the most common, in the international and municipal practice of states: the standard of "national" treatment and that of "most-favored-nation" treatment. The former is to be found in both municipal legislation and diplomatic practice, while the latter belongs almost exclusively to the field of international law and economic relations. The definitions contained in the United States FCN treaties reflect the general usage of these terms. National treatment is defined as

treatment accorded within the territories of a Party upon terms no less favorable than the treatment accorded therein, in like situations, to nationals, companies, products, vessels or other objects, as the case may be, of such Party.[33]

Most-favored-nation treatment, on the other hand, is defined as

treatment accorded within the territories of a Party upon terms no less favorable than the treatment accorded therein, in like situations, to nationals, companies, products, vessels or other objects, as the case may be, of any third country.[34]

Noncontingent standards may be of two general types. On the one hand, the legal rule to be applied may be expressly stated in the treaty or law involved. The provisions on expropriation of property in the United States FCN treaties are an illustration of the deter-

[33] Treaty with Ireland, article XXI(1). Identical provisions are contained in the other U.S. FCN treaties, except those with Iran, Ethiopia, and Muscat and Oman. In article XXIV(1) of the treaty with Greece, this definition is followed by a proviso to the effect that "the term does not imply immunity from the laws and regulations of a Party which apply in a non-discriminatory manner to nationals, companies, products, vessels, or other objects, as the case may be, of both Parties." Cf. also the definition in article 21(1) of the treaty between W. Germany and the Dominican Republic. The recent U.K. treaty with Iran does not give an express definition, but cf. its article 28.

[34] Treaty with Ireland, article XXI(2). Identical provisions in the other U.S. treaties, with the same exceptions as *supra* note 33. And cf. article 21(2) of the treaty between Germany and the Dominican Republic.

mination of such standards.[35] The legal rules to be applied may, on the other hand, be incorporated by reference, as in the case of the application of the standard of international law. In such cases, the content of the rule involved may not always be very clear.[36] The recent FCN treaties of the United States employ this standard in connection with the "protection and security" of aliens.[37] Reference to the same standard may also be found in the ICC Code of Fair Treatment.[38]

The 1959 Draft Convention on Investment Abroad appears at first glance to refer to a similar standard. Its authors mention in the Preamble certain "principles of conduct relating to foreign investment," a restatement of which should contribute to the promotion of the flow of private capital for economic development and to other, more general, aims.[39] In the Comment to their draft, though not in the draft itself, the authors explain that these principles "are believed to be fundamental principles of international law." [40] It is evident, however, that the draft convention's standards belong to the first type of absolute standards mentioned. The rules are stated in great detail, precisely because they are not well-established as principles of international law and grave doubts have been expressed on the validity of at least some of them. In the event the draft con-

---

[35] See *infra*, pp. 167–70.

[36] The epithet "absolute" has in fact a different meaning when applied to each of these two types of standards. In the former case, the standard does not depend on the actions of the state concerned by itself and, also, is not subject to change (except through subsequent agreement of the parties to the treaty). The international law rules, on the other hand, are, by definition, changeable, like all other legal rules, though their change does not depend on the action of any particular state by itself.

[37] For an elaborate discussion of the matter, in its historical setting, see Wilson, *The International Law Standard in Treaties of the United States* 92 *et seq.* (1953). A typical treaty provision is that of article III(1) of the U.S. treaty with The Netherlands. Another standard, equally absolute, but more difficult to define, is the "modern standards of justice" referred to in the treaty with Ethiopia, article VI(2).

[38] *ICC Code*, articles 5(4) and 11(1)(a).

[39] *1959 Draft Convention*, Preamble.

[40] "Comment on the Draft Convention by its Authors," 9 *J. Pub. L.* 119 (1960) and cf. the trenchant criticism in Professor Schwarzenberger's "The Abs-Shawcross Draft Convention on Investments Abroad: A Critical Comment," *idem* 147, at 149.

vention were adopted, the validity of the particular rules would be founded on the treaty's validity as such, not on their being part of international law.

Each type of standard has its own qualities and defects, which should be taken into account when considering state promises concerning the treatment of foreign investors. Noncontingent standards can be generally regarded as offering more certainty, since the content of the legal rules to be applied when the occasion occurs is determined beforehand. Because of their very certainty, however, they are fairly rigid and can adjust to changing circumstances only through variations in the interpretation of their terms, or, in exceptional cases, through an involved procedure of amendment. Moreover, since a great number of possible situations has to be covered, the relevant provisions have to be couched in general language. The certainty of absolute standards is thus in fact diminished, since the more general a term is, the more numerous are the ways in which it can be interpreted. Finally, the rules of international law to which there may be reference are not always clear and well-settled; this is an additional factor of uncertainty.

Contingent standards are certainly more manageable and can cover a great variety of possible situations. But they do not give to the investors a definite picture of the treatment they are to receive, particularly with respect to the future. Moreover, in the case of the standard of national treatment, its content is subject to change through unilateral action of the state concerned. Absolute and contingent standards are not necessarily exclusive of each other. They can be, and often are, used in conjunction, thus complementing each other.

Consideration of the various types of standards is particularly important when examining those provisions of investment laws and treaties which refer to the treatment of investors. Such provisions are to be found in all treaties dealing with such matters, though not in all relevant municipal legislation. They are used not instead of, but together with, more specific provisions, dealing with each of the elements of a country's investment climate.

In the United States FCN treaties, contingent standards are often used. The standard generally imposed is that of national treatment. Within the territory of each party, nationals and companies of the other party are accorded national treatment with respect to business activities [41] as well as to "scientific, educational, religious and philanthropic activities." [42] They are also accorded national treatment with respect to access to local courts and administrative authorities.[43] The most-favored-nation standard is also used; aliens are accorded treatment in accordance with this standard in fields where they are not granted national treatment.[44] The two standards are often applied concurrently as well.[45] We have already noted certain instances where noncontingent standards are used in these treaties.[46]

The recent German investment treaties provide for the application of the same two contingent standards, namely, national treatment and most-favored-nation treatment, in a manner very similar to that of the United States treaties.[47] The 1959 British Treaty with Iran, on the other hand, while still using these standards,[48] seems to place considerable emphasis on a noncontingent standard, that of

[41] Cf. *infra* notes 61, 62.

[42] Treaty with Germany, article VIII(2). Substantially identical provisions in the treaties with Haiti, Israel, Japan, Korea, Nicaragua, The Netherlands, and Pakistan. No corresponding provision in the recent treaty with France.

[43] Cf. treaty with Japan, article IV(1); similar provisions in all the other treaties. And cf. to the same effect, article 7 of the German treaty with Italy, and article 7(1) of its treaty with the Dominican Republic. For a detailed discussion, see Wilson, "Access to Courts Provisions in United States Commercial Treaties," 47 *Am. J. Int'l L.* 20 (1953), also in Wilson, *Treaties* 209–43.

[44] Cf. treaty with Japan, article VII(4) and provisions to the same effect in the treaties with Denmark, Germany, Greece, Haiti, Ireland, Israel, Korea, The Netherlands, Nicaragua, and Uruguay.

[45] Numerous variations exist, on this point, between the various treaties. Cf., e.g., article VI(3) of the treaty with Ireland, articles IV(1), VII(1) and (4), VIII(3), IX(2) and (4) and X of the treaty with Japan, and articles VI(1) and XII(1) of the treaty with Greece.

[46] Cf. *supra* notes 35 and 37.

[47] Cf., e.g., *supra* note 43 and *infra* notes 62, 63, and 69.

[48] For certain clarifications on the manner in which the standards are used, see its article 28.

"fair and equitable treatment." Foreign investors are accorded national and most-favored-nation treatment with respect to the acquisition and disposition of property, within certain limitations,[49] as well as regarding matters of taxation [50] and expropriation.[51] But with respect to the "carrying on of all kinds of business" by companies [52] and to the formation of new companies under the laws of the host state,[53] foreign investors are promised "fair and equitable treatment" as well as most-favored-nation treatment.

The national treatment of foreign investors is stipulated in the Code of Fair Treatment proposed by the International Chamber of Commerce.[54] This standard was also used, in part, in the 1957 Draft Convention for the Mutual Protection of Private Property Rights in Foreign Countries, which also provided for the application of the most-favored-nation standard whenever it was more favorable to aliens.[55] Neither standard is expressly mentioned in the 1959 Draft Convention on Investment Abroad. Its provision on "fair and equitable treatment" as well as on the absence of any "unreasonable or discriminatory measures" [56] may be understood as referring both to certain absolute standards and, by implication, to the standard of national treatment.[57]

Most investment laws do not contain such general provisions. In some of them, however, one finds statements like the following:

Foreign capital in Afghanistan shall enjoy all the exemptions, assistance, and facilities available to Afghan capital under law. No discrimination whatever can be made between foreign and national capital.[58]
Enterprises established with foreign capital, shall receive treatment

[49] Article 12.   [50] Article 10.   [51] Article 15.
[52] Article 6(1).   [53] Article 14(1).   [54] *ICC Code*, article 3.
[55] *1957 Draft Convention*, article IV(4). The proposals of the European League for Economic Cooperation are substantially the same; cf. E.L.E.C., *Common Protection for Private International Investments* 18 (1958). And cf. also [British] Parliamentary Group for World Government, *A World Investment Convention?* 12 (1959).
[56] *1959 Draft Convention*, article I.
[57] Cf. the comments in Schwarzenberger, *supra* note 40, at 152–53.
[58] Afghanistan, Law of April 19, 1954, article 5.

as favorable as that extended to other similar enterprises in this country.[59]

A few other laws contain similar expressions of intent.[60] In many cases, the grant of national treatment to foreign investors is not expressly stated but may be inferred from the various other provisions of the relevant legislative or executive acts. In other cases, however, it is evident from the context that the state issuing the law is unwilling to promise national treatment to all prospective foreign investors.

Restrictions on the Business Activities of Aliens

As already noted, the United States FCN treaties generally provide for the national treatment of foreign investors. In the earlier postwar treaties, it is stated that nationals and companies of each party shall be accorded, within the other party's territory, national treatment with respect to "engaging in commercial, manufacturing, processing, financial, construction, publishing, scientific, philanthropic and professional activities." [61] The language of the more recent treaties is more extensive; national treatment is accorded "with respect to engaging in all types of commercial, industrial, financial and other business activities." [62]

[59] Greece, L.D. No. 2687 of October 22, 1953, article X(1).
[60] Cf., e.g., Nicaragua, Decree No. 10 of February 26, 1955; Turkey, Law No. 6224 of January 18, 1954, article 10; India, Statement at IBRD Meeting, quoted in U.N. Document E/2901, 21 June 1956, Appendix, 14, note; cf. Narayanan "India," in *Legal Aspects* 249, 256–58.
[61] Treaty with Greece, article XII(1); identical or similar provisions in the treaties with Uruguay, Denmark, and Ireland.
[62] Treaty with Japan, article VII(1); substantially identical provisions in the treaties with France, Germany, Haiti, Israel, Nicaragua, Korea and The Netherlands. But cf. article VII of the U.S. treaty with Pakistan. The nonbusiness activities are listed separately and generally accorded national treatment, too; cf. *supra* note 42. In the treaty with Muscat and Oman, article V(1), enterprises engaging in "commercial activities" are distinguished from those engaging in "industrial and other business activities." The former are granted national treatment, the latter most-favored-nation treatment.
To the same effect as the U.S. treaty with Japan, see the treaty between

National and/or most-favored-nation treatment is accorded to nationals and companies of the one party within the territories of the other

with respect to acquiring by purchase, lease or otherwise and with respect to owning and possessing personal property of all kinds, both tangible and intangible.[63]

Almost all treaties,[64] however, contain a provision allowing states to impose restrictions on ownership of such property by aliens, either on grounds of public safety or with respect to ownership of interests in enterprises engaging in activities with regard to which aliens have not been granted national treatment; [65] this is to be done "without impairing the rights and privileges" accorded to aliens by other provisions of the treaties.[66] Aliens are also to be accorded national treatment with regard to leases and other rights in real property (as far as the latter are allowed in local laws).[67]

Some of the treaties provide further that aliens are to be permitted to establish, maintain, control and manage offices, factories or other

---

Germany and Italy, article 8, and the same article in the treaty between Germany and the Dominican Republic. The British treaty of Establishment with Iran, article 6(1), provides for "fair and equitable" as well as most-favored-nation treatment of foreign investors on such matters.

[63] Treaty with Germany, article IX(2). Similar provisions, granting both national and most-favored-nation treatment, are found in the treaties with Haiti, Japan, Korea, The Netherlands, Nicaragua, and Pakistan. The treaties with Denmark, France, Ireland, Israel, and Muscat and Oman accord national treatment only, while those with Ethiopia, Iran, and Uruguay grant only most-favored-nation treatment. No equivalent provision in the treaty with Greece.

The 1959 treaty between the United Kingdom and Iran, article 12, provides for the national and most-favored-nation treatment of foreign investors with regard to such matters. And see also article 11 of the treaty between Germany and the Dominican Republic and article 12 of the treaty between Germany and Italy.

[64] With the exception of those with Ethiopia, Iran, and Muscat and Oman; also the treaty with Greece, on which see *supra* note 63.

[65] Cf. *infra* pp. 146–47.

[66] Cf., e.g., treaty with Germany, article IX(2); treaty with Ireland, article VII(2).

[67] Treaty with Germany, article IX(3). Similar provisions, with minor differences, are found in most of the other treaties. And cf. Wilson, *Treaties* 148–55. See also article 12 of the treaty between the United Kingdom and Iran, and the articles of the German treaties cited *supra* note 63.

establishments.[68] They are to be accorded the right to establish companies in accordance with the applicable local laws and regulations.[69] Some of the more recent treaties also provide that aliens are to be permitted to acquire majority interests in existing companies.[70] In most treaties, however, these provisions are qualified by the general statement that states are allowed to prescribe "special formalities in connection with the establishment of alien-controlled enterprises." Such formalities "may not impair the substance of the rights" granted through other treaty provisions.[71] Of special interest is the provision in the Minutes of Interpretation of the treaty with Denmark, stating the understanding of the parties that the general rule allowing the establishment of companies by aliens does not preclude the maintenance of

> special requirements with respect to the residence or nationality of the founders, members of the boards of directors, and managing directors of companies constituted under [either party's] laws.[72]

Though such a statement is not found in any other treaty or protocol,[73] the similarities in the formulation of the general rule make it probable that the qualification, as well, is of general application.[74]

---

[68] Treaty with Germany, article VII(1). Similar provisions are found in several other treaties; e.g., the treaties with France, Haiti, Japan, Korea, The Netherlands, and Nicaragua.

[69] The relevant provisions are substantially similar in content but present several variations in their form. Cf., e.g., treaty with Uruguay, article VI; treaty with Greece, article XIII; treaty with Ireland, article VI(2); and treaty with Germany, article VII(1). And see, to the same effect, article 8(2) of the German treaty with Italy, and article 8(2) of the German treaty with the Dominican Republic. The British treaty with Iran, article 14(1), provides for fair and equitable treatment and most-favored-nation treatment of foreign investors with regard to the formation of companies.

[70] See article VII(1) of the treaty with Japan; and cf. also the treaties with France, Germany, Haiti, Israel, Korea, The Netherlands, and Nicaragua.

[71] Treaty with Japan, article VII(3). Identical provisions in the treaties with Germany, Haiti, Israel, Nicaragua, Korea, and The Netherlands, and corresponding, though with variations, provisions in the treaties with Greece and Ireland. And cf. article VII(2) of the treaty with Pakistan. No corresponding provision appears in the treaty with Uruguay; cf. its article V.

[72] Treaty with Denmark, Minutes of Interpretation, *ad* article VIII(1).

[73] But cf. treaty with Germany, Protocol, para. 6, mentioning such requirements in connection with the access of foreign companies to the courts of the host state.

[74] In the treaty between the United Kingdom and Iran, article 6(1), most-

Once established, alien-controlled enterprises are accorded national treatment.[75]

In addition to granting national treatment to all foreign investments,[76] the ICC Code provides that the parties to it

> shall not introduce any legislative or administrative provisions of a discriminatory character placing restrictions on: The nationality of the shareholders; The composition of the board of directors and the choice of the directors. . . .[77]

Exceptions are allowed only in the case of enterprises "directly concerned with national defense." [78]

The 1957 Draft Convention provided that the nationals of each state party to it would be guaranteed "freedom in acquiring, administering and utilizing property, rights and interests," in the territory of the other parties.[79] Any limitations on such freedom should "on no account be more restrictive than those applied in respect of nationals." [80] The draft convention further provided that such freedom should not be restricted, by laws or regulations "in so far as these are apt to cause or produce (a) restrictions of the economic activities of non-nationals, particularly foreign shareholders in and managers of legal persons and other membership associations." [81] There is no corresponding provision in the 1959 Draft Convention, in which it is merely stated that "the management, use and enjoyment [of foreign property] shall not in any way be impaired by unreasonable or discriminatory measures." [82]

Apart from their occasional provisions on the grant of national treatment,[83] investment laws generally do not contain provisions

---

favored-nation treatment is accorded to foreign investors with respect to such requirements and limitations.

[75] Cf. the treaty provisions cited *supra*, note 69. For a detailed study, see Walker, "Provisions on Companies in United States Commercial Treaties," 50 *Am. J. Int'l L.* 372 (1956), also in Wilson, *Treaties* 182 *et seq.*

[76] *ICC Code*, article 3.   [77] *Idem*, article 6.   [78] *Ibid.*

[79] *1957 Draft Convention*, article IV(1). The guarantee was qualified only with regard to limitations which might be imposed in certain fields; cf. *infra* p. 146.

[80] *Idem*, article IV(2).   [81] *Idem*, article IV(3).

[82] *1959 Draft Convention*, article I.   [83] Cf. *supra*, pp. 140–41, notes 58–60.

expressly permitting the establishment of foreign owned enterprises. It has already been noted that rarely do the governments of under-developed countries restrict to a minority share foreign participation in all enterprises operating in their territory.[84] Even where the related laws stress the desirability of keeping the control of all enterprises in the hands of local nationals, it is also pointed out that "there can be no hard and fast rule" on the matter,[85] or that "liberal" exceptions may be allowed.[86] Specific decisions on such matters are not to be found in the general provisions of statutes or administrative regulations, but in the instruments of approval or guarantees granted to individual investors.

In no case are foreign investors granted national treatment with respect to all fields of the capital-importing country's economy. Several fields are restricted to local nationals; aliens are either not admitted in them at all, or they are admitted only under strict conditions.[87] In some investment laws, these fields are expressly listed. In its 1948 statement of policy, the Government of Pakistan listed thirteen industries, all enterprises in which should normally be owned by a majority of Pakistani nationals.[88] Mexican legislation limits foreign participation in the ownership of enterprises engaged in a number of specified activities to a minority share.[89] Limitations on the entry of aliens in certain industries are widespread and they constitute today a fact, whose importance has been recognized in the proposed investment codes and in the investment treaties of capital-exporting states.

The ICC Code of Fair Treatment provides that "in the case . . . of investments immediately concerned with national defense, special

---

[84] *Supra* p. 42.

[85] India, Statement of April 6, 1949; cf. Narayanan "India," in *Legal Aspects* 249, 256–58.

[86] Pakistan, Statement of November 18, 1948. Cf. also Burma, Resolution of the Economic Council (1949), section (vi). Indonesia, Statement of December 8, 1955; cf. Wijnberg "Indonesia," in *Legal Aspects* 265, 271.

[87] Cf. the discussion *supra* p. 42.

[88] This restriction is no longer in effect; cf. Ishaque, "Pakistan," in *Legal Aspects*, 397, 404.

[89] Cf. Hidalgo, "Mexico," in *Legal Aspects* 355, 356–57; Friedmann and Pugh, "Comparative Analysis," *idem* 734, 747.

conditions may if necessary be imposed." [90] The 1957 Draft Convention for the Mutual Protection of Private Property Rights goes further in this respect and recognizes the right of each state

to limit the acquisition, utilization and administration of property, rights and interests by non-nationals, and their right to dispose thereof, whenever such non-nationals intend to become active in the fields of public utilities, public transport, the utilization of nuclear energy and the production of arms and war material.[91]

No corresponding provision is found in the 1959 Draft Convention, which permits measures derogating from its provisions only when the state concerned "is involved in war, hostilities or other public emergency which threatens its life; and such measures shall be limited in extent and duration to those strictly required by the exigencies of the situation." [92]

In all United States FCN treaties, it is stated, in more or less similar terms, that their provisions do not preclude the application of measures regulating traffic in gold, silver and other precious metals, or measures relating to atomic materials, traffic in arms, obligations as to war and peace, state security, and some other matters.[93] No standard of treatment is prescribed in such cases. The possibility of limitations in certain other fields is also recognized. It is stated, in one of the more recent treaties, that each contracting party

reserves the right to limit the extent to which aliens may within its territories establish, acquire interests in, or carry on public utilities enter-

---

[90] *ICC Code*, article 3.

[91] *1957 Draft Convention*, article V(1). The second paragraph of this article provides for the protection of enterprises already established in the fields where limitations are imposed.

[92] *1959 Draft Convention*, article V. And cf. the critical observations by Metzger, "Multilateral Conventions for the Protection of Private Foreign Investment," 9 J. Pub. L. 133, 134-36 (1960).

[93] Cf. treaty with Japan, article XXI(1). Similar provisions in the treaties with Denmark, Ethiopia, France, Haiti, Iran, Ireland, Israel, Korea, Nicaragua, Pakistan, and Uruguay. In the treaties with Germany, Muscat and Oman, and The Netherlands, measures reserving rights and privileges with respect to national fisheries are also mentioned, while in the treaty with Greece, article XXIII(1), the export of works of art is added to the list. And cf. the longer list included in article 20 of the German treaty with the Dominican Republic, and article 34 of the German treaty with Italy.

prises or enterprises engaged in shipbuilding, air or water transport, banking involving depository or fiduciary functions, or the exploitation of land or other natural resources.[94]

With respect to such fields, foreign investors are accorded most-favored-nation treatment.[95] The problems arising in this connection as to reciprocity of obligations have been discussed earlier.[96]

It is interesting to note that neither investment treaties nor investment laws contain any general promises with respect to the free entry of foreign capital in the country where it is to be invested. As a matter of fact, in the earliest of the modern FCN treaties of the United States, the one with Uruguay, freedom of entry of capital was stipulated.[97] Doubts were expressed at the time as to the feasibility of the inclusion of this principle in later treaties.[98] Indeed, the principle in question is not to be found in any of the subsequently concluded FCN treaties. On the contrary, it is explicitly stated in the Protocols to some of the treaties that the imposition of requirements or restrictions on the importation of capital is allowed under the terms of the treaties.[99] Moreover, the expressions used in the text of some of the treaties imply clearly that special license or permission may be needed for the importation of capital.[100]

[94] Treaty with Japan, article VII(2); identical or similar provisions in the treaties with France, Germany, Haiti, Israel, Korea, The Netherlands, and Nicaragua. Article VII(2) of the treaty with Pakistan allows limitations on the establishment by aliens of "enterprises engaged . . . in activities for gain (business activities)"; any newly imposed limitation should not affect already operating enterprises. Most of the treaties include a similar proviso to the effect that new limitations should not affect enterprises already carrying on business in the fields enumerated; cf., e.g., treaty with Japan, article VII(2). Cf. also article 8(3) of the recent treaty between Germany and the Dominican Republic.

[95] Cf. *supra* note 44.   [96] Cf. *supra* pp. 98–99.

[97] Treaty with Uruguay, article XV(4). The possibility of limitations on the investment of foreign capital was, however, admitted; see article IV. This treaty, though signed in 1949, is not yet in effect; cf. *supra* Table 1, p. 97.

[98] See, Brown, "Treaty, Guaranty and Tax Inducements for Foreign Investment," 40 *Am. Econ. Rev. Proc.* 486, 487–88 (1950).

[99] See treaty with Germany, Protocol, para. 16; treaty with Denmark, Protocol, para. 7; treaty with Japan, Protocol, para. 6; treaty with Korea, Protocol, para. 7; treaty with The Netherlands, Protocol, para. 14; treaty with France, Protocol, para. 14.

[100] Cf. article VIII(5) of the treaty with Ethiopia: "Nationals and companies . . . which [sic] *are permitted* to establish or acquire enterprises. . . ." And article VII(1) of the treaty with Pakistan: "Enterprises which nationals and companies

Investment laws, as well, provide that permission to enter the country or approval of the competent state agency is a necessary prerequisite to the investment of foreign capital. In the first article of the Japanese investment law, it is stated that

> the purpose of this Law is to create a sound basis for foreign investment in Japan, *by limiting the induction of foreign investment* to that which will contribute to the self-support and sound development of the Japanese economy and to the improvement of the international balance of payments. . . .[101]

Such explicit statements are found in several other investment laws,[102] while in all of them assurances and privileges are granted to "approved" investments only.[103]

Employment of Alien Personnel

The provisions of the United States FCN treaties regarding the employment of skilled personnel of foreign nationality in alien-controlled enterprises are not very forceful. It is stated that nationals and companies of either party

> shall be permitted to engage, within the territories of the other Party, accountants and other technical experts, executive personnel, attorneys, agents and other specialists of their choice.[104]

---

of either Party *are permitted* to establish or acquire. . . ." (Italics mine.) See also Walker, "The Post-War Commercial Treaty Program of the United States," 73 *Pol. Sc. Qu.* 57, 76, note 49 (1958).

[101] Japan, Law No. 163 of 1950, article 1 (italics mine).

[102] Cf., e.g., Afghanistan, Law of April 19, 1954, articles 1 and 2; India, Statement of April 6, 1948.

[103] This is, e.g., the case in Chile, under Decree-Law No. 258 of March 30, 1960, article 4; in Greece, under L.D. No. 2687 of October 22, 1953; in Turkey, under Law No. 6224 of January 18, 1954; in Guatemala, under the Industrial Development Law, Decree No. 1317 of October 23, 1959; in Nicaragua, under Decree No. 10 of February 26, 1955, article 3, now repealed, as well as under the Law of March 20, 1958, articles 25–29, now in force.

[104] Treaty with The Netherlands, article VIII(1). Corresponding provisions are found in all FCN treaties of the United States, with the partial exception of that with Haiti, which contains only a limited provision, of the type mentioned *infra*, text to note 113. Cf. also article 10(1) of the German treaty with the Dominican Republic and article 11(1) of the treaty between Germany and Italy.

In some of the treaties, the words "regardless of nationality" are added to the above rule.[105] Their absence, in the majority of the treaties, probably indicates a corresponding limitation on the investors' rights. In one of the treaties, it is stated that the investors shall be permitted to engage skilled employees "of their choice among those legally in the country and eligible to work." [106] In the Protocols attached to several other treaties, it is stated that the general provision quoted above does not affect existing requirements for "employment permits," but that the states undertake to apply the relevant laws and regulations "in a liberal fashion." [107] Another of the treaties is more explicit on the matter; it qualifies in the following manner the general rule quoted above:

The preceding sentence shall not be construed to preclude a Party from enforcing laws regarding the nationality of employees, but such laws shall not prevent nationals and companies of the other Party from employing personnel, regardless of nationality, who are essential to the conduct of their affairs.[108]

The matter has been dealt with in some detail in the recent Convention of Establishment between the United States and France. In the main body of the instrument, Article VI relates to the employment of technical and other personnel by foreign investors; its terms follow closely the model quoted above.[109] It is stated further that such persons "must fulfill the conditions necessary to the exercise of their calling under the applicable legislation." [110] Another related

---

[105] Cf. the treaties with Denmark, article VII(4), Israel, article VIII(1), Nicaragua, article VIII(1), and Uruguay, article V(4).

[106] Treaty with Greece, article XII(4).

[107] Cf. treaty with Ireland, Protocol, para. 1; treaty with Germany, Protocol, para. 8; treaty with Denmark, Protocol, para. 3; treaty with The Netherlands, Protocol, para. 11.

[108] Treaty with Nicaragua, article VIII(1). Cf. in this connection article 23(3) of the Economic Agreement of Bogota, stating that "it is desirable to permit enterprises, without prejudice to the laws of each country, to employ and utilize the services of a reasonable number of technical experts and executive personnel, whatever their nationality may be."

[109] *Supra*, text to note 104.

[110] Article VI(1). For an exception to this general qualification, see *infra* note 113.

provision, which is found in similar terms in most of the other FCN treaties, is that of Article II, which allows, "subject to the laws relating to the entry and sojourn of aliens," nationals of each party to enter and reside in the territory of the other party, in order to engage in commercial activities or to direct the operation of an enterprise in which they have invested. The precise meaning of this provision is spelled out in the Protocol and in a Joint Declaration annexed to the Convention. In the Protocol,[111] it is stated that each country's laws governing the admission to and exercise of the professions by aliens remain in effect, but such laws should not "impair the substance" of the rights set forth in the treaty. It is further made clear that the provisions on entry and sojourn relate to managerial personnel (persons "occupying a position of responsibility," in the treaty's term) as well as the "investors" themselves.[112] In the Joint Declaration, the parties attempt to "clarify . . . the import of the reservations relating, on the one hand, to the enforcement of the laws governing the entry and sojourn of aliens and, on the other hand, to the enforcement of the laws regulating the access of aliens to the professions and occupations." They express their intention to facilitate "to the greatest possible extent and on a basis of real and effective reciprocity, the establishment of nationals who are not within [the categories of personnel mentioned in the treaty and Protocol] and, in particular, of qualified personnel who are indispensable to the conduct of [foreign-owned] enterprises . . ." and to exercise in this respect "the greatest possible liberality consistent with their national laws. . . ."

Another related provision, common to most of these treaties, allows alien-controlled enterprises to employ alien accountants and other experts on a temporary basis for the making of audits and other technical investigations, even when such experts have not qualified

---

[111] Para. 2.

[112] A similar provision is found in para. 1 of the Protocol to the treaty with Pakistan. And cf. article 13 of the British treaty with Iran, providing for fair and equitable and most-favored-nation treatment with respect to the appointment of agents.

for the practice of their professions within the domain of the capital-importing state.[113]

In the British treaty of Commerce, Establishment and Navigation with Iran, nationals of each party are accorded most-favored-nation treatment with respect to entry and residence in the territory of the other party as well as to employment and the exercise of professions in it.[114] Special emphasis is laid on the need for predictability and certainty in such matters. Any condition imposed on an alien's residence or employment in the host country must be communicated to him at the time of the original grant of his entry or residence permit. The conditions imposed are not to be made more restrictive at any time thereafter.[115]

Of the suggested investment codes, only that proposed by the International Chamber of Commerce goes into any detail concerning this question. According to it, no restrictions should be placed on

The selection or introduction into their territories of such administrative, executive and technical officers and staff, not nationals of those territories, as shall be deemed by the enterprises concerned to be requisite for their efficient operation.[116]

It is to be noted that the enterprise itself is to judge whether it needs alien employees and that such aliens do not have to be strictly indispensable for the operation of the enterprise, but only useful to it. The Draft Convention for the Mutual Protection of Private Property Rights does not deal with the subject at hand, except for a fleeting reference to the freedom from restrictions on "managers of legal persons and other membership associations." [117]

---

[113] Cf. treaty with Haiti, article VIII(1); treaty with France, article VI(2) and corresponding provisions in the other FCN treaties of the United States and Germany, cited *supra* note 104.

[114] Article 3(1) and (4). Para. 2 of this article provides for freedom of travel within the territory of each party, subject to certain limitations.

[115] Article 3(3). For a similar requirement with respect to limitations on the aliens' business activities, see *1957 Draft Convention*, article V(2). And cf. also *supra* pp. 77–78 and note 43.

[116] *ICC Code*, article 6.

[117] *1957 Draft Convention*, article IV(3)(a).

Investment laws are often quite elaborate on this point. The Greek law provides that:

Enterprises established or assisted financially by foreign capital shall be permitted to employ foreign nationals in higher positions of their technical and administrative personnel and to pay them in foreign exchange transferable abroad as provided in the instrument of approval to be executed in each case.[118]

A similar provision is to be found in the Turkish investment statute,[119] while the Egyptian law charges the "special committee for the exploitation of foreign capital," which it sets up, with facilitating "the obtaining of residence visas for business men, experts and foremen from abroad to work in the undertakings where foreign capital is invested." [120] The investment law of Libya provides that "the immigration authorities must give all necessary visas to foreign staff employed in the [approved] projects" and "must facilitate, in general and as far as possible, their entry into Libya, their departure and their movements throughout the country" unless the provision of such facilities is detrimental to the country's interests.[121] At the same time, the Libyan law provides for the imposition of requirements concerning employment and training of local nationals.[122] The same dual emphasis is found in the policy statements of Asian states which recognize the necessity for the employment of foreign personnel, while stressing the importance of training local personnel.[123] In other cases, the right of alien-controlled enterprises to employ alien technical personnel is subject to specific government approval

---

[118] Greece, L.D. No. 2687 of October 22, 1953, article VII; cf. Lambadarios "Greece," in *Legal Aspects* 233, 236–37, 245.

[119] Turkey, Law No. 6224 of January 18, 1954, article 7(a) and (b).

[120] United Arab Republic, Law No. 156 of April 2, 1953, as amended by Law No. 475 of September 2, 1954, article 5(g).

[121] Libya, Foreign Capital Investment Law of January 30, 1958, clause 6.

[122] *Idem* clause 7.

[123] Cf. e.g., Afghanistan, Law of April 19, 1954, article 10; Burma, Resolution of the Economic Council (1949) and sections (1) and (7) of Statement of June 8, 1955; Pakistan, Statement of April 2, 1948, section 13. Indonesia, Statement of December 8, 1955; cf. Wijnberg "Indonesia," in *Legal Aspects* 265, 272.

and its duration is limited to a relatively short period of time, during which local nationals are to be trained in order to replace the aliens.[124] Closely related to the present topic are the provisions in several investment laws permitting the transfer outside the capital-receiving country of the whole or a part of the salaries of alien employees.[125]

Repatriation of Capital and Earnings

The problems arising out of the presence in most capital-importing states of measures of foreign exchange control have received particular attention in most of the instruments designed to encourage foreign private investment.

In the Economic Agreement of Bogota, the American states undertook to "impose no unjustifiable restrictions upon the transfer of [foreign] capital and the earnings thereof." [126] Since the term "unjustifiable" is given no definition, the undertaking seems to have been rather academic.

Most of the later proposals provide for complete freedom of transfer of the earnings and interest on foreign investment as well as of the original capital invested. The ICC Code of Fair Treatment provides that capital-importing states should allow freedom of transfer of current payments arising out of the aliens' investments, including interest, dividends and profits. Similar freedom is to be allowed with respect to payments of principal and other transfers of invested capital as well as all other payments "necessary for the upkeep and renewal of assets" in capital-receiving states.[127] Freedom of transfer is also accorded to all payments arising out of public loans or loans guaranteed by public authority.[128] No restrictions or limitations on the investors' freedom of transfer are recognized ex-

---

[124] Cf. the situation in Colombia, as reported by Kalmanoff and Bernal Salamanca, "Colombia," in *Legal Aspects* 169, 175, and Borges, "Labor Relations in Latin America," 17 *Ohio State L.J.* 290, 294 (1956). See also Friedmann and Pugh, "Comparative Analysis," in *Legal Aspects* 734, 744–45.

[125] Cf. *infra* p. 163.   [126] *Bogota Agreement*, article 22(4).

[127] *ICC Code*, article 9.   [128] *Idem*, article 10.

cept those which "may be authorized under the agreement of the International Monetary Fund." [129]

The relevant provisions of the 1957 Draft Convention for the Mutual Protection of Private Property Rights were less elaborate but similarly far-reaching. It was provided that "the transfer of capital, returns on capital investments, and compensation payments granted for expropriation . . . are guaranteed in every case." [130] This general statement was in no way qualified and no possible exceptions were mentioned. The matter is not touched upon in the latest draft of this convention, except perhaps, to the extent that it may be included in the general provision on "fair and equitable treatment" of the property of foreign nationals.[131] On the other hand, the Draft Convention which was recently submitted by the Swiss government to the OEEC provides in detail for the free transfer to the foreign investor's country of residence of all earnings, amortization payments, and incidental expenses of the enterprise as well as of any sum arising out of the total or partial realization of such investment.

A similar but somewhat qualified rule is found in the report of the European League for Economic Cooperation. It is stated there that "freedom of transfer in a stipulated currency would always be assured" for the earnings of foreign investments, the salary of foreign personnel and "the normal redemptions of capital or of loans." [132] The addition of the word "normal" should be considered as limiting the right of foreign investors to transfer abroad the original capital invested.

The report of the Economic Committee of the Council of Europe Consultative Assembly admits expressly the possibility of "reasonable limitations" on the repatriation of capital, while providing for the free transfer of earnings and interest under normal conditions;

---

[129] *Idem*, article 9(1).

[130] *1957 Draft Convention*, article IV(5); and cf. article IV(3)(e).

[131] Cf. *1959 Draft Convention*, article I. Freedom of transfer is stipulated only in the case of compensation for expropriated property; cf. *infra*, note 201.

[132] E.L.E.C., *Common Protection for Private International Investments* 19 (1958).

under "exceptional conditions" limitations might be allowed even as to current payments.[133] The views of the British all-party Commission's report on a world investment convention are similar in their general effect, though they make no distinction between capital and earnings. Free transfer abroad is to be provided for, "subject to the possibility of exchange control on reasonable balance-of-payments grounds," and to any agreement with the capital-importing country's government with regard to "the rate of withdrawal of capital or limitations of dividends." [134]

The recent FCN treaties of the United States provide in great detail for the modalities of repatriation of the foreign investors' earnings and capital. In the first place, they provide against the use of exchange restrictions solely in order to discriminate against foreign investors, the parties undertaking not to impose restrictions "in a manner unnecessarily detrimental or arbitrarily discriminatory" to the interests and the competitive position of foreign investors.[135] It is quite clear from the context, and it has been on occasion stated expressly,[136] that the treaties provide against discrimination between investors on the basis of their nationality and not against differentiation between currencies.

In a few treaties, a general statement in favor of complete freedom from any exchange restrictions is included, together with an undertaking not to hamper "unnecessarily" the international movement of

---

[133] Consultative Assembly Document 1027, 8 September 1959, at 17–18.

[134] Parliamentary Group for World Government, *A World Investment Convention?* 13 (1959).

[135] Cf. treaty with Germany, article XII(3); treaty with Greece, article XV(4); and corresponding provisions in the treaties with Denmark, France, Haiti, Japan, Korea, The Netherlands, Nicaragua, and Pakistan. The treaty with Israel, article XII(6), provides only for the administration of exchange restrictions in a manner calculated not to alter the competitive position of foreign investors, nationals of either party, as compared with nationals of third countries. Similar provisions are included in the treaties with Ethiopia, Iran, Ireland, and Uruguay. And see article IX(1) and (2) of the treaty with Muscat and Oman for a variant of this position.

[136] Cf. treaty with France, Protocol, para. 13; treaty with Germany, Protocol, para. 14; treaty with The Netherlands, Protocol, para. 13; treaty with Pakistan, Protocol, para. 8. It is stated *inter alia* that the relevant provisions do not preclude "differential treatment of different currencies."

capital.[137] Most treaties contain a general prohibition of exchange restrictions,[138] while at the same time they allow several exceptions to it. It is provided in most cases that restrictions specifically approved or requested by the International Monetary Fund are permitted under the terms of the treaty.[139] In some of the treaties exchange restrictions are also allowed

> to the extent necessary to prevent [the Party's] monetary reserves from falling to a very low level or to effect a moderate increase in very low reserves.[140]

While in certain other treaties, they are allowed

> to the extent necessary to assure the availability of foreign exchange for payments for goods and services essential to the health and welfare of its people.[141]

Beyond these general provisions, the FCN treaties also contain some more specific rules, assuring facilities for the repatriation of the investors' earnings and, possibly, compensation for expropriated

---

[137] Cf. article XII(4) of the treaty with Germany: "The two Parties, recognizing that the international movement of investment capital and the returns thereon would be conducive to the full realization of the objectives of the present Treaty, are agreed that such movements shall not be unnecessarily hampered." Corresponding, though not identical, provisions in the treaties with France, article X(3), and Muscat and Oman, article IX(1).

[138] "Neither Party shall impose exchange restrictions . . . except. . . ." Treaty with Greece, article XV(2), and identical expressions in the treaties with Ethiopia, Denmark, France, Haiti, Iran, Japan, Korea, The Netherlands, Nicaragua, and Pakistan. The treaties with Germany, Ireland, Israel, and Uruguay do not contain such a prohibition. But see the treaty with Israel, article XII(4), providing for the free transfer of earnings, capital, and possible compensation for expropriated property. The Parties are still allowed to impose exchange restrictions; cf. *idem* article XII(5). For a variation on the same theme, see article IX of the treaty with Muscat and Oman.

[139] Cf. the treaties cited in the first part of note 138, *supra*, with the addition of the treaty with Germany, article XII(2), and that with Uruguay, article XV(1).

[140] Treaty with Greece, article XV(2). The other treaties listed in the first part of note 138 *supra*, with the exception of those with Ethiopia and Iran, contain identical or very similar provisions. Note that the wording follows that of article 21(3)(a) of the ITO Havana Charter, which allowed in such situations the imposition of import restrictions.

[141] Treaty with Iran, article VII(1)(a). Similar provisions in the treaties with Denmark and Ethiopia. The treaty with Denmark is the only one which allows both exceptions.

property, even when exchange restrictions are in effect in the capital-receiving country.[142] In general, the parties to the treaty undertake to "make reasonable provision for the withdrawal" of the aforementioned funds. Sometimes, certain specific items are mentioned, which must be assured to the countries imposing the restrictions and which take precedence over the withdrawal of the investors' funds, when a situation of exchange stringency exists. Thus, many treaties provide that each party shall make provision for the withdrawal of the foreign investors' funds only

after making whatever provision may be necessary to assure the availability of foreign exchange for goods and services essential to the health and welfare of its people.[143]

In other cases, other items of absolute priority are mentioned, such as fulfillment of international obligations [144] or "avoidance of serious economic instability." [145] Lastly, whenever multiple rates of exchange are in effect, a rate "specifically approved by the International Monetary Fund" or, in its absence, a "just and reasonable" one is to be applied.[146]

The same treatment is generally accorded to capital transfers, though, in most cases, with some additional qualifications. Capital, including amortization and depreciation payments, is to be transferred abroad, in accordance with the provisions already noted, only "to the extent feasible" [147] and/or "giving consideration to special needs for other transactions." [148] In a few treaties, such special needs

[142] Treaty with Uruguay, article XV(4); treaty with Japan, article XII(3); and corresponding provisions in all the other treaties.

[143] Treaty with The Netherlands, article XII(3); identical provisions in all other treaties save those cited in note 141 *supra* and the treaty with Germany. See also treaty with Ireland, Protocol, para. 8, and Minutes of Interpretation *ad* article XVII(5).

[144] Treaty with Haiti, article XII(3).

[145] Treaty with Greece, article XV(3); and treaty with Korea, article XII(3).

[146] Cf. treaties cited in note 142 *supra*. Corresponding provisions are found in all the treaties, with the exception of that with Ireland.

[147] Treaty with Greece, article XV(3). A similar qualification is found in the treaties with Israel and The Netherlands.

[148] Treaty with Greece, article XV(3). A similar qualification is found in most other treaties, with the exception of those cited *infra* notes 149 and 150.

are to be taken into consideration with respect to transfers of both capital and earnings,[149] while in others, the precise effects of the differentiation between the two are not made clear.[150]

The provisions of the German "investment treaties" on exchange restrictions seem less forceful than those of the United States treaties. In one case, the model of these latter treaties is followed, though only in part.[151] In another, special emphasis is laid on the obligations arising out of the participation of both parties to the treaty in certain international economic organizations, presumably the International Monetary Fund and the European Payments Union and its successors.[152] The parties are expressly allowed to apply their respective legislations on exchange control, though in a "liberal" manner, and they undertake to provide to foreign investors "adequate possibilities" for the transfer abroad of their capital and earnings.[153]

In the recent British treaty with Iran, no express provision prohibits or limits to any important extent the right of each state party to impose exchange restrictions. On the contrary, it may be inferred from some of its provisions that the existence or future imposition of exchange control is deemed wholly legitimate; it is not a measure which should be allowed only under extreme circumstances.[154] The single provision directly relevant accords national and most-favored-nation treatment to nationals and companies of either party who are exporting their moveable property or "the proceeds of the sale of any property, moveable or immoveable, or any interest therein" from the territory of the other party.[155]

Investment laws, as well, contain provisions concerning the repatriation of the capital and earnings of foreign investors.[156] Indeed,

---

[149] Cf. treaty with Germany, article XII(4) and Protocol, para. 15; treaty with Ireland, Minutes of Interpretation *ad* article XVII(5).

[150] Cf. treaty with France, article X(3). No such differentiation is made in the treaty with Muscat and Oman, article IX(1).

[151] Cf. treaty with the Dominican Republic, article 15, whose para. 2 follows closely the provision quoted *supra* note 137.

[152] Cf. treaty with Italy, article 15(1).   [153] *Idem*, article 15(2) and (3).

[154] Cf., e.g., article 18(6) and article 19.   [155] Article 12(3).

[156] The coverage of inconvertibility risks by the United States and the other investment guarantee programs should also be taken into account at this point, though it is not studied in this chapter.

along with provisions on tax arrangements and privileges, provisions on exchange restrictions constitute one of the main elements of modern investment laws. In certain instances, it should be noted, there is no need to formulate promises on such matters, namely, when and where no exchange restrictions are in effect. This is the case in a small number of underdeveloped countries. In the great majority of such countries, however, exchange restrictions are in effect and such promises are necessary, though their precise provisions vary widely.

Most investment laws provide for the repatriation of the earnings of foreign-owned investments. In some cases, the withdrawal of all profits, whatever their amount or proportion to the original capital invested, is allowed. Thus, the Afghanistan investment law provides that "foreign investors will be allowed to transfer abroad the profits accruing on their capital or any portion of those profits (. . .) after paying income taxes." [157] The Turkish law provides that "such net amounts [of profits] as accrue to the owners of the foreign capital base" are entitled, subject to the permission of the Ministry of Finance, to "a transfer abroad in the currency of the country from which the foreign capital base originated and at the prevailing official rate of exchange." [158] The relevant Italian legislation distinguishes productive and nonproductive enterprises and grants unlimited freedom of transfer of "dividends and profits actually received" to the former.[159] Similar provisions are to be found in the legislation of other countries, as well.[160]

In the majority of investment laws, withdrawal of profits is per-

---

[157] Afghanistan, Law of April 19, 1954, article 6.

[158] Turkey, Law No. 6224 of January 18, 1954, article 4(a)1; for more details, see Ansay, "Turkey," in *Legal Aspects* 543, 559.

[159] Italy, Law of February 7, 1956, article 1, as reported by Nobili "Italy," in *Legal Aspects* 303, 313. See also *infra* text to note 164.

[160] Cf., e.g., Colombia, as in Kalmanoff and Bernal Salamanca, "Colombia," in *Legal Aspects* 169, 182. United Arab Republic, Law No. 156 of April 2, 1953, as amended by Law No. 475 of September 2, 1954, article 3(1); cf. Habachy, "United Arab Republic," *idem* 562. India, Statement of April 6, 1949; cf. Narayanan, "India," *idem* 249, 259. Nicaragua, Decree No. 10 of February 26, 1955, article 9. Thailand, Announcement of the Revolutionary Party No. 33, (1958) in 9 *Am. J. Comp. L.* 498 (1960). Chile, Decree-Law No. 258 of March 30, 1960, article 9(b).

mitted within certain limits, usually in proportion to the amount of the initial investment. The relevant Bolivian law provides that the profits which may be withdrawn and transferred abroad each year cannot exceed 15 percent of the original capital invested.[161] The Greek investment law allows the remittance abroad of interest and dividends not exceeding 12 percent a year on the amount of equity capital imported, and 10 percent a year for interest on loan capital.[162] In Italy, a 1948 decree determined this limit in a more complicated manner: the interests and profits transferable abroad could not exceed one percent more than the legal annual rate of interest. That rate being then 5 percent, transferable profits were limited to 6 percent of the initial capital.[163] The Italian legislation now in effect limits the proportion of profits and dividends which may be transferred abroad, in the case of nonproductive enterprises, to a maximum of 8 percent a year.[164]

The Israeli investment law, on the other hand, sets a general limit of not more than 10 percent a year.[165] This law, however, along with the laws of certain other countries, employs an additional criterion in calculating the amount of profits which a foreign-owned enterprise is allowed to transfer abroad. When such an enterprise produces for the export market and thus causes foreign exchange to be imported into the capital-receiving country, then a part or the whole of the foreign exchange thus imported may be used for the transfer abroad of the enterprise's annual earnings.[166] Many investment laws also provide that when the profits transferred one year do

[161] Bolivia, Law of October 9, 1954, article V.

[162] Greece, L.D. No. 2687 of October 22, 1953, article V(2).

[163] Italy, Decree No. 211 of March 2, 1948.

[164] Italy, Law of February 7, 1956, as reported by Nobili, "Italy," in *Legal Aspects* 303, 313. Cf. also *supra* note 159.

[165] Israel, Law No. 30 of 5710–1950, as amended, section 21(a); cf. Sher, "Israel," in *Legal Aspects* 292, 301. Similar provisions are in effect in Japan, under Law No. 163 of 1950, articles 13, 15–(2), 15–(3); cf. Ishii "Japan," *idem* 318, 331–32.

[166] Israel, Law No. 30 of 5710–1950, as amended, section 21(b)–(e); cf. Sher, "Israel," *idem* 292, 301. Similar provisions are in effect in several other countries. Cf. Chile, Decree-Law No. 258 of March 30, 1960, article 9(d); cf. also Aramayo "Chile," *idem* 135, 138. Greece, L.D. No. 2687 of October 22, 1953, article XIV(1); cf. Lambadarios, "Greece," *idem* 233, 245.

not reach the maximum limit set by the law, the difference may be used in subsequent years.[167] Finally, several investment laws provide that reinvested profits from foreign investments are or may, by the application of certain procedures, be regarded as foreign capital and share the latter's position and privileges.[168]

Repatriation of the invested capital, either by amortization, or through the liquidation of the enterprise, is as a rule permitted under more severe restrictions. Very few investment laws allow its free withdrawal and transfer abroad. According to the Turkish law, it is permissible to transfer abroad:

2. The share of the owners of the foreign capital base in the proceeds of the sale, within reasonable prices, of assets in case of partial or total liquidation of an enterprise subject to this law.

3. The proceeds of the sale, within reasonable prices, of part or the whole of the foreign capital base of an enterprise, established or in operation in accordance with this law.[169]

In Iran, as well, the repatriation of the whole amount of the invested capital is permitted, as a rule, except when the amount involved is such that its exportation might upset the country's balance-of-payments. In this case, the repatriation of a part of the capital is to be permitted, in no case less than 30 percent.[170] Similar, though generally less detailed, provisions are found in the laws of a number of states.[171]

Most investment laws impose limitations and conditions to the

[167] Cf. Greece, L.D. No. 2687 of October 22, 1953, article V(2). Bolivia, Law of October 9, 1954, article V.

[168] This may be considered as a partial equivalent of repatriation. Cf. Greece, L.D. No. 2687 of October 22, 1953, article V(3). Turkey, Law No. 6224 of January 18, 1954, article 3; cf. Ansay "Turkey," in *Legal Aspects* 543, 560. Pakistan, as reported by Ishaque, "Pakistan," *idem* 397, 404. Chile, Decree-Law No. 258 of March 30, 1960, article 29.

[169] Turkey, Law No. 6224 of January 18, 1954, article 4(A); cf. Ansay, "Turkey," *idem* 543, 559.

[170] Iran, Law of November 28, 1955, article 5, and article 13 (B) of the related Regulations; cf. Nasr "Iran," *idem* 280, 289.

[171] Cf. Afghanistan, Law of April 19, 1954, article 7. Libya, Foreign Capital Investment Law of January 30, 1958, clause 5. Italy, Law of February 7, 1956, as reported by Nobili "Italy," in *Legal Aspects* 303, 313.

repatriation of the invested capital. Not only must the capital be withdrawn in installments, over a number of years, but in many instances its withdrawal is not permitted before the lapse of a specified period of time after the date of the original investment. The Greek investment law imposes both these limitations; according to it:

No capital shall be repayable before the enterprise begins to operate productively and in no case before the lapse of one year from the date of its importation. The remittance of foreign exchange for the repayment of capital cannot exceed 10 per cent per annum of the amount of capital imported.[172]

Similarly, the investment regulations of Chile provided:

Foreign capital which has been imported in the manner stipulated [in earlier provisions] can be withdrawn from Chile in annual quotas not to exceed 20 percent of the original value, at any time five years after having entered the country.[173]

A 1948 Italian decree, now repealed, provided that after the liquidation of an enterprise, its capital could be transferred abroad after at least two years from the date of the original investment and in amounts not exceeding 50 percent of the total for every two-year period.[174] In Japan, repatriation of foreign capital is permitted at a maximum rate of 20 percent per year, commencing two years after the original investment was made.[175] Similarly, the investment law of the United Arab Republic allows foreign capital to be withdrawn at a rate not exceeding 20 percent of its total registered value, normally commencing five years after its date of entry.[176]

---

[172] Greece, L.D. No. 2687 of October 22, 1953, article V(1).

[173] Chile, Decree No. 427 of May 3, 1954, article 9(1); cf. Aramayo "Chile," in *Legal Aspects* 135, 137–38. The provisions now in force are somewhat less precise; see Decree-Law No. 258 of March 30, 1960, article 9.

[174] Italy, Decree No. 211 of March 2, 1948, article II(2). The legislation now in effect permits the repatriation of the assets of nonproductive enterprises two years after the date of the original investment; cf. Nobili, "Italy," in *Legal Aspects* 303, 313.

[175] Japan, Law No. 163 of 1950, article 15-(3); cf. Ishii, "Japan," *idem* 318, 332.

[176] United Arab Republic, Law No. 156 of April 2, 1953, as amended by Law

Other investment laws impose only one or the other of the afore-mentioned conditions. A Bolivian law provides that capital invested in the country may be transferred abroad at a rate not exceeding 20 percent per year or, in special cases, 30 percent.[177] In vaguer terms, the Burmese Council of Ministers has expressed its willingness to "allow for the repatriation of investment over a reasonable period of time." [178] Provisions of a similar content, with many variations, are found in the legislation of several other states.[179]

Several investment laws also provide that the salaries of personnel of foreign nationality employed by foreign-owned enterprises may be transferred abroad freely or within certain limits.[180] The investment law of Afghanistan allows the transfer abroad of 70 percent of the salaries of foreign employees of foreign or Afghan enterprises,[181] while the Greek law provides for the payment of such personnel "in foreign exchange transferrable abroad." [182] The Egyptian investment law, on the other hand, allows the free transfer abroad of 50 percent of such salaries.[183]

Protection Against Expropriation

Investment codes and bilateral treaties place particular emphasis on the problems arising out of possible measures of expropriation of the property of aliens. Investment laws do not generally attach so much importance to this matter, though relevant provisions are found in several of them.

No. 475 of September 2, 1954, article 3(2); cf. Habachy, "United Arab Republic," *idem* 562.

[177] Bolivia, Law of October 9, 1954, article VI.

[178] Burma, Statement of June 8, 1955.

[179] Cf., e.g., Israel, Law No. 30 of 5710-1950, as amended, section 21.

[180] Cf. the laws cited *infra* notes 181-83, and Turkey, Law No. 6224 of January 18, 1954, article 7(c); Libya, Foreign Capital Investment Law of January 30, 1958, clause 5.

[181] Afghanistan, Law of April 19, 1954, article 11.

[182] Greece, L.D. No. 2687 of October 22, 1953, article VII.

[183] United Arab Republic, Law No. 156 of April 2, 1953, as amended by Law No. 475 of September 2, 1954, article 4; cf. Habachy, "United Arab Republic," in *Legal Aspects* 562.

The ITO Charter's provisions on the matter were vague and of limited effect. Each state member undertook to take no "unreasonable or unjustifiable action . . . injurious to the rights or interests of nationals of other Members in the enterprise, skills, capital, arts or technology which they have supplied." [184] No other related provision is to be found, except for the general commitment of the member states "to provide . . . adequate security for existing and future investments," [185] subject to the Charter's provisions on the rights of capital-importing states.[186]

The Bogota Economic Agreement was more explicit. Not only did it state in strong and clear terms the rule of national treatment in matters of expropriation, in accordance with the constitutional and legislative rules in effect in each state, but it also adopted certain absolute standards by stating the need for "fair compensation in a prompt, adequate and effective manner." [187] However, no fewer than eight, out of a total of twenty-one signatory states, attached express reservations to the Agreement's provision on expropriation.

Some of the proposed codes provide strict conditions for the exercise of the state's power of expropriation with regard to foreign investment. According to the ICC Code of Fair Treatment, expropriations of alien property are to be effected in accordance with certain "principles." The purpose and conditions of any expropriation should be stated explicitly in the relevant national legislation,[188] and the appropriate legal procedures must be followed.[189] The compensation to be paid to the alien should be determined prior to the expropriation and should be paid in cash or in "readily marketable securities," freely transferable to the alien's currency.[190] It is also provided that compensation should be "fair . . . according to international law." [191]

Most of the other proposals lay greater stress on the form and measure of compensation. As a matter of fact, in some of the pro-

---

[184] *Havana Charter*, article 11(1)(b).
[185] *Idem*, article 12(2)(a)(i).
[186] Cf. *supra* p. 71.
[187] *Bogota Agreement*, article 25.
[188] *ICC Code*, article 11(b).
[189] *Idem*, article 11(a).
[190] *Idem*, article 11(c) and (d).
[191] *Idem*, article 11(a).

posals, only the question of compensation is raised. This is true, for instance, of the Swiss proposal to the OEEC which provides for the payment of adequate compensation, to be assessed prior to the taking and to be freely transferable outside the expropriating state. The European League's study also provides for the award of "just compensation" which "must cover the principal, appreciation and outstanding dividends and interest. It must be made payable in a transferable currency, with a gold clause, and be remitted to the investor within a fixed period." [192]

The Council of Europe's report explicitly recognizes that it would be vain to demand guarantees against "dispossession." The proposed convention would stipulate that any expropriation to be effected would follow the legal procedure provided for in the expropriating state and that fair compensation would be forthcoming.[193] The British parliamentary group's study, as well, completely ignores the matter of conditions and concentrates on the need for fair compensation. This study is the only one to admit that, while compensation would normally be "adequate, effective and prompt," the expropriating country's capacity to pay should also be taken into account.[194]

The 1957 Draft Convention of the German Society to Advance the Protection of Foreign Investments dealt in great detail with the problem of expropriation. The Convention made, in this connection, a distinction between foreign investors and other categories of alien property owners. The property of foreign investors was not to be expropriated for at least thirty years after investment.[195] A sole exception was allowed, in the case of a national emergency. It was further stated, however, that expropriation is permissible only when such an emergency cannot be met through temporary restrictive

[192] European League for Economic Cooperation, *Common Protection for Private International Investments* 19 (1958).

[193] Council of Europe Consultative Assembly Document 1027, 8 September 1959, at 18.

[194] Parliamentary Group for World Government, *A World Investment Convention?* 13–14 (1959).

[195] *1957 Draft Convention,* article VI(1).

measures, and that nationalization cannot by itself be considered as constituting a national emergency. The property of other aliens could be expropriated only when the "predominance of public interests demands such action." [196] The modalities of the compensation to be paid were dealt with in some detail. The alien would be granted "substitution and/or compensation equivalent to the value of the expropriated property," at his own choice.[197] The amount and form of compensation would be determined prior to the taking and final payment should be made "as soon as practicable." [198] Such payment should be in cash or in "bonds listed on the Stock Exchange . . . secured against loss of substance and [carrying] commensurate interest, amortization and guarantees." [199]

The Draft Convention prepared under the chairmanship of Lord Shawcross formulated in a somewhat different manner the conditions for the legality of expropriations. Measures depriving aliens of their property had to be taken only for the public benefit, under due process of law, without discrimination and with no violation of any "specific engagement" toward the alien. No taking would be lawful if it were not accompanied by "just and effective" compensation, representing the full value of the expropriated property and paid in transferable form and without undue delay. Provision for the determination and payment of such compensation would have to be made at or prior to the time of taking.[200]

The 1959 Draft Convention, which combines the two earlier proposals, follows, in the matter of expropriation, the Shawcross draft. One of the conditions for the lawfulness of expropriation, namely, the requirement of public interest, has been dropped, but the other

---

[196] *Idem,* article VI(2). According to the comments to the Convention, "the words used . . . are designed to stress the exceptional character of expropriation." *Idem* 54–55.

[197] *Idem,* article VII(1). Compensation is also to be granted in the case of restrictions on alien property; cf. *idem,* article VII(2).

[198] *Idem,* article VII(3).   [199] *Ibid.*

[200] Cf. Brandon, "An International Investment Code: Current Plans," 1959 *J. Business L.* 7, 13.

conditions, as well as the provisions on compensation, remain in substance the same as in the Shawcross draft.[201] Like that draft, too, the 1959 Draft Convention refers explicitly to indirect as well as direct measures of expropriation. The former would presumably include any regulatory government action which affects foreign investors but falls short of an outright taking.[202]

The provisions on expropriation of the United States FCN treaties present certain similarities to those of the investment codes. They are, however, formulated in a different manner, in accordance with past treaty practice of the United States.[203] The treaties assure in the first place that the property of nationals and companies of either party will receive within the territories of the other fair and equitable treatment[204] as well as "the most constant protection and security."[205] The aliens' premises (offices, factory plants, homes, and so on) are to be protected from "unlawful entry or molestation," while any official searches are to be made "according to law and

---

[201] *1959 Draft Convention*, article III. Cf. the cogent criticism of these provisions by Metzger, "Multilateral Conventions for the Protection of Private Foreign Investment," 9 *J. Pub. L.* 133, 139–43 (1960), and Schwarzenberger, "The Abs-Shawcross Draft Convention on Investments Abroad: A Critical Commentary," 9 *idem* 147, 156–60 (1960).

[202] On the virtual impossibility of defining with precision the meaning of "indirect" expropriation, see Metzger, *supra* note 201, at 157. And cf. also *supra* p. 54, note 74.

[203] Cf. Wilson, "Property-Protection Provisions in United States Commercial Treaties," 45 *Am. J. Int'l L.* 83 (1951), also in Wilson, *Treaties* 95 et seq.

[204] Some treaties use both adjectives, but the majority use only the second—"equitable." The variation seems to be of no great importance. Cf. treaty with Ireland, article V; treaty with Israel, article I. Similar provisions are found in all other treaties, save that with Japan. And cf., to the same effect, article 1(1) of the treaty between Germany and the Dominican Republic and article 1(1) of that between Germany and Italy.

[205] Cf. article VI(1) of the treaty with Denmark and corresponding articles in all other treaties. Certain variations as between treaties may be noted. The treaty with Ireland, article VIII(2), and that with Greece, article VII(2), accord, in addition, national and most-favored-nation treatment to alien property. In the treaties with Iran (article IV[2]) and Ireland (as cited) treatment in accordance with the standards of international law is provided; the treaty with Haiti, article VI(1), promises protection and security "under the law," that with France, article I, "full legal and judicial protection" and the treaty with Muscat and Oman, article IV(2), "all possible protection and security." And cf. the German treaty with the Dominican Republic, article 6(1), and that with Italy, same article.

with careful regard to the convenience of the occupants and the conduct of their business." [206] In most treaties, aliens are accorded national and most-favored-nation treatment with respect to such matters.[207] The parties to the treaties also undertake not to take "unreasonable or discriminatory measures" detrimental to the "legally acquired rights or interests" of aliens "in the enterprises which they have established, in their capital, or in the skills, arts of technology which they have supplied." [208]

In most FCN treaties, the inviolability of the property of foreign investors is established as a general rule: "Property of nationals and companies of either Party shall not be taken . . . except. . . ." [209] The exceptions to the rule, that is, the conditions for the legality of such a taking, refer both to the expropriating state's motives and to the payment of just compensation. The only acceptable reason for expropriation is "public purpose," [210] occasionally coupled with considerations of "social utility" [211] or of "due process." [212] The

[206] Treaty with Japan, article VI(2). Similar provisions in all the other treaties. In the treaties with Denmark, Greece and Ireland, the clause "according to law" is omitted. To the same effect as the majority of U.S. FCN treaties, article 6(2) of the treaty between Germany and the Dominican Republic.

[207] Cf. treaty with Japan, article VI(4). Similar provisions in most other treaties, with the exception of those with Ethiopia, Greece, Iran, and Muscat and Oman. National treatment only is accorded in the treaty with France, article IV(4).

[208] Treaty with Japan, article V(1). Identical provisions are found in most of the treaties. Others contain corresponding provisions with variations in the language; cf., e.g., article IV(1) of the treaty with France. To the wording quoted in the text compare article 11(1)(b) of the Havana Charter, quoted *supra* p. 164. And cf. article 6(3) of the German treaty with the Dominican Republic and the same article in the treaty with Italy.

[209] Cf., e.g., treaty with Greece, article VII(3); treaty with Japan, article VI(3). All of the U.S. treaties we are discussing contain such provisions with the exception of that with Uruguay. Cf. in this connection, the language in the German treaty with Italy, article 6(4): "Property of nationals and companies . . . shall be expropriated . . . only. . . ." But cf. article 6(4) of the German treaty with the Dominican Republic, following the American pattern.

[210] Or other expressions of the same general meaning, such as "public benefit" or "public interest." Cf. the treaty provisions cited *supra* note 209. This requirement is found in all treaties, except that with Ireland, which mentions only compensation. Cf. also article 6(4) of the treaty between Germany and Italy.

[211] Treaty with Nicaragua, article VI(4); and cf. the treaty between Germany and the Dominican Republic, article 6(4), mentioning "public utility or social interest."

[212] Treaty with Germany, article V(4). The German treaty cited in the preced-

provisions on compensation of the earlier postwar FCN treaties were rather brief and not very precise.[213] Recent treaties are more detailed and provide for "prompt" and "just" compensation, "representing the full equivalent of the property taken," "in effectively realizable form," and adequately provided for at the time of the taking.[214] These rules are applicable whenever property is wholly owned, directly or indirectly,[215] by nationals and companies of either party. Assurances are also given as to the conversion of the compensation into the investor's national currency and its transfer outside the expropriating state.[216]

With respect to the taking of their property, national and most-favored-nation treatment is accorded to foreign investors.[217] The same standards of treatment are applicable in the case of the taking of property owned in part by aliens.[218] The protection granted in

---

ing note provides for the application of the constitutional provisions of each state party concerning expropriation.

[213] Cf. treaty with Uruguay, article VIII(2); treaty with Ireland, article VIII(2); treaty with Ethiopia, article VIII(2). And compare the provisions in the last mentioned treaty with those of the otherwise very similar treaty with Iran (article IV[2]). The German treaty cited *supra*, note 211 refers only to "just indemnification," subject to judicial review.

[214] These requirements are contained in all treaties, with the exception of those mentioned in the preceding note. The precise language of the provisions varies. For instance, in the treaty with Israel, article VI(3), the requirement of "prompt" payment is omitted; some other treaties, e.g., that with France, article IV(3), provide for payment "without needless delay." Most treaties provide for compensation representing "the full equivalent of the property taken"; cf., e.g., article VI(3) of the treaty with Japan. But in some treaties the word "full" is omitted; cf., e.g., treaty with Germany, article V(4). It is difficult to state with any certainty to what extent the provisions' legal effects are affected by these variations.

The treaty between Germany and Italy, article 6(4), follows on this point the American model and requires in addition that the legality of expropriation and the amount of compensation should be subject to judicial review.

[215] Cf. treaty with Ireland, Protocol, para. 7; treaty with Japan, Protocol, para. 2; treaty with Greece, article VII(3) *in fine*. Similar provisions are found in the Protocols to all the treaties we have been discussing, with the exception of those with Ethiopia, Iran, and Uruguay.

This qualification makes it possible for a company owned by nationals of one of the parties but established in (and generally having the "nationality" of) a third country, to be compensated for the expropriation of its property by the other party to the treaty. See Walker, "Companies" in Wilson, *Treaties* 182, 201-2; Walker, "The Post-War Commercial Treaty Program of the United States," 73 *Pol. Sc. Qu.* 57, 69-70 (1958).

[216] Cf. *supra* pp. 156-57.   [217] Cf. *supra* note 207.

[218] Cf., e.g., treaty with Greece, article VII(4); treaty with Japan, article VI(4).

such a case is more limited, because it applies only to the taking of property into public ownership or control and is established by reference to contingent standards only, without mention of any noncontingent rules, for example, as to compensation.

With respect to the protection of foreign-owned property, the recent German treaty practice seems to follow closely the United States model.[219] On the other hand, the language and the organization, though perhaps not the degree of protection provided, in the recent British treaty with Iran differ considerably from those of the United States FCN treaties. Nationals and companies of each party are accorded "constant and complete protection and security for their persons and property" [220] and the parties undertake to accord to them "fair and equitable treatment" at all times, to "refrain from applying unreasonable or discriminatory measures that would impair their rights and interests" and to "ensure that their contractual rights are afforded effective means of enforcement in conformity with the applicable laws." [221] The foreign investors' premises are to be respected.[222] Finally, the treaty provides that nationals and companies of each party:

> shall receive equitable treatment . . . in respect of any measure of requisition, civil or military, or of disposal, limitation, restriction or expropriation affecting their property, rights and interests, or affecting the property, rights and interests of any company of the host state in which they own interests, and shall receive prompt, adequate and effective compensation for any such measure.[223]

They are accorded in this respect both national and most-favored-nation treatment. The same standards of treatment with respect to

---

In the treaty with Uruguay, article VII(3), national treatment only is accorded. The treaties with Ethiopia, France, Haiti, Iran, and Muscat and Oman do not contain such a provision.

According to the above mentioned provisions, the alien's interest should be "substantial" or even, according to the treaty with Israel, article VI(4), "controlling." See also, to the same effect as the American treaties, article 6(4) of the German treaty with Italy.

[219] Cf. *supra* notes 204–214, 218.

[220] Article 8(1). Compare the United States provision, *supra* note 205.

[221] Article 8(2). And cf. *supra* p. 168.   [222] Article 11. Cf. *supra* pp. 167–68.

[223] Article 15. Compare the American provisions, *supra* pp. 168–69.

expropriation of foreign-owned property are also provided in a number of treaties of Establishment between European states.[224]

Provision for a different kind of protection is found in a 1954 Agreement between Burma and Japan.[225] It is provided therein that Japan will supply Burma with "the services of the Japanese people and the products of Japan," by means of the formation of joint ventures between Japanese nationals and the Government of Burma or Burmese nationals. The agreement further provides (Article III) that at the time the individual contracts establishing such ventures are made, the Burmese Government may grant to the Japanese nationals assurances to the effect that their shares in the enterprises will not be expropriated or nationalized for a given length of time and it may also prescribe certain conditions under which such shares may be expropriated after the lapse of the period provided for.

Certain investment laws go even further in protecting the foreign investors' property against expropriation. The Greek statute states unequivocally:

The assets of enterprises established or substantially assisted financially . . . by the importation of foreign capital shall be exempt from any and all compulsory expropriation.[226]

In Thailand, approved industrial undertakings are guaranteed that "the State will not transfer private industrial establishment to State

---

[224] Cf. Convention of Establishment between France and Italy, of August 23, 1951, articles 4 and 5; 291 UN *Treaty Series* 143. Convention on Conditions of Residence and Navigation between France and Sweden, of February 16, 1954, articles 6(1) and 8; 228 *idem* 137. And cf. UN Document A/AC.97/5/Rev. 1, 27 December 1960, p. 182.

[225] Agreement for Reparations and Economic Cooperation, of November 5, 1954; 251 UN *Treaty Series* 215. Reported in detail in UN Document A/AC.97/5/Rev. 1, 27 December 1960, pp. 182–83.

[226] Greece, L.D. No. 2687 of October 22, 1953, article XI(1); cf. Lambadarios, "Greece," in *Legal Aspects* 233, 246. It should be noted that there have been certain expressions of doubt in Greece concerning the necessity, fairness (from the domestic investor's viewpoint), and constitutionality of so rigid a rule. Its rigidity is considerably strengthened by the extraordinary constitutional position of the law; cf. *supra* p. 121, note 208. See, on this issue, the brief comments by Lambadarios, "Protection accordée par le décret 2687/1953 aux investissements à longue échéance de capitaux venant de l'étranger," 7 *Rev. Hell. Droit Int'l* 219, 238 (1954).

ownership" while in Paraguay, new investments in coffee cultivation may be granted exemption from expropriation proceedings.[227] Declarations to the effect that no industry will be nationalized or otherwise expropriated have been made recently by several governments, including those of Malaya [228] and Viet-Nam.[229]

Several other governments, while not willing to grant such extensive promises, have expressed their readiness to grant to foreign investors exemptions from expropriation for a limited period of time. Thus, the Burmese Council of Ministers, in a statement of policy, has expressed its intention to "guarantee new enterprises against nationalization for an agreed period which will normally be not less than ten years." [230] India follows the same practice. Though no general statement to this effect appears to have been issued, the Indian Government has promised in special agreements with particular foreign investors not to expropriate their properties for a stipulated period of time.[231] A recent Indonesian statute provides that the Government of Indonesia may guarantee foreign investors against expropriation or nationalization for a period of up to twenty years, in the case of industrial enterprises, or up to thirty years, in the case of nonindustrial enterprises.[232] The Cambodian investment statute of May 1956 provides that the instrument of approval of the investment may guarantee against nationalization or expropriation

[227] Thailand, Announcement of the Revolutionary Party No. 33 (1958), in 9 *Am. J. Comp. L.* 498 (1960); Cf. also Koh, "Thailand," in *Legal Aspects* 526, 541. Identical provisions are included in the Industrial Investment Promotion Act of 1960, s. 18 (b), now in force. Paraguay, Decree Law No. 38 of March 31, 1954; cf. United States Dep't. of Commerce, *Investment in Paraguay* 22–23 (1954).

[228] Cf. UN Documents ECAFE/L.122, 12 March 1957, 11 and E/3128, 4 June 1958, ch. II, para. 78.

[229] Cf. UN Document E/3128, 4 June 1958, ch. II, para. 90.

[230] Burma, Statement of Policy of June 8, 1955, section 4(a). Similar, but less definite, views had been expressed in an earlier Resolution of the Burmese Economic Council (1949). The provision has apparently been incorporated in a subsequent statute; see Domke, "Foreign Nationalizations," 55 *Am. J. Int'l L.* 585, 592, n. 53 (1961).

[231] Cf. *supra* p. 127, note 228; Narayanan, "India," in *Legal Aspects* 249, 260–61.

[232] Indonesia, Act 78 of 1958, article 13. See also United States Dep't. of Commerce, *Investment in Indonesia* 2–3 (1956); Wijnberg, "Indonesia," in *Legal Aspects* 265, 273–74.

for a period of ten to twenty years after the importation of the capital.[233] Similar legislative provisions are in effect in the Republic of China (Taiwan) [234] and in that of South Korea.[235]

Instead of, or in addition to, promises of this sort, several investment laws give detailed assurances regarding the payment of fair compensation in case of expropriation and provide for facilities for its conversion into foreign currency and transfer to the foreign investors' home countries.[236] One should note, moreover, in this connection, that in many capital-importing states the matter of expropriation of private property, regardless of the nationality of its owner, is governed by constitutional provisions, making the prompt payment of compensation mandatory for the local executive.[237]

Provisions on Taxation

As has been noted, taxation constitutes a nonbusiness risk for the foreign investor only to the extent that it is discriminatory, excessive, or too uncertain. Accordingly, it is these potential problems in taxation that investment treaties and codes and, in part, investment laws tend to eliminate. The latter, however, often provide also for special tax incentives, that is, for privileges with respect to matters of taxation to be granted to all or some investors under certain conditions.

Investment codes and related proposals do not deal in any detail

[233] Cf. U.N. Document ECAFE/L.122, 12 March 1957, 35.

[234] See Koh "Republic of China," in *Legal Aspects* 155, 158.

[235] Cf. Koh "Korea," *idem* 334, 344; UN Document ECAFE/L.122, 12 March 1957, 106, note 3.

[236] Cf. Burma, Statement of June 8, 1955, section 4(b). India, Statement of April 6, 1949. Iran, Law on the Investment of Foreign Capital, of November 28, 1955, article 3; cf. Nasr, "Iran," in *Legal Aspects* 280, 290. Japan, Law No. 163 of 1950, article 17. Libya, Foreign Capital Investment Law of January 30, 1958, clause 8. Pakistan, Statement of November 1954. Malaya, Statement reported in UN Document E/3128, 4 June 1958, ch. II, para. 79.

[237] For a discussion of the provisions of the various constitutions, see Friedman, *Expropriation* 7–12; on French and English law, in particular, see Wortley, *Expropriation* 25 *et seq*. And cf. UN Document A/AC.97/5/Rev. 1, 27 December 1960, pp. 125 *et seq*.

with taxation. When they refer to it, it is in connection with the elimination of double taxation and the avoidance of discrimination. In addition to the "equitable treatment" promised to foreign investors with respect to all government measures, presumably including taxation,[238] the Economic Agreement of Bogota expressed the willingness of the signatory states to "liberalize" their tax laws in order to eliminate double taxation "and to avoid unduly burdensome and discriminatory taxation, without, however, creating international avenues for tax avoidance."[239] The ICC Code of Fair Treatment provides for national treatment of the foreign investors in matters of taxation[240] and advises the conclusion of bilateral agreements on double taxation.[241] The report of the European League for Economic Cooperation deals with the same two topics. It provides for national treatment of foreign investors with regard to fiscal matters[242] and states that in the proposed Charter of Fair Treatment for International Investments "double taxation will be abolished."[243]

The 1957 Draft Convention for the Mutual Protection of Private Property Rights dealt with only one of these issues. It provided that the freedom of foreign investors concerning property matters is not to be restricted by any laws or regulations resulting in the "levying of incommensurate taxes, duties and charges."[244] This provision was understood chiefly as referring to the need for total lack of discrimination against foreign investors.[245] No express reference to taxation is found in the 1959 Draft Convention on Investments Abroad. Tax measures might create problems under this convention only insofar as they are discriminatory or constitute in fact a form of indirect expropriation.[246]

The United States FCN treaties do not attempt to deal with the

---

[238] *Bogota Agreement*, article 22(3).   [239] *Idem* article 27(1).
[240] *ICC Code*, article 7.   [241] *Idem* article 8.
[242] E.L.E.C., *Common Protection for Private International Investments* 18 (1958).
[243] *Idem* at 19.   [244] *1957 Draft Convention*, article IV(3)(b).
[245] Cf. the comment by its authors, *idem* at 51.
[246] Cf. *1959 Draft Convention*, articles I and III.

bulk of the problems of taxation. They do not deal with any of
the questions which arise out of the uncertainty of tax legislation
in some states and they leave the numerous problems relating to
double taxation to be covered by a body of special agreements.[247]
They provide for most-favored-nation treatment to be accorded
to all nationals and companies of either party, while stating that
national treatment in all instances constitutes an "aim" of the
parties.[248] They do accord national treatment only to resident aliens
and to foreign nationals and companies engaged in business within
the territory of each party.[249] The treaties also provide for the
application of the principle of territoriality in taxing foreign companies and nonresident aliens, on the basis of a "reasonable" ap-
portionment of the respective shares of each country in the investors' income and capital.[250] Finally, the parties to the treaties
reserve their rights to enter into special arrangements with third
countries with respect to certain matters of taxation.[251]

The provisions of the recent treaty between the United Kingdom and Iran are to some extent similar to those just described.
However, while some differentiation is made between the host
state's residents and nonresidents,[252] all nationals and companies of
each party are to receive in the territory of the other party national
and most-favored-nation treatment with respect to taxation.[253]
The German treaties' provisions on taxation are shorter and more
schematic. No definite general pattern seems to have developed as

[247] For an inventory of agreements on double taxation and other international
tax matters, see United Nations, Department of Economic and Social Affairs,
Fiscal Division, *International Tax Agreements,* vol. VIII, World Guide to International Tax Agreements (1958).
[248] Cf. treaty with Germany, article XI(2) and (3); treaty with Iran, article VI(1).
Corresponding provisions are found in all FCN treaties. Note that the clause relating to national treatment being an aim of the parties is omitted from the treaties
with Ethiopia, France, Greece, Iran, Ireland, Muscat and Oman, and Uruguay.
[249] Cf. article XI(1) of the treaty with Germany; article XVI(1) of the treaty
with Greece; and provisions to that effect in all other treaties.
[250] Cf. treaty with Germany, article XI(4); treaty with Greece, article XVI(3);
and similar provisions in the other treaties.
[251] Cf. treaty with Germany, article XI(5); treaty with Greece, article XVI(4);
and corresponding provisions in the other treaties.
[252] Cf. article 10(3) and (4).   [253] Article 10(2) and (6).

yet. In one treaty, nationals and companies of each party are accorded in the territory of the other party national and most-favored-nation treatment with regard to taxation.[254] But in another of these treaties, only most-favored-nation treatment is accorded.[255]

Investment laws abound with provisions on taxation. This is true of those addressed solely to foreign investors as well as those addressed to both foreign and local investors.[256] In addition to general assurances of nondiscrimination in matters of taxation, such laws often contain promises of special treatment of investors through various sorts of arrangements. In the majority of cases, such promises are offered not to all investors but only to those who engage in certain special areas of business activity.

To reduce the uncertainty concerning the future tax burden, certain states offer to approved foreign investments a "freezing" of income tax rates or of some other taxes. The Greek investment law, for instance, provides for the possibility of granting to certain foreign investments

consolidation of the income tax rates in effect at the time of the issuance of the instrument of approval for a period of time not exceeding ten years, with provision for downward readjustment to the level of applicable rates in the event tax rates are lowered; or determination for a like period of a fixed rate of taxation on net or gross earnings which rate may be lower than tax rates in effect at any given time.[257]

According to the Chilean investment law, the foreign investor is guaranteed, through the instrument of approval, that the then existing situation with respect to taxes will constitute the maximum of his tax burden for the next ten years.[258] One should note that such promises do not necessarily result in the granting of a privileged

---

[254] Treaty with Italy, article 14.

[255] Treaty with the Dominican Republic, article 14.

[256] It is, however, true that some of the laws of the former type provide only for foreign exchange facilities and do not deal with matters of taxation. The reverse is true of many of the investment laws of the latter type.

[257] Greece, L.D. No. 2687 of October 22, 1953, article VIII(1)(a).

[258] Chile, Decree-Law No. 437 of February 2, 1954, article 5(b); cf. Aramayo, "Chile," in *Legal Aspects* 135, 139–40. Substantially similar provisions were enacted in Chile's new investment law, Decree-Law No. 258 of March 30, 1960, article 8.

position to foreign investors. They only assure them against the unpredictability of future changes.

Exemptions from certain taxes are often offered to foreign investors. In most instances, such exemptions are valid for a specified period of time, usually five to ten years from the date of investment. In some cases, exemptions are graduated over a number of years, the enterprises paying more taxes year by year, so that by the end of a period of time their tax burdens reach the normal levels effective in the capital-importing country.[259]

One of the exemptions most commonly found is that from customs duties for the importation of machinery, raw materials, and other goods necessary to the operation of the approved foreign-owned enterprise. Thus, the Greek law provides that under the instruments of approval issued to particular enterprises established by foreign capital and engaged in certain types of activities,[260] may be allowed, among other things,

Lowering of or exemption from customs duties, levies or other taxes and charges on imports of machinery, accessories, spare parts and tools, for a period not to exceed ten years.[261]

The Israeli investment law provides that any "goods intended for an approved investment and imported under a license [issued in accordance with the law's provisions] shall be exempt from the payment of customs duties . . . provided that guarantees have been given . . . that the goods will serve the purposes of the enterprise only." [262] Similar provisions are found in the legislation of several other countries, including Chile,[263] India,[264] Libya,[265] The Philippines,[266] and Thailand.[267]

[259] Cf. Friedmann and Pugh, "Comparative Analysis," *idem* 734, 741-42.

[260] "Primarily export manufacturing or mining enterprises, as well as enterprises established in the country for the first time whose operations save substantial amounts of foreign exchange annually." Greece, L.D. No 2687 of October 22, 1953, article VIII(1).

[261] *Idem*, article VIII(1)(b); cf. Lambadarios, "Greece," in *Legal Aspects* 233, 245.

[262] Israel, Law No. 30 of 5710-1950, as amended, s. 24(a); cf. Sher, "Israel," *idem* 292, 296.

[263] Chile, Decree-Law No. 258 of March 30, 1960, articles 5-7. See also Ecuador, Industrial Encouragement Act of June 21, 1957. Mexico, Law for the Development

Investment laws often promise total or partial exemption from income taxation. The Libyan investment law provides for a procedure whereby the Minister of Finance may "exempt projects which are considered as contributing to the country's economic development from such . . . income tax . . . as he thinks fit, and for a period specified by him." [268] In India, company profits from new industrial undertakings, up to 6 percent of the total capital employed, are exempted from income tax, during the first five years of the undertaking's operation.[269] Similarly, Lebanese law provides for the exemption of approved enterprises from any taxation on their income, for a period of six years from the date of their creation.[270] Provisions to the same effect may be found in the relevant legislation of Israel,[271] Pakistan,[272] and several other countries.[273] The investment laws of capital-receiving states provide,

---

of New and Necessary Industries of January 4, 1955, article 14, as reported in World Tax Series, *Taxation in Mexico* 371 (1957). Guatemala, Industrial Development Law, Decree No. 1317 of October 23, 1959, article 7.

[264] Cf. World Tax Series, *Taxation in India* 130 (1960); Narayanan, "India," in *Legal Aspects* 249, 260. See also, Indonesia, Statement of December 8, 1955; cf. Wijnberg, "Indonesia," in *Legal Aspects* 265, 273.

[265] Libya, Foreign Capital Investment Law of January 30, 1958, clause 4(a). Morocco, Dahir No. 1-60-383 of December 31, 1960, articles 4-9.

[266] The Philippines, Tax Exemption Law, Republic Act No. 901; cf. Monzon, "Philippines," in *Legal Aspects* 414, 418-19.

[267] Thailand, Announcement of the Revolutionary Party No. 33 (1958), articles 2(1) and 3(1), in 9 *Am. J. Comp. L.* 498-99 (1960); and cf. Koh, "Thailand," in *Legal Aspects* 526, 528, 536, and sections 19 (2) and 20 (2) of the Industrial Investment Promotion Act of 1960 now in effect.

[268] Libya, Foreign Capital Investment Law of January 30, 1958, clause 4(a).

[269] Cf. [Indian] National Council of Applied Economic Research, *Taxation and Foreign Investment* 41-42 (2d ed. 1958); World Tax Series, *Taxation in India* 283 (1960).

[270] Lebanon, Law of February 12, 1954, article 1.

[271] Israel, Law No. 30 of 5710-1950, as amended, s. 9-16; cf. Sher, "Israel," in *Legal Aspects* 292, 299-300.

[272] Cf. Ishaque, "Pakistan," *idem* 397, 412.

[273] Cf., e.g., The Philippines, Tax Exemption Law, Republic Act No. 901; cf. Monzon, "Philippines," *idem* 414, 418-19. Thailand, Industrial Investment Promotion Act of 1960, s. 19(3). Mexico, Law for the Development of New and Necessary Industries of January 4, 1955, article 14; cf. World Tax Series, *Taxation in Mexico* 370-71 (1957). Puerto Rico, Industrial Exemption Act of 1948, and Industrial Incentive Act of 1954, 13 *Laws of Puerto Rico Annotated* s. 221 et seq. Guatemala, Industrial Development Law, Decree No. 1317 of October 23, 1959, article 6.

moreover, for exemptions from a variety of other taxes, such as municipal and local taxes,[274] property taxes,[275] and taxes of several other kinds.[276] Most states offer also to foreign investors special tax arrangements, such as accelerated depreciation allowances [277] and other "accommodations" of this sort.

A last feature which is common to several investment laws is the partial or total exemption, sometimes only for a limited period, of the salaries of foreign managerial and technical personnel of foreign-owned enterprises from the income tax effective in the capital-importing state. In India, foreign "technicians," whose employment contract has received governmental approval, are exempted from income tax for the first three years of their employment in the country.[278] The exemption applies to strictly technical, and not to managerial, personnel. Employees of foreign enterprises which are not engaged in business in India are also exempted from income tax on any part of their salary earned in India, provided their stay there does not exceed three months.[279] Similar conditions obtain in Pakistan, where foreign technicians, serving under an approved employment contract, are granted a two-year exemption

[274] Cf., e.g., Greece, L.D. No. 2687 of October 22, 1953, article VIII(1)(c). Israel, Law No. 30 of 5710-1950, as amended, section 7. Libya, Foreign Capital Investment Law of January 30, 1958, clause 4(b). Brazil, as reported in World Tax Series, *Taxation in Brazil* 325 (1957).

[275] Cf., e.g., Israel, Law No. 30 of 5710-1950, as amended, sections 2–8.

[276] Such as exemptions from various stamp taxes and fees in connection with contracts, transfer of property, etc. Cf., e.g., Israel, Law No. 30 of 5710-1950, as amended, section 17. Greece, L.D. No. 2687 of October 22, 1953, article VIII(1)(d); cf. Lambadarios, "Greece," in *Legal Aspects* 233, 245; and cf. now the extensive privileges granted to large-scale investments by Law No. 4171 of 1961. Or exemptions from taxes on foreign exchange remittances; cf., e.g., World Tax Series, *Taxation in Brazil* 84–85 (1957).

[277] Cf., e.g., Israel, Law No. 30 of 5710-1950, as amended, s. 10; cf. Sher, "Israel," in *Legal Aspects* 292, 300. Pakistan, as reported in Ishaque, "Pakistan," *idem* 397, 411–12. India, as reported in [Indian] National Council of Applied Economic Research, *op. cit. supra* note 269, at 36–38; World Tax Series, *Taxation in India* 282 *et seq.* (1960). Ecuador, Industrial Encouragement Law of June 21, 1957.

[278] Cf. [Indian] National Council of Applied Economic Research, *op. cit. supra* note 269, at 10–12. A more limited exemption is available to foreign technicians whose employment contract has not received the approval of the government; cf. World Tax Series, *Taxation in India* 149 (1960).

[279] Cf. [Indian] National Council of Applied Economic Research, *op. cit. supra* note 269, at 140–41; World Tax Series, *Taxation in India* 149 (1960).

from all taxes.[280] In Israel, on the other hand, foreign experts are not granted complete exemption from taxation. If, however, they are employed with the approval of the Investment Center, the government body in charge of foreign investments, they may be taxed at a lower income tax rate.[281]

The Settlement of Disputes

An important problem arising in connection with state promises to foreign investors is that of the machinery for the settlement of any related disputes. Provisions concerning such machinery do not constitute, strictly speaking, promises of the type we are studying here. They are, however, highly important because they determine in part the concrete effect of such promises. The importance of this factor has been recognized by the drafters of the recently proposed investment codes as well as by the states which have concluded bilateral treaties dealing with investment.

Both the ITO Charter and the Bogota Economic Agreement stressed the role of diplomatic rather than strictly judicial methods. The former instrument provided for consultation between governments within or outside the Organization, for discussions of the issues in various organs of the Organization and for eventual arbitration, provided the states concerned agreed to it.[282] The Bogota Agreement, in addition to provisions on consultation between governments and possible submission of the disputes to the Council of the Organization of American States,[283] also referred to the "Inter-American Peace System," established by the American Treaty of Pacific Settlement ("Act of Bogota") of April 30, 1948. This instrument provided in great detail for procedures of consultation, arbitration, and recourse to the International Court of Justice.[284]

[280] Cf. Ishaque, "Pakistan," in *Legal Aspects* 397, 412.
[281] Israel, Law No. 30 of 5710-1950, as amended, s. 13; cf. Sher, "Israel," *idem* 292, 300.
[282] *Havana Charter*, articles 92–97.   [283] *Bogota Agreement*, article 38.
[284] *Idem*, article 38(2), in conjunction with chapters IV and V of the Treaty on Pacific Settlement.

Some of the other proposals go so far as to suggest the creation of a special judicial body, which would have jurisdiction to deal with any dispute arising in connection with foreign investments.[285] As early as 1939, the League of Nations Committee for the Study of International Loan Contracts suggested the creation of an International Loan Tribunal, to deal with disputes between states and bondholders.[286] In 1949, the ICC Code of Fair Treatment provided for the creation of an International Court of Arbitration to which any differences which might arise between the states party to the proposed code and which were not settled "within a short and reasonable period by direct negotiation or by any other form of conciliation" were to be referred.[287] The determination of the details of the working and composition of this court were left to the negotiating governments.[288] It was not made clear whether the court would be a permanent judicial body, similar to the International Court of Justice, or would in fact constitute but a blueprint for a series of *ad hoc* tribunals, on the model of the Hague Court of Arbitration.

Some of the arguments for the creation of a special judicial body are stated in the report of the British Parliamentary Group for World Government.[289] The report admits that it would be simpler to refer all related disputes to one of the already existing bodies, such as the International Court of Justice. It points out, however, that in such a case and in view of the statutes of these bodies, no individual investor would be allowed to bring his case before the

---

[285] For a thorough survey of official and unofficial suggestions and attempts, see Sohn, "Proposals for the Establishment of a System of International Tribunals," in *International Trade Arbitration* 63 (Domke ed., 1958). For certain other suggestions by individual scholars, see Re, "Nationalization and the Investment of Capital Abroad," 42 *Georgetown L.J.* 44, 56–58 (1953); Carlston, *Law and Structures of Social Action* 168–71 (1956); Lee, "Proposal for the Alleviation of the Effects of Foreign Expropriatory Decrees Upon International Investments," 36 *Can. Bar Rev.* 351, 357–59 (1958).

[286] League of Nations, Committee for the Study of International Loan Contracts, *Report* (1939).

[287] *ICC Code*, article 13.   [288] *Idem*, article 14.

[289] Parliamentary Group for World Government, *A World Investment Convention?* 18–19 (1959).

court. The report considers this limitation inadvisable insofar as investment disputes are concerned. The creation of a new judicial body is therefore proposed, which would specialize in the problems of international investment. Its permanent seat would be in one of the underdeveloped countries, and it might even hold sessions in several countries, somewhat in the manner of the British High Court on Circuit.

The majority of the investment codes do not seem to favor the creation of a special international tribunal. The evolution of the proposals of the German Society to Advance the Protection of Foreign Investments provides an interesting illustration of a change of opinion on this point. The 1957 Draft Convention provided for the creation of an International Court to deal with the legal disputes arising over the application of the convention.[290] The court was to be a permanent one, composed of members appointed by the states party to the convention for a specified period of time. Its competence would not depend on the previous exhaustion of local remedies. The court was to determine the unlawful character of measures in contravention of the convention and could order the imposition of a number of sanctions.[291] The convention also provided for the creation of Arbitration Committees to decide problems of compensation or substitution arising under the terms of the convention.[292] These committees would be special *ad hoc* bodies competent to deal with the economic matters arising in connection with expropriations and other measures. Lack of prompt compliance with their decisions would constitute an unlawful act against which the International Court might apply the sanctions at its disposal.[293]

The Shawcross Draft's provisions on the settlement of disputes were rather inadequate. Any disputes not settled by diplomatic means were to be submitted to the International Court of Justice.[294]

[290] *1957 Draft Convention*, article X(1); and cf. the comments to it, *idem* 59–61.
[291] *Idem*, article XI; and cf. *infra* p. 229.
[292] *Idem*, article X(2), and comments to it, *idem* 59–61.
[293] *Idem*, article XI. And cf. *infra* pp. 229 *et seq*.
[294] Cf. Brandon, "An International Investment Code: Current Plans," 1959 *J. Business L.* 7, 13–14.

The 1959 Draft Convention went further than that but stopped short of the 1957 Draft's proposals. In an Annex to the Convention, a detailed procedure is set out for the formation of special arbitration tribunals to deal with each particular dispute.[295] If the parties to a dispute do not agree to submit it to arbitration, the dispute may be brought to the International Court of Justice.

The proposals of the European League for Economic Cooperation follow roughly similar lines.[296] The creation of a special permanent tribunal is expressly rejected, on the grounds that it would deprive the proceedings of the necessary flexibility. It is then proposed that a list of arbitrators be drawn up composed of experts in financial and economic as well as legal matters. Alternatively, the arbitrators could be named in advance in each investment contract to be concluded between a foreign investor and the host country's government.

It is to be noted that most of the recent proposals provide for the possibility of recourse of private parties to the court or arbitration tribunal to be created.[297] In one case, this consideration is treated as the determining factor in the choice between a special tribunal and the existing ones.[298] In other cases, the necessity for such recourse is stressed,[299] or it is taken as granted.[300]

This need was emphasized in the 1957 Draft Convention, which provided that private individuals as well as states would be entitled to the rights under it.[301] In the accompanying commentary, it was stated, somewhat cryptically, that "this individualization of rights under the Convention will do much to strengthen private responsibility." [302] It would also eliminate the individual's dependence upon

---

[295] *1959 Draft Convention*, article VII and Annex to the Convention.

[296] E.L.E.C., *Common Protection for Private International Investments* 25–27 (1958).

[297] Such provision is not to be found in the ITO Charter, the Bogota Economic Agreement, the ICC Code of Fair Treatment, and the draft convention proposed to the OEEC by the Swiss Government.

[298] Cf. *supra* p. 181, note 289.

[299] Cf. Council of Europe Consultative Assembly Document 1027, 8 September 1959, at 19.

[300] Cf. ELEC, *op. cit. supra* note 296, at 20, 26.

[301] *1957 Draft Convention*, article IX; cf. *supra* p. 81.   [302] *Idem*, at 59.

the espousal of his claim by the state of his nationality. These provisions were included in an importantly modified form in the 1959 Draft Convention on Investments Abroad.[303] The right of individuals to have recourse to the arbitral tribunals to be instituted under the convention were made contingent upon an "optional clause." Any state party to the convention may file a declaration to the effect that it accepts the tribunal's jurisdiction in respect of claims by nationals of one or more parties.[304]

None of the bilateral investment treaties contains any provision regarding the access of private persons to international jurisdictions. Some of them, however, deal with the enforcement of arbitration agreements between private parties. All recent FCN treaties of the United States, with two exceptions,[305] provide that no arbitration agreement or award is to be deemed unenforceable or invalid merely because the arbitration is to take place or the award was rendered in a foreign country, or because one (or more) of the arbitrators is an alien.[306] In the treaty between Germany and the Dominican Republic, it is provided that the nationals of each party will receive on the part of the other, national treatment with respect to their exercising the functions of arbitrator.[307]

All of the treaties provide for the settlement of disputes which may arise between the parties concerning the treaties' application or interpretation. The United States FCN treaties give precedence to consultation between governments, as the first step toward any settlement. Recourse may be had to the International Court of

---

[303] *1959 Draft Convention,* article VII(2). The Shawcross draft did not provide for the direct access of private parties to international judicial proceedings; cf. Brandon, *supra* note 294, at 13–14.

[304] Cf. the authors' comments, 9 *J. Publ. L.* 119, 121 (1960) and the critical observations in Schwarzenberger, "The Abs-Shawcross Draft Convention on Investments Abroad: A Critical Commentary," *idem* 147, 162–63.

[305] The treaties with Ethiopia and Muscat and Oman.

[306] Cf., e.g., treaty with Germany, article VI(2); and for some variants, treaty with Iran, article III(3); treaty with The Netherlands, article V(2). Provisions to the same effect are found in all other recent FCN treaties (with the exceptions noted *supra* note 305). Cf. Walker, "Commercial Arbitration in United States Treaties," 11 *Arbitr. J.* 68 (1956); Walker, "United States Treaty Policy on Commercial Arbitration—1946-1957," in *International Trade Arbitration* 49 (Domke ed., 1958).

[307] Article 7(2).

Justice, if all other means of settlement, including arbitration, are unsuccessful.[308] The relevant provision of the British treaty with Iran follows almost identical lines, though no emphasis is placed upon settlement by consultation between governments.[309]

The German treaties are more elaborate in their provisions. In the treaty with the Dominican Republic, the parties undertake first to consider "in good will" the objections which either of them might raise regarding the treaty's application.[310] They provide further for the establishment of a consultative Mixed Commission, composed of three representatives of each of the parties, which is to convene at the request of either party.[311] The governments of the parties are to submit any questions concerning the execution of the treaty and not resolved by direct diplomatic negotiations, to the Mixed Commission, which will study them with a view to facilitating their solution and will prepare related reports.[312] Any dispute not resolved by these methods should be submitted to arbitration or, if neither party agrees to it, to the International Court of Justice.[313] The treaty with Italy does not provide for the establishment of a Mixed Commission. If any dispute cannot be settled by diplomatic negotiations, it is to be submitted to the International Court of Justice, if the parties agree to it, otherwise to an arbitration tribunal, at the request of one of the parties.[314] The treaty provides in detail for the constitution and procedure of the arbitration tribunal.

The agreements concluded by the United States concerning the application of the investment guarantee program [315] also provide for a procedure for the settlement of any disputes which might arise after the subrogation of the United States to an investor's

[308] Cf. treaty with Japan, article XXIV; treaty with Greece, article XXVI; and similar provisions in all other treaties. The formulation in article XXVII of the treaty with Germany is a little different, arbitration being given a more important role; but the provision in para. 24 of the Protocol to the same treaty serves to bring it in line with the others.

[309] Article 32.   [310] Article 23(1).   [311] Article 23(2) and (5).

[312] Article 23(3) and (4).   [313] Article 24.

[314] Article 39. Note the curious reversal of the effect of the parties' attitude in determining recourse to arbitration or to the International Court of Justice in the two treaties.

[315] Cf. supra pp. 103–6.

rights. If direct negotiations between the two governments fail to bring about a settlement, the dispute is to be brought to arbitration before a single arbitrator, who is appointed by the mutual agreement of the parties or, if they fail to agree, by the President of the International Court of Justice.[316]

Most investment laws do not contain detailed provisions on the settlement of disputes. But there are some exceptions. The Greek investment law, for instance, provides for the settlement by arbitration of any disputes arising between the Greek government and foreign investors over the interpretation and application of instruments of approval issued by virtue of this law.[317] The procedure to be followed is not described in detail in the statute itself, but it may be found in the particular instruments of approval. One arbitrator (or, in some cases, two) is to be appointed by each of the parties, within certain prescribed periods of time. A third (or fifth) arbitrator who, according to the statutory provision, may be a foreign national, is then elected by those already appointed. If they are unable to agree, the "superarbiter" is appointed either by the President of the Areopagus (the Greek Court of Cassation) [318] or, whenever the investor involved is an alien or a foreign corporation, by the President of the Permanent Court of Arbitration at The Hague.[319] The arbitrators' decision is final and without appeal, binding upon both the Greek Government and the foreign investor.

[316] Cf., e.g., agreement with Pakistan, May 26, 1955, para. 3(c), 6 U.S.T. 2045; agreement with Bolivia, September 23, 1955, para. 3(c), 6 *idem* 3949; agreement with Turkey, January 15, 1957, para. 3(c), 8 *idem* 202. But see the agreement with Colombia, July 14 and November 18, 1955, 6 *idem* 3932.

[317] Greece, L.D. No. 2687 of October 22, 1953, article XII.

[318] Cf. article 9 of the Royal Decree of March 26/April 4, 1955, concerning the approval of the importation of capital from abroad by virtue of Legislative Decree 2687/1953 by the corporation VIELEP, 1955 *Ephimeris tis Kyverniseos* [Official Journal] Fasc. 1, No. 82, 517; article 8 of Royal Decree of May 9/11, 1957, concerning the approval of the importation of capital from abroad . . . by the Greek corporation Olympic Airways, S.A. (A. S. Onassis and others), 1957 *idem* Fasc. 1, No. 83, 560. In both instances the investor was a Greek corporation.

[319] Cf. article 11 of the Royal Decree of May 30/June 23, 1956, concerning the approval of the importation of capital from abroad . . . by the American corporation Kennecott Copper Corporation, 1956 *idem* Fasc. 1, No. 144, 1427. The investor in this case was a foreign corporation.

Provisions on arbitration are also found in a number of countries in their legislation concerning the development of petroleum resources.[320] In India, under the Petroleum Concession Rules in effect, disputes between the Government and the licensee regarding the lease or license, the royalties, any alleged breaches or the amount of compensation to be paid by the government upon acquisition of the concession, are to be submitted to arbitration.[321] The related Pakistani legislation provides for arbitration with respect to disputes arising over certain specified questions, including the cancellation or renewal of petroleum leases or licenses and the amount to be paid by the Government in the case of purchase of the plant after termination of the lease. The Government and the licensee appoint one arbitrator each; if the two arbitrators disagree, an umpire is appointed, who has to be a judge of the Federal Court of Pakistan.[322] Similar provisions may be found in the petroleum laws of Greece,[323] Libya,[324] Morocco,[325] Iran,[326] and the Federation of Mali.[327]

Though not very common in investment laws, provisions on arbitration are frequently included in agreements between states and foreign nationals or companies. They usually describe in detail the procedure to be followed in case of dispute. Many recent agreements follow, with small variations, the pattern of the relevant pro-

---

[320] Recent surveys of relevant legislation are found in Sarre and Unler, "Modern Oil Laws," 1960 *J. Business L.* 161, 182–86; Domke, "International Arbitration of Commercial Disputes," in Southwestern Legal Foundation, *Proceedings of the 1960 Institute on Private Investments Abroad* 131, 167–68 (1960); United Nations, Office of Legal Affairs, *Survey of Mining Legislation* 60–61 (1957); UN Document A/AC.97/5, 15 December 1959, ch. I, para. 63–67, reprinted in 15 *Arbitr. J.* 80 (1960).

[321] India, Petroleum Concession Rules, 1949, as amended, rules 64, 65; as reported in UN Office of Legal Affairs, *op. cit. supra* note 320, at 60.

[322] Pakistan, Petroleum (Production) Rules, 1949, as amended, rule 40; reported *idem*, at 60–61.

[323] Greece, Law No. 3948 of 1959, re: Reconnaissance, Exploration and Exploitation of Liquid and Gaseous Hydrocarbons.

[324] Libya, Petroleum Law, 1955, Law No. 25 of 1955, as amended, article 20 and Second Schedule. Cf. UN Office of Legal Affairs, *op. cit. supra* note 320, at 60, and the other studies cited *supra* note 320.

[325] Dahir No. 1-58-227 of July 21, 1958, article 39; as reported in UN Document A/AC.97/5/Rev. 1, 27 December 1960, p. 74.

[326] Iran, Petroleum Law of July 31, 1957, article 14; cf. *ibidem*.

[327] Cf. Sarre and Unler, *supra* note 320, at 185–86.

vision of the 1954 Agreement between Iran, the Iranian Oil Consortium and the National Iranian Oil Company (NIOC).[328] This agreement provides for initial attempts at conciliation through consultation between the parties or other friendly methods of settlement. When such methods fail, a Mixed Conciliation Commission is to be established. Procedures of arbitration are also provided. In this connection, the agreement distinguishes the disputes which relate to technical matters from those of more general import. In the former case, the parties may request the help of two Swiss institutions (specializing in technical matters and accountancy, respectively) in appointing experts to decide the issues.[329] In the case of disputes of a general character, a more elaborate procedure is to be followed. The parties will first appoint an equal number of arbitrators each. If one of the parties fails to appoint its arbitrators, or if the arbitrators cannot agree on the appointment of an umpire, the arbitrators or umpire will be appointed by the President of the International Court of Justice.[330] If the President refuses, or is unable, to make the appointment, the request should be addressed successively to the International Court's Vice-President, the President of the Swiss Federal Tribunal,[331] and the Presidents of the highest courts of Denmark, Sweden, and Brazil,[332] in that order.

[328] Article 44. Text in 2 Hurewitz, *Diplomacy in the Near and Middle East* 348 (1956). And cf. Sarre and Unler, *supra* note 320, at 184.

[329] Compare Agreement between the Greek State and the Polish firm CECOP concerning the establishment of a sugar processing plant, of March 3, 1960, article 34; 1960 *Ephimeris tis Kyverniseos* Fasc. 1, No. 44, 407 (expert advisors of arbitrators to be of Swiss or Swedish nationality).

[330] Compare the Greek concession cited *infra* note 335; the Libyan oil concessions cited *infra* note 333; Convention between the Government of Iraq and the Turkish Petroleum Co. Ltd., of March 14, 1925, article 40; text in 2 Hurewitz, *op. cit. supra* note 328, 131. And cf. the concession agreements cited in UN Document A/AC.97/5/Rev. 1, 27 December 1960, pp. 74–75.

[331] Compare Agreement between Pan American Petroleum Corporation and the NIOC, of April 24, 1958, article 41; Agreement between Sapphire Petroleums, Ltd., and the NIOC, of June 1958, article 41. The Agreement between AGIP Mineraria and the NIOC, of August 3, 1957, article 44, accords the power of appointment to the President of the Cantonal Tribunal at Geneva, to begin with, then to the President of the same tribunal at Lausanne, and the Presidents of the higher courts of other states, as indicated in text immediately *infra*.

[332] Compare the provisions of the agreements cited in the proceeding note.

Though the general pattern in most other recent concession agreements follows similar lines, several variations may be noted. In some agreements, it is provided that the umpire cannot be a national of the host state or of the investor's state of nationality.[333] In others, a senior judge of the host country is the party competent to appoint the arbitrators or the umpire or is himself designated as the umpire, when the parties fail to agree otherwise.[334] A recent concession contract between the Greek Government and a subsidiary of Standard Oil of New Jersey provides only for the procedure to be followed in arbitrations involving serious matters, such as the possibility of the concessionaire's being penalized by forfeiture of the concession.[335] Other matters are to be governed by the general provisions on arbitration of the Greek Petroleum Law.[336]

[333] Cf. the Libyan oil concessions (1955) cited in Domke, *supra* note 320, at 168.

[334] Cf. the situation in Pakistan, *supra* note 322. See also the Agreement between the Greek State and the Polish firm CECOP, cited *supra* note 329 (President of Athens Court of Appeal appoints missing arbitrators, President of Areopagus to serve as umpire, if no one else is chosen by the arbitrators).

[335] Agreement for the Exploration for and Development of Liquid and Gaseous Hydrocarbons in Greece, between the Greek Government and ESSO Hellenic, Inc., of December 11, 1959, article 26; 1960 *Ephimeris tis Kyverniseos* Fasc. 1, No. 71, 705.

[336] As cited *supra* note 323.

7

The Legal Character
of State Promises

BEFORE examining the concrete effects of the promises of states to foreign investors, it would be useful to study briefly the more theoretical question of their legal character. This is not a search for a chimerical "legal nature" of the promises in question, nor a dispute on definitions.[1] It is rather a preliminary theoretical investigation of the field.

Not all forms of state promises present difficult problems in this connection. Promises made by treaty, either bilateral or multilateral, raise no special issues. FCN treaties and multilateral conventions are evidently instruments of public international law. They are agreements between states under public international law, basically contractual in nature, which impose certain obligations on and accord certain rights to the participating states. Though numerous theoretical questions may and do exist as to the exact meaning and content of the term "treaty," [2] these are not peculiar to the promises studied

[1] For there is no doubt that most of the disputes on the "legal nature" of concepts are due to differences in the original definitions. See, on this point, the thoughtful observations of Professor (now Judge) Jean Spiropoulos in his *Théorie générale du droit international public* 1–24 and *passim* (1930). See also the interesting studies contributed by the logical positivists, such as Weldon, *The Vocabulary of Politics* 17–20, 61–69 (1953); Williams, "International Law and the Controversy Concerning the Word 'Law,'" 22 *Brit. Yb. Int'l L.* 146, 158 *et seq.* (1945); Dias, "Mechanism of Definition as Applied to International Law," 1954 *Cambridge L.J.* 215.

[2] Cf., e.g., Chailley, *La nature juridique des traités internationaux selon le droit*

here. If the treatment promised by treaty to the nationals of the other party to it is not accorded, this constitutes a breach of an international agreement and entails the consequences thereof. Questions may be raised as to the precise legal effects of such instruments, but there can be no doubt as to their legal character.

Neither does there arise any problem as to the legal character of the contracts of guarantee by virtue of which a capital-exporting state insures the foreign investments of its nationals against certain nonbusiness risks. Despite the important international elements which are present in investment guarantee programs as a whole,[3] the particular contracts belong entirely to the municipal law of the guaranteeing state. The performance by this state of its contracts with its own nationals is a matter governed by municipal law. Therefore if the capital-exporting state refuses to perform its contracts with its nationals, its international responsibility will not be engaged.

It is when we study the promises given by capital-receiving states to individual foreign investors by means of special instruments that several complicated questions arise. The legal character of such promises is sometimes difficult to determine with any precision. There is no doubt that, in many instances, these promises belong entirely to the municipal law system of the host state. In other cases, this is not so clear. Similarly, in several instances, such promises clearly constitute unilateral administrative acts of the state involved, with few if any contractual elements.[4] In several other cases, however, the contractual elements are of great importance, so that the instruments cannot realistically be considered as purely unilateral state acts. It may be that in still other cases, the instruments are of an entirely contractual character. The extreme cases do not concern us here. We are dealing rather with the peculiar cases where the instruments involved present both contractual and noncontractual

---

contemporain (1932); Frangulis, *Théorie et pratique des traités internationaux* 5–29 (1934); Houlard, *La nature juridique des traités internationaux* 18–93 (1936); 2 Hyde, *International Law* 1369–73 (1945); Jessup, *A Modern Law of Nations* 123–56 (1949).

[3] Cf. *supra* p. 107.   [4] Cf. *supra* p. 123.

characteristics. It is to these *sui generis* cases that the present chapter is devoted.

Contractual and Noncontractual Elements

It has already been noted that there are three main types of instruments by means of which states give specific guarantees to foreign investors, namely, concession agreements, guarantee contracts and instruments of approval issued by virtue of investment laws.[5] These types of instruments have certain important common elements. They all involve two parties, one of which is a state or a public authority, the other being as a rule [6] a private person, individual or corporation.[7] These instruments present strong similarities in their general contents. Through them, the state grants to private persons certain rights and powers which normally belong to the state. For instance, private persons are permitted to exploit state-owned mineral resources. In several cases, the state may not actually grant its powers to the private persons, but it may undertake to refrain from exercising some of its powers with respect to such persons. In such cases, the latter do not themselves exercise the state's powers, but they nevertheless profit from their not being

[5] For definitions and comparisons, see *supra* pp. 125–28.

[6] When states do participate in concession agreements as concessionaires, they usually do so through a "private" corporation under their control to which the concession is granted. Cf. the case of the Chinese Eastern and the Southern Manchurian Railways and that of the Anglo-Iranian Oil Company. It is interesting to note, with regard to this last, that nowhere in its pleadings before the International Court of Justice did the British Government refer to its control of the Company.

The case of the Panama Canal, where the concessionaire is the United States, is exceptional. The extensive terms of the concession agreement seem to place the concession halfway between an economic concession of the type studied here and a cession of sovereignty over a territory; see, Convention between the United States and Panama of November 18, 1903, 33 U.S. Stat. 2234, and its analysis in Padelford, *The Panama Canal in Peace and War* 45–64 (1942). As such cases are quite exceptional and, for the purposes of this study, largely irrelevant, the term "concession" will be used in the following to refer only to economic concessions to private persons. Cf. Develle, *La concession en droit international* 26 (1936).

[7] For the purposes of the present discussion, the nationality of the other party is immaterial. Instruments of this type may be concluded between a state and aliens or between the state and its own nationals. We are here dealing with the former case.

exercised by the state. A state may, for instance, grant to private persons exemptions from general taxation, or it may undertake not to expropriate their property. The effect is in both cases the same, for the state's promises in fact limit its rights and powers toward certain persons, to the latter's benefit.

There is no doubt that strong contractual elements are present in instruments of this type. An indication to this effect is found in the language of the instruments themselves or of the legislation relating to them. In the Chilean investment law it is stated:

The public instrument referred to in the preceding article will be in the nature of a contract, in which there shall be understood to be fully incorporated all the benefits, privileges, and exemptions of the Supreme Decree approving the investment. Consequently, a natural or juridical person coming within the purview of its provisions shall enjoy the benefits, exemptions, and privileges for the time and under the conditions accorded him, and these may be amended only with the consent of both parties.

However, the President of the Republic may, by means of a decree issued through the Ministry of Economy, cancel any or all of the privileges, benefits, and exemptions granted when it has been proved that the investor or beneficiary has not complied with the provisions of the decree approving the investment.[8]

Similarly, the Preamble of the Industrial Tax Exemption Act, 1948, of Puerto Rico states:

the Legislature . . . declares that it considers all tax exemptions granted under the provisions of [this Act] as being in the nature of a contract or agreement between the Government of Puerto Rico and the industry receiving the benefit of the exemption. . . .[9]

And the Greek investment law, though not employing, as a rule, such terms as the above,[10] declares clearly that the instrument of approval of the investment is "irrevocable" and constitutes

[8] Chile, Decree-Law No. 258 of March 30, 1960, article 25.
[9] Puerto Rico, Industrial Exemption Act, 1948, 13 *Laws of Puerto Rico Annotated* s. 221.
[10] More accurately, while any precise qualification of the instrument's legal character is avoided in the law as a whole, the term "contract" is used in one instance, probably by inadvertence; cf. Greece, L.D. No. 2687 of October 22, 1953, article IV.

the guarantee of the Greek Government vis-à-vis the foreign investor to the effect that his investment shall thereafter be subject inalterably to the status established by the present Legislative Decree. Modification of these terms and conditions shall be permitted only with the consent of the foreign investor. . . .[11]

The contractual character of such promises receives more emphasis in the case of guarantee contracts concluded in the absence of general investment laws. Thus, in Nicaragua, the special instruments promising favorable treatment to foreign investors have been described by the competent government agency as "agreements." [12] The exchange of letters through which the Indian Government granted "assurances" to three foreign oil companies is considered, according to a note in the official publication of the texts, as constituting "the agreement between the Government and the Companies." [13] The term "contract" is also currently used with respect to concession agreements.

The use of such terms is, of course, no proof of the "contractual" character of the state promises in question. The name is but an indication of the way in which some governments and, probably, some investors, as well, regard these promises. Regardless of the term used, the character of a legal instrument must be determined by its substance.

The substantive content of the instruments examined presents important contractual characteristics. The conclusion of such instruments is often preceded by extensive negotiations between the state and the investors. Partly as a result of this, the promises granted are often highly specific, with great differences between instruments. In more general terms, it is evident that states grant concessions

[11] *Idem,* article III(3).

[12] "At present most of the foreign private investments in Nicaragua are guaranteed by agreements entered into by the Nicaraguan Government and the investing corporations." From a paper presented by the Minister of Economy of Nicaragua on October 27, 1953, to the U.S. Senate Committee on Banking and Currency; cf. *Study of Latin American Countries,* Interim Report of the Senate Committee on Banking and Currency 448, 449 (1954).

[13] Government of India, Ministry of Production, *Establishment of Oil Refineries in India, Text of Agreements with the Oil Companies,* title page (1953).

or guarantees in order to attract foreign capital and thus assist the country's economic development. The investment of the capital may then be regarded as the counter-promise of the investor, his "payment" for the state's promises.[14] In return for the guarantees and the other state promises, the foreign investors often undertake additional specific obligations: payment of royalties, in the case of concession agreements,[15] obligations to construct a plant within a certain period of time or to offer part of their product in the domestic market, in other cases.[16]

However, together with these elements which strongly suggest that the instruments under discussion are contractual in character, such instruments also contain important elements whose presence leads to a contrary conclusion. The situation of the parties should be taken into account at this point. Though one of the parties is a private person, the other is a state acting in a sovereign capacity, since it undertakes obligations with respect to its own sovereign powers, that is to say, powers which are essential to it for the protection and welfare of its people. The object itself of the parties' "bargain" is closely related to the welfare of the host state's people. It is presumably for their interest that the government is acting in encouraging foreign investment.

In granting the guarantees, moreover, the state is acting in accordance with its own laws. Its contractual freedom, therefore, is strictly limited. The form as well as the content of the promises to be granted are provided for in, and therefore limited by, preexisting general or specific legislation. The state may grant to investors only those rights which are prescribed in the relevant laws, and it can do so only under certain specified conditions.

It may be held, therefore, that the situation of a private person whose investment is guaranteed by the state, far from being comparable to that of a private party contracting with another private

[14] For a forceful statement of this view, though in a different context, see *supra* p. 90, note 110.

[15] Cf. the agreement summarized *supra*, pp. 126–27.

[16] Cf. the examples summarized *supra* pp. 124 and 128.

party, corresponds in fact to the juridical situation of a taxpayer claiming certain deductions when computing his income tax. The preexisting law having stated certain general rules, the taxpayer, by showing that he comes under their provisions, is entitled to a deduction. Obviously, there is here no contract between the state and the taxpayer. Is the situation of the foreign investor, who, by virtue of an investment law or of the general tax laws, has been granted certain exemptions, significantly different from that of the taxpayer just described?

It is submitted, therefore, in view of the above considerations, that it would be unrealistic to consider the instruments under discussion as wholly contractual in character. Neither are they, however, entirely noncontractual, mere unilateral acts of state. The contractual elements present are too important to be ignored. The only realistic description of such instruments is that they are of a mixed character, both contractual and noncontractual. In the pages which follow, the possibility of and the conditions for the existence of such instruments will be examined.

The Theory of Public Law Contracts

Instruments of the type here considered belong to the domain of public, rather than private, law. The time-honored distinction between these two branches of law corresponds to a certain conception of law and of the state, any discussion of which would be out of place here. For present purposes, it is sufficient to define private law as the law governing the relations between private persons and public law as the law governing the relations between the state and the private persons coming into contact with it.[17] Public differs

---

[17] Compare the Roman definitions of public law as *"ius quod ad statum rei Romanae spectat"* and private law as *"ius quod ad singulorum utilitatem spectat";* *Institutiones,* 1. 1. 4; and cf. Lee, *The Elements of Roman Law* 40 (1949 ed.). And see, more generally, Paton, *Jurisprudence* 258 *et seq.* (2d ed., 1951); Radbruch, "Legal Philosophy," in *The Legal Philosophies of Lask, Radbruch and Dabin* 43, 152–55 (Wilk transl., 1950); Pound, "Public Law and Private Law," 24 *Cornell L. Qu.* 469 (1939).

from private law chiefly in that the former is based on the recognition of a fundamental difference between the state and the private persons. It is misleading to refer to this difference as the "inequality" of the parties in public law relationships. The state does possess certain rights and privileges which private persons lack, but at the same time it has certain obligations toward private persons which no individual has toward the others. There is no inequality but rather a qualitative difference.

The peculiar character of public law is sometimes attributed to the fact that the state is sovereign. From a formal standpoint, this view may be correct, though probably tautological.[18] On a substantive level, however, the peculiarity of public law is founded on the special character of the state as the symbol of a nonvoluntary community of persons. The state as such is nothing but its people. It has no interests of its own, it only represents the collective interests of its citizens. Public law consists then of the rules which govern the relationship between the citizens' collective interests and the particular interests of each citizen by himself. These two types of interests differ in their quality and they cannot be treated as identical or equal. In fact, it is generally accepted that in the case of a conflict the public interests, the interests of the community as a whole, should prevail over the individual interests of each private person.

The typical public law relationships do not arise out of contract (unless one goes back to a hypothetical original "social contract"[19]). The state contracts neither with the criminal nor with the taxpayer, though both are directly affected by the laws or regulations in effect. In certain cases, however, it is to the interest of the state (that is to say, in the public interest)[20] to operate on a voluntary,

[18] For an excellent brief discussion of the role of the concept of sovereignty in the study of the matter at hand, see Mitchell, *The Contracts of Public Authorities* (hereinafter cited as Mitchell, *Contracts*) 2–5 (1954).

[19] But cf. the pertinent remarks of Radbruch, *supra* note 17, at 169.

[20] Grave problems arise because of the impossibility of assuming this identification at all times and in all cases. The state is presumed to act in the interest of the people which constitute it; still, a sometimes very sharp distinction between the governing and the governed has always existed. The sharper the distinction, the

rather than a coercive, basis. The state then enters into agreements with those private persons who are willing to, in order to assure the functioning of the administrative machine or in order to benefit the public in some other way.

No one denies the special character of other public law transactions, apart from state contracts, nor that the principles of private law are not applicable to those transactions. Some of the civil law systems, moreover, take a similar view of government contracts as well. The most complete and elaborate expression of this view is found in French administrative law, which has been followed on this point by the legal systems of several other countries. On the basis of the case law of the country's top administrative tribunal, the *Conseil d'Etat*,[21] French theory has evolved the concept of the *contrat administratif*. This is defined as a contract between the state and a private person, concluded for the sake of the functioning of a public service, and containing provisions which differ from those found in private law contracts ("public law" provisions or *clauses exorbitantes de droit commun*).[22] Since all the above elements should be present, it is evident that not all contracts concluded by

---

less the validity of the identification between state interests and public interests. Furthermore, the possibility of a divergence between the acts of the state and the interests of the public in a given country is of particular relevance to the discussion in this book and it cannot be eliminated by a mere presumption of identity. The discussion in the present chapter, being theoretical in character, can afford to be based largely on such a presumption. In later chapters, however, some of the concrete problems involved will be considered.

[21] The dependence of the theory of the *contrat administratif* on the existence of a system of administrative courts has often been exaggerated. Though certainly assisted in its development by the presence of these courts, the doctrine, as understood today, is founded on the character of the contracts and not on their being under the jurisdiction of this or that tribunal. The point is now well settled after the criticisms by Duguit and others, on which, see Friedmann, *Law in a Changing Society* 349 *et seq.* (1959); Mitchell, *Contracts* 165–68. Note that in Greece, the distinction between administrative contracts and state contracts of private law, as summarized *infra* in the text, is accepted, though both categories of contracts are under the jurisdiction of civil, not administrative, courts.

[22] Cf. 3 Jèze, *Principes généraux du droit administratif* 307 *et seq.* (3d ed., 1926); Péquignot, *Théorie générale du contrat administratif* 66, 178 (1945); Bonnard, *Précis de droit public* 116 (7th ed., 1946); Mitchell, *Contracts* 167–82.

the government are administrative contracts. Some are private law contracts (*contrats de droit privé*) and to them the principles of private law are applicable.[23]

An all-important element in administrative contracts is their close relation to a public service. The execution of the contract is subordinated to the necessity for safeguarding the public interest to the benefit of which the public service is operating. The inclusion of "public law" provisions in the contract is a direct consequence thereof. Such provisions are often found in the *cahier des charges*, the detailed contract form prepared unilaterally by the state and accepted as a whole by the private contractor. Once a contract is defined as administrative, however, certain public law provisions are inferred from its character as such. By virtue of such explicit or implied provisions, the state is allowed extensive rights of supervision and control over the operation of the enterprise involved. It may impose heavy penalties for any infraction of the contract and it may even abrogate the contract without prior recourse to the courts. The state can also modify unilaterally, by direct or indirect action, the terms of the contract to the extent made necessary by reasons of public interest.[24] Generally speaking, the private person's contractual obligations toward the state are to be enforced more strictly than in the case of private law contracts.

To those rights of the state correspond certain definite obligations on its part toward the private person contracting with it. The administrative contract remains a contract in that it is binding upon both parties to it. Although not bound to the precise original terms of the contract, the state may not upset the contract's basic financial

[23] The distinction between administrative contracts and *contrats de droit privé* is a difficult one and no single definite criterion seems to be generally accepted. In the particular cases, the courts tend to judge on the basis of the elements of the definition in the text and of the surrounding circumstances; cf. Mitchell, *Contracts* 168 *et seq.*; Friedmann, *op. cit. supra* note 21, at 372–73.

[24] Cf. Végléri, *Des modifications apportées par l'Administration à ses contrats* (1927); de Laubadère, "Du pouvoir de l'Administration d'imposer unilateralement des changements aux dispositions des contrats administratifs," *Revue du Droit Public* 63 (1954); Péquignot, *op. cit. supra* note 22, at 394 *et seq.*

equilibrium (*équation financière*).[25] The private party to an administrative contract, therefore, is entitled to compensation for any damage suffered through the direct or indirect modification of the contractual terms by the state.[26] Moreover (and this is a definite derogation from private law rules), the private party may claim indemnification for losses due to unforeseeable changes in the external circumstances affecting the contract, for which the state is in no way responsible.[27] Such a claim is limited to part of the damage suffered and it may be raised only when the contractor has continued his performance of the contract, despite the adverse conditions. The theoretical justification of this practice is the same as that of the extensive powers of the state in the matter of contracts, namely, the necessity for the good and continuous functioning of the public services.

The French theory of administrative contracts is not accepted in most of the other legal systems. The civil law systems which follow the German views on the matter insist on the unilateral character of state contracts.[28] The common law systems, on the other hand, emphasize the contractual element in government contracts and their similarities to contracts of private persons. In a simplified form, the argument in favor of this view is that the state may act as such, in the domain of public law, only as long as it imposes its decisions on private persons. Once it decides to cooperate with such persons, on a voluntary basis, it loses its public law character and it has to receive the same treatment as private

[25] Cf. Péquignot, *op. cit. supra* note 22, at 448 *et seq.;* Mitchell, *Contracts* 165–66, 186–87.

[26] Cf. Péquignot, *op. cit. supra* note 22, at 452 *et seq.;* 3 Jèze, *Les contrats administratifs* 88–328 (1934).

[27] This is the so-called *théorie de l'imprévision*, which had its origin in the change in conditions brought about by the First World War. Alibert, *L'imprévision dans les concessions de service public* (1924); Auverny-Bennetot, *La théorie de l'imprévision* (1938); Jèze, *op. cit. supra* note 26, at 31–88; Péquignot, *op. cit. supra* note 22, at 502 *et seq.* For some recent descriptions in English, see Mitchell, *Contracts* 189–93; Friedmann, *op. cit. supra* note 21, at 374; Mewett, "The Theory of Government Contracts," 5 *McGill L.J.* 222, 230–32 (1959).

[28] Cf. Friedmann, *op. cit. supra* note 21, at 375; Langrod, "Administrative Contracts," 4 *Am. J. Comp. L.* 325, 351–58 (1955).

persons. In the language of the United States Supreme Court: "When the United States enters into a contract relation, its rights and duties therein are governed generally by the law applicable to contracts between private parties." [29] Despite such differences in theory, however, the *contrat administratif* of French law has its counterparts in the practice of most modern states.[30] This statement may be illustrated by reference to present United States practice.[31]

The legal problems of government contracts in the United States have received increased attention in recent years.[32] The traditional view is now challenged by several jurists who point out that, in fact, the principles applicable to government contracts derogate in several important respects from the principles accepted in private law.[33]

From the very start, in the procedures relating to the conclusion of government contracts, one notices several departures from the rules applicable to private contracts.[34] The government contract

[29] *Per* Brandeis J. in Lynch v. U.S., 292 U.S. 571, 579 (1934). And cf. Mitchell, *Contracts* 144–46; 9 Williston, *Contracts* 285 *et seq.* (1945).

[30] Several comparative studies have appeared recently. See especially Mitchell, *Contracts;* and see also Langrod, *supra* note 28; Mewett, *supra* note 27; Mewett, "Formalities in Government Contracts," 5 *Wayne L. Rev.* 303 (1959); Friedmann, *op. cit. supra* note 21, at 371–83.

[31] English legal theory and case-law seem to go further than the American in upholding the private law character of government contracts, though several of the elements mentioned with respect to the United States are also present in English practice; e.g. standard contractual clauses permitting extensive state interference. Cf. Mitchell, *Contracts* 24–80; Friedmann, *op. cit. supra* note 21, at 376–81.

[32] Cf. Dimond, "Indexed Bibliography of Articles on Government Contracts in Legal and Related Periodicals," 20 *Fed. Bar J.* 167 (1960).

[33] "A government contract is very different from an ordinary private contract, both in appearance and actual operation." Pasley, "The Non-discrimination Clause in Government Contracts," 43 *Virginia L. Rev.* 837, 846 (1957). "The Government contract is something more than the usual consensual agreement between private individuals. As utilized by the Federal Government, it differs, not in degree, but in type from the historical and traditional idea of contract." Miller, "Government Contracts and Social Control: A Preliminary Inquiry," 41 *Virginia L. Rev.* 27, 56 (1955). The incidence of comparative studies, *supra* note 30, is also an indication of increased awareness of the special character of government contracts. And cf. also Note, "Developments in the Law—Remedies Against the United States and Its Officials," 70 *Harv. L. Rev.* 827, 884–87 (1957).

[34] Cf. Stelzenmuller, "Formation of Government Contracts—Application of Common Law Principles," 40 *Cornell L. Qu.* 238 (1955); Pasley, "Formation of

itself is highly standardized. Though there exists a margin for negotiations either with representatives of the industry involved or with individual contractors,[35] the contractual freedom of the parties appears severely limited. Some of the standard clauses are imposed by legislation or by high-level executive decisions and are therefore immutable, as far as the parties to any particular contract are concerned.[36] Through such clauses, the federal government often attempts to achieve certain aims which, in themselves, are quite unrelated to the purposes of the particular contract. A typical case is that of the nondiscrimination clause, inserted in all federal government contracts, which binds the contractor to a policy of nondiscrimination against any employee or applicant for employment on grounds of race, religion, color, or national origin.[37] Several other standard clauses of the same general type relate to assistance to domestic business, under the "Buy American" Act, aid to small business, or regulation of labor matters.[38]

Through the standard contractual clauses, the government is allowed extensive rights of interference in the performance of the contract. Government officers may inspect the materials to be used by the contractor [39] or they may change the initial specifications provided for in the contract.[40] Government contracts are subject to renegotiation with a view to recapturing any excessive profits made by the contractor. This practice was first established during the First, and then the Second World Wars,[41] but it has remained ap-

---

Government Contracts—Application of Common Law Principles—A Reply," 40 *idem* 518 (1955).

[35] Cf. Pasley, "The Interpretation of Government Contracts: A Plea for Better Understanding," 25 *Fordham L. Rev.* 211, 214-15 (1956).

[36] Cf. Miller, *supra* note 33; Risik, "Federal Government Contract Clauses and Forms," 23 *Geo. Wash. L. Rev.* 125 (1954); Mewett, "Formalities in Government Contracts," 5 *Wayne L. Rev.* 303, 303-13 (1959).

[37] Cf. Pasley, "The Non-discrimination Clause in Government Contracts," 43 *Virginia L. Rev.* 837 (1957). And cf. Miller, *supra* note 33, at 49-52.

[38] Miller, *idem, passim.*   [39] Cf. 9 Williston, *Contracts* 309-10 (1945).

[40] Cf. Mewett, "The Theory of Government Contracts," 5 *McGill L.J.* 222, 238 (1959).

[41] Cf. 9 Williston, *Contracts* 100-122, 461-69 (1954); Symposium, "War Contract Renegotiation," 10 *Law & Contemp. Problems* 185-425 (1944).

plicable to government contracts in peacetime.[42] The Federal Government also possesses extensive powers over the termination of its contracts.[43] It has, moreover, broad competence with respect to the settlement of any disputes arising in connection with a government contract. When the dispute involves a question of fact, the decision of the head of the department concerned is final, unless it is "fraudulent or capricious or arbitrary or so grossly erroneous as necessarily to imply bad faith, or is not supported by substantial evidence." [44] Decisions relating to disputes involving questions of law are not considered final and are subject to judicial review.[45] Some mention should be made, at this point, of the extensive limitations on the liability of the state in contract, which are accepted in United States law. This topic is, however, dealt with at a later stage, when considering the legal effects of state contracts.[46]

From the point of view of concrete effects, therefore, the differences between the French and the American systems (and this holds true *mutatis mutandis* of most of the other systems, as well) do not appear to be as radical as a glance at the prevailing theories would indicate. The concrete situation is often similar in the two cases, but the legal justification adopted is different: in France the public law regime is applicable whenever there is an administrative contract; [47] in the United States, whenever the contractual clauses

[42] See Braucher, "The Renegotiation Act of 1951," 66 *Harv. L. Rev.* 270 (1952); Mewett, *supra* note 40, at 233–36; Friedmann, *op. cit. supra* note 21, at 99–101.

[43] Cf. Mewett, "Formalities in Government Contracts," 5 *Wayne L. Rev.* 303, 309 (1959). For a corresponding British standard clause, see Mitchell, *Contracts* 246–48.

[44] 41 U.S.C.A. § 321 (1960). For a typical disputes clause to that effect, see Lidstone and Witte, "Administration of Government Contracts: Disputes and Claims Procedures," 46 *Virginia L. Rev.* 252, 258, n. 23 (1960). The present formulation of the clause is in part the result of legislation following the decision of the United States Supreme Court in Wunderlich v. U.S., 342 U.S. 98 (1951). For a discussion of the issues in that case, see Etheridge, "Appeals from Administrative Decisions in Government Contract Disputes," 31 *Texas L. Rev.* 552, 563–70 (1953).

[45] 41 U.S.C.A. § 322 (1960). Note, however, that the contract may in some cases provide that a question of law should be treated as a question of fact; cf. U.S. v. Moorman, 338 U.S. 457 (1950). And see Etheridge, *supra* note 44, at 560–62.

[46] Cf. *infra* pp. 270–71.

[47] Note, however, the importance attributed in French administrative law to the presence of *clauses exorbitantes de droit commun;* cf. *supra* pp. 198–99.

provide for its application.[48] In both cases, the private contractor finds himself in an unequal situation; his rights over the other contracting party, the state, are far less extensive than the state's rights over him. Indeed, the application of private law principles seems to be to the detriment rather than the advantage of the contractor.[49] Under the private law regime, he may not receive any compensation for some of the state's actions which have affected the contract, and he will be left to bear the consequences of any unforeseen changes in external conditions.[50] These are situations with respect to which he would often have been entitled to compensation under the administrative law regime.

State Promises as Public Law Contracts

Any conclusion at this point on the legal character of state guarantees to foreign investors can be but tentative; its validity will depend on a determination of the guarantees' legal effects which are not directly at issue here. Since, however, the legal effects themselves are still uncertain, even a tentative conclusion might help in clarifying the issues.

The state guarantees which we are studying do not always correspond closely to the particular forms of public law contracts commonly found in the practice of states. If we use as a test the French definition of an administrative contract, we notice that state promises concerning foreign investments are not necessarily related to a particular public service. However, they affect the public interest directly both because of the importance of the issues involved in the investment of foreign capital in a country (for example, its economic development and eventual industrialization and the exploitation of its natural resources) and because the state, in concluding guarantee agreements, is certainly acting in a sover-

---

[48] But such standard clauses are almost always included in the contract.
[49] Cf., in agreement, Mitchell, *Contracts* 226 *et seq.;* Friedmann, *op. cit. supra* note 21, at 378–81.
[50] Cf., for instance, 9 Williston, *Contracts* 307–9 (1945).

eign capacity and not as a mere administrative machine. Further-more, the provisions of these guarantees differ greatly from those found in private law contracts. Indeed, in view of the very purpose of these guarantees, no contract between private persons can ever have the same content. Though there is no exact identity, therefore, state guarantees to foreign investors do bear definite similarities to public law contracts. This seems to have been recognized in the municipal law of certain states.[51]

It is true that no concept of the public law contract, correspond-ing to that of municipal law theory, has developed as yet in inter-national law. Though cases involving concessions have often come before international tribunals, the latter have avoided giving any general definitions.[52] Nevertheless, existing case law lends support to the idea that concession contracts are of a mixed legal character, pertaining both to private and to public law. The Permanent Court of International Justice has stated in one of its judgments that "a contract granting a public utility concession does not fall within the category of ordinary instruments of private law." [53] Similar expressions are found in several arbitral awards. It is stated, in one of them, that a concession has "a double character; it relates to public as well as to private law." [54] In another, it was held that a concession contract does not "constitute simply a private law con-tract" since it is "by its nature a public service." [55] In another case, the difference between the terms "contract" and "agreement" was examined, the latter term being in the tribunal's view broader than

---

[51] Cf., Baade, *Gesetzgebung zur Förderung ausländischer Kapitalanlagen* 27 (1957), Langrod, *supra* note 28, at 353–55.

[52] See, e.g., the case of the German Reparations in Accordance with Article 260 of the Treaty of Versailles, (1924), 1 UN RIAA 429, 471. The arbitrator under-took to rule only as to whether certain specific cases fell within the category of "concessions" as provided for in article 260 of the treaty of Versailles, refusing to give any more general definition of the term.

[53] Judgment of March 17, 1934, on the Lighthouses case between France and Greece, P.C.I.J. Publ. Ser. A/B, No. 62, 20. The Court also stated, however, that "it is not impossible to grant such concessions by way of contract." *Ibid.*

[54] Affaire de la Compagnie d'Electricité de Varsovie (Fond) (Principe) (France v. Poland, 1932), 3 UN RIAA 1679, 1687.

[55] Societé Rialet c. Gouvernment Ethiopien (1929), 8 *Recueil T.A.M.* 742, 748.

the former.[56] Moreover, there exists some evidence of the application under certain conditions, by international tribunals of concepts similar to that of *imprévision* of French administrative law. The matter will be dealt with in detail in a later chapter.[57]

The legal character of concession agreements has been studied at length in a recent arbitral award, settling a dispute between the Kingdom of Saudi Arabia and the Arabian American Oil Company (Aramco).[58] The arbitrators, in their preliminary examination of the problem, stated "Such is the double character of the concession: it involves, first, a State act and, second, rights of ownership vested in the concessionaire." [59] They then reviewed the legal theories on concessions held in the major legal systems today.[60] With respect to French law, the tribunal pointed out that an oil concession was different from the *concession de service public*, which usually involves the operation of public utilities by private persons.[61] Its conclusion was that "a mining concession in French law is an act *sui generis*, which cannot be completely assigned to any other category. It is an act which partakes of the nature of a unilateral act, in that it depends on the authorization of the State, and of that of a contract, in that it requires an agreement of the respective wills of the State and of the concessionaire." [62]

The tribunal found, further, that the applicable law in the instant case was the *lex situs*, that is, Saudi Arabian law; it admitted the existence of difficulties at this point, since "the regime of . . . oil concessions has remained embryonic in Moslem law." [63] It also found that concessions, in Saudi Arabian law, were of a contractual character. This conclusion was reinforced by the argument that the attribution of the character of a unilateral state act "would presuppose laws and regulations not to be found in Saudi Arabia," while the agreement's contractual elements were evident.[64] The

---

[56] R.C.A. v. China (1935), 3 UN RIAA 1621, 1627-30.
[57] Cf. *infra* pp. 333-38.
[58] Saudi Arabia v. Aramco, award of 23 August 1958 (privately printed).
[59] *Idem* 50.
[60] Namely, the French, German and English legal systems. *Idem* 50-53.
[61] *Idem* 51-53.　　　　[62] *Idem* 53.　　　　[63] *Idem* 55.
[64] *Idem* 56.

arbitrators then dealt with the possibility of a conflict between such a holding and the general principles of law, comparative law, or legal science. Their view was that no such conflict existed, since the theory of administrative contract is found in a single legal system and cannot be considered a general principle. They also emphasized the fact that Moslem law made no distinction between public law and private law contracts.[65] The award examined further the question of the law of the contract, concluding that the agreement itself was in the nature of a constitution and conferred rights on the contracting parties.[66]

On the other hand, in a recent arbitration award in a dispute involving two contracts between Greece and two foreign companies, it was held that a contract for the supply of goods to a state monopoly over a long period of time belonged to administrative rather than private law.[67] The umpire also found that the general principles of private law were still applicable, when not in conflict with the administrative law rules.[68] In fact, he applied such principles extensively, though with acute awareness of the problems faced by a state and the corresponding expectations of the private contractor.[69] The authority of the award is, however, limited, for our present purposes, by the fact that Greek municipal law, and not international law or the general principles of law, was found to be the proper law of the contract.[70]

The scholarly literature on the subject deals exclusively with concession agreements. There is wide agreement among writers that concessions cannot be considered as belonging entirely to

---

[65] *Idem* 57.

[66] *Idem* 57 *et seq.* For a more elaborate discussion of this part of the award, see *infra* pp. 291–93.

[67] Alsing Trading Co., Ltd. and the Swedish Match Co. v. the Greek State (1954), as reported in Schwebel, "The Alsing Case," 8 *Int'l & Comp. L. Qu.* 320, at 332 (1959).

[68] *Idem* at 333.   [69] Cf. *idem* at 335–38, 341–45.

[70] *Idem* at 326–27. Note in this connection the interesting declaration on the part of the Greek Government that "given the interdependence and the common source of the systems of law in force in continental Europe, the question of the law to be applied is rather a question of principle without much practical significance." *Idem*, at 327. The umpire referred frequently to French administrative law and to German and Swiss private law; cf., e.g., *idem* at 335, 338, 342.

municipal private law. Difficulties arise at this point, because there appears to be no other possibility but to consider such agreements as belonging to public international law. Several writers refuse to do this[71] because concessions are not agreements between states or international organizations. They are thus led to the conclusion that concessions are of a "mixed character"; the legal effects which they derive from this conclusion vary widely.[72]

It is submitted that these conclusions are correct to the extent that they reject the applicability of both public international and municipal private law. Both these bodies of law are designed to regulate relations between equals, or, better, between legal persons of similar or comparable juridical qualities. Concession agreements, where the concessionaire is an alien, or other state guarantees of the type we are studying, cannot fit under either of these bodies of law. To call such agreements *sui generis* or of "a mixed character" is a partial solution at best. Such expressions have a negative rather than a positive connotation; they show what these instruments are not, but not what they are. It is not, however, inconceivable that such agreements are in fact governed by another body of law. Or, if this seems too extreme a suggestion, it is possible that international law may apply in the case of such instruments certain rules which differ from those applicable to interstate agreements, in the same manner in which municipal law applies public, and not private, law in the case of government contracts. This possibility will be examined in detail at a later stage, in the concrete and more relevant

[71] But see Miller, "The Corporation as a Private Government in the World Community," 46 *Virginia L. Rev.* 1539 (1960), who proposes "to term the concession agreement as an instrument *sui generis*, and to interpret and construe it under the doctrines of public international law." *Idem*, at 1563. For a discussion of the possible consequences of such a classification, see *infra* pp. 287-89.

[72] See, e.g., O'Connell, "A Critique of the Iranian Oil Litigation," 4 *Int'l & Comp. L. Qu.* 267, 268 *et seq.* (1955); Huang, "Some International and Legal Aspects of the Suez Canal Question," 51 *Am. J. Int'l L.* 277, 289-96 (1957); Farmanfarma, "The Oil Agreement between Iran and the International Oil Consortium: The Law Controlling," 34 *Texas L. Rev.* 259, 274-87 (1955); Guldberg, "International Concessions, A Problem of International Economic Law," 15 *Acta Scandinavica Iuris Gentium* 47, 67-73 (1944). And see also Develle, *La concession en droit international* (1936).

context of the legal effects of such instruments.[73] The purposes of the present chapter will have been accomplished if the unsatisfactory character of the existing concepts and classifications and the need for a concept corresponding to that of the municipal law public contract in international law have been shown.

[73] Cf. *infra*, Chapters 9, 10, and 11.

Part III

LEGAL EFFECTS OF
STATE PROMISES

8

Legal Effects of
Treaty Promises

CONSIDERED in the abstract, the legal effects of state promises
made by instruments of public international law, that is, the manner
and extent of their implementation and the consequences of a possible violation of their provisions, are not difficult to determine.
There is a vast body of legal literature, based on the case-law of
international and municipal tribunals and on the practice of states,
which deals with the effects of treaties, the extent of their binding
force, and other related problems. Treaty promises concerning
matters of investment are not exceptional in their form, so that the
conclusions of such study are certainly applicable. The difficulty,
in their case, does not lie in the determination of their legal effects
in the abstract, but in determining, in each particular case, whether
a violation has occurred. A study of their legal effects should then
of necessity enter into an examination on the treaties' contents and
the possible concrete instances of implementation or violation of
the promises. A jurist's predictions must be uncertain in this respect
because it is not possible to foresee with precision the particular
conditions under which the implementation or violation of the
treaties will become an issue. One can only provide a general frame
of reference, into which possible future cases should fit, even though
the particular concrete solutions cannot be determined beforehand.

The Standards of Treatment of Foreign Investors

The problem is how to apply the provisions of the treaties to any given factual situation and thus determine whether the treaty has been implemented or whether a violation has occurred. In this connection the question of the choice between contingent and non-contingent standards of reference in the treaties is of special importance. Contingent standards, and in particular the standard of national treatment, have definite advantages from this point of view: since they refer to a body of reasonably precise and detailed legal rules, it is easier to determine in any concrete instance whether the treatment given to the foreign investors is in accordance with these rules. This is less true with respect to the most-favored-nation standard, which in any case has a limited role with respect to the problems we are dealing with since it assures nondiscrimination only between aliens of different nationalities.

The application of the standard of national treatment, however, presents certain problems of its own. To begin with, it is difficult to determine with precision the extent to which it is possible to diverge from the general rules applicable to local nationals. We shall have occasion later to study this question in more detail. A second difficulty involves the application of nominally general measures which affect, solely or chiefly, aliens and not nationals. When the oil industry is nationalized in a country where the only existing petroleum-exploiting company is foreign-owned, it is problematical whether this can be called a "general" act in accordance with the rule of national treatment. No general answer can be given and the solution in each particular case will depend on the concrete conditions.

Finally, there is a third difficulty, which relates to the content rather than the application of the rules in question. The rules applicable in the case of nationals may be unsatisfactory to the foreign investor. It may be that the political regime in the host state is corrupt and inefficient and that the existing laws afford little protection against arbitrary government action. It may be that the host state's administrative machinery is still at an early stage of development and is inefficient and subject to favoritism and the exercise of influence. It may be, also, that, with respect to the particular industry in which the foreign investor is engaged, no definite legal or administrative policy has developed in the host state.[1] In such cases, as in several other possible situations, the standard of national treatment might prove insufficient to protect the legitimate interests of the foreign investor.

With respect to this last feature of contingent standards, non-contingent standards present certain advantages in that the treatment they prescribe is determined beforehand and thus, presumably, does not fall below a "minimum standard." The generality and abstraction of these standards, however, remains an important drawback. It is generally difficult to determine whether a certain measure is in accordance with them, that is to say whether, in the usual treaty terms, it is "just," "reasonable," or "equitable."

The Business Activities of Aliens

The problems arising over the application and interpretation of treaty promises to foreign investors are quite evident in the case of the general provisions of the United States FCN treaties with respect to the freedom of aliens to engage in business activities and to own property.[2] It is not easy to determine with any precision the extent of such freedom. The treaties do state the general rule of national treatment, of course, but they also allow certain exceptions.

[1] Cf., for instance, the agreement between the Saudi Arabian Government and A. S. Onassis, of January 20, 1954, 10 *Rev. Egypt. Droit Int'l* 287 (1954), providing *inter alia* for the promulgation of a Saudi Arabian Commercial Code. See also McNair, "The General Principles of Law Recognized by Civilized Nations," 33 *Brit. Yb. Int'l L.* 1, 4 and *passim* (1957) and the discussion *infra* p. 294.

[2] Cf., *supra* pp. 141–43. The discussion in this chapter relates to the legal effects of United States FCN treaties, but the findings are also valid, *mutatis mutandis*, for the recent German and British investment treaties. A joint discussion would have unnecessarily complicated the exposition.

In concrete instances, it may be impossible to determine incontestably where the general rule ends and the special restrictions begin. Extreme cases may well arise of course, where the fulfillment or nonfulfillment of the treaty provisions is evident. It is reasonable to assume, however, that the majority of cases will be less easy. A special case is that of particular restrictions which by their nature affect only aliens. In such a case, the rule of national treatment becomes almost meaningless. Only the general absolute provisions of the treaties, namely, those stating that aliens "shall be permitted to . . . ," might cover such instances.

The treaties provide a general criterion for measuring the compatibility of any restrictions with the treaty promises. Such restrictions should not "impair the substance" of the rights granted by the treaties. The criterion itself is fairly vague and it might be applicable even in the absence of express mention in the text of the treaties, in accordance with the general principles of treaty interpretation. All in all, the main contribution of these provisions of the FCN treaties is their establishing the national treatment of aliens as the general rule, so that the burden of proof that any special restriction does not impair the substance of the rights accorded by the treaty lies normally with the state imposing the restriction.

The same problems arise with respect to the provisions of FCN treaties concerning the elimination of restrictions on the ownership of enterprises in capital-importing countries. In the relevant rules both contingent and noncontingent standards are used. It is expressly stated that aliens are to be permitted to establish companies, but only (and this standard is a contingent one) in accordance with the applicable laws. This latter proviso may well permit the application of extensive restrictions. Still, in the more recent treaties, it is stated unequivocally that aliens are to be permitted to acquire majority interests in companies,[3] and it is reasonable to assume that whatever restrictions may be permitted under the various exceptions, they cannot go counter to the letter of the treaties and thus

---

[3] Cf. *supra* p. 143.

cannot impose ownership of only a minority share by aliens. It is far more debatable whether provisions requiring minority participation of nationals in the ownership of foreign-controlled enterprises [4] constitute restrictions which "impair the substance" of the aliens' rights under the treaties. Indeed, the opposite should be considered as valid in the great majority of cases. Serious evidence must be presented before it can be argued that such requirements are in violation of the treaty provisions. The imposition of a great number of minor formalities which may be highly annoying to the foreign investor should also be considered as allowed under the terms of the treaties. No treaty can wholly eliminate such practices, especially since they are due, in many cases, to the peculiarities and special features of each country's administrative system.

Employment of Foreign Personnel

Even greater discretion is left to capital-importing states with respect to labor legislation. The FCN treaties do not deal at all with possible legislation regarding unskilled labor. The capital-receiving state may then require of all enterprises operating in its territories that they employ exclusively local unskilled labor. As has been pointed out, the matter is of no great importance to foreign investors because in virtually all cases they would not wish to import such labor from outside the country in which they are operating. In the very few cases where they might want to do so, there are very good reasons for their not being allowed to.[5]

Even with respect to skilled personnel, the FCN treaties place few real limitations on the powers of the host state. The foreign-owned enterprise is guaranteed the choice of its skilled personnel, but only with respect to local labor. This is not without any importance, of course, for there are instances where governments of capital-importing states have tried to impose the employment of particular persons. Under the treaties, such direct action is no

[4] Cf. *supra* pp. 42, 43.   [5] Cf. *supra* p. 45.

longer possible, at least not openly. There remain several indirect methods through which the host government may impose its favorites on an enterprise, but it cannot be too obvious about it without running the risk of seeing itself accused of violating the treaty.

The local government, on the other hand, retains almost full powers where the employment of foreign skilled personnel is concerned. Even permission to employ skilled personnel "regardless of nationality" is subordinated to the operation of the immigration and other laws. It could hardly be otherwise, of course, considering that the other contracting state in all these instances is the United States, whose immigration policies and legislation are stricter than those of many underdeveloped countries.[6] It is thus possible for the capital-importing state to regulate the employment of aliens in foreign or locally-owned enterprises as it wishes, with very few, if any, limitations due to the FCN treaties. The latter's provisions in this matter express, at best, the willingness of the states involved to allow, as a rule, the employment of alien technicians or other skilled personnel. Their legal value, however, is more than doubtful; they are phrased in such a manner as to leave to the governments concerned full freedom of action, legislative as well as administrative.

Exchange Restrictions and Taxation

The FCN treaties establish as a general rule that exchange restrictions are not going to be imposed save in the case of exceptional situations.[7] This rule, it should be noted, replaces a preexisting rule of customary international law according to which states are as a rule free to impose whatever restrictions they deem necessary with

[6] Cf. in this connection the language of the treaty between the United States and Uruguay (Protocol, para. 2): ". . . so long as the United States of America permits the entry into its territories of nationals of the Oriental Republic of Uruguay upon terms substantially as favorable as those applicable upon the date of signature of the Treaty, the Oriental Republic of Uruguay undertakes to permit nationals of the United States of America freely to enter its territories, subject to measures necessary to maintain public order and to protect the public health, morals and safety."

[7] For details and qualifications to this statement, see *supra* p. 156.

respect to matters of money and foreign exchange.[8] The new, treaty-made, rule shifts the burden of proof concerning the legality of exchange restrictions from the state of the investor's nationality to the state imposing the restrictions. This is by itself a very important consideration. Moreover, the term "exchange restrictions" is given a broad definition, which includes all possible limitations and charges which might be imposed, under various names, on transactions involving foreign exchange.[9] Finally, the exceptions allowed, though rather general and extensive, are definite enough and susceptible of proof.

This is particularly true as regards the first general exception to the said rule, under which the imposition of exchange restrictions is permitted when they are specifically authorized or requested by the International Monetary Fund. The existence of the specified condition is easy to determine objectively, and the Fund's authorization is an indication of the necessity for exchange restrictions at the particular time.

The existence of the other common exception, relating to a country's monetary reserves,[10] is slightly more difficult to determine with precision. Still the contracting states are not given full freedom. The absolute level of a state's reserves is a matter of record, since member states regularly provide information concerning it to the International Monetary Fund. A comparison of the levels of successive periods will thus determine the relative position of the reserves at any particular moment. Difference of opinion is possible with respect to whether a certain level is low enough to permit the im-

[8] Cf. *supra* p. 49.
[9] "The term 'exchange restrictions' as used in the present Article includes all restrictions, regulations, charges, taxes, or other requirements imposed by either Party which burden or interfere with payments, remittances, or transfers of funds or of financial instruments between the territories of the two Parties." Treaty with Japan, article XII(5). Substantially identical provisions are found in all the other treaties, except that with Israel (but see its article XII[1]); the treaties with Iran, article VII(1), Ethiopia, article XI(1), and Muscat and Oman, article IX(1), contain no definitions but rather summary descriptions covering the same types of transactions.
[10] Cf. *supra* p. 156, note 140.

position of restrictions. It seems difficult to maintain that any state other than the state whose reserves are involved should be the judge as to this question. When a state's reserves are not falling, however, the other contracting state may well invoke the treaty, claiming that the imposition of restrictions is in violation of it. Of course, matters are not so simple as that. It is possible for states to "juggle" with their reserves through the appropriate monetary policies; in the last analysis a state's reserves can always be in the condition the state wants them, at least negatively, that is to say, they can be as bad as it wants them to be, though they cannot always be as good as the state may wish. The effectiveness of the limitations imposed by the treaties should not then be exaggerated.

The treaties further prohibit restrictions imposed "in a manner unnecessarily detrimental" to the investors' interests. This may be considered as a particular instance of the general prohibition against the exercise of treaty or other rights under international law in an "abusive" manner, that is, the prohibition of abuse of rights under international law.[11] The FCN treaties thus impose on any judicial body dealing with disputes arising in connection with exchange restrictions under the treaty the right to examine the possibility of an abuse of rights in the particular case. This provision, however, can only be taken to refer to cases where the lack of necessity for the restrictions is evident. Otherwise, the judgment of the state imposing the restrictions, regardless of its validity in terms of economics or municipal law, should be respected, as far as this particular provision is concerned.[12]

Some degree of control over the imposition of exchange restrictions may then be exercised by virtue of the provisions of FCN treaties. Exchange control is accepted in them as a temporary measure of protection of a state's balance-of-payments position but not as a permanent situation. Unfortunately, the possibility of the existence of such "exceptional" conditions in a state is, today and especially with respect to underdeveloped countries, far from im-

---

[11] Cf. the discussion *infra* pp. 296–98.   [12] See *ibidem* for more details.

probable. This is why, along with these general provisions, the FCN treaties also provide that foreign investors shall be accorded certain facilities for the transfer abroad of their earnings and capital when exchange restrictions are in force.[13]

It cannot be contested that the provisions relating to the transfer abroad of the investors' funds are not very definite or certain. To begin with, the states concerned do not undertake to make such transfer possible, but to "make reasonable provision" for it. Such provision may well consist in making possible the partial transfer of the sums involved. The proportion to be transferred cannot be determined with any precision in the abstract. It has to be judged according to the concrete conditions prevailing at the particular time. A proportion which might be "reasonable" under certain conditions might not be deemed such when the conditions are different. In the second place, provision for transfer of the investors' earnings and capital [14] is to be made only after certain other payments are taken care of. This is the most important limitation to the investors' "right" to be permitted to repatriate their capital and earnings. Such other payments are chiefly those for "goods and services essential to the health and welfare of" the host state's people.[15] This is, of course, an area where many differences of opinion, honest and otherwise, may well exist. It is probably impossible, however, to describe such payments in a more precise manner, because whether certain goods and services are essential to a people's health and welfare depends on the concrete conditions of a country at a particular time. Not only the quality of the goods but their quantity, as well, is a determining factor in their being essential at a particular time.

The treaty promises regarding taxation are similar to those on exchange restrictions chiefly in one respect. They reverse the customary rules of international law in the matter. While the im-

[13] Cf. *supra* p. 157, notes 142–45.

[14] On the special situation of capital transfers, see *supra* pp. 157–58.

[15] Cf. *supra* p. 157, note 143. Other items taking precedence over the investors' funds are described in even more general terms; cf. *ibid.*

position of taxes is a matter of exclusive domestic concern and there is no international law rule condemning discrimination against aliens in matters of taxation, the FCN treaties provide for the national treatment of foreign investors, once certain conditions are fulfilled.[16] The standard they employ is in this case a very appropriate one (even though the possibility of veiled discrimination through nominally general measures is still present) which can safeguard better than any other the investors' interests. The alien may thus refer, before or after investing his capital, to the relevant laws, administrative regulations, and court decisions in the capital-importing state and determine with some degree of precision the tax burden he will have to bear. The treaties, however, do not protect the investor from the effects of any future change in the host state's tax legislation.

Expropriation in Violation of Treaty Promises

The general rule with respect to the violation of state promises of nonexpropriation made by means of an instrument of public international law is clear and well-settled. Expropriation in violation of such promises is in itself unlawful and constitutes an internationally tortious act, for which the expropriating state is fully responsible. This statement holds true regardless of the validity of the act of expropriation in municipal law, the existence or absence of public purpose and even the payment or not of adequate compensation.

The rule of law on the matter has been clearly stated by the Permanent Court of International Justice in its Judgment No. 13 (1928) on the case concerning the factory at Chorzow.[17] In a previous judgment on the same case the Court had found that Poland's action in seizing a German-owned factory was contrary to a convention between Poland and Germany.[18] In its subsequent

[16] Cf. *supra* p. 175. The subject is covered in detail in Wilson, *Treaties* 156–81.
[17] Case Concerning the Factory at Chorzow (Claim for Indemnity) (Merits), Judgment No. 13 of September 13, 1928, P.C.I.J. Publ. Series A, No. 17.
[18] Case Concerning Certain German Interests in Polish Upper Silesia (The

judgment on the merits of the German claim for indemnity, the Court held that such illegal action was to be distinguished from expropriation of foreign property under normal circumstances (that is, in the absence of a treaty provision). The Court's majority opinion stated in part:

> The action of Poland which the Court has judged to be contrary to the Geneva Convention is not an expropriation—to render which lawful only the payment of fair compensation would have been wanting; it is a seizure of property, rights and interests which could not be expropriated even against compensation, save under the exceptional conditions fixed by article 7 of the said Convention. . . .[19]

This distinction, with some variations, is by now generally accepted in international law theory and practice,[20] though it is not found in the holding of any subsequent judgment of the Court or in any arbitral award.[21]

This general rule, however, is of very limited usefulness in con-

---

Merits), Judgment No. 7 of May 25, 1926, P.C.I.J. Publ. Series A, No. 7, at p. 21. Article 6 of a Convention signed at Geneva on May 15, 1922, provided, *inter alia*, that, apart from the exceptions specified in the treaty itself, "the property, rights and interests of German nationals or companies controlled by German nationals may not be liquidated in Polish Upper Silesia." For comments and discussions on this case, see Gidel, "L'arrêt No. 7 de la Cour Permanente de Justice Internationale," 1 *Rev. Droit Int'l* 76 (1927); Williams, "International Law and the Property of Aliens," 9 *Brit. Yb. Int'l L.* 1 (1928), reprinted in *Chapters in Current International Law and the League of Nations* 147, at 154–59 (1929); Friedman, *Expropriation* 75–81.

[19] P.C.I.J. Judgment No. 13, of September 13, 1928, P.C.I.J. Publ. Ser. A., No. 17, at 46.

[20] Cf., e.g., Kaeckenbeeck, "The Protection of Vested Rights in International Law," 17 *Brit. Yb. Int'l L.* 1, 15 (1936); Herz, "Expropriation of Foreign Property," 35 *Am. J. Int'l L.* 243, 253–54 (1941); Doman, "Postwar Nationalization of Foreign Property in Europe," 48 *Columbia L. Rev.* 1125, 1138–39 (1948); Roth, *The Minimum Standard of International Law Applied to Aliens* 171–72 (1949); Bindschedler, "La protection de la propriété privée en droit international public," 90 *Hague Recueil* 173, 186 (1956). For a slightly different interpretation, see Kollewijn, " 'Nationalization' without Compensation and the Transfer of Property," 6 *Ned. Tijdschrift voor Int. Recht* 140, 152–54 (1959).

[21] Distinctions between lawful and unlawful expropriations or other state measures affecting aliens' property rights are found in decisions of international tribunals. There is no other case, however, of expropriations declared unlawful because of violation of specific treaty promises. And see now the discussion in White, *Nationalisation of Foreign Property* 154–61 (1961).

sidering the legal effects of the provisions on expropriation of the various treaty texts we have been studying. It would be directly applicable only in the hypothetical case of expropriation in violation of that particular provision which is found in the 1957 Draft Convention for the Mutual Protection of Private Property Rights and which guarantees the nonexpropriation of the property of foreign investors before the lapse of a certain period of time after the date of their original investment.[22] Such an expropriation would have been unlawful, in accordance with the rule just stated. The provisions in the other proposed investment codes,[23] however, as well as those in the United States FCN treaties are of a different character. They may be stated in the form of general prohibitions of expropriation, but in fact they only state the requirements for a lawful expropriation. They provide that an expropriation is lawful under certain conditions.

In these provisions, there is no attempt to create a new rule in international law concerning the expropriation of foreign-owned property, nor to establish a special rule constituting an exception to existing general rules. What they have in view is giving conventional validity to a customary rule whose validity has been questioned. With regard to this conventional rule, therefore, all the problems which exist with respect to the content of the customary rule will again arise.[24] What cannot be disputed any more between parties to an FCN treaty is the validity of the rule itself, within the limits of the validity of conventional rules of international law.

Accordingly, if a state party to an FCN treaty expropriates the property of a United States citizen protected by it and refuses to grant compensation (on the ground, for example, that no compensation is being paid for the expropriated property of its own nationals)

---

[22] *1957 Draft Convention*, article VI(1). And cf. *supra* p. 165.

[23] As well as the above Convention's provision regarding aliens not belonging to the category of foreign investors; *idem*, article VI(2).

[24] For a discussion and comparison of the provisions of the particular treaties, see Wilson, *Treaties* 113–22 and cf. *supra* pp. 168–70.

its action is internationally unlawful, because it violates the rule established by the treaty. If, however, the state agrees to pay compensation but not the amount demanded by the alien, then the treaty provisions would be of little help. The state might maintain that the compensation offered is "just," while the investor might be claiming the contrary; a deadlock might well ensue whose solution would depend on negotiations between the parties or on the judgment of an international tribunal. The same observations are valid with respect to the requirement of "public purpose" which is found in most FCN treaties. A state would be violating the treaty only if it invoked a purpose other than public. The question as to what constitutes a public purpose (once a purpose is claimed as being public) cannot be determined on the basis of the provisions of the FCN treaties.

The main usefulness of treaty promises regarding expropriation lies then in their establishing a clear conventional rule in the place of an uncertain and strongly contested customary rule. According to the official view of most capital-exporting states, the content of these two rules does not differ substantially. The conventional rule is, therefore, useful only insofar as it clarifies the customary one and makes impossible any contestation of its validity. In fact, since the content as well as the validity of the so-called customary rule is a center of controversy, the treaty rule assumes great importance and usefulness.

The treaties provide an international law standard for judging the lawfulness or unlawfulness of an expropriation. The state whose nationals' property has been expropriated may well intervene diplomatically even before formal exhaustion of local remedies, when the municipal law to be applied by the local tribunals falls short of the standard established by the treaty. Moreover, the question of national treatment versus minimum standards of international law arises in a new form under such treaty provisions. If the treatment accorded to a state's nationals is better than the minimum standards laid down in the treaties, then the expropriating state has to extend such treatment to aliens as well, by virtue of its promise to grant national treatment regarding such matters. If the treatment of its nationals falls short of the treatment prescribed in the treaty, then by virtue of the noncontingent treaty rule, it has to accord to aliens the treatment which the treaty prescribes. A state has now a conventional obligation toward aliens which is quite distinct from its general if qualified obligation (in customary as well as in conventional law) not to discriminate against them.

The existence of treaty promises of the type here discussed makes it possible for an intervening state or (at a later stage) for an international tribunal to examine the motives of the expropriating authorities. It would be an exaggeration, it is submitted, to hold that, in accordance with a strict interpretation of the treaty language, such a foreign state or international tribunal would be allowed to pass judgment on the public character of the purposes invoked for the expropriation. It would, however, be within its rights in examining whether the action of the state authorities involved was impelled by improper motives, that is, whether the authorities which ordered the expropriation were in bad faith when invoking "public purposes." An international tribunal would thus be competent to declare such an expropriation illegal (that is, in violation of the treaty) because of "abuse," or more precisely of "misuse," of power (*détournement de pouvoir*, according to the terminology of French public law) on the part of the expropriating authorities.[25]

Similar considerations apply with respect to the provision of exchange facilities for the transfer abroad of the compensation given to an alien for his expropriated property. Under most FCN treaties, this is now a strict obligation of the expropriating state. A state is legally able to deny such facilities to an alien only under certain specified conditions, which are the same as those applicable to the transfer of an investor's earnings.

[25] Cf. *infra* pp. 296–98.

Concluding Observations

The first important legal effect of the promises to foreign investors which are made through instruments of public international law relates to the possibility and extent of diplomatic intervention on the part of the state of which the investors involved are nationals. There is in this connection an important difference between the effects of promises regarding expropriation and those of promises on other matters, such as exchange restrictions or taxation, due to the differences in the customary law rules pertaining to these two categories of matters.

In the case of expropriation, there already exists in public international law a rule which condemns such action under certain conditions, even though the precise content of the rule and the related conditions are not very clear. The importance of the treaty promises lies in their making the applicable rule clearer and establishing its validity, within the limits of conventional international law.[26]

In the case of exchange and other restrictions affecting the investors' interests, no customary legal rule preexists and, in its absence, such restrictions (when not amounting to confiscation or generally not coming under some other heading of internationally tortious action) are therefore permitted. Treaty promises establish the opposite rule, though with qualifications of varying importance and extent. The diplomatic intervention of the state of the investors' nationality is now legally admissible, being founded on the provisions of the FCN treaties. Moreover, such restrictions have now to conform to certain standards, albeit fairly loose ones, in order to be permitted under international law (meaning in this case the law established by the treaties). To what extent such intervention will be effective depends, of course, on a variety of particular factors.

[26] Cf., in agreement, Wilson, *Treaties* 323.

Generally speaking however, there can be no doubt that, from the investors' standpoint, the situation in the presence of treaty promises constitutes a distinct improvement over the situation in their absence.

If the diplomatic methods of intervention prove not to be effective in any particular instance, there now exists a possibility of bringing the matter before an international judicial body, chiefly the International Court of Justice, but possibly also an arbitration tribunal. Investment codes as well as FCN treaties include provisions making recourse to judicial settlement mandatory and providing, though usually not in detail, for the procedure to be followed in such cases. Under customary international law, such recourse would have been more difficult with respect to disputes involving expropriation, and it would have been impossible in most cases with regard to matters of taxation, exchange restrictions, and the like. Similarly, under such treaty promises, a final decision favorable to the investors' interests is more probable. An investor is far better protected when he can invoke treaty provisions applicable in his particular case. Whatever their interpretation of customary law or general principles of law, international tribunals as well as states have always insisted on the inviolability of treaties. According to all indications, they will keep on doing so in the future, despite the difficulties experienced by jurists when they attempt to theorize on the foundations of this attitude.[27]

In the case of an investment code, especially one adopted semiofficially by some international financial organization, there exists an additional means for settling any eventual disputes. It would be possible to provide for nonjudicial methods of settlement within the organs of the organization involved. Such methods, which permit a more politically oriented treatment of the issues than any international court can afford, have been applied with some success by the various international bodies established by virtue of International Commodity Agreements.[28] With respect to problems where strong

[27] Cf. the studies cited *supra*, Chapter 7, note 2.
[28] Cf. Metzger, "Settlement of International Disputes by Non-Judicial Methods,"

economic and political interests are involved such methods might be more appropriate than judicial settlement. However, few of the investment code proposals seem to have considered this possibility seriously.[29]

It is suggested, instead, in some of the proposed codes, that the enforcement of their provisions be assured by the threat of sanctions. Article XI of the 1957 Draft Convention for the Mutual Protection of Private Property Rights in Foreign Countries provided for the procedure to be followed and the measures to be taken against a state acting in violation of its obligations under the convention. Once the unlawfulness of the state measures involved was established by a court decision, the state at fault would be asked to revoke them within a fixed period of time. If it failed to comply, its conduct would be publicly condemned by the court. The other states party to the convention would refuse to recognize within their territories the measures in question and would make available, for the satisfaction of the judgment, any property of the state at fault which they might have in their power.[30] A list of possible additional economic sanctions is provided in an Appendix. Their application, nature, and extent would depend on the character and the degree of unlawfulness of the state measures involved. Such sanctions would include refusal of public or private loans to the state at fault, denial of investment guarantees to foreign investors operating in it, and recommendations to private or public banks in the capital-exporting states to refuse credits to enterprises intending to invest in the state at fault.

---

48 *Am. J. Int'l L.* 408 (1954); Fischer, "Le mode de règlement des différends adopté par l'Accord International sur le Blé," 1 *Annuaire Français Dr. Int'l* 208 (1955). And see also Morse, "Methods of Pacific Settlement of International Disputes: Difficulties and Revision," 25 *Brooklyn L. Rev.* 20, 32 (1959).

[29] Cf. Gardner, "International Measures for the Promotion and Protection of Foreign Investment," 53 *Am. Soc. Int'l L. Proc.* 255, 265–66 (1959); Parliamentary Group for World Government, *A World Investment Convention?* 16 *et seq.* (1959).

[30] *1957 Draft Convention*, article XI(2) and (4). The commentary to the convention, *idem* 64, made clear that private property of the nationals of the state at fault and property enjoying diplomatic immunity would be excluded from such measures.

Any intergovernmental agreements which would not conform to the convention's standard—for example agreements for lump-sum compensation—would be declared ineffective.[31]

Similar measures are proposed in some detail in the report of the European League for Economic Cooperation concerning the common protection of private foreign investment.[32] The 1959 Draft Convention on Investments Abroad, on the other hand, contains no such elaborate provisions. It only includes a general clause to the effect that when a state fails to comply with an award against it, the other states party to the convention "shall be entitled, individually or collectively, to take such measures as are strictly required to give effect to that judgment or award." [33]

No specific provisions on sanctions are included in the other proposed codes. In some of them the advisability of such provisions is expressly denied. Thus, the report of the British Parliamentary Group for World Government states that "no sanctions in any normal sense of the word, are likely to be generally acceptable at the present time. . . ." [34] The only possible measure would be the publication of the Arbitration Tribunal's award and the consequent exposure of the states at fault before the world public opinion. In discussing the question of sanctions, the Council of Europe report also reaches the conclusion that it is not possible to determine them beforehand with any precision. The states party to the proposed convention would consult in each particular instance and decide on the appropriate steps which they would take.[35] The only general measures which are provided for are the refusal of all states members to recognize any acts contrary to the purposes of the convention and the obligation of the party at fault to pay full compensation.[36]

Finally, the possibility of recourse to the local judicial organs in

---

[31] *Idem*, article XI(7).

[32] Cf. E.L.E.C., *Common Protection for Private International Investments* 16, 24–25 (1958). For a summary of the proposed measures, see *supra* pp. 84–85.

[33] *1959 Draft Convention*, article VIII.   [34] *Supra* note 29, at 19.

[35] Council of Europe Consultative Assembly Document 1027, 8 September 1959, at 19.

[36] *Idem* at 18.

the host state should not be ignored or underestimated.[37] Its value will depend, in part, on the status of the treaty granting the promises in the municipal law of the capital-importing state. If the treaty has force of statute,[38] the foreign investor would be able to invoke its provisions before a local court or administrative agency against any act of administrative authorities which he deems in violation of the treaty. The effectiveness of such recourse would depend on the nature of the question involved as well as on the conditions of administration of justice and the relationship between the branches of government in the host state. Thus, recourse to local authorities might be effective in the case of tax measures, since tax assessments and impositions are often determined by junior state officials subject to judicial or hierarchical control. It might also be effective in the case of disputes arising over the application of exchange restrictions, insofar as they relate to the implementation of existing laws on the subject. In all such cases, it should be remembered, the courts would be bound to examine the formal legality of the acts involved, but not their necessity or advisability.

Local courts would afford little protection to the foreign investors in the case of legislative action in violation of the treaty promises. It is today accepted in the courts of most (though not all) states that a later statute prevails over an earlier treaty. This rule, however, is often applied with caution. Courts generally recognize a presumption in favor of the continuing validity of the treaty and may require direct and clear statutory language in order to admit the treaty's invalidation.[39]

[37] For a discussion of the treaties' provisions on access to courts by aliens, see *supra* p. 139, and Wilson, *Treaties* 209–43.

[38] This could happen either through special legislative action on the part of the host state, or by virtue of the treaty's international validity, in the case of a self-executing treaty in a state which accepts conventional as well as customary international law as "the law of the land."

[39] Cf. 1 Oppenheim, *International Law* 45–46 (8th ed., Lauterpacht, 1955); Rousseau, *Droit International Public* 47–48 (1953); 2 Hyde, *International Law* 1464–65 (1945); 5 Hackworth, *Digest* 186–95 (1943). For a comment on a recent Greek case illustrating this principle, see Fatouros, "Repeal of an International Treaty by Municipal Law Provision," 78 *Journal de la Jurisprudence Hellénique et Etrangère* 376 (1959) (in Greek).

9

Legal Effects of
State Contracts

THE legal effects of state guarantees to foreign investors can be meaningfully studied only when seen against the background of a closely related but more general problem, that of the effects in international law of contractual commitments undertaken by states toward the nationals of other states. Our examination of that problem is preceded by a survey of the forms which such commitments may assume and the types of state measures which may affect them.

Forms of Contractual Commitments of States

The "classical" instance of contractual promises of states to aliens is that of state debts: states issue bonds in foreign markets, promising thus to the alien bondholders that a certain interest will be paid regularly and certain other benefits (including as a rule the reimbursement of the principal at a future date, already specified in the bond, or to be determined later) will accrue to them. It is in the case of such debts that the mixed public and private law character of the contractual commitments of states was first recognized. It is to this fact, as well as to the prevalence of such debts in the state practice of the last century and the first quarter of this one that the remarkable size of the relevant literature should be attributed.[1]

[1] Cf. Borchard and Wynne, *State Insolvency and Foreign Bondholders*, 2 vols.

The problems of state debts have thus received a good deal of attention; even though no definite conclusions as to the law of the matter have been reached, they may be considered as almost exhaustively studied. Chiefly because of this fact they shall not be discussed here in any detail, and we shall refer to them only occasionally. This does not imply, however, that the law applicable in their case is essentially different (except for certain peculiarities and some special legal problems) from the law to be applied in all other instances of state contractual commitments toward aliens.[2]

Another important form of state contracts, already noted, is that of economic concessions. Under this term may be included all types of contracts whereby the state grants to private persons, its own nationals or aliens, certain powers and rights which would otherwise belong to itself only. It thus includes contracts granting to individuals or corporations the right to operate certain enterprises which are monopolistic by nature or as a result of legal regulation. There have been a number of international law cases involving concessions of this type to aliens.[3] The term also includes economic concessions *stricto sensu,* namely, contracts giving to private persons (aliens, in the instant cases) the right to exploit the natural resources of a country.[4] Under the same heading may also be included contracts whereby the right to operate enterprises of public

(1951); VanHecke, "Problèmes juridiques des emprunts internationaux," 18 *Bibliotheca Visseriana* (1955). From among the earlier studies, see Politis, *Les emprunts d'Etat en droit international* (1894); Jèze, "La garantie des emprunts publics d'Etat," 7 *Hague Recueil* 155 (1925); Fischer Williams, "Some Legal Aspects of International Financial Problems" in *Chapters in Current International Law and the League of Nations* 257 (1929).

[2] Cf. in agreement, Mann, "State Contracts and State Responsibility," 54 *Am. J. Int'l L.* 572, 589-90 (1960); and *contra,* Borchard, *The Diplomatic Protection of Citizens Abroad* 302 et seq. (1915).

[3] Cf., e.g., the cases of the Company General of the Orinoco, (France v. Venezuela, 1905), 3 Whiteman, *Damages* 1688; and of the El Triunfo Co., Ltd., (U.S.A. v. Salvador, 1902), *idem* 1680. See also the award in the R.C.A. v. China case (1935), 3 UN RIAA 1621, where the tribunal rejected the plaintiff's allegation that its contract with the defendant constituted such a monopoly.

[4] Cf. *supra* pp. 125, 192. Related international cases involve concessions for the exploitation of mineral and agricultural resources and others of the same general type.

utility is granted to aliens.[5] Such enterprises do not necessarily operate by virtue of a contract of concession, but they may do so, in accordance with the municipal law in effect in each state. In several instances, cases involving enterprises of public utility operating by concession have been adjudicated before international judicial bodies.[6] Closely related to economic concessions of these types, are the special contracts of guarantee and the instruments of approval issued by virtue of investment laws which constitute the particular object of this study.

A state may also undertake contractual commitments of other sorts. Some of the most common are the contracts with various suppliers of goods necessary for the operation of a state's public services. Contracts of this type are rarely of such importance as to warrant diplomatic proceedings; nonetheless, there have been a number of related international cases.[7] Similar in character are the contracts of public works, through which a public authority charges a private person (in this case an alien or a foreign corporation) with the construction of roads, bridges, or public buildings against pay-

[5] It is not possible to give a precise definition of such enterprises. In F.V.N. Beichmann's award in the case of the German Reparations According to Article 260 of the Treaty of Versailles (1924), 1 UN RIAA 426, which dealt in part with this question, it was held that, except for the mention of the very general characteristic of utility to the general public, no other definition could be given to public utility enterprises as a group. More precise qualifications should be made only with regard to specific categories of industries and no exhaustive list of enterprises of this type can be given. *Idem* 453 *et seq.*, 468.

[6] Cf., e.g., the following cases: Delagoa Bay and East African Railway Co. (Gt. Britain, U.S.A. v. Portugal, 1900), 3 Whiteman, *Damages* 1694; Barcs-Pakrac Railway (1934), 3 UN RIAA 1569; Zeltweg-Wolfsberg and Unterdrauburg-Woellan Railways (1934 and 1938), *idem* 1795; Buzau-Nehoiasi Railway (Germany v. Rumania, 1939), *idem* 1827; (all involving transportation enterprises). Cf. also the case of the Compagnie d' Electricité de Varsovie (France v. Poland, 1929, 1932 and 1936), *idem* 1669, 1679, 1689 (involving a power supply concession).

[7] Cf., e.g., the following cases before the Mexican-U.S.A. General Claims Commission: G. W. Cook (1929 and 1930), 4 UN RIAA 506, 661 (contract for the sale of school benches); Illinois Central Railroad Company (1926), *idem* 21, 134 (sale of railway equipment); American Bottle Co. (1929), *idem* 435 (sale of beer bottles to custodian of government-seized private brewery); Dickson Car Wheel Co. (1931), *idem* 669 (sale of car wheels). See also 5 Hackworth, *Digest* 615 *et seq.*

ment for their services. Contracts of this type have also been the object of international claims and awards.[8] Many other kinds of contracts may be concluded in order to take care of particular situations; they all come under the general heading of state contractual commitments toward aliens.[9]

There is no essential difference between the legal effects of the various kinds of contracts described above. It is true that contracts of the first two general types (state debts and economic concessions) are more easily affected by general legislation of an expropriatory or other character and, because of this as well as because of their particular character and relative importance, they are more frequently the object of international claims and disputes than other types of contracts.[10] This, however, is a point of fact and not of law. There is no reason why the same legal rules will not be applicable, *mutatis mutandis*, in all these cases, with necessary allowances for differences due to the type or special content of each contract.

Measures Affecting State Contracts

Not only state contracts, but also the state measures which may affect them, may assume several forms. Such state measures vary

[8] Cf., e.g., the following cases: United Dredging Co. (U.S.A. v. Mexico, 1927), 4 UN RIAA 263 (oral contract for dredging services); heirs of H. F. Rudloff (U.S.A. v. Venezuela, 1904), 3 Whiteman, *Damages* 1864 (building and operation of public market); L. A. Oliva (Italy v. Venezuela, 1904), *idem* 1865 (construction of "pantheon" in cemetery).

[9] Cf., e.g., the Landreau Claim (U.S.A. v. Peru, 1922), 1 UN RIAA 347 (contract for services consisting in indicating to the government the location of guano deposits for exploitation); the J. E. Davies case (U.S.A. v. Mexico, 1927), 4 *idem* 239 (contract for legal services).

[10] On the same premises, one may reach the opposite conclusions. It may be argued that the claims arising in connection with such contracts are, because of their importance, settled more often by diplomatic means. Claims relating to contracts of little importance may be more frequently submitted to international tribunals, because the states concerned can afford to lose them. See, on this point, Cheng, Preface to Roulet, *Le caractère artificiel de la théorie de l'abus de droit en droit international public* 7, 8 (1958).

not only in the degree to which they affect the alien's contractual rights,[11] ranging from slight changes in the contract's normal effects to their complete nullification. They also vary with respect to the manner in which they affect contracts, the alleged causes justifying the state's interference and several other elements of a similar character. No complete description of such measures can be given. They can only be classified into categories, with the help of certain necessarily arbitrary criteria. These categories are of a descriptive, not a normative, character. They do not purport to "reveal" the hidden nature of the measures. They are hypothetical models, like those used in other social sciences, which, it is hoped, will make it easier for us to perceive and describe certain important facets of the problems under discussion. Concrete instances of state measures are never as clearly defined and as distinct from each other as may appear here. In most instances, elements of two or more of these categories are present in any single measure or set of measures. Furthermore, the exact borderline between these categories is hard to find.

The first category of state measures consists of measures taken within the general limits of the contract. Such measures are not necessarily lawful; they may be taken in contravention of the contract's terms. What distinguishes them from other types of state measures is that they do not involve, at least in their first stages, or they involve to no more than a minimal degree, the exercise of the state's sovereign powers.[12] They are measures which, but for certain differences of form, might have been taken by a private person. Even though the question of the state's international re-

---

[11] The term "contractual rights" is used here and in the following to refer to rights founded on a "state contract," i.e., a contract between a state and an alien.

[12] A related criterion is proposed by Professor Carlston, "Concession Agreements and Nationalization," 52 *Am. J. Int'l L.* 260, 265 (1958). He considers the "willingness of [a] state to submit the issues leading to [the termination of a concession agreement] to judicial or arbitral determination" the chief criterion as to whether the state's measures are "an exercise of a claimed contractual right" or are founded on the state's sovereign powers.

sponsibility does, under certain conditions, arise, such measures raise legal questions which are not essentially different from those arising in a dispute over a private law contract. These measures cannot be determined with complete precision, because the grounds on which they are founded may vary widely. Such measures may be accompanied by allegations as to the other contracting party's conduct in its fulfillment of the contract. The state's actions may thus be presented as in response to the contract's violation or nonfulfillment by the private contracting party. Whether this has happened is, of course, a question of fact, to be determined by a national or international court. Such measures are often due to differences in the interpretation of the terms of the contract.[13] Very often, the existence or absence of a breach of contract will depend on the interpretation of certain particular provisions. Again, a court will have to construe the contract and decide on the correctness and the good or bad faith of the parties' conflicting interpretations.

In the records of international tribunals, one finds a large number of cases where states, in canceling or otherwise interfering with their contracts with aliens, maintained that they were exercising a contractual right based on the provisions of the contract involved. The fact that such cases are not more frequent should be attributed to a number of factors. Claims of this sort are often not espoused by the state of the alien's nationality because of their doubtful character. They are often resolved, one way or another, before the capital-receiving state's courts. Finally, in many instances, a dispute starts because of measures of this sort, but as it develops, it acquires additional characteristics, particularly through the employment by the state of the means available to it through the use of its sovereign power. By the time, therefore, that the case reaches an international judicial body, the secondary elements have acquired major importance.

The matter was dealt with in broad terms in the decision of the

---

[13] Cf., in agreement, Mann, *supra* note 2, at 574–75.

United States-Mexican General Claims Commission in the *International Fisheries Company* case.[14] It was claimed by the United States that the cancellation by the Mexican Government of a concession granted to a Mexican company, owned in major part by a United States corporation, was unlawful. The Commission disallowed the claim, relying on a "Calvo clause" in the contract.[15] It also stated, however, that since the possibility of cancellation was provided for in the contract, the state had not acted unlawfully in acting as it did. The majority opinion stated in part:

> There is no ground for an international claim if the annulment of the contract has been made in accordance with its express terms. . . .
>
> This is the situation which is always being aired by private parties before courts having jurisdiction, and no reason is seen why the same fact, for the sole reason that one of the parties to the contract is a government, can constitute an international delinquency.
>
> If every non-fulfilment of a contract on the part of a government were to create at once the presumption of an arbitrary act, which should therefore be avoided, governments would be in a worse situation than that of any private person, a party to any contract.[16]

In several other cases, the interpretation of the contract was at issue. Thus, in the *Hughes* case [17] the main issue was whether the claimant's contractual obligation to "take possession" of a number of mining claims within a specified period included the obtaining of title to the claims or only the application for such title. The tribunal accepted the former interpretation and disallowed the claim, holding that the respondent Government's cancellation of the contract on the ground of failure of performance on the part of the claimant

---

[14] (1931) 4 UN RIAA 691. Opinion written by Mexican Commissioner, F. MacGregor, in which the Presiding Commissioner, H. F. Alfaro, concurred; F. Nielsen, U.S. Commissioner, dissented.

[15] That is, a clause by which the alien renounces his right to appeal to his state of nationality and accepts the exclusive jurisdiction of the host state's courts on all matters relating to the contract. For its history and effects, see Shea, *The Calvo Clause* (1955); Lipstein, "The Place of the Calvo Clause in International Law," 22 *Brit. Yb. Int'l L.* 130 (1945).

[16] 4 UN RIAA 691, at 699, 700.

[17] (U.S.A. v. Mexico, 1930) 4 UN RIAA 617.

was lawful under the terms of the contract. On the other hand, in the *Marion A. Cheek* case,[18] the central issue was whether the contractual obligations of the claimant included the payment at a specified date of interest on a loan extended to him by the Siamese Government. The arbitrator found that such was not the case and allowed the claim, since the claimant had in no way violated his contract with the Government.

A second category of state measures which may affect an alien's contractual rights comprises measures of a punitive character. In taking such measures, a state is exercising its sovereign powers, but its alleged intention is the punishment of the alien for his unlawful conduct.[19] If the penalties are provided in the contract, the state measures may be considered as belonging in the category previously described, since the state is in fact exercising a contractual right. When there is no contractual provision, the penalty, which might consist in the cancellation of the contract or the imposition of extraordinary burdens, would normally be provided by municipal legislation. The crime involved may or may not be connected with the contract itself. In performing his contract, the alien might become guilty of penal or other infractions (for example, involving foreign exchange controls or custom duties), the punishment for which may consist, in part, in the cancellation of his contract or in the imposition of fines. When the alien's delinquency is not related to the contract itself, the punitive measures will rest as a rule on criminal law (for example, confiscation of property, including possible contractual rights, because of infractions of criminal law).

State action of this sort is usually individual in character, that is to say, it applies to a particular person only, though in implementation of general provisions. There may be cases, however, where the punitive action of the state which affected the contractual and other property rights of aliens is of a more general character.[20] A recent

---

[18] (U.S.A. v. Siam, 1898) 3 Whiteman, *Damages* 1646.

[19] See the highly interesting developments in Wortley, *Expropriation* 40 *et seq.*, 105–6.

[20] It is not possible to delimit with precision the borderline between individual

instance of such action is the confiscation of enterprises belonging to persons guilty of collaboration with the enemy during the war. Many such confiscations took place after the Second World War, not only in Eastern and Central Europe, (where they had definite political implications in that they contributed greatly to the "socialization" of these areas) [21] but also in Western European countries such as France.[22]

The third category consists of state measures of an exceptional character which are dictated by considerations of public interest. A state may interfere with the contractual rights of private persons, its nationals or aliens, when it finds that the interests of the public —that is, of the state itself, conceived not as a power organization but as the symbol of a community of persons—require such interference. The state is thus exercising its sovereign powers in a manner calculated to defeat the private persons' normal expectations, based on the provisions of the public contracts. The state's justification lies in the extraordinary exigencies of the public interest and in the latter's prevalence over private interests.

Before going any further, however, it is necessary to make another important distinction between two kinds of state measures affecting aliens' contractual rights. The first consists of individual measures, that is, measures concerned with and aiming at a single contract or a limited class of contracts, while the second one comprises general measures, measures which refer and apply to large categories of contracts and correspond to important changes in a

---

and general measures; see *infra* p. 241. In the instant case, the measures called "general" would be those affecting large categories of persons and rights at the same time.

[21] Cf. Sharp, *Nationalization of Key Industries in Eastern Europe* (1946); Doman, "Postwar Nationalization of Foreign Property in Europe," 48 *Columbia L. Rev.* 1125 (1948); Moodie, "Agrarian Reform in East Central Europe," 8 *Yb. World Affairs* 242 (1954); Foighel, *Nationalization* 58, 64, 65 (1957); Wortley, *Expropriation* 66; Friedman, *Expropriation* 30–34, 39–41, 47.

[22] Cf. Wortley, *Expropriation* 102, 118; Friedman, *Expropriation* 59–60; DeVries and Hoeniger, "Post-Liberation Nationalizations in France," 50 *Columbia L. Rev.* 629, 633 (1950); Robson, "Nationalized Industries in Britain and France," in *Problems of Nationalized Industry* 238, 248–49 (Robson ed., 1952); Katzarov, *Nationalisation* 46.

country's legal and economic structure. This distinction is applicable to all state measures which affect aliens' contractual rights but it acquires special importance in the case of measures of the third category. It is a distinction of fact rather than law; it is not easy to distinguish individual from general measures on legal grounds.[23]

In both cases, a set of general rules is applied to particular situations by means of a number of special rules. In a few cases, we may find obvious formal differences. In the great majority of cases, the differences lie chiefly in the scope and extent of the measures and in the character of the interest they serve. General measures are as a rule closely related to, and constitute in fact manifestations of, vast changes in the legal, economic, and social structure of a state.[24] Individual measures generally do not reflect such changes; they may be taken at any time by any government, conservative, liberal, or revolutionary. Moreover, general measures affect whole categories of interests at about the same time, while individual measures affect small categories of interests to begin with and over a long period of time. Finally, the concept of public interest, which is basic to measures of this category, means different things in the two cases.

The public interest served by individual measures is generally concrete and well-determined or determinable. It consists in the opening up of a road, rendering the elimination of certain buildings necessary; in an increase of the public needs for transportation, resulting in the imposition of additional obligations on a transporta-

---

[23] The matter has been treated in the legal literature chiefly with respect to the distinction between "ordinary" expropriation and nationalization. A question of terminology is, of course, involved, but, apart from that, the distinction between two types of measures does correspond to certain differences in substance. See the discussions and distinctions in 43-I *Annuaire de l'Institut de Droit International* 79, 94, 104-5, 117-21 (1950); 44-II *idem* 262, 267, 283 (1952); Foighel, *Nationalization* 14-23 (1957); Friedman, *Expropriation* 5 *et seq.*; Katzarov, *Nationalisation* 207-12; Cavaré, *La protection des droits contractuels reconnus par les Etats à des étrangers à l'exception des emprunts* (hereinafter cited Cavaré, *Droits contractuels*) 70 *et seq.* (1956).

[24] It is true, however, that in some cases measures of general application may not be related to any radical changes in economic structure. Such is the case of measures leading to the total suppression of activities in certain fields (e.g., prohibition of manufacture and sale of liquor) or establishing state monopolies. Cf. Friedman, *Expropriation* 50-55; Katzarov, *Nationalisation* 27-32.

tion company operating by virtue of a concession; or in the need for better service to the public, making the revocation of an outdated concession necessary. In the case of general measures the general interest is more indefinite and abstract.[25] It involves the indirect effect of changes in the state structure, deemed beneficial by the government effecting them. The typical cases of recent measures of this sort are agrarian expropriations, where large landholdings are expropriated and divided among the landless, or nationalizations of industries, where whole branches of the economy of a country become state property and operate under direct state control.[26] In both instances, the public interest to be served is less immediate than in the case of individual measures and it may usually be understood as operating only in the long run. The benefit of the public is, furthermore, less certain, since the economic or social bases of agrarian expropriations and, even more, of nationalizations are controversial and their acceptance is in large part a matter of ideological conviction. It is not possible, therefore, to apply the same criteria to individual and general measures, nor is it possible to evaluate the public benefit involved in each case in the same manner.

In this discussion of the three major categories of state measures affecting the contractual rights of aliens, we have carefully avoided any qualification of these measures as to their lawfulness or unlawfulness. We have dealt with the external aspects of these measures, not with the truth or falsity of the allegations of the state taking them; we have not examined whether such allegations correspond with actual conditions or with the state's real intentions. We have not even examined whether, had the state's allegations been well-founded, the measures in question would be lawful or not. The

[25] Cf. Cavaré, *Droits contractuels* 113–14; Katzarov, *Nationalisation* 208, 210–11; LaPradelle, "Les effets internationaux des nationalisations," in 43-I *Annuaire de l'Institut de Droit International* 42, 66 (1950) and cf. *idem* 126 *et seq.*; Foighel, *Nationalization* 23–28 (1957).

[26] In the past, repudiations of state debts or temporary suspension of interest payments were the main instances of general measures of this sort. The considerations mentioned in the text also apply, *mutatis mutandis,* in their case.

determination of the lawfulness under international law of state measures of the types just described will constitute the main object of our study in the remainder of this chapter.

The International Law on the Matter

It should be stated from the outset that there are no well-settled and universally accepted international legal rules regarding state measures affecting the contractual rights of aliens. Not only writers and scholars but states and international tribunals, as well, differ in their views on the law in effect. The difference of opinion extends both to the *lex lata*, the legal rules held as effective, and to the *lex ferenda*, the law which, according to the particular views of each state or person, ought to exist. These controversies, far from being merely "theoretical" disputes, are of real practical importance and have far-reaching effects on the life and relations of the nations.

EVOLUTION OF THE LAW

There is a certain evolution in the law regarding state contracts which corresponds closely to the political and economic developments in the international society over the last hundred years. In the state practice of the early nineteenth century, one notices a general reluctance on the part of the then relatively developed states to espouse the claims of their nationals against foreign states, when such claims were founded on contracts. The official position was that such contracts were concluded at the contracting individuals' risk and such individuals had no right to expect the support and intervention of their state of nationality on their behalf.[27] This view was prevalent at a time when, because of the pressing needs for domestic investments, the export of capital was not encouraged, especially since the aliens' activities abroad consisted mainly in

---

[27] Cf., e.g., a Report dated July 27, 1831, by the British Law Officer (Jenner), 2 McNair, *International Law Opinions* 201 (1956); see also *ibidem*, a Report dated January 27, 1830, and cf. Lord McNair's interesting comments, *idem* at 197-98. See also, 6 Moore, *Digest* 705 *et seq.*

trading and financial speculations, and not in the occupations then considered as "productive."

By the end of the last century, economic conditions had changed and foreign investment began to be regarded with increasing favor by the governments of the industrialized countries of the West. Their position on the international law of the matter changed accordingly. It came to be accepted now that contractual claims could form the basis for a state's interposition in support of its nationals, though only under certain conditions. The chief condition was that a denial of justice should be proved, that is, that, before a claim could be raised, it should be shown that the alien had been denied the judicial and other means under local law through which he might obtain reparation for the injury to his interests. This view, with certain qualifications and additions, may be considered as the "classical" international law position with regard to claims based on breach of state contracts and may be found in the main legal studies of the subject.[28]

It should be noted that the classical doctrine does not depart considerably, in theory at least, from the original position on the matter. A breach of contract by a state is still not considered, by itself, as internationally unlawful. It is not the breach of contract, but the denial of justice which follows it, that constitutes the internationally tortious act.[29] Acceptance of such a rule does not indicate any toleration of state measures affecting contractual rights on the part of the then all-powerful capital-exporting states. It expresses rather the "traditional" conception of international law as the law governing the relations between states. Such a rule was adequate and appropriate at a time when there existed general agreement between capital-exporting as well as capital-importing coun-

---

[28] Cf. Borchard, *The Diplomatic Protection of Citizens Abroad* 281 *et seq.* (1915); Eagleton, *The Responsibility of States in International Law* 160–68 (1928); Feller, *The Mexican Claims Commissions* 174 (1935); Freeman, *The International Responsibility of States for Denial of Justice* 111–13 (1938); Friedman, *Expropriation* 153–57. And see Professor Reuter's concise and astute treatment of the topic in his *Droit international public* 179–81 (1958).

[29] For a discussion of some other aspects of denial of justice, see *infra* p. 251–52.

tries (to the extent that the latter were consulted) on the value of the institution of private property and the necessity for its protection.

Today, there is no longer any general agreement on the degree of protection to be accorded to private property and the rights connected with it.[30] Moreover, it begins to be accepted, by states as well as scholars, though more by the latter than the former, that international law is something far more complex than a law between states. Consequently, much criticism has been directed against the classical thesis on the protection of the contractual rights of aliens.[31] Several scholars now consider this thesis as insufficient and outdated, with no relevance to modern legal and economic conditions. They argue that states should be considered guilty of an internationally tortious act whenever they violate, directly or indirectly, their contracts with aliens.[32] There is no need to prove a denial of justice and, accordingly, no necessity for the prior exhaustion of local remedies. Such criticism of the classical doctrine is partly correct in that modern developments have certainly affected at least some of the rules which were once effective. One should not fail to notice, however, that despite controversies and apparently extensive disagreements, there persists a wide measure of substantial agreement between the various views and theories.[33]

Thus, there can be no question as to the relevance of the classical theory with respect to state measures allegedly based on contractual provisions. The normal manner in which a related dispute between a state and an alien can be resolved is by bringing it before the courts of the state involved.[34] If these courts do not give satisfaction to the alien because under the existing legal system they can-

---

[30] Cf. *supra* pp. 50–53.   [31] Cf. *infra* pp. 261 *et seq.*

[32] These arguments are discussed *infra* pp. 261 *et seq.*

[33] See, e.g., in agreement on this point, though holding widely differing positions, Mann, "State Contracts and State Responsibility," 54 *Am. J. Int'l L.* 572, 573–75 (1960); Schwebel, "International Protection of Contractual Arrangements," 53 *Am. Soc. Int'l L. Proc.* 266, 268–69 (1959).

[34] Cf., in agreement, Carlston, "Concession Agreements and Nationalization," 52 *Am. J. Int'l L.* 260, 267 (1958).

not try claims against the state or for any other reason, the latter may ask the protection of his state of nationality, invoking the existence of a denial of justice. Whether such protection will be available or effective depends on the particular facts of each case and does not concern us here. It is evident, however, that the rules as to denial of justice are applicable in such cases and it seems that, under normal conditions, they are sufficient to protect the lawful interests of the aliens.[35]

Punitive state measures do not raise important special problems, either. The issue in their case is twofold: on the one hand, the measures may be lawful in themselves but the alien may contest their applicability in his case. He should then, normally, bring the matter before the competent national authority, judicial or administrative. In the absence of any such authority (and, in exceptional cases, in the event of an unfavorable decision on the part of such authority), he may ask his state of nationality to intervene on the ground of a denial of justice. It is then up to the latter state to espouse his claim or to decline to do so. On the other hand, the alien may claim that the measures which affected his interests are internationally unlawful in themselves, because the crime they are punishing is not considered as such under international law or under the law of civilized states,[36] because the penalties provided are excessive, or because the state's real intent is to deprive him of his rights and not to punish him for a crime. In such cases, the alien is in fact claiming that the state responsible for these measures is abusing its right to punish criminals. Such a claim raises special problems and will have to be studied in more detail in a later section. At this point, we may conclude that, despite certain exceptions (for example, claims of abuse of rights), the classical theory provides sufficient protection to aliens with respect to punitive measures affecting their contractual rights.

[35] Cf. the majority Opinion in the International Fisheries Company case, U.S.A. v. Mexico, award of July 1931, Mexican-U.S.A. General Claims Commission, 4 UN RIAA 691, discussed *supra* p. 238.

[36] See on this point Wortley, *Expropriation* 40–45, 105.

It is only with regard to the third category of state measures here distinguished, namely, measures taken for reasons of public interest, that important difficulties arise when an attempt is made to apply the classical thesis. In order to better understand these difficulties, it is necessary to state more fully the tenets of the theory in question.

THE CLASSICAL THEORY

The classical position concerning state measures affecting the contractual commitments of states toward aliens should not be understood as a wholly formed, well-expressed and systematic theory. In fact, it is found scattered in a number of international judicial decisions and a few scholarly studies,[37] with variations in the emphasis placed on its different aspects and in the importance of several details. Insofar as it can be correctly stated without detailed qualifications, this theory holds that, in the absence of a denial of justice, state measures affecting the contractual (or property) rights of aliens are internationally lawful when (a) they are taken in the public interest and (b) they are not taken in discrimination against aliens as such. When either of these conditions is absent, the measures in question are internationally unlawful and involve the international responsibility of the state which takes them.[38]

The first condition is that state measures affecting the contractual rights of aliens should, in order to be lawful, serve a purpose of public interest. This is a requirement mentioned by most writers on the subject and found in the dicta of several decisions of international tribunals. Apart, however, from one or two doubtful instances,[39] it has not constituted the actual holding of any such decision. International law does not give any detailed definition of

[37] The problem is usually treated incidentally, in the general context of the protection of alien property. Earlier studies of a more specific character dealt chiefly with the question of state debts; see note 1 *supra*. From among the recent studies, special mention is due to Cavaré, *Droits contractuels* and, now, to Mann, *supra* note 33, and White, *Nationalisation of Foreign Property* 162–79 (1961).

[38] Another important question, quite relevant at this point, is that of compensation. It is treated in some detail *infra* pp. 302 *et seq.*

[39] Cf. the case of the Norwegian Shipowners' Claims, discussed *infra* note 43; the W. Fletcher Smith case, *infra* note 256,

the interests that may be considered as public for the purpose of justifying the taking of such measures.[40] The interest involved should be understood as one of the general public and not as a mere financial interest of the state treasury. It might be more immediate, as in the case of measures of protection of the public health or of public safety, or less so, as in the case of measures involving the "general welfare" of the public. It has already been noted that the conception of "public interest" which is operative with respect to general state measures differs considerably from that which applies in the case of individual state measures. The purpose invoked, however, should be connected in some manner with the contractual right affected.[41]

It is by now generally accepted that only the state taking the measures can be the judge as to the character and existence of a public purpose or interest. Most students of the subject accept this view; [42] there is little authority to the opposite effect.[43] Indeed,

[40] Cf. Cheng, *General Principles of Law as Applied by International Courts and Tribunals* 39 (1953); Wortley, "Les problèmes soulevés en droit international privé par la législation sur l'expropriation," 67 *Hague Recueil* 345, 362 *et seq.* (1939); McNair, "The Seizure of Property and Enterprises in Indonesia," 6 *Ned. Tijdschrift voor Int. Recht* 218, 243–45 (1959).

[41] See McNair, *supra* note 40, at 246. Cavaré, *Droits contractuels* 114, holds that, in the case of nationalizations, the public interest involved should be capable of being realized in no other manner and only by means of the measures in question.

[42] See Fischer Williams, "International Law and the Property of Aliens," 9 *Brit. Yb. Int'l L.* 1 (1928), reprinted in *Chapters in Current International Law and the League of Nations* 147, 181–83 (1929); Herz, "Expropriation of Foreign Property," 35 *Am. J. Int'l L.* 243, 251–53 (1941); Bindschedler, "La protection de la proprieté privée en droit international public," 90 *Hague Recueil* 173, 186 (1956); Note: "Nationalization of the Suez Canal Company," 70 *Harv. L. Rev.* 480, 484 (1957).

[43] See Cheng, *op. cit. supra* note 40, at 37–40; Cheng, "Expropriation in International Law," 21 *Solicitor* 98, 99–100 (1954); Memorial submitted by the United Kingdom to the International Court of Justice, *I.C.J. Pleadings, Anglo-Iranian Oil Company Case (U.K. v. Iran)* 64, 85, 94–95 (1951).

In the case of the Norwegian Shipowners (Norway v. U.S.A., 1921), 1 UN RIAA 307, the arbitral tribunal held that the action of the United States in keeping a number of ships of Norwegian ownership after general wartime shipping control had ended was not justified by public need or reasons of public use; *idem* at 336–37. The import of the case in international law is, however, doubtful, because the tribunal had found relevant and, in part, applicable United States constitutional law rather than public international law; cf. *idem* at 330–32.

certain scholars have maintained that there is no international law requirement at all as to the purpose of such measures. They claim that states have complete freedom with respect to the purposes and motives of their measures.[44] This view, however, ignores those extreme cases where the stated purpose of the measures is manifestly not connected with the public.[45] Furthermore, the stated purpose of such measures may in some cases be clearly false, used in order to cover other, manifestly nonpublic, interests. Such a case comes under the general heading of abuse of rights.[46] Instances of these types are admittedly rare. The general rule is that a state or an international tribunal will not question the public character of the purposes stated as such by another state.

The second "classical" requirement for the legality of state measures affecting the contractual rights of aliens is the absence of discrimination. Discrimination, as understood here, consists in the differential and unfavorable treatment of aliens as compared to nationals or of a specific group of aliens as compared to other aliens. It is widely accepted that state measures affecting unfavorably the interests of aliens as such, that is, because of their being aliens, are unlawful in international law. This is a rule stated by almost all writers [47] and frequently found in official statements [48] and in

[44] Cf., e.g., Friedman, *Expropriation* 141–44; Rolin, "Avis sur la validité des mesures de nationalisation décretées par le gouvernement indonésien," 6 *Ned. Tijdschrift voor Int. Recht* 260, 267 *et seq.* (1959). In support of this position, the language of the award in the Shufeldt Claims (U.S.A. v. Guatemala, 1930), 2 UN RIAA 1079, may be cited. In stressing the obligation on the part of Guatemala to compensate Shufeldt, the arbitrator stated that this state was perfectly competent to enact any decree it liked and for any reasons it saw fit, and he went on to state that "such reasons are no concern of this tribunal." *Idem* at 1095.

[45] See, on this point, Schwarzenberger, "The Abs-Shawcross Draft Convention on Investments Abroad: A Critical Commentary," 9 *J. Pub. L.* 147, 156 (1960).

[46] Cf., for instance, the W. Fletcher Smith case (U.S.A. v. Cuba, 1929), 2 UN RIAA 913, discussed *infra* p. 299.

[47] Among the more recent studies, see Cheng, *op. cit. supra* note 40, at 36–37, 49; Friedman, *Expropriation* 189–93; Bindschedler, *supra* note 42, at 186; Verzijl, "The Relevance of Public and Private International Law Respectively for the Solution of Problems Arising from Nationalization of Enterprises," 19 *Zeitschrift für ausländisches öffentliches Recht und Völkerrecht* 531, 536 (1958); McNair, *supra* note 40, at 247–49; Rolin, *supra* note 44, at 269–70.

[48] See, e.g., 3 Hackworth, *Digest* 555, 654; 3 Whiteman, *Damages* 1557.

the dicta of the decisions of international tribunals.[49] It has not, however, constituted the holding of any such decision.[50] This is not accidental. It is to be attributed to a number of factors, one of which may be that the principle of nondiscrimination is often taken for granted by writers or judges.[51] In recent years, the main emphasis has been placed on the existence and determination of an international minimum standard of justice, independent of the relative standard of national treatment. Moreover, the whole question of nondiscrimination is far from being clear, because of the existence of several possible meanings of that term as well as of the fact that some discrimination against aliens is generally recognized as internationally lawful. The problem thus becomes often one of establishing a borderline between just and unjust discrimination.[52]

A cardinal problem with respect to the requirement of nondiscrimination is that states rarely discriminate openly against aliens in peacetime. Frequently, state measures which are apparently general in character affect in fact only aliens. This happened, for instance, in the nationalization of the oil industry in Iran, which, at the time it occurred, affected solely the Anglo-Iranian Oil Company, or, even more plainly, in the case of the nationalization of the Universal Suez Maritime Canal Company by Egypt. International

[49] See, e.g., the Norwegian Shipowners' Claims, *supra* note 43; the case of the British Properties in Spanish Morocco (U.K. v. Spain, 1925), 2 UN RIAA 615.

[50] The problem of discrimination has been discussed thoroughly by the Permanent Court of International Justice in the Oscar Chinn Case, Judgment of December 12, 1934, PCIJ Publ. Ser. A/B, No. 63. However, the import of the case is limited, for the majority of the judges found no discrimination and, at any rate, the claim was founded on specific treaty provisions. In a different context, discrimination between foreign companies with respect to the award of compensation for war damage, in the absence of any positive obligation on the part of the compensating state, was held to be "perfectly legitimate"; cf. the case of the Eastern Extension, Australasia and China Telegraph Co. (Great Britain v. U.S.A., 1923), 6 UN RIAA 112.

[51] But see Anzilotti, "La responsabilité internationale des Etats à raison des dommages soufferts par des étrangers," 13 *Rev. Gén. Dr. Int'l Public* 5, 19 (1906) who held that nondiscrimination was not yet a principle of positive international law.

[52] Cf. Schwarzenberger, *supra* note 45, at 158–60; 6 Moore, *Digest* 698 *et seq.;* Friedman, *Expropriation* 192–93. And see *supra* p. 56.

law, however, does not consider such measures unlawful, since there is no actual discrimination between aliens and nationals.[53] The discrimination is only hypothetical and, in the absence of proof to the contrary, it is assumed that the state involved would have taken the property of its nationals, as well.[54] However, the opposite view, to the effect that general measures are discriminatory when they affect solely or chiefly aliens, has received considerable support.[55] In one occasion, the United States Government stated that the land expropriations decreed by the then Guatemalan Government raised "a serious question of discrimination against aliens," because about two thirds of the total acreage of expropriated landholdings belonged to a company owned by American nationals.[56]

With respect to individual measures affecting state contracts, the problem arises in a different form. The state may interfere in the execution of such contracts, alleging that it does so in accordance with the general rules governing public contracts. It may in fact be a case of covert discrimination, but it has to be proven as such.

The classical theory was completed by the doctrine of denial of justice. According to it, it is only where access to local remedial procedures is denied the foreign national or where such local reme-

---

[53] Cf., in agreement, Delson, "Nationalization of the Suez Canal Company: Issues of Public and Private International Law," 57 *Columbia L. Rev.* 755, 767–68 (1957); Note, *supra* note 42, at 484; Rubin, *Private Foreign Investment* 16 (1956).

[54] In a recent decision dealing with the legality of the Indonesian expropriations of Dutch enterprises, a German court went further than that. It found the discriminatory treatment of the nationals of a former colonial power by the government of the former colonial territory did not constitute a violation of the principle of equality. The court stated that "the equality concept means only that equals must be treated equally and that the different treatment of unequals is admissible. . . . For the statement to be objective, it is sufficient that the attitude of the former colonial people toward its former colonial master is of course different from that toward other foreigners." Quoted in Domke, "Indonesian Nationalization Measures before Foreign Courts," 54 *Am. J. Int'l L.* 305, 315 (1960).

[55] See, e.g., Mann, *supra* note 33, at 575–76, who considers the Iranian nationalization of the oil industry as a clear case of discriminatory expropriation.

[56] Cf. Thomas, "Protection of Property of Citizens Abroad," in Southwestern Legal Foundation, *Proceedings of the 1959 Institute on Private Investments Abroad* 417, at 438–39 (1959).

dies are nonexistent or so inadequate as to provide no reasonable means of redress, that an international delinquency arises. Such a delinquency, termed a denial of justice, warrants the intercession of a state on behalf of its national. In the absence of a treaty, a state has no right to intercede on behalf of one of its nationals, whose interests have been affected by measures taken by another state, unless that national can establish that his resort to local remedial procedures has resulted in a denial of justice. It is not feasible to discuss here at any length the concept of denial of justice, particularly since there have been several excellent studies of it.[57] We are here concerned only with those aspects of the problem which are closely connected with our topic. Today, the requirement of previous exhaustion of local remedies is often (though by no means always) meaningless. When the state measures involved are legislative in form, as often happens, national courts cannot ordinarily refuse to apply them, even though, in states where the courts may refuse to apply a statute which they deem unconstitutional, a further remedy may still exist.[58] Therefore, the alien whose interests have been affected has in fact no local remedy against such measures. His state of nationality may then intervene on his behalf from the very start.[59] From the special standpoint of the present topic, denial of justice provides definite though perhaps not very extensive protection to aliens.

[57] See Ch. de Visscher, "Le déni de justice en droit international" 52 *Hague Recueil* 369 (1935); Eustathiades, *La responsabilité internationale de l'état pour les actes des organes judiciaires et le problème du déni de justice en droit international* (1936); Freeman, *The International Responsibility of States for Denial of Justice* (1938).

[58] This apparently was the case in the recent Cuban expropriations. For a description of the efforts of the American enterprises involved to have the Nationalization Law of July 6, 1960, declared unconstitutional by the Cuban Supreme Court, see Allison, "Cuba's Seizures of American Business," 47 *Am. Bar Ass'n. J.* 48, at 50-51 (1961).

[59] Cf. Reuter, "Quelques remarques sur la situation juridique des particuliers en droit international public," 2 *La technique et les principes du droit international public: Etudes en l'honneur de Georges Scelle* 535, 543 (1950); Carlston, "Concession Agreements and Nationalization," 52 *Am. J. Int'l L.* 260, 264, 275 (1958). And see also Schwebel, "International Protection of Contractual Arrangements," 53 *Am. Soc. Int'l L. Proc.* 266, 269 (1959).

GENERAL PRINCIPLES OF LAW

Apart from the requirements discussed above, traditional international law also includes the application of general principles of law, recognized among civilized nations. Two such principles are of particular relevance in connection with the legality of state measures affecting the contractual rights of aliens. These principles were not, it is true, an integral part of the "classical" international law doctrine on the matter, but they are applicable within the general framework of the traditional law of nations.

The first of the principles in question is that which prohibits unjustified enrichment. This is a principle of very broad application and its relevance to the present topic is generally acknowledged. It is, however, closely related to the problem of compensation, so that its discussion will be deferred for the time being.[60] The second principle is that of estoppel; it has not been often associated with the present topic, but it is of particular relevance. At this point, only its more general aspects will be discussed.

The principle of estoppel is found in municipal law in most modern legal systems [61] and it has been formulated in several ways. It involves two distinct elements, and the presence of both is required before a successful plea of estoppel can be raised in any particular instance. First, there has to be an inconsistency in the position of one of the parties to a legal relationship. Second, an objective element is needed, namely, a prejudicial change in the situation of one of the parties which is due to its reliance on the other party's previous position. In the result, the inconsistent party is precluded from altering its initial position. The two elements of estoppel are clearly indicated in the Latin maxims often used in this connection. On the one hand, *allegans contraria non est audiendus*, and, on the other, *non concedit venire contra factum proprium*.

---

[60] See *infra* pp. 308 *et seq.*
[61] Though the term of estoppel comes from English law, the principle itself is found in most other legal systems as well. Cf. Lauterpacht, *Private Law Sources and Analogies of International Law* 203–4 (1927); W. Friedmann, *Legal Theory* 391 (3d ed., 1953).

With respect to the first element, the traditional formulation of estoppel by conduct [62] in English law refers to an inconsistency as to a state of facts, which has been represented as existing by the party now estopped from asserting otherwise. American legal theory has added the concept of promissory estoppel, which arises when a party may be injured because of its reliance on the other party's gratuitous promise.[63] In the result, the promise is held binding, despite the absence of consideration. In both instances, estoppel arises under strict conditions. In the case of a statement of fact, its meaning must be clear and unambiguous.[64] In the case of a promise, the reliance of the other party on it must have been foreseen by the promisor or, at least, must be reasonably foreseeable.[65]

Great emphasis is also laid on the objective element of estoppel. The action of the party injured must have been clearly induced by the other party's representation, conduct, or promise;[66] and there must be a definite injury to the former party's interests.[67] In the

[62] English law distinguishes three kinds of estoppel, namely, estoppel by record, estoppel by deed, and estoppel *in pais;* estoppel by conduct is the main form of the third of these estoppels. See Ewart, *Estoppel* 1 (1900); 2 Street, *Foundations of Legal Liability* 241–48 (1906); 15 Halsbury, *Laws of England* 168 (3d ed., Simonds, 1956); 1 Williston, *Contracts* 601–7 (3d ed., Jaeger, 1957).

It is suggested in a recent study that estoppel by deed has its close counterpart in international law in estoppel by treaty, *compromis* or other undertaking in writing; Bowett, "Estoppel before International Tribunals and Its Relation to Acquiescence," 33 *Brit. Yb. Int'l L.* 176, 181–83 (1957). It is not suggested that estoppel of this type may be founded on a contract between a state and an alien. In view of the importance of the formal element in estoppel by deed, it would be difficult to support such an argument.

[63] Cf. the definition in Restatement, *Contracts* 90 (1932), where, however, the term "promissory estoppel" is not used. And see Williston, *op. cit. supra* note 62, at 607–19; Boyer, "Promissory Estoppel: Requirements and Limitations of the Doctrine," 98 *U. Pa. L. Rev.* 459 (1950); Fridman, "Promissory Estoppel," 35 *Can. Bar Rev.* 279 (1957).

[64] Cf. Halsbury, *op. cit. supra* note 62, at 225–26; Ewart, *op. cit. supra* note 62, at 14–17; Sheridan, "Equitable Estoppel Today," 15 *Mod. L. Rev.* 325, 327 (1952).

[65] Cf. Restatement, *Contracts* 90 (1932); Fridman, *supra* note 63, at 289; Boyer, *supra* note 63, at 461–65. For the intent required in the case of estoppel *in pais,* see Halsbury, *op. cit. supra* note 62, at 228; Ewart, *op. cit. supra* note 62, at 155–62.

[66] Cf. Halsbury, *op. cit. supra* note 62, at 229–30; Ewart, *op. cit. supra* note 62, at 140–46, 163–76; Boyer, *supra* note 63, at 471–74.

[67] Cf. Halsbury, *op. cit. supra* note 62, at 229–30; Ewart, *op. cit. supra* note 62, at 146–49; Wilson, "Recent Developments in Estoppel," 67 *L. Qu. Rev.* 330, 332, 348–49 (1951).

case of promissory estoppel, the action or forbearance induced must be of a definite and substantial character.[68] Estoppel will arise only when grave injustice will be avoided by its operation.[69]

The applicability of the principle of estoppel in international law seems today well-established. The principle has been applied in a number of decisions of international tribunals,[70] and it has been favorably considered, though found not applicable in the particular instance, in many others.[71] Several other judgments may be interpreted as applying estoppel in substance, though not expressly.[72] The principle has often been put forward by states in diplomatic correspondence or in pleadings before international tribunals.[73] It has been favorably considered by several scholars [74] and, recently, several detailed studies have been devoted to it.[75]

[68] Cf. Boyer, *supra* note 63, at 474–82.   [69] Cf. *idem* at 482–94.

[70] See, e.g., the case of the Yukon Lumber Co. (Great Britain v. U.S.A., 1913), 6 UN RIAA 17, on which see Bowett, *supra* note 62, at 187–88; and the cases discussed *infra*, text to notes 84, 87, 97, 101. Cf. also the cases cited and discussed in the studies cited *infra* notes 74 and 75.

[71] See, e.g., cases cited *infra* notes 88, 91, 93, 99, 104.

[72] Cf., e.g., the Pious Fund case (U.S.A. v. Mexico, 1902), 1 *The Hague Court Reports* 3 (Scott ed., 1916); the Venezuelan Preferential case, (Germany, Great Britain, Venezuela, and other states, 1904), *idem* 56; the Russian Indemnity case (Russia v. Turkey, 1912), *idem* 532; the case of The Eastry (Great Britain v. U.S.A., 1914), 6 UN RIAA 36. For an interpretation of these and other cases contrary to that indicated here, see Holohan, "Legal Aspects of the Inter-Allied Debt," 14 *Boston U. L. Rev.* 47, 78–79 (1934).

[73] See Lauterpacht, *op. cit. supra* note 61, at 232 *et seq.;* MacGibbon, "Estoppel in International Law," 7 *Int. & Comp. L. Qu.* 468, 480–86 (1958). See also *idem*, 487–99, for an interesting survey of the application of the principle of estoppel in the Opinions and Reports of the Law Officers to the British Government.

[74] See McNair, "The Legality of the Occupation of the Ruhr." 5 *Brit. Yb. Int'l L.* 17, 34–35 (1924); Lauterpacht, *op. cit. supra* note 61, 205 *et seq.;* Witenberg, "L'estoppel—Un aspect juridique du problème des créances américaines," 60 *J. Droit Int'l* (Clunet) 529 (1933); Witenberg, "La théorie des preuves devant les juridictions internationales," 56 *Hague Recueil* 1, 27–28 (1936); Friede, "Das Estoppel-Prinzip im Völkerrecht," 5 *Zeitschrift für ausländisches öffentliches Recht und Völkerrecht* 517 (1935). See also more recently, 2 Guggenheim, *Traité de droit international public* 158–59 (1954); W. Friedmann, *Law in a Changing Society* 456–57 (1959); 1 Schwarzenberger, *International Law* 608, 609 (3d ed., 1957) (on which, see MacGibbon, *supra* note 73, 475–76).

[75] Cheng, *General Principles of Law as Applied by International Courts and Tribunals* 141–49 (1953); MacGibbon, "The Scope of Acquiescence in International Law," 31 *Brit. Yb. Int'l L.* 143, 147–50 (1954); Bowett, *supra* note 62; Meron, "Repudiation of *Ultra Vires* State Contracts and the International Responsibility of States," 6 *Int'l & Comp. L. Qu.* 273, 282–86 (1957); MacGibbon, *supra* note 73.

In international law, there is often more emphasis on the first element of estoppel than on the second. Some writers go as far as to identify this principle with the general, logical as well as moral, principle of consistency, emphasizing its close relation to the concept of good faith.[76] Such alleged "rules" are then based on it as that a state is precluded from asserting claims the legality of which it has previously contested or from challenging claims the legality of which it has previously asserted.[77] It is, however, open to serious doubt whether estoppel in such a broad sense constitutes a legal principle rather than a policy rule or a moral principle. It is surely an exaggeration to say that international law today holds states strictly to all their previous assertions and conduct.[78]

On the other hand, the principle of estoppel cannot be considered as a mere rule of evidence. It is true that it has been so regarded traditionally in municipal law.[79] But it seems now well accepted that, in the words of an eminent British judge, "the whole concept is more correctly viewed as a substantive rule of law." [80] The same evolution of opinion seems to have occurred in international law. Earlier writers have treated estoppel as part of adjective law,[81] probably because of wholesale acceptance of the municipal law theories prevailing at the time. Today, it is widely accepted that the principle of estoppel is part of the substantive law of nations.[82]

The principle of estoppel is certainly applicable with respect to

[76] Cf. MacGibbon, *supra* note 73, at 471–73.   [77] *Idem* at 487 *et seq.*

[78] For instance, though a state is estopped from denying the existence of a state or government which it has recognized (cf. MacGibbon, *supra* note 73, at 473–75), it is not precluded from asserting claims against a government which it has refused to recognize. In the Tinoco case (Great Britain v. Costa Rica, 1923), 1 UN RIAA 369, a plea of estoppel on the above grounds was rejected, the arbitrator holding that no estoppel could lie when the non-recognition did not lead the government involved or its successor to change its position upon the faith of it.

[79] Cf., e.g., the citations in Halsbury, *op. cit. supra* note 62, at 168, note (c).

[80] *Per* Lord Wright, in Canada & Dominion Sugar Co. v. Canadian National (West Indies) Steamships, Ltd. (1946), [1947] A.C. 46, at 56.

[81] Cf., e.g., Lauterpacht, *op. cit. supra* note 61, at 203; Witenberg, "La théorie des preuves devant les juridictions internationales," 56 *Hague Recueil* 1, 27–28 (1936). And cf. more recently, Guggenheim, *op. cit. supra* note 74, at 158–59.

[82] This view is implicit in the treatment of the subject in the studies cited *supra* note 75; and see especially, MacGibbon, *supra* note 73, at 478–79.

state measures affecting aliens' contractual rights, especially with regard to individual measures.[83] A state will be estopped from asserting the invalidity of a public contract if it has treated it as valid for some time and has profited from the other party's fulfillment of its obligations under the contract.[84] A case very much in point is that of the *Shufeldt Claim*[85] where the claimant argued that "the Guatemala Government having recognized the validity of [Shufeldt's] contract for six years and received all the benefits to which they were entitled under the contract and allowed Shufeldt to go on spending money on the concession, is precluded from denying its validity."[86] The arbitrator held that, in view of his finding that the contract was valid, there was no need for him to discuss this point, but he went on to state that he had "no doubt that this contention . . . is sound and in keeping with the principles of international law."[87] In another instance, an arbitral tribunal held that by not objecting to the allegedly *ultra vires* appointment of a lawyer by a United States Consul, of which it was aware through official correspondence, the United States Government ratified the contract entered into by its consul and was thus estopped from declaring it invalid.[88]

It should be noted, moreover, that the act or conduct of the state which may lead to estoppel need not be of an international character or form. It need not be made by international instrument or be directly connected with the state's international relations. It might consist of administrative or other acts which originally are not taken in view of and do not involve another state. Such acts need

---

[83] The present discussion deals with the role of estoppel in public international law, that is, as between states. The municipal law doctrines or precedents regarding the admissibility of estoppel against the Government or the Crown are therefore of no relevance.

[84] See Meron, *supra* note 75, at 282–86.

[85] (U.S.A. v. Guatemala, 1930) 2 UN RIAA 1079.   [86] *Idem* at 1094.

[87] *Ibid.* This is an alternative holding rather than a pure *obiter dictum*.

[88] H.J.R. Hemming case (Great Britain v. U.S.A., 1920), 6 UN RIAA 51. Similar holding in the J. E. Davies case (U.S.A. v. Mexico, 1927), 4 UN RIAA 139 (contract with lawyer held ratified by partial payment of compensation provided for in it).

only relate to the alien and his rights. This view is well-founded on existing case-law as well as on the logic of the principle itself and of its application in international law.

It is true that there exists some authority to the opposite effect. In the *Croft Case* [89] the arbitrator held that a request submitted by the Portuguese Government to its Council of State, requesting the annulment of a certain decree on the grounds of the existence of a denial of justice, did not preclude that government from later denying the existence of such denial of justice. The tribunal based its holding on the grounds that the admission was not contained in "a note or a diplomatic communication," or, more generally, in "an international act between the two governments." [90] The tribunal also noted, however, that the document in question was a "request" (*requête*) addressed to an administrative tribunal and thus in the nature of a pleading. The state's final position was expressed by the Council's decision rather than the request.[91]

In the case of *The Newchwang* [92] the tribunal held that a letter, never officially published, of the United States Secretary of the Navy to the Chairman of the Committee on Claims of the United States House of Representatives "was merely a personal or private recommendation" and could not be regarded as an admission of liability.[93] More recently, in its judgment on the *Nottebohm Case* (*Second Phase*) [94] the International Court of Justice stated, in rejecting a plea of estoppel, that the measures of Guatemala which might be considered as recognizing Nottebohm's Liechtenstein na-

---

[89] (Great Britain v. Portugal, 1856) 2 LaPradelle and Politis, *Recueil des arbitrages internationaux* 22 (1923).

[90] *Idem* at 25.

[91] The fact that both this request and a subsequent decree were due quite obviously to British pressure on the Portuguese Government seems also to have influenced the tribunal; see the editors' *note doctrinale idem* 34–35. Bowett, *supra* note 62, at 186, distinguishes this case on the ground that the request was not directed to the person pleading the estoppel and thus could not form the basis for such a plea.

[92] China Navigation Co. case (Great Britain v. U.S.A., 1921), 6 UN RIAA 64.

[93] *Idem* at 66. This holding, however, refers to the official or unofficial, rather than the international, character of the document involved.

[94] (Liechtenstein v. Guatemala), 1955 *I.C.J. Reports* 4.

tionality did not in fact create an estoppel, because they related "to the control of aliens in Guatemala and not to the exercise of diplomatic protection" and "there did not thus come into being any relationship between governments." [95] The Court concluded that "there is nothing here to show that . . . Guatemala had recognized Liechtenstein's title to exercise protection in favour of Nottebohm and that it is thus precluded from denying such a title." [96]

The authority of these cases with respect to the matter at hand is, however, rather limited.[97] The view here submitted, on the other hand, has the support of several decisions of international tribunals. Thus, it is well-settled that states espousing claims of their nationals may be estopped on the basis of some previous action or assertion of the nationals involved. Such action or assertion can obviously have no international character. In the *SS. Lisman* case [98] it was held that the claimant (a private person whose claim had been espoused by his state) by his previous position before a municipal court "affirmed what he now denies, and thereby prevented himself from recovering there or here upon the claim he now stands on." [99] Similarly, in the *Serbian Loans Case*,[100] the Permanent Court of International Justice considered the possibility of estoppel by reason of the previous conduct of the bondholders, albeit rejecting the contention that this did in fact happen.[101]

Furthermore, government acts of a clearly domestic character have sometimes constituted the basis of an estoppel. In the case of

---

[95] *Idem* at 18.

[96] *Idem* at 19. It might be maintained, however, that this argument was not really necessary to the holding, since the rejection of the plea of estoppel was also based on certain other characteristics of the Guatemalan measures, such as their being founded on nothing more than a statement of the person concerned. *Idem* at 17. For criticisms of this part of the Judgment, see, among others, Van Panhuys, *The Rôle of Nationality in International Law* 96, 166 (1959); Kunz, "The Nottebohm Judgment (Second Phase)," 54 *Am. J. Int'l L.* 536, 547–48 (1960).

[97] Cf. *supra* p. 258 and notes 91, 93, and 96.

[98] Disposal of Pecuniary Claims Arising Out of the Recent War (1914–1918) (U.S.A. v. Great Britain, 1937), 3 UN RIAA 1767.

[99] *Idem* at 1790. And cf. the case of The Tattler (U.S.A. v. Gt. Britain, 1920) 6 UN RIAA 48, and the criticism in Briggs, *The Law of Nations* 723 (2d ed., 1952).

[100] P.C.I.J. Judgment No. 14 (July 12, 1929), P.C.I.J. Publ. Ser. A, Nos. 20/21.

[101] *Idem* at 38–39.

The Lindisfarne,[102] the arbitral tribunal held that the United States Government had admitted its liability for a collision between two ships by passing an Act of Congress providing for the payment of the cost of repairs of the damaged British ship.[103] There can be no doubt that this legislation and the related Reports on which the tribunal in part based its decision were by themselves devoid of international character and in no way constituted diplomatic communications. And in several cases involving the nationality of some of a state's residents, it has been held that, the state in question having treated in the past such residents as aliens, it was now precluded from treating them as its own nationals, and vice-versa.[104] Several other decisions contain similar applications of the principle of estoppel.[105]

It could hardly be otherwise, since claims based on state conduct toward nationals of another state are not "international" to start with. Acts and documents of an international character begin to be of importance when the subject of the dispute or claim is already formed. To disregard the conduct of the private persons involved or that of the states toward them at the earlier stages of the dispute would be to miss wholly the substance of the claim.

The principle of estoppel is therefore a useful tool in limiting the powers and assuring the bona fide conduct of states in connection with their contractual obligations to foreign nationals. Excessive reliance should not be placed upon it, however. Contractual commitment on the part of a state should not be confused with conduct leading to estoppel.[106] The latter may in some cases arise because of the former, but this is not always the case and when it

---

[102] (Great Britain v. U.S.A., 1913), 6 UN RIAA 21.

[103] *Idem* at 23.

[104] Cf. the Kunkel case (Germany v. Poland, 1925), [1925–1926] *Annual Digest* Case No. 318; the Kahane case (Roumania v. Austria, 1929), [1929–1930] *idem* Case No. 131. And see Bowett, *supra* note 62, at 187.

[105] Cf., e.g., the Eastry case (Great Britain v. U.S.A., 1914), 6 UN RIAA 36; the Landreau Claim (U.S.A. v. Peru, 1922), 1 UN RIAA 347, 366.

[106] Cf. on this point the observations in connection with the English law of estoppel in Wilson, "Recent Developments in Estoppel," 67 *L. Qu. Rev.* 330, 330–31 (1951).

happens their substance is not identical. With respect to general measures affecting state contracts, and in view of the particular types of measures prevalent today, it is only in exceptional instances that the principle of estoppel will be wholly applicable. A state may be estopped from asserting the invalidity of a contract, when it has treated it as valid for some time, thus inducing the private party to act in reliance on its validity.[107] But this does not mean that contracts concluded illegally by a state's government should always be held valid by subsequent governments. A state may also be estopped from changing the legal justification for a particular measure; if it has asserted initially that the measure was based on contractual provisions, it cannot claim later that it was based on criminal law. On the other hand, the existence of a state contract does not estop a state from applying general measures which might affect the contract. The application of the principle of estoppel in the particular case of state guarantees will be discussed later.[108]

Unlawfulness of State Measures Affecting Aliens' Contractual Rights

Our discussion of the public international law rules on the protection of the contractual rights of aliens leads to the conclusion that it is only in exceptional instances that general measures of states affecting such rights are considered unlawful. This situation has led several modern jurists to advocate the rejection of the "classical" theory on the matter and the adoption of new legal rules. It is submitted, however, that the rules which they have proposed are neither practically acceptable nor theoretically correct. There are other legal means available for the protection of aliens' contractual rights which do not depend on an assertion of the unlawfulness of all state measures affecting these rights. After a discussion of the suggested reasons for rejecting the newly proposed theories, some of these available means will be examined.

[107] Cf. *supra* note 84.   [108] *Infra* p. 345.

THEORETICAL ISSUES

The basic assertion of the proposed modern theory is that the violation by a state, in whatever manner and for whatever purpose, of its contractual commitments to aliens constitutes in and by itself an internationally unlawful act. The legal effects of state contracts with individuals of a foreign nationality are thus identified with those of agreements between states, since, according to traditional international law, only the violation of the latter constitutes an internationally unlawful act.[109] It is thus held that even state measures which are dictated by reasons of public interest and are not discriminatory in character should be considered unlawful when they serve to defeat the normal expectations of the private contracting party.[110]

Though the central position itself is clear enough, the same cannot be said of the legal and other grounds on which its proponents base it. The fundamental and most widely encountered argument is that any action of the state which results in a violation of its contractual obligations to aliens is a contravention of the legal and moral principle according to which *pacta sunt servanda*. The position in question is thus presented as already effective in international law,

---

[109] In the past, as well, there have been certain expressions of dissatisfaction with the prevailing theory and attempts to state it in terms such as the above; cf., e.g., Fauchille, *Traité de droit international public* (1st part) 529–30 (1926).

[110] For the ablest expositions of this view, see Carlston, "Concession Agreements and Nationalization," 52 *Am. J. Int'l L.* 260 (1958); Wadmond, "The Sanctity of Contract between a Sovereign and a Foreign National," address delivered at the London Meeting of the American Bar Association (mimeo., 1957); 1 Sibert, *Traité de droit international public* 329–33 (1951); Schwebel, "International Protection of Contractual Arrangements," 53 *Am. Soc. Int'l L. Proc.* 266 (1959); Domke, "Foreign Nationalizations," 55 *Am. J. Int'l L.* 585 (1961). And see also, in addition to the studies cited in the notes *infra*, Domke, "American Protection against Foreign Expropriation in the Light of the Suez Canal Crisis," 105 *U. Pa. L. Rev.* 1033 (1957); Brandon, "Legal Aspects of Private Foreign Investments," 18 *Fed. Bar J.* 298, 337–40 (1958); American Branch of the International Law Association, Committee on the Study of Nationalization, "Nationalization of the Property of Aliens," 13 *Record of N.Y.C. Bar Ass'n* 367 (1958); Kissam and Leach, "Sovereign Expropriation of Property and Abrogation of Concession Contracts," 28 *Fordham L. Rev.* 177, 194–214 (1959); and the discussions in International Law Association, *Report of the Forty-Eighth Conference* 130 *et seq.* (1958).

not as *lex ferenda*. Most of the relevant discussions may be reduced to this argument. Though the validity of the principle itself cannot be contested, its applicability in the instant case is open to doubt. By itself, the maxim is too general to permit any definite concrete conclusions.[111] There is no doubt that it is applicable in the case of interstate agreements and it is also generally applicable in the case of contracts between private persons, according to the municipal law of all states.[112] But is the case of contracts between states and individuals exactly similar to the above two cases? Evidently, this is the real issue; and this can also be inferred from the argumentation of the proponents of the views under discussion. Thus, a learned author emphasizes the similarity between interstate agreements and state contracts with private persons:

A State cannot unilaterally abrogate its treaties with other states without violating international law, and there is no real difference in this respect between a treaty and a concession, except that the latter is an agreement, not between two states, but between a State and a person of private law.[113]

In line with this approach, another recent study stresses the fact of the actual involvement of capital-exporting states in the investments of their nationals.[114] There is no doubt that the governments of such states have often assisted their nationals in the conclusion and performance of contracts with foreign states. Still, this does not make foreign investors the official representatives of their states of nationality. It is not suggested, after all, that the investor's state should also be responsible for any breach of contract on the part of the investor, only that the investor's claims would arise under international law, as if they were *ab initio* claims of the state of na-

---

[111] Cf. the relevant general observations of Lauterpacht, "Codification and Development of International Law," 49 *Am. J. Int'l L.* 16, 17–19 (1955).

[112] See, e.g., Jenks, *The Common Law of Mankind* 143–45 (1958).

[113] O'Connell, "Legal Issues in the Persian Oil Dispute," 28 *New Zealand L.J.* 57, 58 (1952). And see also Wehberg, "Pacta Sunt Servanda," 53 *Am. J. Int'l L.* 775, 786 (1959).

[114] Schwebel, *supra* note 110, at 267.

tionality. Apart from the problems raised by the application of the concept of nationality to this thesis,[115] it seems that, in this manner, the foreign investor is going to have the best of two worlds. He is to be allowed to operate under private law and to invoke international law whenever this is to his benefit. No cogent reason is advanced as to why he should be favored thus.

From the point of view of the investor's state of nationality, on the other hand, no claim can be raised on the sole ground of its involvement with the investment. Today, as in the past, a state is free to operate internationally under its own name as a trader or investor. If its government chooses not to do so, because of ideological reasons or in order to enjoy the advantages of private law status, it is precluded from invoking later its character as a sovereign state. This is certainly valid in the case of companies owned in major part by foreign governments. And it is characteristic that nowhere in its pleadings before the International Court of Justice in the Anglo-Iranian Oil Company case did the United Kingdom refer to its ownership of a majority share in the company.[116] This view would be *a fortiori* applicable in the cases where the foreign investor is a private person or a company owned by private persons, regardless of the importance of the investment or of the actual interference of the investor's state of nationality in the conclusion or performance of the related state contract. This last point may be considered as settled after the decision of the International Court of Justice in the Anglo-Iranian Oil Company case.[117] The Court expressly rejected the submission of the United Kingdom that because of the manner in which the concession agreement had been negotiated, with the assistance and intervention of governments and of the League of Nations, it was in fact an international law instrument rather than a private law contract.

---

[115] See on this point, Griffin, Comments, 53 *Am. Soc. Int'l L. Proc.* 281, 282 (1959).
[116] Cf. the Memorial Submitted by the United Kingdom to the International Court of Justice, *I.C.J. Pleadings, Anglo-Iranian Oil Company Case (U.K. v. Iran)* 64 *et seq.* (1951).
[117] Anglo-Iranian Oil Company Case (U.K. v. Iran), 1952 *I.C.J. Reports* 93.

Certain other recent studies also emphasize the similarities between treaties and state contracts with aliens. They point to the power and importance of the modern big corporations operating internationally and conclude that their agreements, between themselves or with foreign states, are more in the nature of treaties than private law contracts.[118] It is submitted, however, that such views do not necessarily lead to an acceptance of the applicability to state contracts of strict international law rules relating to the violation of contractual obligations. On the contrary, the scholars expressing the views in question stress the need for flexibility in the performance and the legal effects of state contracts of this type or deplore the absence of an international regulatory machinery, corresponding to those already existing in the municipal law of most advanced states.[119] These views will therefore be discussed later, in a more appropriate context.[120]

Other writers prefer to refer to the general recognition of the principle of the binding force of contracts and reach the obvious conclusion that this principle must be applicable in the case of state contracts with individuals, as well. According to one of them,

Any party has a duty to perform its obligations under a valid contractual agreement. . . . As all legal systems seem to enforce contracts between individuals who are subject to their jurisdiction, it is indeed paradoxical for the states of the world community to refuse to apply this same standard to their own agreements with individuals.[121]

[118] Cf. Berle, *The 20th Century Capitalist Revolution* 116 *et seq.* (1954); W. Friedmann, *Law in a Changing Society* 305-9, 429-31 (1959); Miller, "The Corporation as a Private Government in the World Community," 46 *Virginia L. Rev.* 1539 (1960).

[119] Cf. Berle, *op. cit. supra* note 118, at 134-35; Miller, *supra* note 118, at 1566 *et seq.;* and see Guldberg, in International Law Association, *op. cit. supra* note 110, at 172, 174.

[120] *Infra* p. 285.

[121] Olmstead, "Nationalization of Foreign Property Interests, Particularly Those Subject to Agreements with the State," 32 *N.Y.U.L. Rev.* 1122, 1136 (1957). But see Carlston, *supra* note 110, at 261 who, though generally in sympathy with the views discussed here, rejects such a "crude" method and founds his arguments on a review of the relevant case-law of the international tribunals and on policy considerations.

This view may seem attractive at first glance, but its accuracy in practice as well as in theory is highly doubtful. Even if private and international law were completely analogous, the analogy would refer to relations between private persons, on the one hand, and relations between states, on the other.[122] The analogy has no relevance to the relations between states and private persons. Moreover, grave doubts may be entertained as to the validity of the analogy itself, insofar as it is held to cover all the domain of international law. One cannot ignore the fact that the modern state is a highly complex unit whose processes and functions have little similarity to those of individuals.[123] Furthermore, municipal private law and international law are today at different stages of development; the former has reached a stage of maturity (at least in civilized countries) while the latter is still at an earlier stage.[124] It is not possible, therefore, to pass freely from one system of law to the other.[125] The difficulty is compounded by the absence of a well-developed system of international adjective law and of a judicial system comparable to the systems of municipal private law. Thus, questions of fraud or duress are examined as a matter of course by municipal courts, while they are rarely raised before international tribunals. This should be attributed mainly to the imperfections and incompleteness of existing substantive and adjective international law,

---

[122] See the classical exposition of Lauterpacht, *Private Law Sources and Analogies of International Law* (1927), especially his discussion of the meaning of analogy, *idem* at 81–84.

[123] See Dickinson, "The Analogy between Natural Persons and International Persons in the Law of Nations," 26 *Yale L.J.* 564 (1917); Brierly, "The Rule of Law in International Society," 7 *Acta Scandinavica Iuris Gentium* 3, 8–10, 12–13 (1936).

[124] These necessarily oversimplified and brief statements are based on Dean Pound's "The End of Law as Developed in Legal Rules and Doctrines," 27 *Harv. L. Rev.* 195 (1914). To employ his terminology, international law seems today to be reaching the stage of "equity" but it has not yet attained a more stable ("mature") combination of its strict and equitable elements. See also the same learned author's thoughtful observations in his "Philosophical Theory and International Law," 1 *Bibliotheca Visseriana* 71 (1923).

[125] Lauterpacht, *op. cit. supra* note 123, at 84–87, seems to accept this contention in part. And see, in this connection, Professor Verzijl's observations quoted *infra* p. 295, note 242.

but also, in part, to the complexity of the possible forms of duress or fraud, in the international setting,[126] and to the play of certain psychological and sociological factors affecting the conduct of states and of state officials.[127]

There exists an additional reason why the maxim *pacta sunt servanda* should not be applied to contracts between states and aliens in the same manner in which it is applied in private contracts. In the municipal practice of states, public contracts, that is, contracts between the state and private persons, while generally considered as binding on both parties, are as a rule treated in a different manner than private contracts.[128] The general principle *pacta sunt servanda* is still applicable, but with certain qualifications and differences. Generally speaking, public contracts are subject to the overriding interest of the public, as conceived in good faith by the state. They are accordingly more flexible than private contracts.

It is sometimes argued, nevertheless, that such a principle is not applicable in the case of contracts with an alien for a number of reasons. First, it is said that the alien "is, by virtue of the diplomatic intervention of his own state that he may in some circumstances seek, placed under the protection of international law." [129] This argument seems to involve a *petitio principii*, since the problem being considered is precisely whether the taking of measures affecting the alien's contractual rights is one of the "circumstances" making

---

[126] *Vide* the difficulties met by the jurists of the International Law Commission in their undertaking to furnish a definition of aggression. Stone, *Aggression and World Order* (1958); and cf. Professor (now Judge) Spiropoulos' first report on the matter, "The Possibility and Desirability of a Definition of Aggression," U.N. Doc. A/CN.4/44, at 47-70 (1951).

[127] A disregard for these realities may be ground for reproach even to so excellent a study as Wadmond, *op. cit. supra* note 110. In discussing the possible situations where strict application of the rules he advocates would be manifestly unjust, the learned writer mentions that such rules can be qualified by "other legal rules, such as those of fraud in the making, lack of capacity, frustration and impossibility of performance" and even by the concept of *rebus sic standibus. Idem* at 63. It is difficult to see how these rules could be applied *in concreto*, under the prevailing conditions in the international society and in international law.

[128] Cf. *supra* pp. 197-204.

[129] Schwebel, *supra* note 110, at 271. And cf. Wortley, *Expropriation* 21-22 and *passim*.

possible the diplomatic intervention of the alien's state of national-ity. The fact that "in some circumstances" an alien may be pro-tected by his state cannot be held to determine his position in the cases in which he may not be so protected.

It is further argued that since the rules mentioned above are founded on the need for the protection of a state's general welfare, they are not applicable in the case of contracts with aliens, because by virtue of the very operation of such rules, the alien is cast out of that particular society and does not share in the resulting welfare.[130] It should be noted that this objection relates only to measures of an expropriatory character, thus presumably admitting the legality of any measures short of expropriation affecting the contractual rights of aliens. But its very legal basis is doubtful. A person is not subject to the laws of a particular state, especially the laws relating to the state's general welfare, merely because of the future benefits he may derive. A tourist will derive no benefit from the continued keeping of public order or from the future welfare of the country in which he happens to be visiting. This would not make him im-mune to criminal prosecution or to the payment of customs duties.[131]

As far as the "normal" expectations of the private parties to state contracts are concerned, again there is no need to distinguish be-tween nationals and aliens. It is sometimes argued that no alien would conclude a contract with a foreign state, if he expected the state to violate the contract.[132] When phrased in this manner, the argument cannot be refuted. What in fact happens, however, is that the alien, like the national, contracts in the hope that no ex-ceptional circumstances will arise which will make it necessary

---

[130] Schwebel, *supra* note 110, at 271; and see also Carlston, *supra* note 110, at 263; Carlston, "Nationalization: An Analytical Approach," 54 *Nw. U.L. Rev.* 405, 429 (1959); Van Panhuys, *The Rôle of Nationality in International Law* 50 (1959).

[131] Note that the argument was first used in connection with the measure of compensation to which an alien is entitled in cases of nationalization; cf. Judge Carneiro's Dissenting Opinion in the Anglo-Iranian Oil Company Case (U.K. v. Iran), 1952 *I.C.J. Reports* 151, 162. In that particular context, the argument is more relevant, if not wholly convincing; cf. *infra* p. 328.

[132] Cf. Dunn, *The Protection of Nationals* 165 *et seq.* (1932); Wadmond, *op. cit. supra* note 110, at 62; Schwebel, *supra* note 110, at 269–70.

for the state to take any measure which would affect the contract. But any experienced investor is aware of the possibility that such circumstances may arise. This view finds strong support in a recent arbitral award in a dispute between the Greek Government and two Swedish companies.[133] The umpire pointed out that the particular circumstances of the contract made it possible for the claimant companies to foresee that Greece might not be able to pay back the amount lent to her.[134] He then stated, in more general terms,

To this must be added that, in long-term contracts, the parties must reckon with rather considerable fluctuations due to public disturbances whose origin cannot be foreseen. . . . If the [claimant] certainly could not foresee the events of the 1939–45 war, it should, nevertheless, have expected that in the course of the 28 years of the contract, more or less serious difficulties would arise as a result of internal or external events.[135]

It may be concluded, therefore, that an analogy between municipal public contracts and state contracts with aliens is valid, certainly more so than an analogy between state contracts with aliens and municipal private contracts.[136]

A particular consequence of the theory under discussion is that it distinguishes contractual rights from other property rights. As to the latter, it admits the state's right to expropriate them under certain conditions, but, with regard to the former, it holds that such state action would be always internationally unlawful.[137] One might

[133] The Alsing Trading Co., Ltd. and the Swedish Match Co. v. the Greek State (1954), reported in Schwebel, "The Alsing Case," 8 *Int'l & Comp. L. Qu.* 320 (1959).

[134] "Greece is not a country with great national resources. It had already experienced serious financial crises. At the time of the contracts, the payment of its public debt was supervised by an international financial committee." Quoted in Schwebel, *supra* note 133, at 344.

[135] Quoted in Schwebel, *ibid.* To the same effect, see the Transvaal Concession Commission report (1901), in 1 Moore, *Digest* 411, at 413–14. And cf. de Visscher, *Théories et réalités en droit international public* 248 (3d ed., 1960).

[136] See, in agreement, Wall, "The Iranian-Italian Oil Agreement of 1957," 7 *Int'l & Comp. L. Qu.* 736,744 (1958). And cf. *infra* pp. 295–96.

[137] "Quand il s'agit d'une confiscation des biens d'un étranger, c'est l'omission de payer une indemnité adéquate qui est illicite. Quand il s'agit d'un engagement pris par l'état par un contrat conclu avec un étranger, par exemple une concession, la

see in this distinction the influence of the relevant rules of United States constitutional law.[138] These rules are chiefly based on section 10 of Article I of the United States Constitution which prohibits any state legislation "impairing the obligation of contracts." [139] Public and private contracts are thus effectively distinguished from land and other property rights. However, the application of this provision to public contracts is today very limited. As regards contracts with private persons concluded by the particular states of the Union, it is now generally accepted that the state "police power," that is, the power relating to the general welfare of the public, is inalienable; no state can limit itself by contract in the exercise of its police power.[140] Certain exceptions are, nevertheless, admitted, and the power of the state legislature to bind itself in matters of tax exemption,[141] the grant of franchises of public service companies [142] and the fixing of public utilities rates [143] is still accepted by the courts.[144] Like all state contracts, however, contracts of the above types are construed strictly in favor of the retention of state powers.[145] The state's power of eminent domain, that is to say, of

---

violation commise par l'état de cet engagement est par elle-même illicite. . . ." Gihl, Comment in International Law Association, *op. cit. supra* note 110, at 135, 138–39. See also Wadmond, *op. cit. supra* note 110, at 60–62; Carlston, "Nationalization: An Analytical Approach," 54 *Nw. U.L. Rev.* 405, 428 (1959).

[138] Cf. Q. Wright, "Arbitration as a Symbol of Internationalism," in *International Trade Arbitration* 3, 12 (Domke ed., 1958).

[139] Cf. *The Constitution of the United States of America. Analysis and Interpretation* 329 *et seq.* (Corwin ed., 1952); Wright, *The Contract Clause of the Constitution* (1938); Hale, "The Supreme Court and the Contract Clause," 57 *Harv. L. Rev.* 512, 621, 852 (1944); Note, "The Contract Clause of the Federal Constitution," 32 *Columbia L. Rev.* 476 (1932); Mitchell, *Contracts* 81 *et seq.* For two opposed views, in the special context of state contracts with aliens, see Kissam and Leach, "Sovereign Expropriation of Property and Abrogation of Concession Contracts," 28 *Fordham L. Rev.* 177, 200–03, 210–11 (1959); Mann, "State Contracts and State Responsibility," 54 *Am. J. Int'l L.* 572, 584–86 (1960).

[140] Stone v. Mississippi, 101 U.S. 814 (1880). On the impossibility of defining with precision the limits of "police power," see Mitchell, *Contracts* 88 *et seq.*

[141] Cf., e.g. Piqua Branch of the State Bank of Ohio v. Knoop, 16 How. 369 (1853).

[142] Cf., e.g., New Orleans Gas Co. v. Louisiana Light Co., 115 U.S. 650 (1885).

[143] Cf., e.g., Los Angeles v. Los Angeles City Water Co., 177 U.S. 558 (1900).

[144] For discussions of the reasons for this limitation, see Mitchell, *Contracts* 114 *et seq.*, 125 *et seq.*; Note, *supra* note 139, at 482 *et seq.*

[145] Cf. Charles River Bridge v. Warren Bridge, 11 Pet. 420 (1837). For applications in the particular case of tax exemptions, see Hale v. Iowa State Board of As-

taking private property (including contractual rights) upon payment of compensation, is wholly inalienable and it overrides any contractual obligations of the state.[146] Similar rules apply, *mutatis mutandis*, to contracts entered into by the Federal Government.[147]

Apart from these rules (which bring American law on public contracts in line with the law of most modern states) one might argue that a rule based on the express formulation of a constitutional text should not by itself be regarded as of universal application. Moreover, there is every reason to apply the same international law rules in the cases of contractual rights and of other rights of property. The relation between these two categories is so close that attempting to distinguish between them might create considerable difficulties. In the case of agrarian expropriations, for instance, some of the lands may be held by virtue of contracts between the state and the landholders (concessions or other, more archaic, forms). The application of a different set of rules for such a category of landholdings would certainly be impractical both for the expropriating state and for the state interposing in support of its nationals' claims.

THE POSITIVE LAW

So much for the purely theoretical considerations. Some supporters, however, of the theory of the unlawfulness in international law of any state action in violation of contractual commitments to aliens use a different line of argument.[148] Holding that this theory

---

sessment, 302 U.S. 95 (1937); Atlantic Coast Line R. Co. v. Phillips, 322 U.S. 168 (1947).

[146] West River Bridge Co. v. Dix, 6 How. 507 (1848); Pennsylvania Hospital v. Philadelphia, 245 U.S. 20 (1917).

[147] "The United States when sued as a contractor cannot be held liable for an obstruction to the performance of the particular contract resulting from its public and general acts as sovereign." Horowitz v. U.S., 267 U.S. 458, 461 (1925). But when the government action does not fall within the federal police power or some other "paramount power," it is held invalid; cf. Lynch v. U.S., 292 U.S. 571 (1934). And see Stack, "The Liability of the United States for Breach of Contract," 44 *Georgetown L.J.* 77 (1955).

[148] See especially Carlston, "Concession Agreements and Nationalization," 52 *Am. J. Int'l L.* 260 (1958). But cf. Mann, *supra* note 139, at 577-79.

is the one accepted in positive international law, they base their assertion on the official statements of states and on a number of cases settled among the states involved by diplomatic means or decided upon by international tribunals.

When dealing with official state pronouncements, a great deal of caution is necessary. Indeed, according to an eminent international jurist, "the very name of authority when applied simply to the arguments used by one party to an international dispute is a misnomer." [149] This is particularly appropriate in cases such as those we are concerned with, since the arguments cited are usually those of claimant states in whose interest, in each particular instance as well as generally, it was to have such views accepted as effective in international law.[150]

Cases of diplomatic settlement are important evidence of state practice, though it is often difficult to determine their value from a legal point of view. They are apt to be dismissed offhand in any controversy as instances of "gunboat diplomacy" or of the predominance of political over legal considerations. As far as state contracts are concerned, there exist certain early cases where states agreed to drop measures which interfered with the property rights of aliens.[151] In most instances, however, the main object of the diplomatic intervention was the grant of compensation, without any clear-cut statement as to the lawfulness of the measures involved, once compensation is paid. Recent cases of disputes settled by diplomatic methods can serve to show that state measures affecting the contractual rights of aliens create only an obligation to compensate

[149] Williams, "International Law and the Property of Aliens," 9 *Brit. Yb. Int'l L.* 1 (1928), reprinted in *Chapters in Current International Law and the League of Nations* 147, 153 (1929).

[150] Cf., for instance, the oft-cited pleadings of the Swiss Government in the Losinger case (1936), P.C.I.J. Publ., Ser. C, No. 78, at 32, on which see Kissam and Leach, *supra* note 139, at 208; Mann, *supra* note 139, at 577-78.

[151] Cf. the case of the Insurance Monopoly in Uruguay (1911), where the project for the establishment of such a state monopoly was dropped after the intervention of foreign powers. In the similar case of the Italian Insurance Monopoly (1912), however, diplomatic intervention had very limited success; a ten-year delay was granted to foreign insurance companies, but no compensation was paid. See Friedman, *Expropriation* 52-54.

on the part of the state.[152] This point will be discussed more in detail later.[153]

The decisions of international tribunals deserve more attention. One should not forget, of course, that even such decisions are of "varying degrees of authority," [154] since international judges are but scholars, diplomats, or international lawyers under a (very thin, in some cases) judicial gown. Regardless of such general considerations, however, the cases cited by the authors in support of the theory we are discussing do not appear convincing.

A study of these cases leads to certain general conclusions. First, one should eliminate the cases which deal in fact not with the problem at hand but with those of the legality and binding force of the acts of de facto or revolutionary governments [155] or with the problems of state succession.[156] Among the cases that are left, one observes that in many instances, the lawfulness of state action in contravention of contractual commitments was not an issue before the tribunal, often because there was sufficient agreement on the law of the matter between the parties and there remained for the tribunal to determine what were the exact facts and to fix the amount of compensation due.[157] In perhaps the majority of cases, the tribunals' holding related only to the existence of an obligation on the part of the host state to compensate the aliens for the losses caused by such measures, regardless of their lawfulness under international

---

[152] Thus, after the nationalization of private industries in the states of Eastern and Central Europe after the Second World War, agreements were concluded between these states and the Western states principally concerned providing for compensation to be paid in lump sums by the nationalizing states. For a list of such agreements, see UN Document A/AC.97/5/Rev. 1, 27 December 1960, pp. 195–99.

[153] *Infra* pp. 305 *et seq.*   [154] Williams, *supra* note 149, at 154.

[155] Cf., e.g., the Tinoco Claims (Great Britain v. Costa Rica, 1923), 1 UN RIAA 369.

[156] Cf., e.g., the P.C.I.J. Judgments in the Mavrommatis case, P.C.I.J. Publ. Ser. A, No. 5 (1925); the Alsop case (U.S.A. v. Chile, 1911), 3 Whiteman, *Damages* 1662.

[157] Cf., e.g., the Landreau Claims (U.S.A. v. Peru, 1922), 1 UN RIAA 347; the Harrah Claim (U.S.A. v. Cuba, 1930), 3 Whiteman, *Damages* 1718; the Thurston case (U.S.A. v. Dominican Republic, 1898), *idem* 1674; the May case (U.S.A. v. Guatemala, 1900), *idem* 1704, *Foreign Relations of the United States 1900* 659 (1902).

law.[158] This, it is submitted, is a quite distinct proposition, for states may be bound to pay compensation even in the case of lawful measures.[159]

One can scarcely deny that the statements of international judges in a number of cases indicate clearly that, in their view, state action in violation of contractual obligations toward aliens should be considered internationally unlawful. In the more recent judgments, especially those of the International Court of Justice, such statements are found only as dicta or in certain dissenting or separate opinions.[160] In the earlier cases, the courts' statements are often not very clear on the matter,[161] while the frequent presence of an element of denial of justice serves to complicate the issues further. Moreover, in many instances, the courts take special pains to point out that the state measures involved were "unjust" or "arbitrary," so that we may validly infer that they are in fact referring to the existence of an abuse of rights on the part of the state in question.[162]

Finally, even if it were shown conclusively that in a number of instances the international judges have decided as they did in the belief that state measures affecting the contractual rights of aliens

[158] Cf., e.g., the Shufeldt Claims (U.S.A. v. Guatemala, 1930), 2 UN RIAA 1079; the de Garmendia case (U.S.A. v. Venezuela, 1904), 3 Whiteman, *Damages* 1683; also, in part, the Delagoa Bay case, on which see more *infra* note 161.

[159] Cf. *infra* pp. 307 *et seq.*

[160] Cf., e.g., Judge Carneiro's Dissenting Opinion in the Anglo-Iranian Oil Company Case, 1952 *I.C.J. Reports* 93, 151.

[161] See, e.g., the relevant statements in the otherwise very articulate award in the Delagoa Bay and East African Railway Company case (U.S.A., Great Britain v. Portugal, 1900), 3 Whiteman, *Damages* 1694. In discussing the measure of damages, the tribunal formulated three initial queries, the first of which was "Is the 'compensation' to represent reparation for an injury done unlawfully?" In this case, it was stated, "the compensation will be in the nature of damages (*dommages et intérêts*)." *Idem* at 1697. The tribunal found that such should be the compensation to be paid, but then it went on to state: "Whether one would, indeed, brand the action of the Government as an arbitrary and despoiling measure or as a sovereign act prompted by reasons of State which always prevails over any railway concession, or even if the present case should be regarded as one of legal expropriation, the fact remains that . . . the State . . . is bound to make full reparation for the injuries done by it." *Idem* at 1698.

[162] Cf., e.g., the El Triunfo Company case (U.S.A. v. Salvador, 1902), 3 Whiteman, *Damages* 1680; the Walter Fletcher Smith case (U.S.A. v. Cuba, 1929), 2 UN RIAA 913.

are internationally unlawful, it would still be difficult to conclude that this is today the law on the matter. It may have been that this was the law in the last years of the nineteenth century, when the great majority of these cases were adjudged.[163] Should one accept, however, that today, when all the environing legal, economic, social, political, and even cultural conditions have changed, these outdated cases should constitute binding precedents? The municipal law of most states, and in particular the law relating to property and state powers, has changed fundamentally since the beginning of the century. Should international law remain immutable? If such a view should represent the dominant opinion among international jurists, then it is not surprising that, the more recent the period, the fewer the relevant cases brought before international tribunals. States have preferred the methods of diplomatic settlement in order to be certain that the existing conditions would not be disregarded.

POLICY CONSIDERATIONS

Supporters of the view that any state action in contravention of contractual commitments to aliens is internationally unlawful employ an additional argument, quite different from the preceding. They hold that acceptance of this view is indispensable for the security of international investment.[164] In its absence, there can be no increase in the private capital exported from the developed countries. It is, therefore, to the interest of capital-importing states, they maintain, to adopt a similar view on the existing law. This is evidently a question of policy rather than law, and one might

---

[163] Thus, out of 23 cases cited by Carlston, "Concession Agreements and Nationalization," 52 Am. J. Int'l L. 260, 261–63, notes 5, 7, 9, 10, 11, 13, and 16 (1958) only 3 date later than 1910. Note also that this strict view was not adopted in the "classical" statements of the law on the matter, one or two decades later; cf. supra note 28.

[164] For an early statement of this view, see Anderson, "Basis of the Law Against Confiscating Foreign-Owned Property," 21 Am. J. Int'l L. 525 (1927). The view is found in most postwar writings on the subject. See, among the more recent ones, Carlston, "Concession Agreements and Nationalization," 52 Am. J. Int'l L. 260, 274–75 (1958); Abs, "The Safety of Capital," in Private Investment: The Key to International Industrial Development 69 (Daniel ed., 1958).

evade the issue by limiting oneself to strict *de lega lata* considerations. It would, however, be unrealistic to disregard the importance of policy considerations in the formation of positive law, especially international law. It is then necessary to enter into the substance of this argument.

It was noted, in the first chapter, that a great number of factors influence the investment of foreign private capital in underdeveloped areas. The security which might be provided by a general adoption of the theory under discussion would be at best but one favorable factor, whose practical effects would be uncertain since they would depend on a host of other factors. Thus, an accidental change in a country's terms-of-trade would influence much more and much faster the international movement of private capital in relation to that country. Furthermore, it has not been proven that the only manner in which legal security of private investment can be achieved is the general acceptance of this theory. There may be several other solutions, as our investigation into the various forms of state guarantees has shown. Finally, it is certainly very doubtful whether this view can ever be accepted by a great number of countries, and especially by the capital-importing countries.

A recent more sophisticated version of the policy argument, one particularly relevant to contracts of concession, combines moral with pragmatic considerations.[165] The authors emphasize the dependence of Western Europe and the United States on raw materials whose source is located in underdeveloped countries. They argue that, since the latter countries cannot by themselves develop or find any productive use for their resources, they should not have an absolute right over their disposition. They stress accordingly the

[165] The most articulate exposition of this argument is found in Carlston, "Nationalism, Nationalization and International Law," 7 *Rev. Dr. Int'l Moyen-Orient* 1 (1958); Carlston, "Concession Agreements and Nationalization," 52 *Am. J. Int'l L.* 260, 277–79 (1958); and especially, Carlston, "Nationalization: An Analytical Approach," 54 *Nw. U.L. Rev.* 405 (1959). See also Levy, "Issues in International Oil Policy," 35 *Foreign Affairs* 454 (1957); Elliot, "Colonialism: Freedom and Responsibility," in *The Idea of Colonialism* 430, 444–51 (Strausz-Hupé and Hazard ed., 1958); Murdock, Comment, in International Law Association, *Report of the Forty-Eighth Conference* 174, 176 (1958).

rights of the "international community," as represented by the Western states and their investing nationals and corporations, and the corresponding limitations on the rights and powers of the primary-producing countries.

This is a persuasive argument, especially because it is difficult to dispute the validity of its theoretical foundations. It is true that "the image of the international society as a society of separate and independent nations, an image still held by the systems of public and private international law, no longer adequately reflects the true nature of that society." [166] And it is certainly not possible to ignore the facts of the economic as well as political and military interdependence of the world's "independent states." [167] Unfortunately, it is possible to draw a variety of conclusions from these premises. And the conclusions drawn in the studies here discussed seem open to several important objections.

To begin with, they seem to identify closely the interests of the Western nations with those of the international community. Though one may accept that their long-term interests do coincide, it is far from certain that they always do so in the short run as well. It may well be that, in certain cases, the short-term economic interests of the Western nations are opposed to those of the international community as a whole and more particularly to those of any other group of nations.[168]

Moreover, the argument is one-sided, since it emphasizes the need for Western interference within the underdeveloped countries but disregards completely the reverse possibility. The underdeveloped countries depend heavily on the Western ones, and they also have no voice in the determination of the economic policies of the Western countries. To raise but a single point, fluctuations in the prices of the international commodity market affect a great number of

---

[166] Carlston, "Nationalization: An Analytical Approach," 54 *Nw. U.L. Rev.* 405, at 405 (1959). And cf. Rubin, *Private Foreign Investment* 73 (1956).

[167] Cf. Carlston, *supra* note 166, at 407–10.

[168] Cf. Myrdal, *Economic Theory* 50 *et seq.*; Miller, "Protection of Private Foreign Investment by Multilateral Convention," 53 *Am. J. Int'l L.* 371, 375–76 (1959).

countries at least as much as (if not more than) the availability and pricing of petroleum affects the Western countries.[169] Yet one does not find the proponents of the interests of the "international community" combining their proposals for the control of petroleum or other resources with plans for the stabilization of the prices of primary products.

A truly international control of the natural resources which are essential to the economy of all countries might be possible in the not too distant future. But such a plan would have to take into account the interests of, and try to offer important advantages to, all parties concerned. For, in the final analysis, even if the underdeveloped countries are today using the natural resources located in their territory as a tool in political bargaining rather than in an economically more productive manner, on what grounds can they be denied their right to dispose of them in such a way? Political bargaining is but an indirect way of deriving strength from these resources and there is no immanently "moral" way in which one may employ existing natural resources. To limit these countries' power, in a world of power politics, without any further step toward a solution of their economic and noneconomic problems seems a less than equitable solution, and a rather impractical one, too.

Contemporary Developments in the Law

Refusal to adopt the theory of the unlawfulness of all state measures affecting the contractual rights of aliens does not necessarily imply acceptance of the opposite view, according to which the state is the sole judge of the legality of its measures and municipal law is the only relevant body of law.

In the first place, one may acknowledge frankly that in complex

---

[169] But see Carlston, *supra* note 166, at 408. For recent reports on this topic, see: United Nations, Department of Economic and Social Affairs, *World Economic Survey 1958* 17–176 (1959); G.A.T.T., *Trends in International Trade* 51–54, 65 *et seq.* (1958). See also the earlier studies of the UN Economic Affairs Department, *Relative Prices of Exports and Imports of Underdeveloped Countries* (1949); *Instability in Export Markets of Underdeveloped Countries* (1952); *Commodity Trade and Economic Development* (1954).

situations such as those we are dealing with, the only general statement which can be made with certainty is that no general rule,
covering all possible cases, can be found. A recognition of this fact
is found in the "Basis of Discussion" on the subject at hand, adopted
by the Preparatory Committee of the League of Nations Conference
for the Codification of International Law in 1929. It was stated in
part,

It depends upon the circumstances whether a State incurs responsibility
where it has enacted legislation general in character which is incompatible with the operation of a concession which it has granted or the
performance of a contract made by it.[170]

In the second place, a considerable number of possible cases may
be covered by application of the classical doctrine on the matter.
As has been already pointed out, this theory considers as unlawful
any state measure which affects the contractual rights of aliens
while at the same time being either unjustly discriminatory or not
taken for a public purpose. A claim may also arise on the basis of a
denial of justice occurring in connection with state measures of this
type. Moreover, the lawfulness or unlawfulness of a state measure
does not necessarily affect the existence, under international law, of
a duty to compensate on the part of the state responsible, though it
does affect the measure of the compensation to be awarded.[171]

The vitality and relevance of the classical doctrine on state contracts is made evident in its successive reformulations in the numerous drafts of proposed international conventions codifying the law
of state responsibility. Thus, the related article in the 1929 Harvard
Research draft consists of a brief statement of this doctrine, without qualifications or details:

A state is responsible if an injury to an alien results from its non-
performance of a contractual obligation which it owes to the alien, if
local remedies have been exhausted without adequate redress.[172]

---

[170] Basis of Discussion No. 3, 2d para., 24 *Am. J. Int'l L. Supp.* 50 (1930).

[171] For a discussion of this problem, see *infra Chapter* 10, pp. 307 *et seq.*

[172] Harvard Law School, Research in International Law, "The Law of Responsibility of States for Damage Done in Their Territory to the Person or Property
of Foreigners," Article 8(a), 23 *Am. J. Int'l L. Sp. Supp.* 131, 134, 167–73 (1929).

The Preparatory Committee of the League of Nations Conference for the Codification of International Law prepared a more elaborate text, which distinguished between state debts and other state contracts, between legislative measures and measures of the executive, and between individual and general measures. It provided that

A State is responsible for damage suffered by a foreigner as the result of the enactment of legislation which directly infringes rights derived by the foreigner from a concession granted or a contract made by the State.[173]

The legal effect of general measures was said to depend upon the particular circumstances.[174] Denial of justice, public purpose or nondiscrimination were not mentioned as requirements for the legality of state measures affecting the contractual rights of aliens.

A few years later, a Committee of Experts on the Codification of International Law prepared at the request of the 1936 Inter-American Conference for the Maintenance of Peace a draft which seems to follow the Harvard Research formulation. The proposed text stated that

The High Contracting Parties agree not to intervene diplomatically in support of claims arising out of contracts, unless there has been a denial of justice or infraction of a generally recognized international duty.[175]

Recent attempts at codification have generally resulted in more detailed texts. In his second report on international responsibility, the International Law Commission's Special Rapporteur proposed the following formulation, which follows closely, but in modern terms, the classical doctrine:

---

[173] Basis of Discussion No. 3, 1st para., 24 *Am. J. Int'l L. Supp.* 50 (1930). Similar provision with respect to damages caused by executive action was included in Basis of Discussion No. 8, *idem* at 54.

[174] *Supra,* p. 279, note 170.

[175] As quoted in Garcia Amador, Second Report on International Responsibility, 1957-II *Yearbook of the International Law Commission* 104, 119 (1958). The following paragraph of the proposed text provided for arbitration in cases of unjustified repudiation or breach of contract by the state.

1. The State is responsible for the injuries caused to an alien by the non-performance of obligations stipulated in a contract entered into with that alien or in a concession granted to him, if the said non-performance constitutes an act or omission which contravenes the international obligations of the State.

2. For the purposes of the provisions of the foregoing paragraph, the repudiation or breach of the terms of a contract or concession shall be deemed to constitute an "act or omission which contravenes the international obligations of the State" in the following cases, that is to say, if the repudiation or breach:

(a) Is not justified on grounds of public interest or of the economic necessity of the State;

(b) Involves discrimination between nationals and aliens to the detriment of the latter; or

(c) Involves a "denial of justice" within the meaning of article 4 of this draft.[176]

The new draft of the Harvard Research, on the other hand, is formulated in a different manner:

1. The violation through an arbitrary action of the State of a contract or concession to which the central government of that State and an alien are parties is wrongful. In determining whether the action of the State is arbitrary, it is relevant to consider whether the action constitutes:

(a) a clear and discriminatory departure from the proper law of the contract or concession as that law existed at the time of the alleged violation;

(b) a clear and discriminatory departure from the law of the State which is a party to the contract or concession as that law existed at the time of the making of the contract or concession, if that law is the proper law of the contract or concession;

(c) an unreasonable departure from the principles recognized by the principal legal systems of the world as applicable to governmental contracts or concessions of the same nature or category; or

(d) a violation by the State of a treaty.

2. If the violation by the State of a contract or concession to which the central government of a State and an alien are parties also involves

[176] Garcia Amador, *supra* note 175, at 116–17.

the taking of property, the provisions of Article 10 shall apply to such taking.

3. The exaction from an alien of a benefit not within the terms of a contract or concession to which the central government of a State and an alien are parties or of a waiver of any term of such a contract or concession is wrongful if such benefit or waiver was secured through the use of any clear threat by the central government of the State to repudiate, cancel, or modify any right of the alien under such contract or concession.[177]

Other provisions of the Draft Convention lay down the requirement of the exhaustion of local remedies [Articles 1(2)(a) and 19], while subsequent articles provide in detail for the form and purposes of the reparation which states are required to make (Articles 27 and 34).

In addition to the requirements of nondiscrimination and exhaustion of local remedies, the recent Harvard Draft Convention has introduced certain new elements in the formulation of the classical doctrine. The requirements of legality and nondiscrimination are related to the "proper law of the contract," whether this is the municipal law of the state party to the contract, the municipal law of some other state or public international law.[178] The requirement of public purpose is not expressly mentioned in connection with the annulment of state contracts, but it is with respect to the taking of property.[179] On the other hand, in referring to the application of general principles of law, the Draft Convention makes clear that it is to public, not private, law that reference is intended.

---

[177] Draft Convention on the International Responsibility of States for Injuries to Aliens, article 12, 55 *Am. J. Int'l L.* 548, 566–67 (1961).

[178] This is made quite clear in the explanatory note accompanying article 12, *idem* 569.

[179] Article 10 of the Draft Convention provides that the taking of alien-owned property is wrongful "if it is not for a public purpose clearly recognized as such by a law of general application in effect at the time of the taking." In the explanatory note accompanying this article, however, the authors confess to some hesitation on the point and they state that "because the verbal formula has so often been employed, it was considered unwise to omit it at this point, empty though it may be of any operative legal content." 55 *Am. J. Int'l L.* 548, at 556 (1961). On the related question of possible abuse of rights, see *infra* p. 300.

This is, perhaps, the most important of the innovations introduced by this article of the Harvard Draft.[180]

The successive formulations quoted above show clearly that the classical theory of state contracts is flexible and adaptable and may still be employed with profit within the framework of traditional international law. It remains true, nevertheless, that this theory is not adequate, under modern conditions. It may take care of the extreme cases, where a state action is found to be internationally tortious, but it is of little help with respect to the functioning of the contracts. In this respect, the proposed theory which holds that all state action affecting the contractual rights of aliens is unlawful is equally inadequate. A whole body of law is needed which will regulate the performance of state contracts, a body of law which, while taking into account the fundamental difference between the parties to such contracts, will not decide all points in the abstract in favor of the one or the other of the parties. Recourse to public international law is possible and desirable, but only as a last resort, when the state actions involved clearly violate its rules.

It is today becoming increasingly accepted that a new body of law, differing from both international and municipal law, is in the process of developing. The trend was first noted several years ago,[181] but it is only recently that it has become manifest and has attracted the attention of jurists.[182] It is still on their studies that the differentiation of this body of law is chiefly based, rather than on the limited evidence of the practice of states [183] and international

---

[180] Cf. *infra* pp. 295–96.

[181] Cf. Williams, "Some Legal Aspects of International Financial Problems," in *Chapters in Current International Law and the League of Nations* 257, 258, note 3 (1929).

[182] As the discussion in the text will make evident, there exist several variations in the approach of jurists to this matter. For present purposes, it is the factual observation of the existence of a distinct body of law that is important and not the possible theoretical constructions founded on this fact. Such variations will not always be pointed out, since it is the common ground of agreement that is here examined.

[183] As manifested chiefly in concession contracts and other instruments involving states and individuals of another nationality; see *infra* pp. 289–93.

organizations [184] and that of international judicial bodies.[185] This body of law, variously named "extranational" [186] or, better, "transnational," [187] governs those situations where neither municipal law nor the traditional public international law would be wholly appropriate. Such situations are mainly those where, in the terms of traditional international law, a subject and an object of international law are involved. For instance, relations between an international organization and an individual [188] and perhaps certain types of transactions between states and international organizations.[189] Contractual relations between states and aliens would also seem to fall within this general category and it is to these that the present discussion is devoted.

The applicability of transnational law to state contracts is supported by the same considerations which militate against the application of public international or municipal law each by itself. The relation between the two parties to such contracts is a peculiar one. As has been noted,[190] it is not so much a question of equality or inequality as it is a matter of difference in the character and purposes of the parties and in the interests involved on each side. If

[184] Cf. *infra* notes 188 and 189.

[185] Chiefly certain awards of arbitral tribunals, *infra* notes 209, 218, and 221, and decisions of international administrative tribunals, *infra* note 188.

[186] Williams, *ubi supra* note 181.

[187] Jessup, *Transnational Law* (1956). This term has been adopted in the present discussion, though its use does not wholly conform to that proposed in the above cited study. For criticism of the term and suggestion of several others, see Rice, Book Review, 10 *J. Leg. Ed.* 122, 128 (1957).

[188] The so-called international administrative law would therefore fall within the domain of transnational law. See Jessup, *op. cit. supra* note 187, at 82 *et seq.;* Bastid, "Les tribunaux administratifs internationaux et leur jurisprudence," 92 *Hague Recueil* 343 (1957); Friedmann and Fatouros, "The United Nations Administrative Tribunal," 11 *Int'l Organization* 13 (1957); Carlston, "International Administrative Law: A Venture in Legal Theory," 8 *J. Pub. L.* 329 (1959).

[189] Certain loans by international financial agencies might fall under this category; cf. Adam, "Les accords de prêt de la Banque Internationale pour la Reconstruction et le Développement," 55 *Rev. Gén. Dr. Int'l Public* 41, 55 *et seq.* (1951); and see Mann, "The Proper Law of Contracts Concluded by International Persons," 35 *Brit. Yb. Int'l L.* 34, 38–41 (1959). It is also possible that this category may include the law of the international public authorities described by Adam, *Les établissements publics internationaux* (1957).

[190] Cf. *supra* p. 197.

equality is understood as referring to a power relationship, then the parties to many modern state contracts should certainly be considered equal.

The big corporations which operate in the international economy are certainly as powerful as, and often more powerful than, many of the states with which they enter into agreements. And it is such big corporations that constitute today the great majority of "foreign investors." [191] In this sense, therefore, the agreements between states and foreign investors are contracts *inter pares*.[192] Nonetheless, the ultimate purposes sought and the interests represented and served by the parties differ sharply. The foreign investors' purposes remain essentially "private" in character, since they relate to the financial interests of a limited voluntary group of individuals. The state, on the other hand, represents the general (not only economic or financial) interests of a nonvoluntary community of persons. It is on this difference, and not on the possible inequality of the parties in terms of power, that the special character of state contracts, in transnational as in municipal law, is based.

The precise classification of "transnational" law, in its relationship to traditional international law and to the numerous bodies of municipal law, is still a matter of dispute. Some writers seem to consider transnational law as an entirely distinct body of law. Thus, Professor Verdross maintains that state contracts of the type here considered are founded on "an independent legal order," namely, the *lex contractus* of the parties, which regulates exhaustively their relations.[193] This argument is based on two main grounds. First, the

[191] For instance, ten corporations account for 40 percent of United States foreign investment, and 62 corporations for over 70 percent. 26 companies account for 97 percent of petroleum investments abroad and twelve companies account for over 90 percent of foreign investment in agriculture. See Barlow and Wender, *Foreign Investment and Taxation* 17–76 (1955), as cited in Surrey, "Current Issues in the Taxation of Corporate Foreign Investment," 56 *Columbia L. Rev.* 814, 851–52 (1956).

[192] Cf., e.g., 1 Schwarzenberger, *International Law* 578 (3d ed., 1957). For a discussion of this problem from the viewpoint of the state of nationality, see Garcia Amador, "State Responsibility: Some New Problems," 94 *Hague Recueil* 365, 469–72 (1958).

[193] Verdross, "Protection of Private Property under Quasi-International Agree-

contracts in question ("quasi-international agreements" in the author's terminology) have their "reason of validity" not in municipal or international law but "in the general principle of law 'pacta sunt servanda,' which the parties concurringly recognize in entering into the agreement." [194] Secondly, an agreement does not necessarily have to be based on "the legal order of a preexisting legal community"; the agreement may itself create such a legal community.[195] This thesis cannot be considered convincing, at least not to anyone not sharing the jurisprudential views of the eminent Austrian jurist. It is not convincing from a theoretical point of view since it is generally accepted that contracts have to be based on some existing legal system.[196] And it is not helpful from a practical standpoint, since the most difficult problems and disputes arise over these contractual provisions which are not by themselves clear and have to be construed and applied in accordance with some legal system.

A similar, but importantly qualified, thesis has been propounded by Lord McNair who supports the application of "general principles of law recognized by civilized nations" (which, for present purposes, may be considered as corresponding to the body of law here called "transnational") to concessions and other state contracts. The eminent jurist, however, expressly distinguishes such principles from "public international law *stricto sensu*." [197] It would appear that this is an empirical distinction between the traditional body of

---

ments," in *Varia Juris Gentium. Liber Amicorum J.P.A. François* 355, 356, 358 (1959).

[194] *Idem* at 357.

[195] *Ibid.* The learned author cites in support of his thesis the existence of agreements between the Dutch and British India Companies and Indian princes and between European states and African (and, he could well add, American Indian) tribes.

[196] Cf. the trenchant criticism of Mann, *supra* note 189, at 48–50. The agreements cited in support of Professor Verdross' thesis, *supra* note 195, may be distinguished from state contracts of the type here studied. Colonial Companies may be considered (and were often treated) as agents of their respective states, while the African and American Indian tribes had all the attributes of sovereignty, except, sometimes, that of a permanent territory.

[197] McNair, "The General Principles of Law Recognized by Civilized Nations," 33 *Brit. Yb. Int'l L.* 1, 10 (1957) and cf. *id.* at 6.

international law and the law applicable to state contracts, and not a dogmatic classification into three separate bodies of law.[198]

In his discussion of "transnational law," Professor (now Judge) Jessup does not make clear his view on the character of the law of state contracts. Such law would certainly be included under the general heading of "transnational law," in the sense in which he uses this term, but so would the whole of public and private international law.[199] It may be that traditional public international law, private international law, the law of state contracts and international administrative law would constitute separate branches of transnational law.[200]

Finally, certain writers advocate the inclusion of the law of state contracts under public international law. This is, in a sense, a more traditionalist approach. In a recent article, Dr. F. A. Mann attacks the view of those writers who suggest the existence of a "third" body of law and maintains that it is to public international law that state contracts should refer if they are not to be subject to municipal law.[201] He seems to admit, however, the difficulty of deriving the principles to be applied from existing international law and favors the use of the comparative method in order to determine the applicable principles and rules.[202]

The International Law Commission's Special Rapporteur on state responsibility takes a similar position in his recent report on the protection of acquired rights.[203] The learned writer distinguishes

[198] But see the critiques of Calvert, "The Law Applicable to Concessions," 1 *U. Malaya L. Rev.* 265 (1959); Mann, *supra* note 189, at 45.

[199] ". . . I shall use, instead of 'international law,' the term 'transnational law' to include all law which regulates actions or events that transcend national frontiers. Both public and private international law are included, as are other rules which do not wholly fit into such standard categories." Jessup, *Transnational Law* 2 (1956).

[200] Cf. *idem* Chapter 3, 72 *et seq.* International administrative law and the law of state contracts might perhaps be considered as a single branch.

[201] Mann, *supra* note 189, at 41–56.

[202] Cf. Mann, "Reflections on a Commercial Law of Nations," 33 *Brit. Yb. Int'l L.* 20, 33–40 (1957). This article refers to a different, though closely related, problem, but it would appear that the observations on the general principles of law would be applicable in the case at hand, as well.

[203] Garcia Amador, "Responsibility of the State for Injuries Caused in Its Ter-

two categories of state contracts, namely, those of the "traditional type," where municipal law is applicable, and "internationalized" contracts, that is, state contracts which either refer, expressly or by implication, to public international law, the general principles of law "or some other legal system described in less precise terms but substantially similar in content," or contain arbitration clauses.[204] The classical doctrine applies only to the first category of contracts; nonperformance of such a contract will constitute a violation of international law only when (and because) it is "arbitrary" in character. The breach of a contract of the second type constitutes in itself a violation of public international law; nonperformance thus gives rise to the international responsibility of the state. It is, in itself, "unlawful." [205]

It is not always easy to determine the real importance of these alternative classifications or the precise effect of the differences among them.[206] It is submitted that the existence of a "separate" body of law, applicable to state contracts, is today accepted by the majority of legal opinion.[207] Whether this is a completely independent body of law or is subordinated to international law or to

---

ritory to the Person or Property of Aliens—Measures Affecting Acquired Rights" (Fourth Report to the International Law Commission), 1959-II *Yearbook of the International Law Commission* 1 (1960).

[204] *Idem* at 31.

[205] *Idem* 33 *et seq.* On the important distinction between "unlawful" and "arbitrary" acts, on which the Special Rapporteur places special emphasis, see *idem* 13 *et seq.*

[206] But see in this connection Dean Pound's wise observations on the purpose of classification in law, in 5 Pound, *Jurisprudence* 13 *et seq.* (1959).

[207] Cf. the studies already cited: Jessup, *Transnational Law* (1956); Verdross, *supra* note 193; McNair, *supra* note 197; Mann, "The Proper Law of Contracts Concluded by International Persons," 35 *Brit. Yb. Int'l L.* 34, 41 *et seq.* (1959); And see also Mann, "The Law Governing State Contracts," 21 *Brit. Yb. Int'l L.* 11 (1944); Farmanfarma, "The Oil Agreement between Iran and the International Oil Consortium: the Law Controlling," 34 *Texas L. Rev.* 259, 269 *et seq.* (1955); O'Connell, "A Critique of the Iranian Oil Litigation," 4 *Int'l & Comp. L. Qu.* 267, 268–76 (1955); Huang, "Some International and Legal Aspects of the Suez Canal Question," 51 *Am. J. Int'l L.* 277, 296 (1957); Meron, "Repudiation of *Ultra Vires* State Contracts and the International Responsibility of States," 6 *Int'l & Comp. L. Qu.* 273, 276–78 (1957); Wall, "The Iranian-Italian Oil Agreement of 1957," 7 *idem* 736, 744 *et seq.* (1958). And cf. Fragistas, "Arbitrage étranger et arbitrage international en droit privé," 49 *Rev. Critique Dr. Int. Privé* 1, at 14–20 (1960).

some other, more inclusive body of law, is in itself immaterial, as long as it is understood that it is distinct from the traditional body of international law. The need for determining its relative position with respect to international and municipal law cannot be denied. It may be, however, that the limited factual material [208] available today does not permit yet any definite classification, at least not before such material has been subjected to considerably more study.

Such legal material as there exists indicates clearly that transnational law is founded on the general principles of law common to civilized nations. Reference to such principles is found in several agreements between states and aliens. Indeed, before the jurists began to refer to the possibility of the existence of a distinct body of law, drafters of state contracts or arbitrators in proceedings between states and foreign companies had begun to refer to the general principles of law applied by civilized nations. The award in the *Lena Goldfields* case [209] is probably the first in which direct reference was made to the general principles of law, as distinguished from both municipal and international law. A contention to that effect was made by counsel for one of the parties and the court accepted it and went on to apply one such principle, namely, the principle of unjustified enrichment.[210] Probably quite independently from this award, reference to general principles of law found its way into several petroleum concession agreements concluded during the 1930s, more particularly in their provisions regarding the law to be applied in any future arbitration between the parties. The 1933 Convention between the Anglo-Persian Oil Company and the Government of Iran (then Persia) mentioned the "juridical principles contained in Article 38 of the Statutes of the Permanent Court of International Justice." [211] Another agreement stated that "the award shall be consistent with the legal principles familiar to

[208] Cf. *supra* notes 183–85 and the text *infra* to p. 293.

[209] Lena Goldfields Co., Ltd. v. U.S.S.R. (1930), 36 *Cornell L. Qu.* 42 (1950).

[210] *Idem* at 51.

[211] Article 22 (F); text in 2 Hurewitz, *Diplomacy in the Near and Middle East* 188 (1956).

civilized nations." [212] Still other concession contracts concluded before the Second World War referred to good faith and equity without direct reference to general principles of law.[213]

In the postwar years, references to such principles multiplied, both in concession agreements and in arbitral awards. In the Agreement concluded in 1954 between the Iranian Oil Consortium and the Iranian Government, it is provided:

In view of the diverse nationalities of the parties to this agreement, it shall be governed by and interpreted and applied in accordance with principles of law common to Iran and the several nations in which the other parties to the agreement are incorporated, and in the absence of such common principles, then by and in accordance with principles of law recognized by civilized nations in general, including such of those principles as may have been applied by international tribunals.[214]

Similar provisions are found in several other recent agreements dealing with the exploitation of petroleum resources.[215] Mention of such general principles is also found in some relevant municipal legislation. Thus, the Libyan Petroleum Law provides for arbitration in case of dispute between the state and the concessionaire; it further provides that concessions are to be "governed and interpreted in accordance with the laws of Libya and such principles and rules of international law as may be relevant." [216] The relevant Iranian legis-

---

[212] Agreement between the Ruler of Qatar and the Anglo-Persian Oil Co., Ltd., of May 17, 1935, quoted in the arbitral award in Ruler of Qatar v. International Marine Oil Co., Ltd. (1953), 1953 *Int'l L. Rep.* 534, 545.

[213] Cf. article 89 of the Agreement between the U.S.S.R. and Lena Goldfields Co., Ltd. (1925), quoted in the related arbitral award, *supra* note 209, at 42; clause 17 of the Agreement between the Ruler of Abu Dhabi and Petroleum Developments (Trucial Coast) Ltd. (January 11, 1939), quoted in the award in the related case, 1 *Int'l & Comp. L. Qu.* 247, 249–50 (1952).

[214] Article 46; text in 2 Hurewitz, *Diplomacy in the Near and Middle East* 348 (1956).

[215] Cf. Agreement between the National Iranian Oil Co. and A.G.I.P. Mineraria of September 5, 1957, article 40, quoted in Wall, *supra* note 207, at 739; Offshore Concession Agreement between the Shaikh of Kuwait and the Arabian Oil Co., Ltd., (Japan), of July 5, 1958, article 39, quoted *idem* at 751–52. And compare the advice to prospective concessionaires by Wadmond, "Basic Problems of Foreign Oil Operations," in Southwestern Legal Foundation, *Proceedings of the 1960 Institute on Private Investments Abroad* 537, 549–52 (1960).

[216] Libya, Petroleum Law, Law No. 25 of 1955, Second Schedule, clause 28(7);

lation leaves the determination of the applicable law to be made in the particular concession agreements. Some, though not all, of these agreements have included reference to general principles of law.[217]

Certain recent arbitration awards also refer to such principles in construing and applying concession agreements. The arbitrator in the *Abu Dhabi* case [218] held that, since no relevant law could be found in the "state" of Abu Dhabi,[219] the proper law of the contract consisted of "principles rooted in the good sense and common practice of the generality of civilised nations—a sort of 'modern law of nature.' " [220] In a similar case,[221] two years later, the arbitrator again found that the law of the conceding power could not be considered as the proper law of the contract,[222] and therefore the agreement was governed by "the principles of justice, equity and good conscience." [223]

It is evident that it is not clear as yet which precisely are the legal rules that govern such agreements. The confused state of the law on the matter is shown in the provisions of an important recent award in a dispute between the Kingdom of Saudi Arabia and the

---

reported in Wall, *supra* note 207, at 746; Sarre and Unler, "Modern Oil Laws," 1960 *J. Business L.* 161, 182.

[217] Iran, Petroleum Law of July 1957, reported in Sarre and Unler, *supra* note 216, at 182. Agreements which include such provisions are cited *supra* notes 214, 215; some other agreements (e.g. with the Pan-American Petroleum Corporation and with Sapphire Petroleum, Ltd.) do not contain such provisions; cf. Sarre and Unler, *idem* at 185.

[218] Petroleum Developments (Trucial Coast) Ltd. v. the Sheikh of Abu Dhabi (1951), text of award in 1 *Int'l & Comp. L. Qu.* 247 (1952).

[219] The arbitrator, Lord Asquith of Bishopstone, found that "the Sheikh administers a purely discretionary justice with the assistance of the Koran; and it would be fanciful to suggest that in this very primitive region there is any settled body of legal principles applicable to the construction of modern commercial instruments." *Idem* at 250–51.

[220] *Idem* at 251.

[221] Ruler of Qatar v. International Marine Oil Co. Ltd. (1953), in 1953 *Int'l L. Rep.* 534.

[222] The learned arbitrator found that Islamic law, as the law of Qatar, was *prima facie* applicable; but he did not apply it in this case because (a) the law in question was not developed enough and was not sufficient for construing the contract and (b) the whole agreement was not initially made under such law and was not consistent with Islamic law. *Idem* at 544–45.

[223] *Idem* at 545.

Arabian-American Oil Company (Aramco).[224] It has already been noted that the tribunal in this case found that the proper law of this contract was the law of Saudi Arabia and that according to the scant evidence available, such law considered concession agreements as private law contracts.[225] The tribunal had difficulty in determining the legal system on which the concession was based. It found that it could not be public international law, and that Saudi Arabian law was appropriate only as to certain matters.[226] It therefore concluded that "the Concession Agreement is thus the fundamental law of the Parties" and that "the Concession has the nature of a Constitution which has the effect of conferring acquired rights on the contracting Parties."[227] Resort to the general principles of law was found necessary for interpreting and supplementing the contractual provisions.[228] The Tribunal cited in this connection the *Lena Goldfields* and the *Abu Dhabi* cases and concluded that "the same character of public rights inevitably mixed with the grant of private rights to the concessionaire is to be found in the Aramco Concession Agreement."[229] The tribunal held further that the Saudi Arabian Government had granted to Aramco "irretractable rights," stressing the fact that the grant of such rights is not incompatible with state sovereignty and that it is by virtue of its sovereignty that a state binds itself irrevocably.[230]

The precise import of this award for the law of state contracts is not easy to determine. The facts of the case were not typical of "modern" cases. What was involved was not a general measure (such as nationalization) taken in order to promote the general welfare of the people of the state, but the grant to an individual of certain transportation rights which were found to have been already granted to Aramco. Only the financial interests of the state were directly involved; the general welfare of its people was affected only indirectly, if at all. It was therefore a case of a simple breach

---

[224] Saudi Arabia v. Aramco (1958) (privately printed).   [225] *Supra* pp. 206–7.
[226] Saudi Arabia v. Aramco (1958) at 57–60.   [227] *Idem* at 60–61.
[228] *Idem* at 61.   [229] *Idem* at 62.   [230] *Idem* at 61, 109–10.

of contract, which could easily have occurred in a similar manner between private companies.[231] The fact that the issue of the exercise of sovereign powers was raised is in itself of little importance.[232] In view of the facts before them, the arbitrators had no reason to distinguish between totally irrevocable rights and rights revocable, for reasons of public interest, upon payment of compensation. In their statement of the law, the arbitrators refer in passing to the existence of "rules of public policy." [233]

It is clear that there is today a developing practice involving the application of general principles of law to state contracts. There still remain several problems, of course, the most important of which are the determination of the conditions under which such principles are to be applied and the establishment of a method for finding the precise content of the rules involved.

It is not yet quite clear under what conditions transnational law is applicable to particular state contracts. There is little doubt as to its applicability when the parties include in the contract itself a provision to the effect that the "proper law of the contract" is transnational law or the general principles of law recognized by civilized nations.[234] Apart from such express statements, a similar intent of the parties may be inferred when the parties provide that any dispute is to be adjudged by an international court.[235] Provision

[231] The case was clearly one belonging to the first category of cases discussed *supra* pp. 236–39. In the same sense, see Mann, "The Proper Law of Contracts Concluded by International Persons," 35 *Brit. Yb. Int'l L.* 34, 48, 55 (1959).

[232] The unsatisfactory and purely formal character of the concept of sovereignty in this context has been noted *supra* p. 197 and note 18.

[233] The relevant statement reads: "Should a new concession contract incompatible with the first, or a subsequent statute, abolish totally or partially that which has been granted by previous law or concession, this would constitute a clear infringement, by the second contract, of acquired rights, or a violation, by the subsequent statute, of the principle of nonretroactivity of laws, *with the only exception of rules of public policy*." Saudi Arabia v. Aramco (1958) at 61 (emphasis supplied). The exception, as it is worded, is certainly of very limited effect, relating only to the nonretroactivity of statutes.

[234] Cf., in agreement on this point, Verdross, "Protection of Private Property under Quasi-International Agreements," in *Varia Juris Gentium. Liber Amicorum J.P.A. François* 355, 357 (1959); Mann, *supra* note 231, at 45 *et seq.*

[235] Cf. Mann, *idem* at 51–52.

for arbitration may also be an indication of the existence of such intent, though probably not in all cases.[236] Finally, transnational law may sometimes be applied when no other system of law may be said to govern the contract, or in order to supplement other applicable rules of law. The situation of the parties in each particular instance will certainly be a most important factor in determining whether such law is applicable. There is no cogent reason, however, for limiting the applicability of transnational law to the cases where one of the parties to the contract, presumably the state, does not have a sufficiently developed legal system.[237] It is true that in such cases, it is more probable that transnational law will be referred to, but the insufficiency of some legal systems should not be considered as the main cause of the development of transnational law.[238]

The close relationship between transnational law and public international law makes it probable that the former will depend on the latter for the determination of the precise content of the general principles to be applied. Whatever view one may have on the extent of the distinction between the two bodies of law, it remains true that the adoption by international law of certain "general principles of law recognized by civilized nations" is adequate evidence of their validity as legal principles and of their wide acceptance by civilized nations. This has been understood by the drafters of some concession agreements which, when providing for the application of general principles of law, mention especially the prin-

---

[236] But see, strongly in favor of such a presumption, Verdross, *supra* note 234, at 358–59. Carlston, "International Role of Concession Agreements," 52 *Nw. U.L. Rev.* 618, 640 (1957), suggests, on the other hand, that an obligation to have recourse to negotiations and arbitration for the settlement of any dispute is imposed to the parties of state contracts by the "living law" of their contract. See also Carlston, "Concession Agreements and Nationalization," 52 *Am. J. Int'l L.* 260, 265 (1958).

[237] Cf. McNair, "The General Principles of Law Recognized by Civilized Nations," 33 *Brit. Yb. Int'l L.* 1, 4, 19 (1957). The language used by the learned writer may perhaps tend to mislead, but it is clear that he states only a strong probability to that effect, not a necessary limitation.

[238] But see, on this point, Calvert, "The Law Applicable to Concessions," 1 *U. Malaya L. Rev.* 265, 280 (1959).

ciples "applied by international tribunals." [239] A recent agreement goes further in this respect and provides for the application of "the principles of law recognized as normal by civilized nations, *in particular* such principles as have already been applied by the International Tribunals." [240]

Municipal law, on the other hand, still retains its importance as the ultimate source of the principles to be applied. Extensive comparative research and study are needed in order to clarify the still vague content of most general principles.[241] It should be noted, at this point, that just as not all principles of private law are applicable in international law,[242] so, too, not all general principles of law recognized in international law are applicable in the case of state contracts. The peculiar character of these contracts, which is, after all, the chief reason for the application of special legal rules, should be kept in mind. It is in this connection that the latest Harvard Research draft makes a significant contribution, in referring to "the principles recognized by the principal legal systems of the world as applicable to governmental contracts or concessions." [243] One of the directors of the research project made clear the implications of this provision when he stated that

[239] Cf. *supra* p. 290.

[240] Agreement between the National Iranian Oil Co. and A.G.I.P. Mineraria, September 5, 1957, article 40, quoted in Wall, "The Iranian-Italian Oil Agreement of 1957," 7 *Int'l & Comp. L. Qu.* 736, 739 (1958) (emphasis supplied).

[241] Cf. on this point, Gutteridge, *Comparative Law* 60–71 (1949); Mann, "Reflections on a Commercial Law of Nations," 33 *Brit. Yb. Int'l L.* 20, 33–40, 48–51 (1957); Schlesinger, "Research on the General Principles of Law Recognized by Civilized Nations," 51 *Am. J. Int'l L.* 734 (1957).

[242] ". . . the fundamental fallacy of reasoning on the lines of private law concepts in matters of public international law—a fallacy which should be avoided also in construing point 3) of Article 38 of the Statute of the Court dealing with 'the general principles of law recognised by civilised nations,' as incorporating lock, stock and barrel into the body of rules to be applied by the Court the traditional rules and concepts of municipal private law, as though they were really susceptible of direct and automatic application to inter-State relations, without careful separation of chaff from wheat." Verzijl, "The International Court of Justice in 1957 and 1958," in *Varia Juris Gentium. Liber Amicorum J.P.A. François* 363, 370–71 (1959).

[243] Article 12(1)(c), quoted *supra* pp. 281–82, note 177.

The theory of the rule is that a modern law of government contract is under development and thus the rule to be applied would be based on an analogy from the rules relating to government contracts.[244]

It is to be noted that in another branch of transnational law, namely, international administrative law, which is perhaps more systematically developed than the law of state contracts, public law concepts are applied in regulating the relations between international organizations and the members of their staff.[245]

That such an application of general principles of law is both important and appropriate may be illustrated by reference to a well-known legal principle whose applicability in public international law is still a matter of controversy. The principle in question is that which prohibits the abuse of rights. According to it, legal rights should be exercised in good faith and in accordance with their social and economic purposes, so that they will not have manifestly unjust consequences prejudicial to others.[246] This principle is accepted in certain legal systems (for example, those of France and Switzerland), it is not found at all in other systems (for example, those of Italy and of the common law countries) or it is found with severe limitations on its extent (for example in the German legal system).[247]

At the same time, most advanced legal systems arrive at roughly similar results, in their regulation of the exercise of rights, regardless of their acceptance of the principle regarding abuse of rights. This paradoxical fact is given different interpretations by the jurists,

[244] Sohn, in 54 *Am. Soc. Int'l L. Proc.* 117 (1960). But see *contra*, Verdross, *supra* note 234 at 356–59, who supports the existence of a separate body of law applicable to "quasi-international agreements" precisely in order to avoid applying to such instruments the rules applicable to municipal law administrative contracts.

[245] Cf. *supra* p. 284 and note 188. And see also *infra* note 255.

[246] For a discussion of the various elements of the principle and the controversies regarding them in municipal law theory, see the able account of Roulet, *Le caractère artificiel de la théorie de l'abus de droit en droit international public* 35–43, 53–76 (1958). See also Lauterpacht, *The Function of Law in the International Community* 286 *et seq.* (1933); W. Friedmann, *Legal Theory* 392–93 (3d ed., 1953); W. Friedmann, *Law in a Changing Society* 76–80 (1959).

[247] Cf. the discussions and citations to the related literature in Roulet, *op. cit. supra* note 246, at 14–34.

according to their position with respect to the principle's applicability in international law. Proponents of such applicability regard this as confirmation of the principle's validity; they maintain that it is in fact applied even in those systems which formally reject it.[248] Their opponents tend to regard the doctrine of abuse of rights as a specific legal technique rather than a general principle of law. They contest its necessity and usefulness in international law, claiming that whenever the states' rights are limited by existing legal rules (and this, in their view, is true of most such rights) no margin is left for an application of the theory of abuse of rights. Any action which goes beyond these limits is illegal in itself and not as an abuse of the corresponding rights.[249]

This argumentation may not be conclusive but it does raise certain important doubts as to the extent of the principle's application in international law. Since its first appearance in the literature of international law [250] a large number of studies have been devoted to this principle.[251] Although not all of them avoid a certain semantic confusion in their treatment of the subject, they make apparent the principle's relevance to international law. Its acceptance would give greater elasticity to the sometimes very strict rules of traditional international law, for it would serve to temper the extensive rights of states which are admitted under that law. On the other hand, this doctrine is a difficult one to apply between sovereign nations, because of its implications of bad faith. Evidence of this may

[248] Cf. Lauterpacht, *op. cit. supra* note 246, at 292–97; W. Friedmann, *Law in a Changing Society* 76–80 (1959).

[249] Cf. Schwarzenberger, "The Fundamental Principles of International Law," 87 *Hague Recueil* 191, 305 *et seq.* (1955); Schwarzenberger, "Uses and Abuses of the 'Abuse of Rights' in International Law," 42 *Grotius Soc. Transactions* 147 (1956); Roulet, *op. cit. supra* note 246, *passim.*

[250] Politis, "Le problème de la limitation de la souveraineté et la théorie de l'abus des droits dans les rapports internationaux," 6 *Hague Recueil* 1 (1925).

[251] Scerni, *L'abuso di diritto nei rapporti internazionali* (1930); Séléa, *La notion de l'abus de droit dans le droit international* (1940); Kiss, *L'abus de droit en droit international* (1953). Roulet, *op. cit. supra* note 246 at 161, cites more than a dozen studies devoted specifically to the theory of abuse of rights and its application in public international law. And see, more recently, Garcia Amador, "State Responsibility: Some New Problems," 94 *Hague Recueil* 365, 376–82 (1958).

be found in the absence of any judicial decision openly basing its holding on abuse of rights.[252] Even in their diplomatic statements and their pleadings before international tribunals, states are loath to invoke this principle. It seems thus certain that, under present conditions, the doctrine of abuse of rights will be of limited application in public international law.

In the case of transnational law, there would be fewer difficulties in applying this principle. Since, as here submitted, this law relates to relations between states or international organizations and individuals, abuse of rights on the part of the former would normally take the form of a "misuse of power" (*détournement de pouvoir*).[253] According to this concept, familiar to students of French administrative law and of those legal systems based on it, the unlawfulness of the act involved consists in the employment of powers attributed by law to certain state organs in pursuit of purposes differing from those in view of which the powers were attributed.[254] There is no necessary implication of bad faith on the part of the state or of its agent. This concept does take into account the inequality of the parties involved in the related dispute. The responsible official is allowed full discretion in judging whether an act or omission is appropriate or necessary. But certain extreme limits are set to his right to do so.[255]

The law granting the powers allegedly misused would be, in the case of a state contract, either the contract itself or public international law, or both. No one can deny that, in the case of state con-

---

[252] For a list of references to the principle in separate and dissenting opinions of I.C.J. judges, see Roulet, *op. cit. supra* note 246, at 45, note 4.

[253] See in this connection Roulet, *op. cit. supra* note 246, at 41–43; Fawcett, "*Détournement de Pouvoir* by International Organizations," 33 *Brit. Yb. Int'l L.* 311 (1957).

[254] See, e.g., Duez and Debeyre, *Traité de droit administratif* 391 (1952); Waline, *Droit Administratif* 443 *et seq.* (8th ed., 1959).

[255] The principle of abuse of rights, under the form here discussed, has been adopted and is applied in international administrative law. Cf. Bedjaoui, "Jurisprudence comparée des tribunaux administratifs internationaux en matière d'excès de pouvoir," 2 *Annuaire Français Dr. Int'l* 482 (1956); Fawcett, *supra* note 253, *passim*; Friedmann and Fatouros, "The United Nations Administrative Tribunal," 11 *Int'l Organization* 13, 26, 28 (1957).

tracts, extreme importance is, and should be, given to the contractual provisions. They are often quite extensive and detailed and constitute clearly the basic law of the parties. However, both parties
to such a contract may act in a manner which, without being in
direct breach of the contract, may still constitute an abuse of the
parties' rights under the contract. A foreign investor may, in order
perhaps to serve some of his other interests, outside the host country, act in a manner highly detrimental to the host state's national
economy. There are often provisions for such cases in the state
contracts themselves; but if there is no relevant provision it may
be possible to invoke the principle condemning abuse of rights. Or
the state may unnecessarily delay the grant of certain permissions
or licenses which are required under the contract and thus damage
the investor. Again, abuse of rights may be claimed by the injured
party.

International law, on the other hand, is particularly important
with respect to the state party to the contract. International customary law or specific treaty provisions attribute to states certain
rights and powers in view of certain purposes. The employment of
such powers by the state in pursuit of other ends would constitute
a "misuse of power." This would occur, for instance, if the reasons
of public interest invoked by a state when taking measures affecting
the contractual rights of aliens are manifestly false, or nonexistent,
or of the state's own creation, if the existing laws and regulations
are, in the particular instances, applied in bad faith, or if there is
complete absence of due process, as required by the local municipal
law or by the international minimum standard of justice.

The case law of international tribunals on this point is very limited. A patent case of abuse of rights by local authorities is described
in the award in the *Walter Fletcher Smith* case.[256] The arbitrator
found, in this instance, that the expropriation of the claimant's property by municipal Cuban authorities was in violation of the laws
and Constitution of the country. He further found

[256] (U.S.A. v. Cuba, 1929), 2 UN RIAA 913.

that the expropriation proceedings were not, in good faith, for the purpose of public utility. They do not present the features of an orderly attempt by officers of the law to carry out a formal order of condemnation. The destruction of the claimant's property was wanton, riotous, oppressive. It was effected by about one hundred and fifty men whose action appears to have been of a most violent character. . . .

While the proceedings were municipal in form, the properties seized were turned over immediately to the defendant company, ostensibly for public purposes, but, in fact, to be used by the defendant for purposes of amusement and private profit, without any reference to public utility.[257]

In one of the successive drafts of the Harvard Draft Convention on the International Responsibility of States for Injuries to Aliens, it was provided that the annulment by a state of a contract with an alien is wrongful if it is "inconsistent with the law of the State as it existed at the time of the making of the contract . . . and is effected with the purpose of securing to the State or to other persons for its or their economic advantage benefits owed to the alien under the terms of the contract. . . ." [258] The term "economic," insofar as it relates to the state's advantage, is evidently to be understood here in a limited sense. It refers, not to the general benefit of the national economy, but to the possible financial benefit of the state treasury, the "fisc." This provision should then be considered as a clear reference to possible "misuse of power" on the part of the state. The language quoted above has been omitted from the latest draft of the Convention.[259] This, however, should not be understood as implying a denial of the applicability of the principle regarding abuse of rights, even though it may indicate a certain decrease of emphasis. In the explanatory note accompanying the amended text of the related article, the authors, after discussing illustrations of lawful and wrongful state action, state that

[257] *Idem* at 917. The term "municipal" denotes in this context local authorities, in contradistinction to the central government.

[258] Draft No. 11 (June 1, 1960), article 12(1)(a), as quoted in 54 *Am. Soc. Int'l L. Proc.* 102, 104–5 (1960).

[259] Draft No. 12 (1961), article 12, quoted *supra* at pp. 281–82.

"the evil with which this sub-paragraph is intended to deal is action which is clearly violative of the contract under the state of law existing at the time of its conclusion and which is intended to deprive the alien of the fruits of his contract without any other purpose than the enrichment of the State with which the agreement was made." [260] Moreover, in the article dealing with the taking of property,[261] it is provided that "an uncompensated taking of property of an alien" which results from the application of legal provisions of general application, such as tax laws or penal legislation, will not be wrongful, unless, *inter alia,* it is "an abuse of the powers specified in this paragraph for the purpose of depriving an alien of his property." [262] It is certain, therefore, that under the Draft Convention, an international claim with respect to state contracts could be founded on the principle prohibiting the abuse of rights and, more specifically, the misuse of power.

[260] 55 *Am. J. Int'l L.* 548, at 572 (1961).

[261] Article 10, 55 *Am. J. Int'l L.* 548, 553–54 (1961). This article would be applicable in most cases of annulment of state contracts; cf. article 12(2), quoted *supra* pp. 281–82.

[262] Article 10(5)(d), 55 *Am. J. Int'l L.* 548, 554 (1961).

IO

Problems of Compensation

A MOST important element of the classical international law theory regarding the effects of state measures affecting the contractual rights of aliens is its requirement that the states responsible for such measures compensate the aliens for the damage to their interests. The existence of such a requirement under international law cannot today be contested. It is supported by the existing case law of international tribunals, by state practice, particularly as manifested in treaties, and by the consensus of competent legal opinion.

Recent State Practice

The relevant case law is perhaps of more value as evidence of state practice than as a set of judicial precedents.[1] In many cases, the chief question submitted to arbitration was the amount of compensation to be paid, the states involved having agreed beforehand that some compensation was due. This is, for instance, true of the award in the *Delagoa Bay* arbitration,[2] where the tribunal was instituted in order "to fix, as it shall deem most just, the amount of the compensation due from Portugal to the claimants of the two other countries in consequence of the cancellation of the concession

---

[1] Cf. the observations *supra* pp. 272–73.

[2] Delagoa Bay and East African Railway (U.S.A. and Great Britain v. Portugal, 1900), 2 Moore, *International Arbitrations* 1865; text of award, *Foreign Relations of the United States 1900* 903 (1902); 3 Whiteman, *Damages* 1694.

of the Lourenco-Marques Railway and of the taking possession of said railway by the Portuguese Government." [3] In the few other cases, however, where the arbitrators' function was less limited, the tribunals found that, under certain conditions, compensation was due. In the *El Triunfo* case,[4] the majority of the arbitrators found that a company owned by United States citizens was "entitled to compensation for the result of the destruction of the concession and for the appropriation of such property as belonged to that company." [5] In the *Shufeldt Claim* [6] the arbitrator held that "where such a decree, passed even on the best of grounds, works injustice to an alien subject . . . the Government ought to make compensation for the injury inflicted." [7] A similar view may be inferred from the judgment of the Permanent Court of International Justice in the *Chorzow Factory* case.[8]

If the requirement of compensation should today be considered as established, it is chiefly by virtue of recent diplomatic practice. In virtually all cases where expropriatory measures have affected the property and contractual rights of aliens, compensation has ultimately been paid by the expropriating state, usually on the basis of an agreement between that state and the aliens' state of nationality.[9]

Thus, the dispute between the United States and Mexico regarding Mexico's expropriation of land and petroleum holdings (including concessions) of United States nationals was finally settled in 1941 by the conclusion of two agreements. By the first of these

[3] Protocol of June 13, 1891, Article I, 2 Moore, *International Arbitrations* 1865, 1874. And cf. *supra* p. 274 note 161.

[4] Salvador Commercial Company v. Salvador (U.S.A. v. Salvador, 1902), *Foreign Relations of the United States 1902* 838 (1903).

[5] *Idem* at 872. The majority decision was based on a finding that the Salvador Government was guilty of a denial of justice because of their imposing on the company "the extreme penalty of forfeiture" without due process; *idem* at 870-71.

[6] (U.S.A. v. Guatemala, 1930), 2 UN RIAA 1079.

[7] *Idem* at 1095.

[8] Judgment No. 13, September 13, 1928, P.C.I.J. Publ., Ser. A. No. 17, at 46.

[9] The most recent cases, of course, have not yet been settled and thus constitute, for the time being, exceptions to the statement in the text. Note, however, that some compensation has been offered in all recent instances of expropriation.

instruments, Mexico undertook to pay, over a number of years, a lump sum as full compensation for the value of all expropriated land holdings and for certain other claims.[10] The second agreement provided for the appointment of experts to determine the compensation to be paid to the United States for the petroleum properties of their nationals expropriated by Mexico.[11] The report was submitted a few months later and the two governments undertook to implement the experts' recommendations.[12] Similar arrangements were made between Mexico and the governments of the United Kingdom and The Netherlands, providing for compensation to be paid to the latter states for the expropriated petroleum properties of their nationals.[13]

Compensation was also given for the contractual and other property rights affected by the postwar nationalizations in the "people's democracies" of Southern and Central Europe. A series of bilateral agreements were concluded between the expropriating states and the states whose nationals had been affected.[14] In most of these agreements, provision was made for the payment of lump-sum compensation.[15]

In the case of the nationalization of the petroleum industry in

---

[10] Convention Providing for the Final Adjustment and the Settlement of Certain Unsettled Claims, of November 19, 1941, U.S. Treaty Series No. 980, 36 *Am. J. Int'l L. Supp.* 179 (1942). Cf. more generally, Gordon, *The Expropriation of Foreign-Owned Property in Mexico* (1941); Kunz, "The Mexican Expropriations," 17 *N.Y.U.L. Qu. Rev.* 327, 342–59 (1940); and on the final settlement, Briggs, "The Settlement of Mexican Claims Act of 1942," 37 *Am. J. Int'l L.* 222 (1943).

[11] Agreement on Expropriation of Petroleum Properties, of November 19, 1941, 36 *Am. J. Int'l L. Supp.* 182 (1942).

[12] Agreement of Experts, April 17, 1942, *idem* 185. And cf. Person, *Mexican Oil. Symbol of Recent Trends in International Relations* 81 (1942); Kunz, *supra* note 10, at 359–68.

[13] Cf. Wortley, "The Mexican Oil Dispute 1938–1946," 43 *Grotius Soc. Transactions* 15 (1957); Foighel, *Nationalization* 95 (1957).

[14] For lists of such agreements, see Foighel, *idem* 127–33; UN Document A/AC.97/5/Rev. 1, 27 December 1960, pp. 195–99.

[15] For discussions of the provisions of the agreements, see Foighel, *Nationalization* 88–101 (1957); Bindschedler, "La protection de la propriété privée en droit international public," 90 *Hague Recueil* 173, 257–67, 272–88 (1956); Drucker, "Compensation for Nationalized Property: The British Practice," 49 *Am. J. Int'l L.* 477 (1955). And see now the exhaustive systematic analysis in White, *Nationalisation of Foreign Property* 193–232 (1961).

Iran, only about 10 percent of the compensation was paid by the state. The rest was paid to the Anglo-Iranian Oil Company by the seven other foreign oil companies constituting the Iranian Oil Consortium, which had profited from the nationalization.[16] Finally, compensation has also been paid for the nationalization of the Universal Suez Maritime Canal Company. By the same Act by which it nationalized the company, the Egyptian Government offered to compensate its shareholders.[17] The exact sum to be paid was determined, after negotiations, by a preliminary agreement,[18] and the matter was finally settled by a formal agreement between the nationalizing government and the company's shareholders.[19] The latter were given all external assets of the company and a further lump sum to be paid in installments.

State practice is, of course, always open to the objection that it is politically inspired and does not reflect acceptance or application of legal principles. And it is certainly true that states have been led to conclude agreements concerning compensation by a variety of economic or political motives. In his study of nationalization, Professor Foighel lists four main categories of such motives, citing instances of their presence in recent treaty practice.[20] These categories are: force,[21] release of accounts and assets of the expropriating state, located in and blocked by the claimant state, remission of earlier debts owed by the expropriating state and the securing of commercial and other economic advantages. This last

[16] Cf. Farmanfarma, "The Oil Agreement Between Iran and the International Oil Consortium: The Law Controlling," 34 *Texas L. Rev.* 259, 261 (1955); Carlston, "Concession Agreements and Nationalization," 52 *Am. J. Int'l L.* 260, 273–74 (1958).

[17] Nationalization Law, July 26, 1956, Law No. 285 of 1956, text in *The Suez Canal: A Selection of Documents* . . . 41 (1956).

[18] Heads of Agreement, April 29, 1958, text in 62 *Rev. Gén. Dr. Int. Public* 444 (1958); *The Suez Canal Settlement: A Selection of Documents* . . . 3 (Lauterpacht ed., 1960).

[19] Agreement between the Government of the United Arab Republic and the Compagnie Financière de Suez, July 13, 1958, *idem* 6.

[20] Foighel, *Nationalization* 79–85 (1957).

[21] *Idem* at 79–80. The applicability of this category of motives may be limited today, since in most cases pressure will be exerted by economic or other means. The case cited by the author, namely, the blocking of Yugoslav gold reserves by the United States, belongs rather to the second category of motives.

category is perhaps the most important and certainly the most widely found. Apart from the agreements concluded with the Southern and Central European states,[22] several other recent agreements on compensation have been expressly coupled with commercial arrangements. This is true, for instance, of the Mexican-United States agreements of 1941 which were accompanied by extensive commitments on the part of the United States.[23] Compensation for the nationalized tin mines in Bolivia was also secured chiefly by the promise of increased United States technical and economic assistance and of certain commercial arrangements.[24]

The evidence of state practice, however, cannot be dismissed on the basis of these considerations. As has been pointed out,[25] the methods used are not objectionable, under international law; in fact, they are the chief available means of exercising pressure in peacetime and they have their counterparts in private business practices. In certain cases, of course, state practice may justifiably be attributed solely to considerations of temporary convenience, but this is not always the case. Compensation represents today the only possible common ground between the various states, in view of the divergence in their social and economic systems. It is to the interest of both capital-exporting and capital-importing states, since it makes possible the continuation of international trade and economic relations. This is today the consensus of juristic thought[26] despite certain earlier divisions of opinion.[27] Even the proponents of the

[22] Discussed *idem* 81–84.

[23] The United States undertook to negotiate a trade agreement, to cooperate in the stabilization of the Mexican currency by purchasing pesos with dollars, to purchase Mexican silver at favorable prices, and to extend Export-Import Bank loans. Cf. Woolsey, "The United States Mexican Settlement," 36 *Am. J. Int'l L.* 117, 118 (1942); Briggs, *supra* note 10, at 232.

[24] Cf. Thomas, "Protection of Property of Citizens Abroad," in Southwestern Legal Foundation, *Proceedings of the 1959 Institute on Private Investments Abroad* 417, 437–38 (1959).

[25] Foighel, *Nationalization* 84–85 (1957). And see also, Wortley, "The Protection of Property Situated Abroad," 35 *Tulane L. Rev.* 739, 744–45 (1961).

[26] See Bindschedler, *supra* note 15, at 187 *et seq.* and citations therein; Wortley, *Expropriation* 33–35; de Visscher, *Théories et réalités en droit international public* 247, 249 (3d ed., 1960); White, *op. cit. supra* note 15, at 231–35.

[27] Cf. the famous controversy between Alexander Fachiri and Sir John Fischer Williams, in 6 *Brit. Yb. Int'l L.* 159 (1925), 9 *idem* 1 (1928), and 10 *idem* 32 (1929).

recognition of the complete freedom of states to nationalize private property admit that a "synthesis of divergences on a world scale" [28] is needed and tend to consider the award of compensation as the best possible solution.[29]

Compensation for Lawful and Unlawful Measures

A state's obligation to compensate aliens may arise either out of an unlawful interference with their contractual rights or out of interference which in itself is lawful under international law but still creates a duty to compensate. As has already been noted,[30] measures taken in violation of treaty commitments or in pursuit of no public purpose, or measures discriminatory against the alien, are unlawful under international law. A subsequent denial of justice also entails the state's responsibility for an international tort, so that measures which are followed by a denial of justice are similar in their effects to measures unlawful *ab initio*. Lawful measures are those which are taken for a public purpose and do not otherwise violate international law.[31] This distinction, which now appears to be well established [32] is of considerable practical importance because it corresponds to a difference in the manner in which the compensation is to be calculated.

The reason for this difference lies in the different legal founda-

---

[28] ". . . une synthèse des divergences à l'échelle mondiale," Katzarov, *Nationalisation* 436.

[29] Cf. Friedman, *Expropriation* 206–11; Katzarov, *Nationalisation* 429–39; Seidl-Hohenveldern, "Communist Theories on Confiscation and Expropriation. Critical Comments," 7 *Am. J. Comp. L.* 541, 546–48, 549 (1958); R.H.G., "Rome Conference on International and Comparative Law," 7 *Int'l & Comp. L. Qu.* 585, 586–87 (1958). And see also Foighel, *Nationalization* 85–87 (1957); Delson, "Nationalization of the Suez Canal Company: Issues of Public and Private International Law," 57 *Columbia L. Rev.* 755, 765–67 (1957).

[30] *Supra* pp. 222, 244 *et seq.*

[31] Measures taken in accordance with the contract's provisions do not entail compensation (in the absence of special provision to that effect) and are not discussed in this chapter. The same is true, for different reasons, of measures of a punitive character.

[32] It was forcefully expressed by the Permanent Court of International Justice in its judgment in the Chorzow Factory case, quoted *supra* pp. 222–23. And cf. Bindschedler, *supra* note 15, at 245–46.

tions of the duty to compensate in the two cases. With respect to unlawful measures, compensation constitutes reparation for an international tort and has therefore a mixed punitive and compensatory character. Such compensation aims at restoring the exact *status quo ante*, at least in financial terms.[33] It has to cover the alien's loss, as promptly and effectively as possible.

Different considerations apply in the case of lawful measures. The chief ground on which compensation is founded in this case is the general principle of law condemning unjustified (or unjust)[34] enrichment.[35] This principle holds that "a person who has been unjustly enriched at the expense of another is required to make restitution to that other."[36] It is accepted today, under varying forms and names, in most advanced legal systems including the major civil and common law jurisdictions.[37] It has been considered favorably by international jurists, sometimes in its most general form, as a principle on which state responsibility is founded[38] and sometimes only as a principle of limited application, helpful in con-

[33] But see *infra* pp. 310–14 on the question of restitution versus compensation.

[34] The latter adjective seems to be more in use, though the former is more accurate. It is possible to distinguish between "unjustified enrichment" (i.e., enrichment without legal cause, *sine causa*) and "unjust enrichment" (i.e., enrichment in an unjust manner), and attribute different legal effects to each of them. See, in this line, the decision of the Roumanian-German Mixed Arbitral Tribunal in the case of Direction Générale des ports et voies de communication par eau v. A. Schwartz et Cie, (1927), 7 *Recueil T.A.M.* 738, 742, and Dr. Cheng's comments on it, in his "Justice and Equity in International Law," 8 *Current Legal Problems* 185, 200–1 (1955). The advisability of such a distinction in international law is doubtful and it is not followed in the present limited treatment of the subject.

[35] Cf. Cheng, *General Principles of Law* 47–49 (1953); O'Connell, *The Law of State Succession* 131–32 (1956); Carlston, *supra* note 16, at 266; Cheng, "The Rationale of Compensation for Expropriation," 44 *Grotius Soc. Transactions* 267, 290–93 (1959). And cf. *infra* note 38.

[36] Restatement, *Restitution* s. 1 (1937).

[37] See the following comparative law studies: Gutteridge and David, "The Doctrine of Unjustified Enrichment," 5 *Cambridge L.J.* 204 (1934); W. Friedmann, "The Principle of Unjust Enrichment in English Law: A Study in Comparative Law," 16 *Can. Bar Rev.* 243, 365 (1938); Dawson, *Unjust Enrichment* (1951); O'Connell, "Unjust Enrichment," 5 *Am. J. Comp. L.* 2 (1956).

[38] See Ripert, "Les règles du droit civil applicables aux rapports internationaux," 44 *Hague Recueil* 565, 631–32 (1933); O'Connell, "A Critique of the Iranian Oil Litigation," 4 *Int'l & Comp. L. Qu.* 267, 270–71 (1955); 1 Schwarzenberger, *International Law* 580–81 (3d ed., 1957); Wortley, *Expropriation* 95 *et seq.*; W. Friedmann, *Law in a Changing Society* 456 (1959). And cf. also *supra* note 35.

nection with the assessment of damages.[39] In very few instances has the principle itself constituted the holding of a decision by an international tribunal.[40] It should be noted in this connection that the concept of unjustified enrichment has no necessary implication of bad faith [41] and it is thus easily applicable in interstate relations.

The application of this principle in the case at hand means that the compensation to be awarded will have to be assessed on the basis of the state's profit from the measures involved, not on the basis of the alien's loss. Certain other considerations of an equitable character might also be operative and further reduce the amount or availability of compensation.[42]

Such a difference in the measure of compensation in each case is then a necessary consequence of the distinction between lawful and unlawful state measures affecting the contractual and property rights of aliens.[43] The recent movement in support of the view that any interference with the contractual rights of aliens is internationally unlawful may be said to be founded on the acceptance of

[39] Cf. DeSzassy, "The Protection of Acquired Private Rights of Foreigners in International Law," International Law Association, Report of the Thirty-Sixth Conference 583, 587–89 (1931); Cheng, "Expropriation in International Law," 21 Solicitor 98, 100 (1954); 1 Schwarzenberger, International Law 655–56 (3d ed., 1957).

[40] The case most in point is that of Lena Goldfields Co., Ltd., v. U.S.S.R., (1930), 36 Cornell L. Qu. 42 (1950). See also the Anglo-German Mixed Arbitral Tribunal's decisions in the cases of Burroughs Welcome & Co. v. Chemische Fabrik (1926), 6 Recueil T.A.M. 13, and Leslie Caro v. Norddeutsche Lloyd (1927), 7 idem 398, which however, being partly based on treaty and German law provisions, are not of general application. The early case of Putegnat's Heirs (1871), 4 Moore, International Arbitrations 3718, is less clear.

The application of the principle in question in international law was explicitly rejected by the Mexican-U.S.A. General Claims Commission in the Dickson Car Wheel Company case, (U.S.A. v. Mexico, 1931), 4 UN RIAA 669, 676. The Commission's statement, however, is clearly a dictum, since the Commission held that, in any case, the theory of unjustified enrichment would be inapplicable in the instant case; cf. idem at 676–77.

[41] But see supra note 34. "Unjust," as opposed to "unjustified," enrichment may have a connotation of bad faith.

[42] See infra pp. 326–33.

[43] Cf. Judgment No. 13, September 13, 1928, of the Permanent Court of International Justice in the Chorzow Factory case, P.C.I.J. Publ., Ser. A, No. 17, at 47–48. But see contra the dissenting opinions of Lord Finlay and Judge Ehrlich, idem at 70–72, 90.

this distinction. It is in fact a movement in favor of the application of the strictest measure of compensation in cases of interference with aliens' contractual rights.[44]

In connection with this distinction, two important problems arise, each of which is closely related to one of these two kinds of measures. With respect to unlawful measures, the question of the principal character of restitution or of compensation arises. In considering lawful measures, on the other hand, the problem of the legal character of compensation, as a condition precedent or as a duty arising out of the measures in question, has to be considered.

It has been widely held in the theory of international law that *restitutio in integrum* or, in common law terminology, "specific performance," is the principal mode of reparation of a material wrong, pecuniary compensation being subsidiary in character, applicable only when *restitutio* is not possible or not claimed.[45] On the other hand, it is generally admitted that in practice *restitutio* is possible only in exceptional cases and that in the overwhelming majority of cases the responsibility of the state is discharged by the

[44] For two opposing statements, both supporting this inference, see Schwebel, in International Law Association, *Report of the Forty-Eighth Conference* 150–51 (1958), and Delson, *idem* 156–57. And cf. Kissam and Leach, "Sovereign Expropriation of Property and Abrogation of Concession Contracts," 28 *Fordham L. Rev.* 177, 214 (1959).

[45] Among the authors supporting this view and discussing it at some length, see 1 Anzilotti, *Cours de droit international* 526–27 (Gidel transl., 1929); 1 Sibert, *Traité de droit international public* 320–25 (1951); 2 Cavaré, *Droit International Public Positif* 394 (1951); Personnaz, *La réparation du préjudice en droit international public* 74 et seq. (1938); Reitzer, *La réparation comme conséquence de l'acte illicite en droit international* 171–74 (1938); Wortley, *Expropriation*, 78 et seq.; 1 Schwarzenberger, *International Law* 656–57, 660 (3d ed., 1957).

Several others merely mention the rule, as stated in the text, but discuss at length only the problems of compensation; cf. Yntema, "The Treaties with Germany and Compensation for War Damage–II," 24 *Columbia L. Rev.* 134, 137 (1924); Decencière-Ferrandière, *La responsabilité internationale des états à raison des dommages subis par des étrangers* 245–46 (1925); Eagleton, *The Responsibility of States in International Law* 182–83 (1928); Eagleton, "Measure of Damages in International Law," 39 *Yale L.J.* 52, 53 (1929); Salvioli, "La responsabilité des Etats et la fixation des dommages et interêts par les tribunaux internationaux," 28 *Hague Recueil* 231, 237 (1929). In this connection, see also the award in the case of the Forests in Central Rhodope (Greece v. Bulgaria, 1933), 3 UN RIAA 1405, 1431 et seq.

payment of pecuniary compensation.[46] The latter view is supported by the case law of international tribunals as well as by the prevailing diplomatic practice. In fact, it is only in exceptional cases that reparation is made through *restitutio*,[47] especially whenever compensation is manifestly insufficient as a remedy.[48] Instances of restitution may also be found in the provisions of peace treaties,[49] but these cannot be considered as expressing the established practice of states in peacetime. There exists thus a contradiction between theory and practice, which cannot be resolved by merely arguing that theory accounts for the practice since it allows for the possibility of compensation in exceptional cases. In reality, practice follows a pattern which is exactly the opposite of the one accepted

[46] See especially, Personnaz, *op. cit. supra* note 45, at 83–93; Eagleton, *The Responsibility of States in International Law* 189 (1928); Rousseau, *Droit International Public* 356, 383 (1953). Borchard, *The Diplomatic Protection of Citizens Abroad* 381 *et seq.*, 413 *et seq.* (1915), discusses the problems of pecuniary compensation only, without mention of *restitutio*. The same is true of Ripert, *supra* note 38, at 622–25. Lauterpacht, *Private Law Sources and Analogies of International Law* 147 *et seq.* (1927), uses the term *restitutio in integrum* with reference to the full character of the reparation, not in the sense of specific performance. De Visscher, "La responsabilité des Etats," 2 *Bibliotheca Visseriana* 87, 118 (1924), mentions the two methods of reparation without any indication of precedence.

In its Judgment in the Chorzow Factory case, the Permanent Court of International Justice has stated that "an indemnity corresponding to the damage which the nationals of the injured State have suffered . . . is . . . the most usual form of reparation." P.C.I.J. Judgment No. 13, September 13, 1928, P.C.I.J. Publ., Ser. A, No. 17, at 27–28.

[47] Cf., e.g., the case of the Expropriated Religious Properties (France v. Portugal, 1920), 1 UN RIAA 7, 11 (restitution ordered with respect to very few claims). In the case of the Chorzow Factory in Poland, the Permanent Court of International Justice found the factory's expropriation by Poland unlawful and ordered its restitution; Judgment No. 7, May 25, 1926, P.C.I.J. Publ., Ser. A, No. 7. In a later judgment, after Poland's refusal to restore the factory and subsequent agreement to accept compensation, the Court ordered the payment of compensation; Judgment No. 13, September 13, 1928, P.C.I.J. Publ., Ser. A, No. 17.

[48] This is eminently the case in instances of internationally unlawful imprisonment, where only specific performance, namely, release, is appropriate. Payment of indemnity in such cases constitutes largely "satisfaction" for the moral wrong against the alien rather than compensation properly speaking. See Personnaz, *op. cit. supra* note 45, at 277–82; Bisonette, *La satisfaction comme mode de réparation en droit international* 78–80 (1952).

[49] See Robinson, "Reparations and Restitution in International Law as Affecting Jews," 1948 *Jewish Yb. Int'l L.* 186 (1949); Wortley, *Expropriation* 80 *et seq.*; 1 Sibert, *Traité de droit international public* 321–23 (1951).

in theory. In practice, compensation constitutes the principal remedy, *restitutio* being clearly an exceptional one.

There is, moreover, no compelling reason for accepting in theory the rule that *restitutio* is the principal remedy. It is evident that the adoption of this rule is due to the importation into international law of certain private law concepts.[50] In several modern legal systems, restitution in kind is the principal mode of discharging an obligation, compensation being either an alternative method, open to the injured party's choice, or a clearly subsidiary remedy, available only when *restitutio* is impossible.[51] Nonetheless, such a view is neither generally held nor rationally necessary. In classical Roman legal theory, pecuniary compensation was the sole mode of reparation.[52] Modern common law systems, too, accept specific performance only as an exceptional remedy, to be granted in a limited number of cases or when compensation is clearly insufficient.[53]

Several theoretical and practical reasons may be adduced in support of this position.[54] At the present stage of development of the international legal order, its organs have the right and the power (that is, the competence) to declare an action of a state organ unlawful in international law; they cannot declare it invalid (that is, nullify its legal effects) in municipal law.[55] Consequently the

[50] See Lauterpacht, *op. cit. supra* note 46, at 147 *et seq.* and remarks in the same note; Personnaz, *op. cit. supra* note 45, at 74–75.

[51] This is true of most civil law systems, especially the German and French ones. See Von Mehren, *The Civil Law System* 502 *et seq.* (1957); Szladits, "The Concept of Specific Performance in Civil Law," 4 *Am. J. Comp. L.* 208, 214 *et seq.* (1955).

[52] The rule was expressed in the maxim *omnis condemnatio pecuniaria est*; cf. Gai *Institutiones* IV, 48. The rule was altered at the time of Justinian's codification. See Buckland and McNair, *Roman Law and Common Law* 412–13 (2d ed. by Lawson, 1952).

[53] See Holmes, *The Common Law* 300–1 (1881); 5 Corbin, *Contracts* 608 *et seq.* (1951); Paton, *A Text-Book of Jurisprudence* 393–95 (2d ed., 1951); Szladits, *supra* note 51, at 208–14, 231–34. Whether specific performance is, in such cases, a matter of right or of discretion is, for present purposes, irrelevant.

[54] See also Personnaz, *op. cit. supra* note 45, at 88–93; Kopelmanas, "Du conflit entre le traité international et la loi interne," 18 (3d ser.) *Rev. Dr. Int. Legisl. Comp.* 88, 128–33 (1937); 1 Anzilotti, *Cours de droit international* 527 (Gidel transl., 1929).

[55] See Kopelmanas, "Du conflit entre le traité international et la loi interne— II," 18 (3d ser.) *Rev. Dr. Int. Legisl. Comp.* 310, 356–60 (1937); Guggenheim,

unlawfulness of an act entails an obligation of reparation through compensation; matters cannot be brought to the *status quo ante* by the annulment of the internationally unlawful act by the international organ.[56]

Furthermore, international disputes usually take a long time to settle. By the time the unlawfulness of the state act has been established internationally, it will have created several effects in municipal law. Third parties will in all probability be involved who will by then have adjusted to new conditions, any radical alteration of which would have clearly unjust consequences with respect to them. This argument is even more cogent in the case of general measures radically affecting a country's economic structure. It is evident that, independently of any possible unlawfulness in the state measures involved, it would be impossible to make the economy of the state return to the situation where it was before the measures in question. Pecuniary compensation may, moreover, offer in some cases certain advantages to the private person, since it may cover losses which would not be covered by simple restitution. It is therefore submitted that, in international law, pecuniary compensation constitutes the principal mode of reparation.[57] Restitution is possible only in a limited number of special cases.

It is true that, if this view is accepted, then a strong similarity appears to exist between the legal effects of lawful and unlawful measures affecting the contractual rights of aliens. In both cases, there arises on the part of the state taking the measures an obligation to compensate the aliens involved. However, the difference in

---

"La validité et la nullité des actes juridiques internationaux," 74 *Hague Recueil* 191, 201 (1949); Fachiri, "International Law and the Property of Aliens," 10 *Brit. Yb. Int'l L.* 32, 49 (1929).

[56] Cf. on this point the Observations of the Preparatory Commission for the Hague Codification Conference of 1929, 24 *Am. J. Int'l L. Supp.* 46, 50 (1930).

[57] See the strong arguments, in the same sense, in Baade, "Indonesian Nationalization Measures Before Foreign Courts—A Reply," 54 *Am. J. Int'l L.* 801, 814-30 (1960). And see also Braybrooke, "The 'Persian Oil' Dispute—The 'Rose Mary' Case," 29 *N. Zealand L.J.* 59, 76, 92, at 93-94 (1953). But cf. strongly *contra*, 1 Sibert, *Traité de droit international public* 320-25 (1951); Wortley, *Expropriation* 101-2 and *passim*; Kissam and Leach, *supra* note 44, at 212-14.

the character of the measures in each case is sufficiently reflected in the applicable measure of compensation. In practical, oversimplified, terms, a state which interferes with an alien's contractual rights will probably have to pay much more if its actions are deemed unlawful than otherwise.

No problem as to restitution arises in the case of lawful measures. Another problem, however, has to be considered in this case. The traditional formulation of the relevant legal rule is that the lawfulness of state measures affecting aliens' contractual rights depends, in international law, on the payment, or at least the offer, of just compensation.[58] Another opinion, however, considers compensation as a legal duty arising out of the related measures, not as a condition precedent to the lawfulness of these measures.[59] In accordance with this view, if a state takes measures which affect the contractual rights of aliens without offering to compensate them

[58] Cf. 1 Hyde, *International Law* 710–17 (2d rev. ed., 1945); 1 Sibert, *Traité de droit international public* 524–26 (1951); Cheng, *General Principles of Law* 38 *et seq.* (1953); Schwarzenberger, "The Protection of British Property Abroad," 5 *Current Legal Problems* 295, 309 *et seq.* (1952); Re, "The Nationalization of Foreign Owned Property," 36 *Minn. L. Rev.* 323, 327 *et seq.* (1952); Carlston, "Concession Agreements and Nationalization," 52 *Am. J. Int'l L.* 260, 267 (1958); Verzijl, "The Relevance of Public and Private International Law Respectively for the Solution of Problems Arising from Nationalization of Enterprises," 19 *Zeitschrift für ausländisches öffentliches Recht und Völkerrecht* (Festgabe für A. N. Makarov) 531, 536 (1958); Wortley, *Expropriation* 33 and *passim;* Kollewijn, " 'Nationalization' Without Compensation and the Transfer of Property," 6 *Ned. Tijdschrift voor Int. Recht* 140 (1959); Kissam and Leach, *supra* note 44, at 190–92; Lauterpacht, in International Law Association, *op. cit. supra* note 44, at 162. The same view was partly accepted in our earlier discussion of the topic, Fatouros, "Legal Security for International Investment" in *Legal Aspects* 699, 726.

[59] Cf. Herz, "Expropriation of Foreign Property," 33 *Am. J. Int'l L.* 243, 254–55 (1941); Doman, "Postwar Nationalization of Foreign Property in Europe," 48 *Columbia L. Rev.* 1125, 1127 (1948); Roth, *The Minimum Standard of International Law Applied to Aliens* 172 (1949); Rubin, "Nationalization and Compensation: A Comparative Approach," 17 *U. Chicago L. Rev.* 458, 461 (1950); Rubin, *Private Foreign Investment* 9–10 (1956); Foighel, *Nationalization* 75 (1957); Bindschedler, *supra* note 15, at 246; Delson, *supra* note 29, at 763–64; Rolin, "Avis sur la validité des mesures de nationalisation décretées par le gouvernement indonésien," 6 *Ned. Tijdschrift voor Int. Recht* 260, 270–71 (1959).

Gihl, "Two Cases Concerning Confiscation of Foreign Property," in *Liber Amicorum of Congratulations to Alcot Bagge* 56, 61–62 (1956), and in International Law Association, *op. cit. supra* note 44, at 137, accepts this view as to property but rejects it as to state contracts.

for their losses, it is responsible internationally for its unlawful nonpayment of compensation, but the measures themselves remain internationally lawful. It is submitted, on the basis of the relevant state practice and of pertinent theoretical considerations, that the latter is the better view.

Since the amount of compensation to be paid depends on the lawfulness or unlawfulness of the measures involved, it is necessary to determine the latter before assessing the former. It is reasonable to assume, therefore, that the lawfulness of the measures is independent of the payment of compensation. This is evidently true of measures which are unlawful because they are taken in violation of treaty commitments or in discrimination against aliens. The mere payment of compensation does not render such measures lawful.[60] There is no cause to apply a different reasoning in the case of lawful measures. Otherwise, if we had to determine the compensation to be paid in the case of state measures unlawful because of lack of compensation, we would be running in a vicious circle or certain arbitrary borderlines would have to be established. The statements found in many judicial decisions and the writings of scholars to the effect that compensation is a prerequisite for the lawfulness of the state measures involved may, from a substantive point of view, be considered as a means for stressing the right of aliens to compensation.[61]

Assessment of Compensation

The first step in the determination of the amount of compensation in any particular case is logically the assessment of the damages for which the compensation is to be paid. The diversity of the possible measures which may affect the contractual rights of aliens

[60] Cf. the P.C.I.J. Judgment quoted *supra* pp. 222-23.

[61] See, in agreement, Seidl-Hohenveldern, "Communist Theories on Confiscation and Expropriation: Critical Comments," 7 *Am. J. Comp. L.* 541, 544-45 (1958). Note that most of the relevant decisions of international tribunals may be restrictively interpreted to hold only that compensation is to be paid.

results in a diversity of possible forms and degrees of damages, which cannot be discussed here in any detail. The present discussion will be concerned with the most radical as well as the most important of these measures, namely, the revocation of concessions, nationalization of industries and other such measures which bring to an end the alien's contractual relationship with the state. Measures of a less radical character do not present essentially different problems; the principles found applicable in the case of the more radical measures will also be applicable, *mutatis mutandis*, to less radical measures.[62]

An important difficulty in assessing damages is that international claims are as a rule presented in greatly exaggerated amounts. The sums demanded often have little relation to the actual loss suffered. In the recent case of claims for compensation for properties of United States citizens nationalized in Yugoslavia, the claims originally submitted to the Foreign Claims Settlement Commission (a United States Government agency) amounted to $148,472,773, out of which the Commission allowed $18,817,904.89.[63] This is neither an extreme nor an exceptional case. There is, therefore, some need for caution when dealing with any particular claims.

Damages to property rights are usually classified in international law under the two broad headings of direct and indirect damages. The same categories are applicable in the case of losses resulting from measures affecting state contracts. Direct damages will include in this case all capital already invested by the alien, e.g., in factory plants, offices or machinery. They will also include any stocks of raw materials or goods taken along with the enterprise as well as other possible actual damages.[64] Indirect damages will in-

---

[62] See also *infra* pp. 345–47 for a discussion of the particular problems arising in the case of state guarantees.

[63] *Settlement of Claims by the Foreign Claims Settlement Commission of the United States and Its Predecessors from September 14, 1949 to March 31, 1955* 4, 330 (1955). And cf. the earlier examples cited by Williams, "International Law and the Property of Aliens," 9 *Brit. Yb. Int'l L.* 1 (1928), reprinted in *Chapters in Current International Law and the League of Nations* 147, 176–77 (1929).

[64] Such other damages would include, for instance, those suffered because of the

clude the intangible assets of the enterprise involved (such as good-will) and the prospective profits of the investors had there been no interference with the contract. Which of these elements will be included in the compensation in any particular case depends on several factors, the most important of which is the lawful or un-lawful character of the measures involved. In the case of losses re-sulting from lawful measures, compensation will probably include only direct damages, while, if the measures were unlawful, it may include prospective profits or other indirect damages. Apart from this question, however, difficult problems arise in connection with the initial determination of the losses.

In the municipal law of most states, the compensation to be paid in the case of a lawful taking of property is assessed on the basis of the market value of such property.[65] This standard is also used in international law, when the property involved is such as to make the determination of its market value possible. But in many cases where a state contract is involved, this standard is inappropriate. Part of the difficulty is due to the character of the measures and the assets involved in recent cases. Earlier cases, and, in particular, the majority of international judicial decisions are of little help in this connection. They relate to relatively simple situations, where the state measures involved were individual in character and the in-terests affected consisted in goods already delivered,[66] services al-ready rendered,[67] or other interests of a similar nature. The market

---

cancellation of a contract for the sale of goods to the government, when the price at which the goods were ultimately sold elsewhere was inordinately low.

[65] This is, for instance, the practice in the United States; cf. 1 Orgel, *Valuation Under Eminent Domain* s. 20 (2d ed., 1953); Crouch, "Valuation Problems under Eminent Domain," 1959 *Wisconsin L. Rev.* 608, 609 *et seq.* Similar views obtain in English law; cf. e.g., Wortley, *Expropriation* 27–28.

[66] Cf., e.g., the Pacific Press Publishing Company case (U.S.A. v. Guatemala, 1900–1928), 5 Hackworth, *Digest* 615 (involving payment for schoolbooks de-livered to Guatemalan authorities in 1895, settled through diplomatic channels); the Yukon Lumber case (Great Britain v. U.S.A., 1913), 6 UN RIAA 17 (involving payment for timber delivered to U.S. authorities in 1900).

[67] Cf., e.g., the J. E. Davies case (U.S.A. v. Mexico, 1927), 4 UN RIAA 139 (pay-ment of services of lawyer); the Landreau claims (U.S.A. v. Peru, 1921), 1 UN RIAA 347 (payment for the indication of guano deposits).

value of such interests was not difficult to determine with a fair degree of precision. The corresponding situations today are widely different. The state measures involved are as a rule general in character, affecting whole sectors of the national economy. They often result in a radical alteration of the country's economic structure which, in its turn, affects the value of the particular interests involved. Enterprises functioning by virtue of concession contracts, for instance, may often have no "market value" because of their relative position and size within the capital-importing country's economy. The Anglo-Iranian Oil Company in Iran and the Universal Suez Maritime Canal Company in Egypt are the most obvious examples of such enterprises.

No simple solution can therefore be offered; no permanent and stable criteria may be used to determine the measure of compensation in all instances. In their place, we have several factors whose presence, extent, form, or quality play an important role in the determination of the amount of compensation. The importance of each variable is not the same in each case, nor are the same criteria always used.

The value of an enterprise's plants and inventories, or of the original investments therein, evidently are not an appropriate measure of its value at the time of a nationalization or revocation of the concession. A company's balance sheet and other accounting statements cannot as a rule serve as the sole basis for assessment of its value. Their function is, normally, a relative one; they facilitate comparison of costs and profits of successive periods. They do not give and, in the modern economy, they are not intended to give, absolute values; they do not tell what the company is worth.

A related method of assessment is that which bases the amount of compensation on the valuation of the properties involved by the investors themselves in their latest tax declaration. This method has been applied in the Mexican land expropriations,[68] and, most

----

[68] Cf. Gordon, *The Expropriation of Foreign-owned Property in Mexico* 45–47 (1941); and cf. Kunz, "The Mexican Expropriations," 17 *N.Y.U.L. Qu. Rev.* 327,

recently, it forms the proposed basis of assessment of compensation for the landholdings expropriated under the 1959 Cuban Agrarian Reform Law.[69] From a purely economic point of view, there is no compelling reason for accepting such valuation as conclusive. The purposes for which the valuation was originally made are not related to those for which it is to be used and, presumably, a new valuation would be more satisfactory.[70] There is, however, a strong policy argument in favor of the proposed method. It creates in fact a kind of estoppel against property owners who had managed, or were permitted, under previous regimes, to declare a false value for their properties in order to pay lower taxes. It is submitted that this argument is persuasive.[71] Foreign investors should be held to the same standards of good faith to which the host government is held. It follows, however, that such valuation is acceptable only when the investor himself is responsible for it, not if the expropriating government itself had made it.[72]

Another possible method, particularly appropriate to enterprises of great size operating under concessions, is the assessment of the enterprise's value on the basis of the price of its shares of capital stock.[73] This method has been adopted in many recent nationalizations, especially those effected within the framework of a funda-

---

348 (1940). The same standard was proposed (and objected to by the United States) in the 1953 land expropriations in Guatemala; cf. Thomas, "Protection of Property of Citizens Abroad," in Southwestern Legal Foundation, *Proceedings of the 1959 Institute on Private Investments Abroad* 417, 438–40 (1959).

[69] Cuba, Agrarian Reform Law, June 3, 1959, as reported in Note, "Foreign Seizure of Investments: Remedies and Protection," 12 *Stanford L. Rev.* 606, 606–7 (1960).

[70] See, in this sense, Note, *supra* note 69, at 610; Note, "Expropriation of Alien Property," 109 *U. Pa. L. Rev.* 245, 251, note 37 (1960).

[71] See, in agreement, Snyder, "Measure of Compensation for Nationalization of Private Property," 3 *Catholic U.L. Rev.* 107, 116 (1953); Seidl-Hohenveldern, *supra* note 61, at 549–550. And see *contra*, Note, *supra* note 69, at 610–11; Domke, "Foreign Nationalizations," 55 *Am. J. Int'l L.* 585, 608 (1961).

[72] On the Cuban situation in this respect, see Note, *supra* note 69, at 610, note 28. And see also, on the situation in Guatemala, Thomas, *supra* note 68, at 439.

[73] Another method, used in some of the British postwar nationalizations, is the capitalization of net maintainable revenue, that is, a calculation of the value of the enterprise concerned on the basis of its average annual net earnings. Cf. Note, "British Nationalization of Industry—Compensation to Owners of Expropriated Property," 97 *U. Pa. L. Rev.* 520, 521–22, 525 (1949); Snyder, *supra* note 71, at 116.

mentally capitalist economy. Though far from perfect itself, it constitutes, where appropriate, the most practical and the fairest of available methods. Shares of stock are of relatively small value and numerous enough; they therefore have a market, namely, the Stock Exchange, and a market price, their quotation in it.[74]

Since there is no single permanent price of shares but rather a series of successive prices, the central issue is which price will be selected as the one on which the calculation of the corporation's value will be based. The situation in the stock exchange at various times before the taking of the measures in question constitutes one of the variables which have to be taken into account. The difference between full and partial compensation is often reduced to variation in the choice of dates, the Stock Exchange quotation on which is taken as the basis of assessment. Such choice involves ideological and political rather than legal considerations.[75] When the iron and steel, transport, electricity and gas industries were nationalized in Great Britain, shareholders of the related corporations were compensated in Treasury-guaranteed Government stock, on the basis of the average price of the nationalized corporations' shares in the Stock Exchange during specified alternative periods.[76] In France, substantially the same method was used in compensating shareholders of banks and electricity and gas companies,[77] while the

[74] How far such a price corresponds in fact to a mathematical fraction of the whole enterprise's value as a going concern is open to doubt. Large blocks of shares, permitting the control of an enterprise, are usually sold at higher prices in the Stock Exchange. Cf. Walker and Condie, "Compensation in Nationalized Industries," in *Problems of Nationalized Industry* 54, 60–66 (Robson ed. 1952).

[75] Cf. Robson, "Nationalized Industries: General Conclusions," in *Problems of Nationalized Industry* 275, 286 et seq. (Robson ed., 1952); Vedel, "La technique des nationalisations," 9 *Droit Social* 49, 56–57 (1946).

[76] Cf. Cairns, "Some Legal Aspects of Compensation for Nationalized Assets," 16 *Law & Contemp. Problems* 594, 604 et seq. (1951); Walker and Condie, *supra* note 74, at 57 et seq.

[77] Cf. DeVries and Hoeniger, "Post-Liberation Nationalizations in France," 50 *Columbia L. Rev.* 629, 640–41, 643–44 (1950); Loiseau, *L'indemnisation des entreprises électriques et gazières nationalisées* (1950); Auby, "La nationalisation du Gaz et de l'Electricité," in 1 *Les nationalisations en France et à l'étranger: Les nationalisations en France* 111, 123–26 (De La Morandière and Byé ed., 1948); Thomas, "La nationalisation des Banques," *idem* 145, 151–54.

price of coal companies' shares was determined by adopting an average price and multiplying it by certain "coefficients," varying according to region.[78] The methods were similar, but the practical result was not. The compensation awarded in France was generally partial, because war and the existing expectation of nationalization had already lowered the price of the shares at the dates adopted as basic.[79] In Britain, this had not happened, at least, not to the same extent; the dates adopted as basic were such that no predictions as to future nationalizations were operative. Accordingly, the compensation paid was more nearly full.[80]

There exists in international law a dispute of long standing regarding the existence of an obligation to compensate for indirect damages.[81] To a large extent the question is one of semantics only, arising because of a lack of clarity in the terms used. It is very doubtful, however, whether complete clarity can ever be achieved, because, as has been pointed out by good authority, the whole problem "resolves itself ultimately into a question of fact." [82]

Intangible assets of enterprises present particular problems. The value and, in fact, the very existence of such assets depend on the surrounding legal, social, and economic conditions. Any change in these conditions entails a variation in the value of the assets involved. In one instance, the Permanent Court of International

[78] Cf. DeVries and Hoeniger, *supra* note 77, at 636; Personnaz, "La nationalisation des houillères françaises," 10 *Droit Social* 81, 86–87 (1947); Gueullette, "La nationalisation des houillères," in 1 *Les nationalisations en France et à l'étranger: Les nationalisations en France* 85, 94–95 (De La Morandière and Byé ed., 1948).

[79] Cf., e.g., Roblot, "La nationalisation du gaz et de l'électricité," 9 *Droit Social* 179, 183 (1946).

[80] But see *contra* Katzarov, *Nationalisation* 416–17, 423, who claims that even in Britain the compensation paid was partial. See, in this sense, Note, *supra* note 73, at 530–33. The practice as to compensation in recent nationalizations is reviewed in Einaudi, "A Comparative Study of Nationalization Policies," in Einaudi, Byé, and Rossi, *Nationalization in France and Italy* 3, 39–42 (1955).

[81] Cf. Hauriou, "Les dommages indirects dans les arbitrages internationaux," 31 *Rev. Gén. Dr. Int. Public* 203 (1924); Personnaz, *La réparation du préjudice en droit international public* 127–51 (1938); Eagleton, "Measure of Damages in International Law," 39 *Yale L.J.* 52, 66–75 (1929). For a thorough survey of the cases, see 3 Whiteman, *Damages* 1765–1876.

[82] Lauterpacht, *Private Law Sources and Analogies of International Law* 148 (1927). And see 1 Schwarzenberger, *International Law* 668–73 (3d ed., 1957).

Justice has held that "the possession of customers and the possibility of making a profit" cannot be considered a vested right of the owner of an enterprise. Consequently, a change in these conditions caused by otherwise lawful governmental action cannot be construed as an unlawful act.[83] Furthermore, a radical change of the existing conditions may eliminate altogether the value of certain intangible assets. Thus, in a socialist economy operating under a strict state plan, the concept of good will or of possession of customers largely loses its meaning.[84] Under such conditions, even certain professions may disappear. The aliens' interests may thus be damaged; but as long as their losses do not correspond to any direct enrichment of the state or of the public, it does not seem that they are entitled to compensation.[85]

Another category of indirect damages which presents serious problems is that of prospective profits (*lucrum cessans*). When the state measures which affect the aliens' contractual rights are internationally lawful, compensation aims at the elimination of the aliens' loss and not at the restoration of the *status quo ante*. Accordingly, inclusion in it of payment for future profits is not indicated.[86] The state, in such cases, pays to the extent of its own

[83] The Oscar Chinn Case, Judgment of December 12, 1934, P.C.I.J. Publ., Ser.A/B, No. 63, at 88. Cf. also the Trail Smelter Arbitration (U.S.A. v. Canada, 1938), 3 UN RIAA 1905, 1931. See *contra* Wortley, *Expropriation* 112–13; and cf. Foighel, *Nationalization* 102–3 (1957).

[84] Cf. 1 Guggenheim, *Traité de droit international public* 335 (1953); Bindschedler, "La protection de la propriété privée en droit international public," 90 *Hague Recueil* 173, 268 (1956).

[85] Two instances of United States practice on the matter are relevant. Neither when slavery was abolished nor when Prohibition was established did the U.S. Government recognize that it had any obligation to compensate aliens or nationals whose interests were affected unfavorably by these measures. See Friedman, *Expropriation* 50–51. Note that good will and similar intangible assets are as a rule not included in compensation for takings under eminent domain, according to United States practice; cf. Orgel, *op. cit. supra* note 65, s. 72–76; Crouch, *supra* note 65, at 619, 623–24; McCormick, "The Measure of Compensation in Eminent Domain," 17 *Minn. L. Rev.* 461, 476–82 (1933).

[86] In agreement with this position, see Bindschedler, *supra* note 84, at 246–47; Farmanfarma, "The Oil Agreement between Iran and the International Oil Consortium: The Law Controlling," 34 *Texas L. Rev.* 259, 285 (1955); Cheng, *General Principles of Law* 50–51 (1953); Seidl-Hohenveldern, *supra* note 61, at 549. For the views *contra* see note 88 *infra*.

enrichment. Payment for profits lost would be an addition to the aliens' loss or the state's enrichment. This rule prevails in the municipal law of several states with respect to compensation for takings in exercise of the power of eminent domain.[87] Furthermore, acceptance of the view that there exists an obligation to compensate for future profits would certainly lead to severe practical difficulties. The lost profits in the Anglo-Iranian Oil Company case, for instance, would amount to huge sums, many times higher than the value of the original investments, the factory plants and any other concrete assets of the enterprise in question. In fact, allowance for future profits in all cases of general measures of a radical character would render the cost of such measures prohibitive to most states.

Advocates of the view that *lucrum cessans* should always be included in compensation usually recognize this fact. They even use it sometimes as an argument in support of their thesis.[88] Such a view, however, is acceptable only if it is admitted that all state measures affecting the contractual rights of aliens are unlawful.[89] If this view is rejected, as it should be,[90] then it is necessary to impose differing conditions in the case of lawful and unlawful measures. Lawful measures, if the term is to have any meaning, are those which are permitted by international law, even though not encouraged by it. The legality of such measures should not be made to depend on conditions which can be fulfilled only rarely and with the utmost difficulty. When the measures are unlawful, on the other hand, the aliens should be compensated not only for their actual loss but also for prospective profits, since the state is in such

[87] On United States practice, see Crouch, *supra* note 65, at 619-20; McCormick, *supra* note 85, at 476-82.

[88] Cf. Olmstead, "Nationalization of Foreign Property Interests, Particularly Those Subject to Agreements with the State," 32 *N.Y.U.L. Rev.* 1122, 1133-34 (1957); P. De Visscher, "Les aspects juridiques fondamentaux de la question de Suez," 62 *Rev. Gén. Dr. Int. Public* 406, 434-35, 442-43 (1958); Verzijl, in 43-I *Annuaire de l'Institut de Droit International* 104 (1950).

[89] This is in fact admitted by the scholars cited *supra* note 88. And see Dr. Eli Lauterpacht's explicit statement to that effect in International Law Association, *Report of the Forty-Eighth Conference* 162-64 (1958).

[90] Cf. *supra* pp. 261-78.

a case bound to restore the exact *status quo ante*. Possible hardship to the state cannot then be taken into account, in view of its responsibility for unlawful action.

The international judicial and diplomatic practice offers little guidance on the subject at hand. In the earlier cases, compensation for lost profits was awarded in principle, but such claims were quite often rejected on a variety of grounds.[91] The high proportion of rejected claims may be interpreted as indicating the reluctance of international tribunals to allow compensation for lost profits in the absence of flagrant illegality in the states' actions. Recent practice tends to support the rule that, generally speaking, compensation for contractual rights affected by general measures of a state should cover only actual losses and not prospective profits. Thus, for instance, in the course of negotiations leading to the agreement on compensation for the nationalization by Egypt of the Universal Suez Maritime Canal Company, the representatives of the latter's shareholders abandoned their claim to compensation for the loss of revenue expected during the remaining years the concession had to run.[92]

Municipal state practice offers another possibility with respect to compensation for lost profits. In the postwar British and French nationalizations, the shareholders of most of the expropriated enterprises received in compensation government bonds or other negotiable securities paying interest or dividends equal to those normally paid by the shares of the expropriated corporations.[93] Such a practice takes into consideration the conduct of many large corporations which strive to keep their annual dividends on the same level over long periods of time and the consequent attitude of share-

---

[91] See the survey in 3 Whiteman, *Damages* 1836–40, 1858–66, 1871–74. And cf. 1 Schwarzenberger, *International Law* 668–73 (3d ed., 1957).

[92] See notes 18, 19 *supra*. For some related figures, see "Issues Before the Thirteenth General Assembly," 1958 *Int'l Conc.* No. 519, at 67; Thomas, *supra* note 68, at 445–46. For a criticism of the Suez settlement preliminary agreement precisely on the ground that it does not provide for compensation for lost profits, see De Visscher, *supra* note 88, at 442–43.

[93] See citations *supra* notes 76, 77.

holders toward such corporations.[94] This mode of compensation also brings to the fore the close interdependence between measure and form of compensation and the importance of surrounding circumstances. If an underdeveloped country with an unstable and inflationary economy proposed to compensate aliens in a similar manner the latter might well reject the offer. They could argue that such compensation was neither prompt nor effective, not even adequate, since according to every reasonable expectation the currency of the underdeveloped state would be devaluated after a few years.[95]

The Elements of "Just" Compensation

The qualities usually required of a just compensation are its adequacy, promptness, and effectiveness.[96] Each of these qualities should not be conceived by itself, independently of the others. It should rather be seen in its close relationship to them, from which its value in any particular instance depends. Discussing them one by one, as we have to do, means only that one of them is, each time, in focus, while the two others constitute the background against which it is seen.[97]

To be adequate, compensation should correspond fully to the value of the alien's interests affected by the state measures. Ordinarily, the alien's actual loss will correspond to the state's gain, so

[94] The Bank of England, for instance, had paid the same annual dividend for twenty-three years prior to its nationalization. See Cairns, *supra* note 76, at 602; Walker and Condie, *supra* note 74, at 55; Note, *supra* note 73, at 532.

[95] See also *infra* pp. 331-33.

[96] Cf. 1 Hyde, *International Law* 710-11 (2d rev. ed., 1945). These requirements have been repeatedly set out in official statements of the position of the United States; cf. the Note of August 22, 1938, to the Mexican Ambassador, 3 Hackworth, *Digest* 658, and a 1953 Note to the Government of Guatemala, 29 *Dep't State Bull.* 357 (1953). And compare the relevant provisions of the recent United States FCN treaties, *supra* pp. 168-69.

[97] In the terms of phenomenological philosophy, such other qualities are part of the "horizon" of the quality in focus, that is, part of that infinite sum of aspects and relations which, though at the moment out of our immediate consciousness, are implied in the particular aspect we are conscious of. See Kuhn, "The Phenomenological Concept of 'Horizon,'" in *Phenomenological Essays in Memory of Edmund Husserl* 106 (Farber ed., 1940).

that by calculating the former, the latter is also determined. In certain instances, however, this may not happen because of the nature of the assets involved,[98] or because of the character of the state acts. In such a case, and provided the measures involved are internationally lawful, it is the state's gain, and not the investor's loss that should determine the amount of compensation. This follows necessarily from the foundation of the state's duty to compensate for the effects of lawful measures.[99]

In recent state practice, compensation has seldom been adequate, that is, commensurate with the full value of the assets involved. In all instances of nationalization (with the possible exception of those in Great Britain) [100] the indemnity paid has been partial, though this fact has often been obscured by the methods of assessment used.[101] In the particular case of the agreements between the "socialist" states of Eastern and Central Europe and the Western countries, in no instance was the lump sum awarded equal to the total of the individual claims. In fact, the difference between the two seems to have been considerable in the great majority of cases.[102] Exceptions to this rule may be attributed to special circumstances resulting in increased bargaining power on the part of the claim-

---

[98] Cf. *supra* p. 322 and note 85.

[99] Cf. *supra* note 38. And see also Cheng, *General Principles of Law* 47–49 (1953). In a more recent study, Dr. Cheng states that the rationale of compensation for expropriation consists of two elements: "First, the community has been enriched by the sacrifice of the individual or individuals concerned. Secondly, this sacrifice has fallen on individual citizens without its being shared by others, and compensation for expropriation is required in order to equalise this sacrifice among all members of the community." Cheng, "The Rationale of Compensation for Expropriation," 44 *Grotius Soc. Transactions* 267, 298 (1959), and cf. cases cited *idem* 298–300. It is, however, problematic—and the learned author is certainly aware of it (see *idem* 300–5)—to what extent the second element is operative in the absence of the first, that is, whether compensation should be paid even when the community is not enriched by the state action (and the individual's sacrifice). It would rather seem that the second element (or principle) is subordinated to the first and serves to qualify its application.

[100] But see *supra* note 80.   [101] Cf. *supra* pp. 320–21.

[102] Cf. the cases discussed in Foighel, *Nationalization* 117–19 (1957). See also Schwarzenberger, "The Protection of British Property Abroad," 5 *Current Legal Problems* 295, at 306, 307 (1952).

ant state.[103] The practice of partial compensation has found theoretical support in the writings of several jurists,[104] though the majority of writers on the subject condemn it unreservedly.[105]

The main argument in support of the practice is its economic necessity, that is, the fact that, if full compensation had to be paid, the nationalizations would have been impossible or the nationalizing state would have been led into bankruptcy. Opponents of the practice in question point out that if a state cannot afford to nationalize, it should not do so. This argument ignores the fact that nationalizations are not effected as an end in themselves, but as a means to social and economic progress, even though their effectiveness as

[103] This is true of the 1948 agreement between the United States and Yugoslavia. According to the report of the competent United States Government agency, the aggregate amount of awards made in pursuance of this agreement was $18,817,904.89, which exceeded by less than two million dollars the fund of $17 million provided by Yugoslavia. See *Settlement of Claims by the Foreign Claims Settlement Commission of the United States and Its Predecessors from September 14, 1949 to March 31, 1955* 4, 330 (1955). As to the conditions surrounding the conclusion of the 1948 agreement, see Viénot, *Nationalisations étrangères et interêts français* 180 *et seq.* (1953); Rubin, *Private Foreign Investment* 93–95 (1956).

[104] Cf. 1 Oppenheim, *International Law* 352 (8th ed., Lauterpacht, 1955); 1 Guggenheim, *Traité de droit international public* 335 (1953); Cheng, *General Principles of Law* 47–49 (1953); De Visscher, *Théories et réalités en droit international public* 248–249 (3d ed., 1960); Cavaré, *Droits contractuels* 116 *et seq.*; Foighel, *Nationalization* 118–19 (1957); La Pradelle, in 43-I *Annuaire de l'Institut de Droit International* 42 *et seq.* (1950); Kuhn, "Nationalization of Foreign-Owned Property in Its Impact on International Law," 45 *Am. J. Int'l L.* 709, 711–12 (1951); Delson, "Nationalization of the Suez Canal Company: Issues of Public and Private International Law," 57 *Columbia L. Rev.* 755, 765–66 (1957); Rolin, "Avis sur la validité des mesures de nationalisation décretées par le gouvernement indonésien," 6 *Ned. Tijdschrift voor Int. Recht* 260, 272 (1959); Katzarov, *Nationalisation* 439–48; Note, "Expropriation of Alien Property," 109 *U. Pa. L. Rev.* 245, 261 (1960).

[105] See, among several others, 1 Sibert, *Traité de droit international public* 523–26 (1951); Viénot, *op. cit. supra* note 103, at 32 *et seq.*; Wortley, *Expropriation* 118 *et seq.*; Re, "The Nationalization of Foreign-Owned Property," 36 *Minn. L. Rev.* 323, 333–36 (1952); Schwarzenberger, *supra* note 102, 309 *et seq.*; Bindschedler, *supra* note 84, at 248–51; Carlston, "Concession Agreements and Nationalization," 52 *Am. J. Int'l L.* 260, 274–76 (1958); Brandon, "Legal Aspects of Private Foreign Investments," 18 *Fed. Bar J.* 298, 318 (1958); Becker, "Just Compensation in Expropriation Cases: Decline and Partial Recovery," 40 *Dep't State Bull.* 784, 53 *Am. Soc. Int'l L. Proc.* 336 (1959); Kissam and Leach, "Sovereign Expropriation of Property and Abrogation of Concession Contracts," 28 *Fordham L. Rev.* 177, 188–89 (1959); Note, "Foreign Seizure of Investments: Remedies and Protection," 12 *Stanford L. Rev.* 606, 609–11 (1960).

such may be open to doubt.[106] Moreover, nationalizations are meant to benefit the nation as a whole; everybody, including those affected by the measures, stands to profit from them in the long run.[107] Opponents of partial compensation argue at this point that the alien does not profit from the nationalization because he is not a national of the nationalizing state and because "by the very fact of nationalization [he is] cast from the national community in whose favour nationalization has been carried out." [108] It is generally accepted, however, that, by investing in a country, an alien submits himself, to a reasonable extent, to the fortunes of its nationals. It is submitted that partial compensation covering a major part of the alien's losses is, under certain conditions, reasonable. Refusal of any compensation at all, on the other hand, or an offer of compensation covering a minimal part of the losses should be considered as unreasonable, and therefore unlawful.

Acceptance of the possible lawfulness of partial compensation does not necessarily result in acquiescence to arbitrary state measures. Certain criteria and conditions serve to limit the state's power of granting inadequate compensation to the aliens affected by its measures. The first, and perhaps most important, requirement is that the measures involved have to be *bona fide* measures of a general character, such as nationalizations or general expropriations for purposes of land reform.[109] The offer of partial compensation

---

[106] Indeed, Katzarov, *Nationalisation* 424–29, points out that the nationalizing governments in the postwar years not only could not, but also would not, pay full compensation, because of their attitude toward private property which was expressed by these very nationalizations. This point should be kept in mind, however irrelevant it may seem at first glance from the claimant states' point of view.

[107] Cf. Cheng, "Expropriation in International Law," 21 *Solicitor* 98, 100 (1954); Reuter, "Quelques remarques sur la situation juridique des particuliers en droit international public," 2 *La technique et les principes du droit public: Etudes en l'honneur de Georges Scelle* 535 (1950). And see now, Cheng, "The Rationale of Compensation for Expropriation," 44 *Grotius Soc. Transactions* 267, at 300–5 (1959).

[108] Dissenting Opinion of Judge Carneiro in the Anglo-Iranian Oil Company case, 1952 *I.C.J. Reports* 93, 151, 162.

[109] Note that even Professor Katzarov, *Nationalisation* 395, 398–400, insists that partial compensation is internationally lawful only in cases of *bona fide* nationalizations. And see, to the same effect, de Visscher, *op. cit. supra* note 104, at 246.

in the case of measures which do not reflect a radical change in the economic structure of the expropriating state, even where the takings are otherwise lawful, would be insufficient and insistence on it would constitute an international tort. In the second place, certain definite considerations have to be taken into account in determining the amount of compensation. In addition to the interests of the particular private person involved, the interests of the general public will have to be considered.[110] The character of the property involved is also important, that is to say, the extent to which it is imbued with public interest; different rules may apply in the case of a public utility concession and in that of a manufacturing enterprise. Finally, the financial possibilities of the state at the time of the taking will certainly have to be taken into account.[111]

It is true that no precise rule may be stated, no definite proportions which in all cases will constitute just compensation for nationalized property. But this is to be expected when dealing with such a new phenomenon, whose principles and consequences have not yet been determined with precision. Moreover, it is improbable that the question of partial compensation will ever arise in a definite form and with respect to a single undertaking. In all probability it will be closely related to, and perhaps confused with, the questions of promptness and effectiveness of compensation, and it will be settled by an agreement between states or some other instrument of a nonjudicial character. The recent practice of lump-sum agreements is indicative of this trend.

It is difficult to point out a single factor as the cause of the recent preponderance of agreements on lump-sum compensation. To begin with, such agreements may have been less common in the past,

---

[110] Cf., in this sense, Article 14(3) of the Basic Law (Constitution) of the Federal Republic of Germany, providing that "the compensation is to be determined in a just balancing of the interests of the community and the parties." Schubert, "Compensation under New German Legislation on Expropriation," 9 *Am. J. Comp. L.* 84, 86 (1960). 2 Peaslee, *Constitutions of Nations* 30, 33 (2d ed., 1956), uses a slightly different translation which refers to "just consideration of the interests of the general public and the participants."

[111] That is to say, the financial capacity of the state treasury, as distinguished from the general interests of the public, referred to *supra* text to note 110.

but they were by no means unknown.[112] It is rather the virtual dis-appearance of other methods of settling compensation disputes that lends importance to the practice of lump-sum settlements. In view of the number of persons affected in the postwar nationalizations, it is evident that this method of settlement has considerable ad-vantages, in that it eliminates the difficulties which would other-wise have to be met in dealing with each claim by itself. In the language of the Swiss Federal Council:

Il est certainement plus avantageux d'obtenir une indemnité déterminée dans un temps relativement court que de chercher à recevoir une somme qui peut-être [sic] plus élevée, mais dont la fixation pourrait trainer pendant des dizaines d'années.[113]

The prevailing political conditions and, in particular, the "polariza-tion" of the world in the years after the Second World War, made it impossible for any judicial body, such as a "Mixed Claims Com-mission," to operate satisfactorily. Moreover, the settlement of mat-ters of compensation by governments is in line with the generally more active role of present day governments in economic affairs.[114] And, of course, the practical fact that states have greater bargaining power than private persons should not be ignored. In negotiating on an economic question such as that of compensation, a state can offer to the other negotiating party, not only several other eco-nomic, but also purely political inducements.[115]

As to their content, there can be little doubt that the lump-sum agreements under consideration represent a compromise between what the claimant states asked for and what the debtor states were

---

[112] Cf. 3 Whiteman, *Damages* 2061 *et seq.*; Bindschedler, *supra* note 84, at 280–82.

[113] Message concerning the agreement between Switzerland and Yugoslavia, October 29, 1948, quoted in Bindschedler, *supra* note 84, at 279–80.

[114] Cf. on this point Reuter, *supra* note 107, at 539–42.

[115] On lump-sum agreements generally, see LaPradelle, in 43-I *Annuaire de l'Institut de Droit International* 60–66, 69 (1950); Viénot, *op. cit. supra* note 103, at 73–83, 223–35; Bindschedler, *supra* note 84, at 274–95. And cf. the critiques of Drucker, "The Nationalization of United Nations Property in Europe," 36 *Grotius Soc. Transactions* 75, 95–110 (1950); Schwarzenberger, *supra* note 102, at 305–8. And see note 116 *infra*.

prepared to pay. But this does not necessarily mean that these agreements represent nothing more than temporary political expediency.[116] There was, in their case, considerable uniformity of practice, so that they may be considered as having set a precedent, at least insofar as they indicate the locus of possible agreement between states with different political and economic tendencies.

The two other attributes of just compensation need not be considered at as great length as the first one. In order to be prompt, compensation must be paid either before the taking or within a short time thereafter. Payment may be further delayed if an appropriate rate of interest is determined, so that the claimant will not suffer any additional loss through delay.[117] In most recent instances of general measures affecting aliens' rights, however, the payment of the compensation provided was spread over a number of years. The compensation for the agrarian and petroleum properties of United States citizens expropriated by Mexico was paid in sixteen annual installments.[118] The 1948 agreement between France and Poland provided for payments by the latter, in compensation for the nationalized properties of French nationals, over a period of fifteen years,[119] while the agreement between Switzerland and Poland provided for thirteen years of payments.[120] Deferred payment of this sort seems to be generally acceptable, with respect to lawful measures.[121]

[116] This view has been advanced by several jurists opposing the lawfulness of partial compensation; cf. Carlston, in International Law Association, *Report of the Forty-Eighth Conference* 181 (1958); Carlston, "Nationalization: An Analytical Approach," 54 *Nw. U.L.Rev.* 405, 430–31 (1958); Wortley, *Expropriation* 124, 157.

[117] Cf. 1 Hyde, *International Law* 718 (2d ed., 1945).

[118] See *supra* notes 10–12. Compensation for British properties was paid in fifteen annual installments; cf. Wortley, *Expropriation* 65.

[119] Cf. Viénot, *op. cit. supra* note 103, at 115; Bindschedler, *supra* note 84, at 262–63. The agreement between Belgium and Poland provided for payments over the same period; cf. Viénot, *idem* at 110–11.

[120] Cf. Viénot, *op. cit. supra* note 103, at 112; Bindschedler, *supra* note 84, at 264.

[121] Cf. Foighel, *Nationalization* 120–22 (1957). The Draft Convention on the International Responsibility of States for Injuries to Aliens prepared by the Harvard Law School provides that in the case of takings of property "in furtherance of a general program of economic and social reform, the just compensation . . . may be paid over a reasonable period of years," provided there is no discrimination, "a

"Effectiveness" usually refers to the precise form of the indemnity, and especially to the possibility of its immediate utilization by the recipient.[122] It is evident that it is an essential requirement.[123] The requirement is often taken to refer exclusively to payment in hard currency. Though this is the usual form that effective payments tend to take in recent years, it is not the sole one. Payments in kind are also common in international practice. The compensation paid by Poland to France and Belgium for the nationalized properties of their nationals was effected by exports of Polish coal.[124] Even payments in hard currency may assume particular forms, as in the case of the compensation to Switzerland for the properties of its nationals expropriated in Poland and Yugoslavia, which was paid in Swiss francs by earmarking a specified part of the revenues from Polish and Yugoslav exports to Switzerland.[125] It is obvious that the surrounding conditions are of crucial importance in such cases. It was only because of the need for exports of the countries in question that agreements such as the last mentioned were profitable to both parties.

The question of the certainty of the compensation is closely related to that of its effectiveness; in fact, the former question may be considered a side aspect of the latter. If the provision on compensation made in the nationalizing legislation is so vague as to leave the matter unsettled, the compensation cannot be considered effective.[126]

---

reasonable part" of the compensation is paid promptly and interest-bearing bonds are given to the alien. Article 10(4), 55 *Am. J. Int'l L.* 548, 553–54 (1961). And see also *infra* p. 346, note 23.

[122] Cf. Foighel, *Nationalization* 122–26 (1957); Bindschedler, *supra* note 84, at 269–71; Brandon, *supra* note 105, at 316.

[123] "Quant au caractère effectif de l'indemnité, il ne saurait être sacrifié pour la bonne raison qu'une indemnité non effective serait illusoire." Bindschedler, *supra* note 84, at 251.

[124] Bindschedler, *idem* at 262–63; Viénot, *op. cit. supra* note 103, at 115, 110–11 respectively.

[125] Cf. Viénot, *idem* 112, 116; Bindschedler, *supra* note 84, at 264.

[126] See Note, "Foreign Seizure of Investment: Remedies and Protection," 12 *Stanford L. Rev.* 606, 611 (1960). And cf. de Nova, Note, in 47 *Rev. Critique Dr. Int. Privé* 534 *et seq.* (1958).

This may happen when the nationalizing state proposes to pay compensation when its financial condition permits it or mentions some other vague contingency. It may also happen (but a good deal of caution is needed in determining that this is in fact happening in any concrete instance) when the financial condition of the state is obviously such that its keeping its promises as to compensation is extremely improbable. The claimant states may in such cases seek guarantees of the effective character of the compensation.

There is a very close relationship between the three requirements here discussed. In most cases, the states and aliens involved have to choose between alternative forms and amount of compensation. The value of each one of them depends on the circumstances. When the debtor state is under a socialist regime, effectiveness becomes the ruling consideration, since there are no other investment opportunities in that state to absorb the capital paid to the alien. Prospects of devaluation of currency or of government instability may increase the value of promptness, while in a capitalist state of relative economic stability, it is the amount of compensation that becomes all-important. Thus, it is only by looking at all three interrelated elements of compensation—adequacy, promptness and effectiveness—that the extent of its compliance with international law may be determined.

Effect of Unforeseen Circumstances

Before concluding this chapter, another possible ground for compensation should be mentioned, which obtains in the absence of any state measures affecting the contractual rights of aliens. The municipal public law of some states accepts the principle, that, when, by reason of unforeseen circumstances, the fulfillment of the private contractor's obligations under a state contract has become excessively onerous to him, the state should compensate him and should allow the contract to be revised to take account of the new situation. This principle is most cogently expressed in the theory of *imprévision* of French administrative law.[127] It is not accepted in Anglo-American law with respect to state contracts,[128] though a corresponding principle is accepted in private law, in the form of the doctrine concerning the frustration of contracts.[129] There is also a similarity between this principle and the theory of the *clausula rebus sic standibus* in international law.[130] In all these cases, the law attempts to take into account, in construing or applying a contract, the unforeseen changes in the circumstances surrounding and affecting the contract.

There is some evidence that the theory of *imprévision* may be applicable in public international law in the case of state contracts.[131] The few international cases on which this assertion is based are, admittedly, of limited value as general precedents because of their dependence on the provisions of particular treaties. It is possible, however, to derive certain general conclusions with respect to the conditions under which the doctrine in question may be applied.

The first condition is that the contract involved has to be a state contract; in fact, in all the cases where this theory has been applied, a contract of concession was involved. It is noteworthy that in some of these cases the contract involved was not initially a contract between a state and an alien.[132] It was a contract between a state and one of its own nationals. In the territorial changes which followed the First World War, the whole or part of the territory involved passed to another state, and this resulted in a difference of nationality between the conceding (successor) authority and the concessionaire. Moreover, the theory cannot apply to all state con-

---

[127] Cf. *supra* p. 200 and note 27.   [128] Cf. *supra* p. 204, text to note 50.

[129] And note that this principle is accepted to a very limited extent in French private law, which tends to insist on the sanctity of contractual commitments.

[130] See generally 1 Schwarzenberger, *International Law* 538–45 (3d ed., 1957).

[131] See the interesting study of Dr. Durand, "L'imprévision dans les contrats internationaux de concession d'après la jurisprudence internationale," 19 *Travaux juridiques et économiques de l'Université de Rennes* 63 (1956), on which the present section is based in part. See also Cavaré, *Droits contractuels* 123–31.

[132] See Durand, *supra* note 131, at 80–82.

tracts, but only to those which depend on a continuous relationship between the state and the private contractor.[133] In all relevant cases, the contracts involved the operation of public utilities.[134] There is no reason, however, for not applying the doctrine to concessions of mineral rights, as well, as long as they conform with the conditions described.

The second condition for the application of the theory of *imprévision* is that the performance of the contract should be disrupted, to the detriment of the private contractor, by events which could not be foreseen at the time of the conclusion of the contract and which upset the initial economic equilibrium of the contract.[135] Events of such a type are wars, economic crises, or, in some cases, the very fact of the change in the sovereignty over the territory involved. Thus, after the First World War, the railway companies operating by virtue of concessions in the territories previously belonging to the Austro-Hungarian monarchy found themselves operating in the territory of one or more other states.[136] The Peace Treaties dealt with this problem by providing for the conclusion of agreements between the railway companies and the successor states to regulate the reorganization of the railways on the basis of the new conditions.[137]

In the presence of both these conditions and assuming, for the moment, that the case has been submitted to an international tribunal,[138] there are two ways in which a conflict may be resolved.[139] On the one hand, the state may take over the contract, paying appropriate compensation to the concessionaire. On the other hand,

---

[133] *Idem* at 82–83.

[134] The cases relate to the operation of railways, *infra* notes 140, 141, and 142, and of an electrical power company, *infra* note 145.

[135] Cf. Durand, *supra* note 131, at 83–87.

[136] Cf. the cases cited *infra* notes 140, 141, and 142.

[137] Treaty of Trianon (1920), article 304; Treaty of Saint-Germain-en-Laye (1919), article 320.

[138] Cf. *infra* p. 337. For a discussion of the international judge's problems in such a case, see Durand, *supra* note 131, at 87 *et seq.*

[139] For a discussion of these two solutions in the context of French administrative law, see *idem* at 90 *et seq.*

the international tribunal may proceed to adjust the contractual provisions to the now existing conditions; it may also provide for some compensation to be given to the concessionaire to cover the losses which he has already suffered. Illustrations of both methods of settlement may be found in the related case law.

In the case of the *Sopron-Koszeg Railways*,[140] the arbitrators held that the two states concerned should purchase the sections of the railway line located in their respective territories. The contractual relationship was thus brought to an end without any damage to the interests of the concessionaire. The same solution, in the presence of similar facts, was given in the case of the *Zeltweg-Wolfsberg and Unterdrauburg-Woellan Railways*.[141]

In the case of the *Barcs-Pacrac Railway*,[142] however, the tribunal applied a different method. It stated that, though the public contract involved, concluded in 1884, should be respected in its general lines, it could not be strictly applied any more. The tribunal held that it was itself competent to adjust the terms of the contract to the conditions prevailing after the war and to events which had altered radically the position of the parties and which were "unforeseeable in the common intention of the parties at the time of the conclusion" of the concession contract.[143] It was further stated that the provisions of the contract could be considered neither as wholly invalidated by these events nor as wholly valid and binding on the parties; they had to be revised to conform to present conditions.[144]

A similar solution was given to the dispute in the *Electricity Company of Warsaw* case.[145] The arbitrator held that the concession contract in this case was of a "mixed" private and public character, and thus could be considered as coming under the provisions

---

[140] (Hungary, Austria, 1929), 2 UN RIAA 961, 3 *idem* 1810.

[141] (Austria, Yugoslavia, 1934), 3 UN RIAA 1795, 1805.

[142] (Hungary, Barcs-Pacrac Railway Co., 1934), 3 UN RIAA 1569. In all three cases, the railway company involved was a party to the arbitration proceedings.

[143] *Idem* at 1575.   [144] *Idem* at 1576.

[145] (France v. Poland, 1932 and 1936), 3 UN RIAA 1669, 1679. Another award of 1933, supplementary to that of 1932, is summarized in the 1936 award.

of a treaty between France and Poland which related to private contracts between their nationals.[146] He stated further that, when the continued execution of contracts entailed, for one of the parties, "because of the change in the conditions of commerce, a considerable prejudice, an equitable indemnity could be awarded to the damaged party." [147] He held therefore that the company in question was entitled to a prolongation of the duration of its concession, to an increase of its rates and to the payment of compensation.[148] In a later award in the same case, the payment of additional compensation was ordered, because of the nonexecution of the earlier award.[149]

In view of the limitations imposed by their particular facts (especially, the application of specific treaty provisions), the cases just discussed are not sufficient to establish a general rule of international law. They indicate, however, the existence and importance of certain principles, applicable to state contracts. The scarcity of judicial authority on this point should be expected, since, in most instances, modifications of state contracts are effected by negotiations leading to an agreement between the parties rather than by arbitration or judicial determination. It is interesting to note, in this connection, that a recent study suggests that there is a "living law" of state contracts which imposes on the parties the obligation to have recourse to negotiations and, possibly, to arbitration for the settlement of any related dispute.[150] Whether by negotiations or by arbitration, the parties to a state contract of long duration should be expected to seek to adjust its provisions to changing conditions. This means that both parties should be prepared to cooperate rather than compete in the performance of the contract. Whenever, because of unforeseen changes of external conditions, or

[146] Convention concerning private property, rights and interests, of February 6, 1922, 53 *League of Nations Treaty Series* 399.
[147] Award of November 24, 1932, 3 UN RIAA 1679, 1686.
[148] Award of June 20, 1933, summarized 3 UN RIAA 1689, 1690–91.
[149] Award of March 23, 1936, 3 UN RIAA 1689.
[150] Carlston, "International Role of Concession Agreements," 52 *Nw. U.L.Rev.* 618, 640 (1957).

because of the indirect effects of state measures of a general character,[151] the private contractor suffers considerable damage, the
state should be willing to cooperate in restoring the financial equilibrium of the contract.[152]

[151] Durand, *supra* note 131, at 86, distinguishes the two cases, in accordance with
the distinction between *imprévision* and *fait du prince* of French administrative
law. He seems to accept that the international responsibility of the state would be
engaged in the latter case. But, as has been shown, this is not necessarily so, in the
case of general measures of a nondiscriminatory character.

[152] Durand, *supra* note 131, at 91, suggests that while in French administrative law,
the doctrine of *imprévision* involves two considerations, namely, the regular functioning of the public service involved and the financial equilibrium of the parties, in
international law only the latter consideration is taken into account. The validity
of this distinction appears doubtful. The public interest, one manifestation of which
is the need for the regular functioning of public services, is certainly taken into
account in cases relating to state contracts in international law.

II

Legal Effects of Guarantees to Foreign Investors

STATE guarantees to foreign investors granted by virtue of investment laws are one species of contractual commitments of states to aliens. The conclusions in the preceding chapters are, therefore, generally applicable in their case. It would be useful, however, to examine in more detail their particular legal effects.

Effects in International Law

In accordance with the conclusions in Chapter 9, state measures affecting in whole or in part the operation of state guarantees to foreign investors are not necessarily unlawful in international law. They may be so under certain conditions, but, in the absence of discrimination, of abuse of the state's rights or of other exceptional circumstances of this type, they should be considered as lawful under international law. The requirements previously noted in a more general context are also applicable here. The measures in question should be taken for a public purpose and they should be nondiscriminatory with regard to the aliens affected. Moreover, such measures create an obligation on the part of the state taking them to compensate the aliens for their losses. These general requirements are applicable with qualifications or alterations made necessary by the particular character of the promises. Apart from such minor exceptions, however, the general principles remain essentially the same.

It has been argued that, independently of the general situation with respect to state contracts, specific promises of special treatment constitute a distinct class of contractual commitments, whose direct or indirect violation constitutes in all cases an internationally unlawful act. This position has been powerfully urged, with respect to the particular case of promises of nonexpropriation, by the United Kingdom Government in its Memorial to the International Court of Justice in connection with the *Anglo-Iranian Oil Company* case.[1] Its argumentation requires special attention. The British Government's basic thesis was that there is

a fundamental difference between an ordinary concession, even if granted for a term of years, and a concession in which the State has expressly divested itself of the right to exercise the power of terminating it by unilateral sovereign action, whatever the grounds for such action.[2]

The grounds of this difference are to be found first of all in the variation between the investor's expectations in the two cases. In the case of a regular concession, it may be argued that the investor realizes that the conceding government may at any time terminate the concession. According to the Memorial, however,

the position is quite different, as a matter of law and good faith, if the foreign company or national expressly stipulates in the contract—a stipulation formally accepted by the other contracting party—that the concession shall be immune from termination by legislative or other governmental action. . . . The question whether in any particular case a cancellation, for the purpose of nationalization, of a concession granted

---

[1] *I.C.J. Pleadings, Anglo-Iranian Oil Company Case (U.K. v. Iran)* 64, 86–93 (1951). It should be noted that the main British contention was that the concession agreement between Iran and the Anglo-Iranian Oil Company was an international agreement; the alternative contention was that, even if it were not, its violation would still be internationally unlawful, on the grounds summarized in the text; see *idem* 74–78, 86–87, 90. The Court rejected the principal contention and did not examine the alternative one.

[2] *Idem* at 87.

for a fixed term of years involves a breach of international law may be a matter of dispute, but there is . . . no room at all for controversy in relation to a case in which the State in question has expressly renounced such power of legislative action.[3]

The Memorial rejected the possible contention that the difference between the two cases is one of degree only or that the specific promise of nonexpropriation is "essentially redundant and without effect." The inclusion of such a promise, according to it, renders the termination of the contract "illegal in *all* circumstances, including those in which, apart from the explicit undertaking, cancellation would be legal," and it removes any doubt as to the possible presence in the contract of an *"implied* term that the concession may be terminated by lawful nationalization." [4] After developing the thesis that the legislative freedom of the state may be limited by contract as well as by treaty,[5] the Memorial summarized its argument in the following three points: firstly, the nationalization was in violation of an express undertaking of the Iranian Government; secondly, this undertaking was "a most material consideration" for the company in concluding the contract; and thirdly,

the violation of that undertaking, in addition to being a breach of the contract between the Iranian Government and the Company, is, from the point of view of international law and *vis-a-vis* the United Kingdom Government, a tortious act on the part of the Iranian Government.[6]

It was found necessary to summarize the United Kingdom's Memorial at some length because it is the most complete and articulate exposition of the particular thesis it is defending. The problem has also been touched upon by some of the jurists writing on the *Anglo-Iranian Oil Company* case.[7] It was discussed at more length

---

[3] *Idem* at 87, 88.   [4] *Idem* at 89 (emphasis in the original).
[5] *Idem* at 89–92.   [6] *Idem* at 92–93.
[7] See especially Lissitzyn, "Iranian Oil, Foreign Investments and the Law," 2 *Foreign Affairs Reports* (Delhi) 17, 17–18, 28–29 (1953). See also Hoveyda, "Les aspects juridiques de la nationalisation des industries petrolières en Iran," 1 *Rev. Dr. Int'l Moyen-Orient* 127, 136–37 (1951–52); Schwarzenberger, "The Protection of British Property Abroad," 5 *Current Legal Problems* 295, 313–14 (1952).

at the 1952 meeting of the *Institut de Droit International* in Sienna.[8] During the discussion of a draft resolution on the legal effects of nationalization, it was proposed that a provision be included declaring internationally unlawful any nationalization in violation of express or implied undertakings toward aliens. The proposal was not adopted but the close division of the vote and the high number of abstentions [9] are indicative of the present day lack of a common consensus on the matter.

It is evident that the central issue is whether the undeniable difference in content between specific promises of special treatment and other contractual promises is sufficient to warrant the application of widely different legal rules in the two cases. It is submitted that there is no compelling reason for accepting that the existing difference is of such a high order of importance. Even if the investors' expectations are as different as is suggested in the United Kingdom Memorial, it should be noted that such expectations are not the only factor to be taken into account.[10] The lawfulness of state measures affecting the contractual rights of aliens is founded not on the character of the latter's expectations but on that of their legal relations with the state. In fact, most of the Memorial's argumentation seems founded on considerations of good faith [11] and on the investors' reliance on the state's promises.[12] It has been pointed out already that a state is not necessarily acting in bad faith when taking measures affecting the aliens' interests. Moreover, both

---

[8] See 44-II *Annuaire de l'Institut de Droit International* 307 *et seq.* (1952). And cf. also 43-I *idem* 42 *et seq.* (1950).

[9] Twenty members and associates of the Institute voted against the proposal, sixteen for it and twenty-two abstained; 44-II *idem* 318 (1952).

[10] Cf. in this connection Verzijl, "The Relevance of Public and Private International Law Respectively for the Solution of Problems Arising from Nationalization of Enterprises," 19 *Zeitschrift für ausländisches öffentliches Recht und Völkerrecht* (Festgabe für A. N. Makarov) 531, 535 (1958). The eminent jurist denies that there exists any important difference between specific promises of special treatment and general contractual commitments; he strongly disagrees, however, with the views here submitted as to the lawfulness of state measures affecting such commitments. And see now, White, *Nationalisation of Foreign Property* 173–79 (1961).

[11] See, e.g., the U.K. Memorial, *supra* note 1, at 64, 87.

[12] See, e.g., *idem* at 88, 89, 92.

of the Memorial's considerations do not necessarily lead to acceptance of the unlawfulness of such state measures but rather to the recognition of the existence of an obligation on the part of the state to compensate equitably the aliens damaged by its measures.

International judicial and diplomatic practice is not very helpful with respect to guarantees of special treatment. The few relevant cases which may be found involve state measures in violation of promises of exemption from taxation. None of them, however, seems to be quite to the point. In the case of *J. B. Okie* [13] the claimant, a citizen of the United States, had received from the Mexican Department of Finance and Public Credit an assurance that he would be allowed to import sheep into Mexico "without the collection of any charges." When importing them, however, he was required to pay certain fees which he paid under protest. The issue in dispute before the Tribunal seems to have been whether the Mexican assurance covered all charges or only import duties.[14] The Tribunal found that, whatever the correct interpretation of the assurance, the Mexican Government was, under the particular circumstances, responsible for the claimant's misunderstanding of its meaning. The claim was therefore allowed.[15] In the *G. W. Cook* case [16] the claimant had erected a building on the understanding that it would be exempted from any taxation on real estate. Such exemption was granted by subsequent legislation. Several years later, a special tax was imposed which the claimant paid under protest. The Tribunal rejected the claim on the twofold grounds that there existed no contract between the state authorities and the claimant [17] and that the tax collected was not of the kind referred to in the statute granting the exemption.[18] This case is relevant only insofar as it can be inferred from the Commissioners' *obiter dicta*

---

[13] (U.S.A. v. Mexico, 1926), 4 UN RIAA 54.   [14] *Idem* at 56.
[15] *Idem* at 56, 57.   [16] (U.S.A. v. Mexico, 1930), 4 UN RIAA 593.
[17] *Idem* at 594, 595–96. In a Separate Opinion, the United States Commissioner concurred in this part of the holding; *idem* at 596.
[18] *Idem* at 594–95. The United States Commissioner dissented as to this part of the holding; *idem* at 596–98.

that the situation in law would have been different, had the existence of a contract been proven.[19]

In the absence of relevant precedents, the legal effects of contractual promises of special treatment will have to be discussed on the basis of the content of the particular promises, the theoretical conclusions in the preceding chapters, and certain general considerations, not exclusively legal in character.

Promises of nonexpropriation should be distinguished from other types of promises. The violation of such promises means, in effect, that not only the state contract possibly related to the promises (for example, concession) is terminated, but also that any other relationship, apart from any possible claim of the alien, is at an end. In the case of other guarantees, such as those concerning exchange restrictions, taxation, or labor legislation, their violation does not necessarily lead to the severance of all economic relations between the state and the alien. The original concession may still be effective, the enterprise established by foreign capital still functioning, though the amount or availability of profits or its efficiency may have been affected. Accordingly, the investor is still interested in its operation and, in many instances, there may still exist some other contractual relationship between him and the capital-receiving state. The means available to the investor in protection of his interests are thus affected. The investor may now have a greater bargaining power, since he is still in control of his enterprise; but he may also be in no position to react as strongly as he otherwise would or even to address himself officially to his state of nationality, because of the possible consequences of such action on the operation of his enterprise (for example, further restrictive measures by the state, or indirect measures, such as withholding of government contracts).

The main advantage of state guarantees to foreign investors is that their existence provides grounds for the interposition of the aliens' state of nationality. This is not strictly true with respect to

[19] *Idem* at 594, 595–96.

promises of nonexpropriation, where such interposition would be in most cases possible even in the absence of guarantees.[20] With respect, however, to measures imposing exchange restrictions or new taxes the contractual relationship arising out of the state guarantees is the only ground upon which such interposition is possible, in the absence of treaty provisions or other special conditions. The effectiveness of such interposition is, of course, a quite distinct question. State interposition will be normally founded in such cases on the existence of a denial of justice, possibly consisting in that the investor's contractual claims have not been properly honored by the courts of the capital-receiving state. The object of the claim will again be, in most instances, the award of compensation to cover the investor's losses. Such an obligation would exist in all cases of state measures affecting contractual guarantees to foreign investors, regardless of the international lawfulness or unlawfulness of the measures [21] or of the existence or not of a denial of justice.

The application of the principle of estoppel may be in certain instances of particular importance. The state taking these measures cannot now deny its liability to the alien, by invoking the general or nondiscriminatory character of its measures. By granting special legal guarantees to the particular foreign investor, it has acknowledged the investor's special position and it has induced him to act on the basis of this recognition. Both elements of the classical form of estoppel are thus present.[22]

The award of compensation in the case of promises of special treatment presents certain particular problems. With respect to guarantees of nonexpropriation, the main problem is whether their existence has any concrete effect on the measure of compensa-

[20] Interposition would be founded either on the taking of the alien's property or, if the enterprise involved operated by virtue of a concession, on the effect of the state measures upon it, followed by a denial of justice. In both cases, the expropriatory measures would create a duty on the part of the state to compensate the alien affected.

[21] Even though the measure of compensation would differ in the two cases.

[22] See *supra* p. 253. But see also *supra*, pp. 260–61.

tion to be awarded. The conclusions already reached regarding the lawfulness of state measures affecting such guarantees lead to a negative answer. To recognize any particular effect on the measure of compensation would, in fact, mean that compensation in such cases would be different from that applicable to cases of lawful expropriation. Though there exists here a sort of "double expropriation," there is no justification for applying the rules relating to unlawful expropriations. Nonetheless, the existence of state guarantees does have some effect in that it reinforces the existing obligation to compensate the alien for the taking of his property or the cancellation of his contract.[23]

In the case of guarantees regarding other matters, such as labor legislation, taxation, or exchange restrictions, the problems which arise are largely different. The state's obligation to compensate the investor is now founded solely on these guarantees. In their absence, no such obligation would normally exist. The difficulty lies not in determining the measure of compensation, which will presumably be the one applicable to internationally lawful state measures affecting aliens' contractual rights, but in assessing in each particular case the compensation to be awarded. This is generally difficult, though not always impossible. In the case of promises of tax exemption, the alien's loss will normally consist in the amount of additional tax he had to pay. In the case of promises regarding the removal of exchange restrictions, the alien's loss may be determinable, for instance when the foreign currency denied to the investor is needed for the purchase of raw materials or equipment outside the capital-importing state. In other cases, however, the

[23] According to Article 10 of the Harvard Draft Convention on the International Responsibility of States for Injuries to Aliens, the taking of property "in violation of an express undertaking by the State in reliance on which the property was acquired or imported by the alien," is not in itself wrongful. The lawfulness of the taking, however, depends on the prompt payment of compensation. Even in the case of measures "in furtherance of a general program of economic and social reform," the payment of compensation cannot be deferred (while it could be, in the absence of such an undertaking). This is an interesting way of giving effect to state guarantees and one that would be applicable in a great number of, though not in all, cases. See 55 Am. J. Int'l L. 548, 553–54, 560–61 (1961).

loss may be difficult to determine with any precision, though it may be no less real. The same is largely true with respect to promises regarding labor legislation. In certain exceptional cases, when the state measures have affected the enterprise's operation greatly, the alien's loss may become apparent.[24] But in the majority of cases, this does not happen.

In several cases, the object of the international claim may be "specific performance" (that is, revocation of the measures involved) rather than compensation. In the case of promises of tax exemption, the related claim, in seeking the return of the amounts paid for taxes imposed in violation of the guarantees, may be said to be demanding the effective revocation of the measures in question. Matters are somewhat simplified when the state measures affecting the guarantees are imposed on an admittedly temporary basis, for instance, when exchange restrictions are imposed because of a crisis in the capital-importing country's balance-of-payments. Later revocation of the measures may then remove the necessity for compensation.

It is evident from this discussion that it is not possible to generalize with regard to measures of so diverse a character, which may be based on such a wide variety of causes. In many cases, though by no means in all, it may not be possible to determine with any precision the amount of the compensation to be granted to the alien. In other cases, specific performance rather than compensation may be the appropriate remedy.

Other Legal Effects of State Guarantees

The discussion up to now has stressed the limitations of the effectiveness of state guarantees in international law. Considerations

---

[24] In cases of manifest abuse of rights, the compensation to be awarded would have to reconstitute the exact *status quo ante*. In cases of indirect expropriation, when, that is, the state measures affect the alien's interests to the extent of making him lose control of his enterprise, the rules applicable in the case of direct expropriation are appropriate.

of a strictly legal character, however, are hardly ever sufficient by themselves and this is particularly true with respect to the present topic. The value of state guarantees to foreign investors may be relative, but it nevertheless exists. In order to perceive it in its proper perspective, it is necessary to take into account certain other effects of such guarantees, which go beyond strictly legal considerations.

First of all, the mere fact that state guarantees are granted, indicates the existence in the capital-importing state of an understanding of the need for foreign private capital and an attitude favorable to it. This is an intangible factor, the importance of which should by no means be underestimated. It can never be assumed that a state gives guarantees to foreign investors with the intention of not keeping them. Such cases may occur, but they are clearly exceptional. When a state violates its own guarantees, it usually does so because of a radical change of government policy, due either to a change of regime or to the presence of unforeseen circumstances. A capital-importing country has important economic reasons for keeping its guarantees. The need for capital in underdeveloped countries is not a temporary one. Such countries, therefore, cannot afford, in the great majority of cases, to alienate foreign investors by failing to fulfill their promises. Such behavior is possible only in extreme cases, for example when the country's resources and products are so important to other countries that the latter may have to accept unfair treatment without strong reaction. Such cases involve, after all, but the old play of power politics in a relatively modern form.

Certain elements of a formal character should also be taken into account. Once specified treatment has been promised to the investor, any government action in contravention of it must fulfill certain additional formal conditions (that is, conditions which would not have been required had there been no guarantees) in order for such government action to be lawful by municipal law standards. Legislative, rather than merely administrative, action will often have to be taken, since the guarantees are usually granted by virtue of special legislative provisions.[25] From the standpoint of substance, this makes the decision to act in contravention of the guarantees a "top level" one. The possibility of arbitrary action by minor government officials is thus almost wholly eliminated. This is a particularly important consideration with regard to guarantees concerning taxation, exchange control and other such measures short of expropriation of property. Matters of this sort are usually regulated by administrative action, insofar as they affect particular persons or enterprises. Indeed, it may be said that one of the hazards of investment in an underdeveloped country is the dependence on actions and judgments of minor government officials whose ability and efficiency may be highly doubtful. This hazard is to a large extent eliminated by the grant of state guarantees of the type here studied. Considerations of this sort are not as important with respect to measures of expropriation, where the related decision would as a rule be a "top-level" one, even in the absence of guarantees.

From a municipal law standpoint, the existence of guarantees may also be important in that it makes recourse to the local tribunals possible. Such recourse may be had against administrative acts in contravention of the guarantees, the competent court being either a special administrative tribunal or a regular court. The investor is thus better protected against any formally illegal action of the guaranteeing government. In the case of legislation, such recourse will probably not be possible, at least in the majority of instances. The partly contractual character of state guarantees by special instrument might be of some importance in this connection. According to the law of several modern states, the government has no power to revoke a tax exemption or other privilege when it is granted by contract, though it may do so when it is accorded by general legislation.[26] In other instances, states do have the power to modify their contracts unilaterally but are bound to compensate the other party

---

[25] In cases such as that of the Greek Legislative Decree 2687 of October 22, 1953, a constitutional amendment would be needed. This is the strictest formal condition which may be imposed.

[26] This is, for instance, the case of United States law with regard to tax exemptions; cf. *supra* p. 270 and see also Baker, "Puerto-Rico's Program of Industrial Tax Exemption," 18 *Geo. Wash. L. Rev.* 327, 349–56 (1950).

to the contract.[27] In such cases, recourse to the local judiciary might prove to be an effective remedy.

Certain other considerations should also be taken into account. By the conclusion of a contractual or semicontractual instrument, a whole system of legal relations between the state and the foreign investor comes into being. Its breakdown, though possible, is more difficult than it may seem at first glance. Given some adaptability and good faith on the part of both parties to the agreement, such systems may operate under considerable stress and adjust successfully to changing conditions.

The system's flexibility and durability depends to some extent on the content of the particular promises included in the instrument involved. The imposition of specific limits on the extent of the privileges or other promises granted to the investors may thus be seen as an indication of the good faith and seriousness of the government granting them. Promises which are too broad or too generous to the investor may have less chance of being kept faithfully by the government granting them, not necessarily because of any lack of good faith on its part but because of economic difficulties which may be partly due to the broad scope of these promises. The fact that, in most instances of state guarantees by special instrument, the specific content of the promises is determined after negotiations between the state and the prospective investors is of great importance. The guarantees are thus formulated with regard to the particular investment and they represent an express or implied bargain. The effects of both the investment and the guarantee on the country's economy are presumably taken into account when the instrument is drafted. It is up to the government concerned, and, indirectly, up to the investor, as well, to see that the guarantees granted will not be such that they will have to be violated at the first sign of adverse conditions.[28] In the last analysis, therefore,

[27] See the discussion of French law, *supra* pp. 198–200. See also *supra* p. 252.
[28] See, in this sense, in a broader context, Metzger, "The Nature and Extent of Legal Limitations upon a Nation's Freedom of Action," 1961 *Wisconsin L. Rev.* 277, 288–93.

the fate of the promises granted to foreign investors depends in major part on the technical competence of the persons responsible for the drafting of the instrument granting them.[29]

Similar considerations obtain with particular force in the case of the provisions on settlement of disputes which are sometimes included in state contracts.[30] It has been cogently argued [31] that instruments of approval or guarantee contracts should not be understood as final, immutable agreements. They are better seen as instruments indicating the kind of relationship which will prevail and establishing a frame of reference for the future relations between the government of the host state and the foreign investor. And it has been further said [32] that negotiation, not arbitration, is the principal mode of settlement of any disputes relating to concession contracts. Both the state and the foreign investor who are party to the contract favor negotiation because it permits the open discussion and weighing of the economic and political considerations which in fact determine the attitude of the parties. Even if the parties do not reach complete agreement, they may succeed in narrowing down the issue, so that it may be submitted to arbitration, in a manner acceptable to both parties. The role of the specific provisions on the matter which may be included in state contracts will be to make clear and more precise the methods to be employed.

The role of international organizations and of the international economic agencies, in particular, can be all-important in this connection. They have a reputation of impartiality and they are trusted to a considerable extent by the governments of capital-exporting as well as capital-importing countries. Such organizations, or their high-level personnel, can serve as mediators, bringing together the parties and encouraging them to express their views around the

[29] The importance of this factor has been stressed in a related context by Jenks, *The Common Law of Mankind* 408–42 (1958).

[30] Cf. *supra* pp. 186–89.

[31] Cutler, Address, in Am. Soc. Int'l L., *First Investment Law Conference* 10 (mimeo., 1956).

[32] Carlston, "International Role of Concession Agreements," 52 *Nw. U. L. Rev.* 618, 640 (1957). And see, more generally, Jenks, *op. cit. supra* note 29, at 156–58.

conference table. They may also prepare and suggest to the parties plans for possible solutions. The role of the President of the World Bank in bringing about the settlement of a dispute between the City of Tokyo and the French bondholders of its 1912 loan [33] is an illustration of such possibilities. The function assigned to the World Bank in the agreement concerning compensation for the nationalization of the Suez Canal Company [34] is indicative of the possibility of an even more extensive role. The World Bank gave considerable assistance during the negotiations leading to the agreement in question and it was itself a party to the agreement, though for limited purposes only. It was provided that the Bank would act "as fiscal agent for the purpose of the payments to be made" pursuant to the Agreement.[35] It was further provided that

> In case of any disagreement between the Parties concerning the interpretation or implementation of this Agreement, the Parties will request I.B.R.D. to use its good offices to assist them in composing their differences.[36]

Such active participation of the World Bank and its affiliates provides a substantially new method of settlement of foreign investment disputes. Apart from the limitations which the Bank may impose on itself in order to retain a high degree of effectiveness, its role in connection with such disputes may increase in extent and importance. In cases of lawful measures affecting state contracts with aliens, the World Bank may help to reach a settlement not only by advising the parties but also, perhaps, by more direct methods. It may, for instance, guarantee the bonds issued by the state

[33] Cf. Domke, "International Arbitration of Commercial Disputes," in Southwestern Legal Foundation, *Proceedings of the 1960 Institute on Private Investments Abroad* 131, 172 (1960).

[34] Agreement between the Government of the United Arab Republic and the Compagnie Financière de Suez, July 13, 1958, in *The Suez Canal Settlement* 6 (Lauterpacht ed., 1960).

[35] Article 10 and Annex 12, *idem* at 15, 29.

[36] Article 11. A first illustration of this role of the Bank is provided by a letter of the Bank's representative to the representatives of the parties, settling by a compromise a difference of opinion on the interpretation of the Agreement's provision on the currency of payment; Appendix 2 to Annex 12, *idem* at 31.

of investment in deferred payment of compensation to aliens. An admittedly inconclusive precedent in this direction may be found in the loans issued "under the auspices of" the League of Nations in the early 1920s.[37] The Bank's guarantees might be informally arranged, rather than openly expressed as such. The Bank may, for instance, undertake to supervise the payment of deferred compensation (as in the Suez Canal case), while the state concerned may bind itself toward the Bank and not only toward the alien investors to provide the related payments. The Bank and its affiliated agencies would be in a position to exert great pressure on the debtor state, in case of unjustified default, through the withholding of loans and of IMF assistance in currency matters or perhaps, by the blocking of the currency held by the IMF. Of course, great caution would be needed before the undertaking of any such obligation by the Bank, but thus far the Bank has not been found wanting in caution.

The provisions of concession agreements, instruments of approval or guarantee contracts concerning the settlement of disputes may therefore usefully include reference not only to judicial international bodies, such as the International Court of Justice or the Permanent Court of Arbitration, but also to international financial agencies or other functional bodies, though with regard to conciliation rather than adjudication proceedings. In this manner, the cooperation of these agencies might be secured for the purpose of enforcing measures against internationally unlawful state action.

In addition to the provisions on settlement of disputes by negotiation or other conciliatory procedures, state guarantees to foreign investors sometimes also provide for arbitration. As has been noted,[38] such provisions appear to be included in a minority of investment laws. This reluctance is not accidental and it may be considered as

---

[37] But in that case the League itself did not guarantee the loans. Cf. Williams, "L'entre-aide financière internationale," 5 *Hague Recueil* 109 (1924); Jèze, "La garantie des emprunts publics d'Etat," 7 *idem* 155, 225–30 (1925); 1 Borchard and Wynne, *State Insolvency and Foreign Bondholders* 296–99 (1951); Wells, "Guarantees in International Economic Law," 4 *Int'l & Comp. L. Qu.* 426 (1955).

[38] Cf. *supra* pp. 186–87.

a manifestation of the general unwillingness of underdeveloped capital-importing countries to submit to obligatory international arbitration. The unwillingness is to be attributed to a refusal to acquiesce, *a priori* and without limitations, to the existing rules of international law, especially those pertaining to economic matters. The governments of underdeveloped countries seem to fear that arbitration or other international tribunals will tend to ignore the substantive problems involved and to apply rigid legal principles, evolved in the nineteenth century under different international conditions.[39]

In view of this attitude, the extensive use of arbitration would seem possible only under certain conditions. First, technical matters which do not affect the vital interests of the parties involved may be easily settled by impartial technical experts. This course has been adopted, as has been already noted,[40] in several recent state contracts. Second, the arbitrators may be given power to adjudicate *ex aequo et bono* and not in accordance with strict law. Again, this course has been adopted to some extent in recent practice, either expressly,[41] or by implication.[42] Arbitration of strictly legal matters may also be useful in connection with some contracts, depending on the particular circumstances.

A final problem relates to the possible refusal of a state to submit

[39] For a discussion of such attitudes, see Castaneda, "The Underdeveloped Nations and the Development of International Law," 15 *Int'l Organization* 38, 38–44 (1961). And cf. Metzger, *supra* note 28, at 285–88.

[40] Cf. *supra* p. 188.

[41] "The arbitrators judging ex aequo et bono are neither bound by any special law, nor by any rules of procedure in carrying out the arbitration." Agreement between the Greek State and the Polish Firm CECOP concerning the establishment of a sugar processing plant, March 3, 1960, article 34, 1960 *Ephimeris tis Kyverniseos* Fasc. 1, No. 44, 407. An identical provision is found in a similar contract with three German firms dated December 10, 1959, 1960 *idem* No. 22, 133. But note that in a contract concerning petroleum exploration and production, signed on December 11, 1959, between the Greek State and a subsidiary of Standard Oil of New Jersey, 1960 *idem* No. 71, 705, the provision on arbitration (article 26) merely states that "the arbitrators are not bound by any rules of procedure in carrying out the arbitration."

[42] The provision of recent petroleum concessions on the application of general principles of law may, perhaps, be considered as allowing an equitable, rather than strictly legal, settlement of disputes.

to arbitration, in breach of an express guarantee to that effect. Several procedures have been devised for the appointment of arbitrators by an impartial body, in case of failure of one of the parties to effect such appointment. The direct usefulness of such provisions may be open to doubt. Despite the legal considerations which may be adduced in its favor, the enforcement against a state of the decision of an arbitral tribunal in the formation of which it has not participated remains problematical. The provisions in question may be useful indirectly in inducing the parties to submit to arbitration. Arbitration without the cooperation of one of the parties may be impractical and of limited effect but an unfavorable award, even under these conditions, would be to the detriment of the nonparticipating party. Both parties therefore have an interest in participating in the arbitration. It is difficult to determine beforehand whether refusal to arbitrate constitutes in all cases a denial of justice. It may well be that this is so in certain cases but in other instances, depending on the contract and the state measures involved, the necessity for the exhaustion of local remedies may still exist.

Nonlegal Aspects and Measures

Several other important considerations make it difficult, though, of course, not impossible, for a capital-importing state to violate its promises to foreign investors. Perhaps the most important of these is apprehension over the probable reaction of foreign investors in general to such violation. It has already been noted that such action will probably lead to a significant decrease of private foreign investment in the country in question. The concerted action of foreign investors may affect in other ways, as well, the interests of capital-importing states. It is widely recognized, for instance, that the major oil concerns control world petroleum distribution channels to the extent of being able to prevent a petroleum-producing country from selling its product, were it in their interest to do so.[43]

[43] See, for instance, Penrose, "Profit Sharing between Producing Countries and Oil Companies in the Middle East," 69 *Econ. J.* 238, 250 (1959).

Large international corporations would also be in a position to employ other means of a similar character in order to exert pressure on unwilling capital-receiving states. An instance of possible means of this sort is the proposals during and after the Suez Canal crisis for the building of "super-tankers" in order to bypass the Suez Canal or the development of other sources of petroleum so as to cease to depend on that of the Middle East.[44] It is apparent even to the superficial student of world economic conditions today that there exist large margins for exerting economic pressure of such "nonlegal" character.

Not only investors, however, but their states of nationality as well may react to the actions of capital-importing states by applying certain measures which, explicitly or not, are intended to exert pressure in order to make them respect the interests of foreign investors. This is an obvious fact of international life which should not be ignored because of its very obviousness. Political considerations play, it is true, a most important role in determining the form and extent (and the very existence) of such reaction on the part of capital-exporting states. The measures employed may differ depending on the circumstances in each concrete case and the general political atmosphere of the times. During the nineteenth century, the capital-exporting states managed, partly through measures of this sort, to impose their own conception of the protection due to foreign interests, especially insofar as the then "backward" states were concerned. Today, states are far more limited with respect to the measures to which they may resort, not so much because of a change in substantive public international law but rather because of a general change in the atmosphere prevailing in the international society.[45] There still remains, however, a vast variety of possible measures, principally of an economic character, by means of which capital-exporting states can exert pressure on capital-receiving countries.[46] The legality of some of these measures in international law

---

[44] Cf., e.g., Levy, "Issues in International Oil Policy," 35 *Foreign Affairs* 454, 467–68 (1957).

[45] Cf. Castaneda, *supra* note 39, at 41–43.

[46] Cf. Wortley, *Expropriation* 99, 152 *et seq.;* Seidl-Hohenveldern, "Communist

is not wholly established, but neither can they be regarded as unlawful, under existing international law.

One possible measure of this type is the blocking of the assets of the capital-importing state which are within the capital-exporting state's jurisdiction. This method of exerting pressure in connection with economic matters has been much favored in recent years. Thus, after the Second World War, the United States refused to return to the Yugoslav Government the gold of the Central Bank of Yugoslavia deposited during the war in the Federal Reserve Bank, until Yugoslavia agreed to compensate the United States nationals whose property had been expropriated by it.[47] During the Suez Canal dispute, the governments of France, the United Kingdom and the United States blocked all assets belonging to the Egyptian government and the Suez Canal Company, until a settlement was reached between the former and the shareholders of the latter.[48]

There exist several other measures which may be employed by capital-exporting against capital-importing states. Measures of a noneconomic character similar to those employed in other cases of international disputes, may also be used. They range from diplomatic protests[49] to the interruption of diplomatic relations or to the non-recognition of the state or government involved. The rules of general public international law with respect to the form, legality or extent of such measures are evidently applicable in these cases. Again, their effectiveness should not be underestimated.

Theories on Confiscation and Expropriation: Critical Comments," 7 *Am. J. Comp. L.* 541, 552–54 (1958).

[47] Cf. Friedman, *Expropriation* 45; Viénot, *Nationalisations étrangères et interêts français* 180 et seq. (1953); Rubin, *Private Foreign Investment* 93–95 (1956).

[48] Cf. Domke, "American Protection against Foreign Expropriation in the Light of the Suez Canal Crisis," 105 *U. Pa. L. Rev.* 1033, 1038 (1957); Wortley, *Expropriation* 154–55. The measures were lifted on the basis of the agreement between the United Arab Republic and the United Kingdom of February 28, 1959 (article II) and that between the United Arab Republic and France of August 22, 1958 (article 3); texts in *The Suez Canal Settlement* 48, 64 (Lauterpacht ed., 1960).

[49] For an able advocacy of the possible use of diplomatic protests even before the actual taking of the measures depriving an alien of his property or affecting his contract with a state, see Wortley, *Expropriation* 72–75; Wortley, "The Protection of Property Situated Abroad," 35 *Tulane L. Rev.* 739, 742–45 (1961).

12

Conclusions

WITHIN their limitations, guarantees to foreign investors can play a very useful role in promoting international investment in the underdeveloped countries. Their main significance is of a non-legal character. It lies in their providing an indication that a favorable attitude toward foreign investment prevails in the particular capital-importing state.[1] No country gives guarantees merely in order to defraud the investors, if only because it does not pay to do so even in the short run. The grant or offer of guarantees shows that the state concerned is conscious of its own need for private investment and of the foreign investors' desire for security. Such an attitude is in itself reassuring to the investors.

As has been shown in the preceding chapters, each form of guarantee has its own advantages and limitations. The latter are perhaps more prominent in the case of the proposed investment code; they seem to effectively outweigh the advantages of certainty and universality that a code would presumably possess. The existing difficulties are such that no satisfactory international code seems possible.

The investment guarantees provided by capital-exporting countries are of greater usefulness. They, too, have limitations, though

[1] This observation applies also to investment guarantees by capital-exporting states, since, in most cases, the grant of such guarantees is conditional upon the conclusion of a related international agreement with the state of investment. Such an agreement (and, in the case of the United States program, the assent of the capital-importing state to the insurance of the particular investment) is sufficient indication of a favorable attitude.

not all of them are necessary or unavoidable. Some other limitations, however, are inherent in this type of guarantee. They can cover a relatively small number of risks and there is little possibility for significant variations to serve the needs of each particular investment. They relate only to the future, in the sense that they insure against future changes of conditions, without directly affecting existing situations. Finally, despite the fact that their real role is far more complex,[2] they appear to the investor as providing insurance only, rather than assurance of fair treatment. Investors may find that such insurance is not adequate to protect their interests.

The two forms of guarantees which are most widely used and probably most effective are the investment treaties and the guarantees given by capital-importing countries by means of instruments of approval. The former are international instruments, binding upon the party states under public international law. The protection they guarantee is backed by the existing machinery of international law, such as it is. This advantage is, however, coupled with certain important drawbacks. The guarantees by treaty are necessarily general in character and abstract in language, so that, under certain conditions, differences of interpretation may greatly limit their effectiveness. Furthermore, the protection of the particular foreign investor depends on the willingness of his state of nationality to espouse his claim. The governments of capital-exporting states are not, it is true, as reluctant to do this as foreign investors often claim. Still, the requirement of espousal of the claim does bring in a number of considerations, political or other, which bear no relevance to the investment.

The content of the guarantees given by virtue of investment laws is as a rule well-determined; the guarantee refers in each case to a particular investment. Several difficulties of interpretation are thus eliminated or can be eliminated, though a few still remain. On the other hand, such guarantees lack the binding force of international treaties. And it has been submitted that, under present conditions,

[2] Cf. *supra* p. 64.

it is not possible to claim successfully that the violation of such guarantees is in fact a breach of public international law, save in certain rather exceptional circumstances. The effectiveness of these guarantees is therefore limited, despite their precision, by the fact that they are subject to an important extent to state action, on the part of the capital-importing state's government. The existence of a possibility of compensation is not always sufficient to reassure the prospective investors.

The effectiveness of guarantees also varies according to their particular content. A guarantee concerning repatriation of earnings will be effective under different conditions than a guarantee of nonexpropriation.[3] Moreover, in some cases there exist other methods of protection apart from guarantees, while in other cases the guarantees provide the only protection available to the investor.

In view of the above, it is clear that there exists today a need for all the forms of guarantees discussed in the present study, with the possible exception of the guarantees by international code, due to its probable lack of effectiveness. The other forms of guarantees are complementary to each other. Each of them has a certain function which it can perform better than the other forms, while on the other hand, it cannot perform certain other functions as well as some of the other forms.

Apart from their individual limitations, state guarantees to foreign investors also have certain other basic common limitations which should be taken into account in assessing their effectiveness.

In the first place, state guarantees relate, almost by definition, to the encouragement of private foreign investment. It is clear, however, that such investment today plays a secondary role in the development of the more backward countries. The role is still one of considerable importance, just how important depends on the stage of development of each particular economy; but it is not the central or the most important role, certainly far less so than it was a hun-

[3] Cf., e.g., *supra* pp. 344–47.

dred years ago.[4] The guarantees' importance is affected thereby and so is the willingness to grant such guarantees or extend existing ones, on the part of the governments of capital-importing states. The world political situation is such that they generally cannot be coerced into doing so against their will.

Second, it should be remembered that, even with respect to private foreign investment only, state guarantees are but one set of factors among a great number of others. By themselves, they cannot determine the existence, amount, or direction of international investment. When unfavorable, they may serve to prevent it; but the reverse is not equally true. When legal factors are favorable, they are not by themselves sufficient as investment incentives and they cannot attract foreign capital; other factors, as well, will have to favor investment in the country concerned. It is, therefore, no paradox that some countries offer guarantees of all forms without attracting foreign investors, while foreign capital is invested in others which do not offer such guarantees.

Moreover, no guarantee can today provide complete security, even from nonbusiness risks only. The lack of security of investments in foreign, and especially underdeveloped, countries is due to, and is a manifestation of, the general lack of stability in today's economic and political situation. It is not possible to provide complete security for investment where the underlying economic and political conditions are unstable. Legal means can be useful, since they provide some degree of relative security, but there are definite limits to their effectiveness.

Closely related to this point is the problem of the fate of legal guarantees in times of revolution. It is not possible to state that any of the guarantees here discussed are certain to survive a radical change in the guaranteeing country's general political, economic,

---

[4] Cf. *supra* pp. 59 *et seq.* And note the pessimistic conclusions of an eminent authority: "I am regretfully forced to the conclusion that foreign capital, in the absence of major changes in the international scene, will make but a marginal contribution to the capital needs of under-developed countries." Viner, *International Trade and Economic Development* 111 (1953).

and social structure. Survival is highly uncertain, though not impossible, since, even with regard to revolutions, there are degrees and stages which have to be taken into account. Still, it remains generally true that after or during a revolution little attention might be paid to formal guarantees made by a previous regime. It is not possible, however, to provide in law for a change which nullifies the existing law. It is in the case of a revolution or other radical change that one sees clearly what otherwise often remains in the background, namely, that it is the continuing community of interests between foreign investors and the capital-receiving state which provides the real basis for the investors' security.

Legal instruments and techniques cannot by themselves create such a community of interests where it does not exist; but, where it does exist, they can help to make its existence clearer and to protect it from hasty and arbitrary actions. They can also provide the methods through which the relationship between the parties will adapt itself successfully to changing conditions. Security cannot be found in the mere assertion of strict rules providing for the protection of foreign investors. This would be true even if the rules in question were well-established in the past, since conditions have by now changed significantly. Even more so, when the rules have never been clearly established and seem to have been accepted without protest only by those whose interests they serve. The statement of abstract general rules will tend to hamper rather than assist the development of an atmosphere of security, since it will necessarily focus attention on the occasional breach rather than on the more usual substantial compliance.

What is needed today is flexibility, adaptability to the changing circumstances. To this end, it is necessary to emphasize not the legal forms and relations but the concrete realities behind them. Legal concepts are relevant and meaningful only to the extent that they correspond to the economic and political facts in each situation. The problem of international investment is basically an economic problem, as well as a political one, to the extent that no serious world problem can avoid being political. Application of legal rules and concepts is of course necessary but not without a continuing awareness of the economic and political realities.[5] When state A restricts significantly its importation of a certain basic product from state B, this is no doubt an internationally lawful action and no legal rule has been infringed (in the absence, of course, of treaty or other special commitments). In retaliation, state B expropriates without compensation the property of state A's citizens within its territories. This is prima facie an internationally unlawful action (because of its discriminatory character, the denial of compensation being also unlawful by itself). In law, therefore, the quality of the actions of the two states is diametrically opposed, one being lawful and the other unlawful. In economic or political terms, however, it may well be that state A's action was far more detrimental to state B's interests than the latter state's action was to the interests of state A. This fact, of course, cannot by itself determine the legality of the respective actions of the two states, but should it be completely ignored when examining the legal aspects of the incident?

This is *ex hypothesi* a conflict between governments. Private persons are materially affected by the states' actions but there is little they can do to alter the course of events, which is presumably governed by political considerations only (though it may be that their impotence in this connection is sometimes exaggerated). It may still be true in some cases that where the community of interests between the foreign enterprise and the capital-importing state is powerful enough, the latter will be less liable to take measures against the enterprise. In the main, however, this is another situation where private persons, individuals or corporations, are caught in the middle and are made to pay for state actions in the

[5] It is obvious that the illustration that follows has been inspired by the recent events in the relations between Cuba and the United States. The case as here described, however, is only a hypothetical model; the surrounding political and non-political factors in the Cuban situation (as well as a number of other events) have been altered to fit present purposes.

inception of which they had no say. It is certainly not a unique situation, as it is sometimes made to appear. In peacetime as well as in war, the individual is often made to suffer because of conflicts between governments. Today, not only wars but peacetime conflicts as well tend to become "total." Moreover, the struggle for economic development in the underdeveloped areas is akin to war. It is to them as vital and as urgent as any armed conflict. Historically, as well, their drive toward economic development is a continuation of their liberation struggles.[6]

Where the main conflict arises between a foreign enterprise and the host state, different considerations obtain. It is in such cases that one expects the modern giant corporations to show some of the flexibility and adaptability which has been at the foundation of their economic success. They should realize the grave difficulties which the local governments are facing and tolerate (or perhaps resign themselves to) a certain amount of inefficiency in the operation of the host country's administrative machinery. What is basically needed on the investors' part is an awareness of the fact that their profits and the continuation of the operation of their enterprise depend not on an initial "good bargain" but on a continuing contribution to the welfare of the country of investment. In spite of official pronouncements on either side, such an awareness is not absent in fact in the great majority of cases; the recent increase in private foreign investment in underdeveloped areas is, at least in part, attributable to it.

[6] In discussing the lawfulness of the Indonesian expropriations of Dutch enterprises, a German Court of Appeals pointed out that the nonpayment of compensation "may be objected to in case of individual expropriations of the usual kind and may then be contrary to the rules of international law. Here, however, the expropriation of the Dutch companies constitutes at the same time a shifting of proprietary relations which was effected by a former colony after its independence, in order to change the social structure. The opinion has often been advanced recently and not without reason, that by the nature of the matter alone, the same principles cannot prevail for such overall expropriations and for individual expropriations of the conventional type. . . . Thus the long-standing principle of strong protection of private property clashes here with the modern concept that underdeveloped countries must be given the possibility of using their own natural resources." Quoted in Domke, "Indonesian Nationalization Measures before Foreign Courts," 54 *Am. J. Int'l L.* 305, at 317 (1960).

The international jurist's urgent task today is not the statement of new rules but the search for solutions of concrete problems as well as for methods by which future problems might be resolved or avoided. Such solutions and methods will necessarily be largely of a political character. It is the parties themselves, governments and private investors, as well as third parties acting as conciliators, rather than impartial judges that will develop the international law relating to foreign investment. No need to decry such predominance of, and reliance on, political and generally nonlegal elements in international law. In municipal law, as well, it is not the judiciary but Parliament or Congress which is entrusted with legislation. The latter are political bodies and their criteria are necessarily political ones. The need for political, rather than solely legal, wisdom is perhaps greater in international than in municipal law; international legal rules are generally less certain than those of municipal law, the judicial structure is far less developed and the importance of each "individual" state is far greater than that of each citizen in municipal law.

Awareness of political factors in no way implies disregard or underestimation of the role of law, in general, and international law, in particular. Indeed, it would rather enhance its importance, since it would tend to make it more effective. Law has a very important function to perform in connection with the economic development of underdeveloped areas, but if this is to be a creative function, it is necessary that in each case the concrete content and effect of the legal rules involved should be examined, not only their formal validity or logical appropriateness. Strict abstract rules should therefore be avoided. Equitable general principles should rather be used, for they would be more adaptable to changing conditions and situations.[7] Following the lead of successful diplomats, jurists should not allow themselves to be trapped in "either/or" positions. They

[7] The development of a "transnational law," as discussed *supra* pp. 283–301, is part of the movement in this direction. Other developments take place within the context of public international law *stricto sensu;* e.g. the development of non-judicial procedures for the settlement of disputes relating to certain economic matters; cf. *supra* Chapter 8, note 28.

should be able to offer a variety of solutions to fit each particular case without relying solely on judicial proceedings. There is today ground for development of extrajudicial procedures which would lead to settlements of disputes through recognition and utilization of the economic and political factors operative in each case.

The operation of the international financial agencies provides perhaps the best available example. The World Bank and its affiliates are financial agencies with a definite political function. They have been able to operate with a fair degree of success, because they have moved not on a single plane, say that of financial transactions and relations, but on several planes at the same time, making use of political, economic, or legal tools. With few exceptions, they have avoided putting themselves in situations where they would have to choose between two opposed directions, managing more often than not to find some half-way point which would satisfy the parties involved. Instead of censuring, they have advised and by so doing they have on occasion succeeded in affecting the particular state policies with which they were concerned.[8]

The fact that most recent investment disputes have been settled by political rather than by judicial means is highly significant. Such settlements have reached widely varying solutions. The postwar nationalizations in Eastern and Central Europe resulted in the conclusion of agreements between the nationalizing states and the states of nationality of the investors providing for lump-sum compensations. The nationalization of the oil industry in Iran resulted in a new arrangement which, despite differences in detail, is not basically different from the earlier one and may indeed be more accurately described as a modification of it. The Suez Canal nationalization, on the other hand, was settled by a compensation agreement between the nationalizing state and the shareholders of the nationalized company. It is not the legal relationships between the parties that were different in each case but the political and economic realities behind them. The latter, not the former, were found controlling in arriving at a settlement.

[8] Cf. *supra* pp. 351–53.

Legal guarantees to foreign investors are peculiarly appropriate in developing a flexible and adaptable body of law. The instruments of approval issued by capital-importing states by virtue of investment laws have already been described as instruments designed to promote further collaboration between the state and the investor rather than strictly enforceable legal documents.[9] The same is true, though perhaps in a different sense, with respect to investment treaties. Both these forms of guarantees are chiefly useful in that they provide inducements and procedures for consultation and for the solution of future problems by cooperation rather than by adversary proceedings. Neither are state guarantees necessarily limited to the forms already in use and discussed in this study. New forms and combinations are both possible and desirable.

Legal guarantees may also play an important part in promoting a "renaissance" of indirect foreign investment. Such investment is today of secondary importance, almost insignificant as far as the underdeveloped countries are concerned.[10] It is improbable that portfolio investment, in its earlier forms, will develop sufficiently to assist the underdeveloped countries. New forms of indirect investment are, however, possible, perhaps through association with public capital or through assumption of a limited degree of control over the enterprise involved. The operations of the International Finance Corporation or the involvement of firms from the advanced countries in the establishment of industries in underdeveloped areas through "management contracts" are cases in point.[11] State guarantees could help greatly by assuring a minimum of security and by assisting in the development of new forms of indirect investment.

[9] Cf. *supra* p. 351, note 31. [10] Cf. *supra* pp. 23, 26.
[11] See on this question, "The Promotion of the International Flow of Private Capital," UN Document E/3492, 18 May 1961, Chapter I, on "contractual devices for the channelling of technical and managerial know-how from enterprises in industrialized countries into enterprises in under-developed countries," (prepared by Professor R. C. Pugh.)

Selected Bibliography

THE present bibliography covers studies relating to the obstacles, incentives and guarantees to private foreign investment in underdeveloped countries. A limited number of works dealing with some more general aspects of the subject have also been included. To provide some guidance to the reader without unduly complicating the bibliography by divisions into sections and subsections, a key indicating the particular aspects to which each title chiefly relates has been provided. The letter (or letters) to the left of each entry refers to the topics listed below.

A Problems of Economic Development
B Public International Investment
C Private International Investment
D General Surveys of Obstacles and Incentives to Private Foreign Investment
E Regulation of Entry, Ownership and Personnel of Foreign Enterprises
F Exchange Control and the Repatriation of Capital and Earnings
G Taxation as an Obstacle and as an Incentive
H Expropriation: Recent Practice
I Expropriation: Problems of International Law
J International Investment Code Proposals
K Investment Treaties
L Guarantees by Capital-Exporting Countries
M Investment Laws in Capital-Importing Countries
N Concessions and State Contracts: Legal Character, Applicable Law, and Settlement of Related Disputes

J Abs, Hermann J., "The Protection of Duly Acquired Rights in International Dealings as a European Duty," in Society to Advance the Protection of Foreign Investment, *Foundation and Purpose* 51 (1956).
J —— "The Safety of Capital," in J. Daniel, ed., *Private Investment: The Key to International Industrial Development* 69 (New York, 1958).
D Advisory Committee on Overseas Investment, *Report*. Ottawa, 1951.

A   Agarwala, A. N., and S. P. Singh, eds., *The Economics of Under-development*. Bombay, 1958.

G   Albrecht, A. R., "The Taxation of Aliens under International Law," 29 *Brit. Yb. Int'l L.* 145 (1952).

DM Alexander, C. H., "Foreign Investment Laws and Regulations of the Countries of Asia and the Far East," 1 *Int'l & Comp. L. Qu.* 29 (1952).

H   Allison, Richard C., "Cuba's Seizures of American Business," 47 *Am. Bar Ass'n J.* 48, 187 (1961).

G   Allix, Edgard, "La condition des étrangers au point de vue fiscal," 61 *Hague Recueil* 541 (1937).

G   American Management Association, International Management Division, *The Taxation of Business Income from Foreign Operations: Studies in U.S., Foreign and International Tax Law*. New York, 1958.

I   Anderson, Chandler P., "Basis of the Law Against Confiscating Foreign-Owned Property," 21 *Am. J. Int'l L.* 525 (1927).

B   Asher, Robert E., *Grants, Loans, and Local Currencies: Their Role in Foreign Aid*. Washington, D.C., 1961.

A   Aubrey, Henry G., "The Role of the State in Economic Development," 41 *Am. Econ. Rev. Proc.* 266 (1951).

AB Aubrey, Henry G., assisted by Joel Darmstadter, *Coexistence: Economic Challenge and Response*. Washington, D.C., 1961.

DM Baade, Hans W., *Gesetzgebung zur Förderung ausländischer Kapitalanlagen*. Frankfurt-am-Main, 1957.

HI —— "Indonesian Nationalization Measures before Foreign Courts—A Reply," 54 *Am. J. Int'l L.* 801 (1960).

GM Baer, W., "Puerto-Rico: An Evaluation of a Successful Development Program," 73 *Qu. J. Econ.* 645 (1959).

I   Bagge, Alcot, "Intervention on the Ground of Damage Caused to Nationals, With Particular Reference to Exhaustion of Local Remedies and the Rights of Shareholders," 34 *Brit. Yb. Int'l L.* 162 (1958).

GM Baker, Robert M., "Puerto Rico's Program of Industrial Tax Exemption," 18 *Geo. Wash. L. Rev.* 327, 443 (1950).

GM —— "Tax Exemptions as a Means of Attracting Industry," 20 *Geo. Wash. L. Rev.* 253 (1952).

GM Baker, Robert M., and James E. Curry, "Taxpayer's Paradise in the Caribbean," 1 *Vand. L. Rev.* 194 (1948).

A   Balandier, Georges, "Sociologie des régions sous-développées," in 1 G. Gurvitch, ed., *Traité de Sociologie* 332 (Paris, 1958).

A   Baran, Paul A., *The Political Economy of Growth*. New York, 1957.

G   Barlow, E. R., and Ira T. Wender, *Foreign Investment and Taxation*. New York, 1955.

G — *United States Tax Incentives to Direct Private Foreign Investment.* New York, 1954.

A Bauer, P. T., and Basil S. Yamey, *The Economics of Underdeveloped Countries.* Cambridge, Eng., 1957.

IJ Beale, W. T. M., Remarks before the 1958 Investment Law Conference, 39 *Dep't State Bull.* 967 (1958).

I Becker, Loftus, "Just Compensation in Expropriation Cases: Decline and Partial Recovery," 40 *Dep't State Bull.* 784 (1959), 53 *Am. Soc. Int'l L. Proc.* 336 (1959).

B Berliner, Joseph S., *Soviet Economic Aid: The New Aid and Trade Policy in Underdeveloped Countries.* New York, 1958.

I Bindschedler, Rudolf L., "La protection de la propriété privée en droit international public," 90 *Hague Recueil* 173 (1956).

G Bittker, Boris I., and Lawrence F. Ebb, *Taxation of Foreign Income.* Stanford, 1960.

H Bliss, Brian, "Nationalization in France and Great Britain of the Electricity Supply Industry," 3 *Int'l & Comp. L. Qu.* 277 (1954).

E Bonsal, Dudley B., and Milo A. Borges, "Limitations Abroad on Enterprises and Property Acquisition," 11 *Law & Contemp. Problems* 720 (1946).

IN Borchard, Edwin M., *The Diplomatic Protection of Citizens Abroad or the Law of International Claims.* New York, 1915.

I —— "Protection of Foreign Investments," 11 *Law & Contemp. Problems* 835 (1946).

E Borges, Milo A., "Labor Relations in Latin America," 17 *Ohio St. L.J.* 290 (1956).

J Boyle, D. A. V., "Some Proposals for a World Investment Convention," 1961 *J. Bus. L.* 18, 155.

ABCD Brand, W., *The Struggle for a Higher Standard of Living. The Problem of the Underdeveloped Countries.* Glencoe, Ill. and The Hague, 1958.

J Brandon, Michael, "An International Investment Code: Current Plans," 1959 *J. Bus. L.* 7.

DEFI —— "Legal Aspects of Private Foreign Investments," 18 *Fed. Bar J.* 298 (1958).

DEFI —— "Legal Deterrents and Incentives to Private Foreign Investments," 43 *Grotius Soc. Transactions* 39 (1957).

I —— "Nationalization Before the United Nations," in International Bar Association, *Fifth International Conference of the Legal Profession, Monte Carlo, 1954* 38 (The Hague, 1954) (separate print).

J —— "Recent Measures to Improve the International Investment Climate," 9 *J. Pub. L.* 125 (1960).

I —— "The Record in the United Nations of Member States on Nationalization, 1951–1955," Report Submitted to the International Law Association (48th Conference, New York, 1958) (mimeo.).

H   "British Nationalization of Industry—Compensation to Owners of Expropriated Property," 97 *U. Pa. L. Rev.* 520 (1949).

AI   Bronfenbrenner, M., "The Appeal of Confiscation in Economic Development," 3 *Economic Development and Cultural Change* 201 (1955).

GKL   Brown, William A., "Treaty, Guaranty and Tax Inducements for Foreign Investment," 40 *Am. Econ. Rev. Proc.* 486 (1950).

B   Brown, William A., and Redvers Opie, *American Foreign Assistance.* Washington, D.C., 1953.

ABC   Buchanan, Norman S., and Howard S. Ellis, *Approaches to Economic Development.* New York, 1955.

I   Bullington, John P., "Problems of International Law in the Mexican Constitution of 1917," 21 *Am. J. Int'l L.* 685 (1927).

H   Cahen-Salvador, Jean, "La régie nationale des usines Renault," 8 *Droit Social* 208 (1945).

H   Cairns, Mary Bell, "Some Legal Aspects of Compensation for Nationalized Assets," 16 *Law & Contemp. Problems* 594 (1951).

N   Calvert, H. G., "The Law Applicable to Concessions," 1 *U. Malaya L. Rev.* 265 (1959).

IN   Carlston, Kenneth S., "Concession Agreements and Nationalization," 52 *Am. J. Int'l L.* 260 (1958).

F   —— "Import and Export Controls," 11 *Law & Contemp. Problems* 794 (1946).

N   —— "International Role of Concession Agreements," 52 *Nw. U.L. Rev.* 618 (1957).

IN   —— "Nationalism, Nationalization and International Law," 7 *Rev. Dr. Int'l Moyen-Orient* 1 (1958).

IN   —— "Nationalization: An Analytical Approach," 54 *Nw. U.L. Rev.* 405 (1959).

G   Carroll, M. B., "Tax Inducements to Foreign Trade," 11 *Law & Contemp. Problems* 760 (1946).

IN   Cavaré, Louis, *La protection des droits contractuels reconnus par les Etats à des étrangers à l'exception des emprunts.* Barcelona, 1956.

H   Celier, Charles, "Quelques données historiques du problème des nationalisations," 8 *Droit Social* 94 (1945).

I   Chargueraud-Hartmann, P., "Les interêts étrangers et la nationalisation," 1 *Etudes Internationales* (Haarlem and Brussels) 331 (1948).

H   Cheng, Bin, "The Anglo-Iranian Dispute," 5 (n. s.) *World Affairs* 387 (1951).

I   —— "Expropriation in International Law," 21 *Solicitor* 98 (1954).

IN   —— *General Principles of Law as Applied by International Courts and Tribunals.* London, 1953.

I —— "The Rationale of Compensation for Expropriation," 44 *Grotius Soc. Transactions* 267 (1959).

G Chrétien, Maxime, *A la recherche du droit international fiscal commun.* Paris, 1955.

G —— "Contribution à l'étude du droit international fiscal actuel: le rôle des organisations internationales dans le règlement des questions d'impôts entre divers états," 86 *Hague Recueil* 1 (1954).

G —— "Le problème des réglements juridictionnels des litiges internationaux d'ordre fiscal," 78 *J. Droit Int'l* (Clunet) 30, 508 (1951).

H Christenson, Gordon A., "The United States-Rumanian Claims Settlement Agreement of March 30, 1960," 55 *Am. J. Int'l L.* 617 (1961).

I Clay, H. J., "Recent Developments in the Protection of American Shareholders' Interests in Foreign Corporations," 45 *Georgetown L.J.* 1 (1956).

C Collado, Emilio G., and J. F. Bennett, "Foreign Investment and Economic Development," 35 *Foreign Affairs* 631 (1957).

C Committee for Economic Development, *Economic Development Abroad and the Role of American Foreign Investment.* New York, 1956.

N Corbett, Percy E., "The Search for General Principles of Law," 47 *Va. L. Rev.* 811 (1961).

CDE Coudert, Alexis, and A. Lans, "Direct Foreign Investment in Undeveloped Countries: Some Practical Problems," 11 *Law & Contemp. Problems* 741 (1946).

DE Crawford, Henry Paine, "Going into Business in Latin America," in Washington Foreign Law Society, *A Symposium on the Law of Latin America* 25 (Washington, D.C., 1959).

MN Cutler, Lloyd N., Address, in 1 American Society of International Law, *Investment Law Conference* 10 (mimeo., 1956).

B —— "U.S. Government as a Source of Capital for Private Investment Abroad," in Southwestern Legal Foundation, *Proceedings of the 1959 Institute on Private Investments Abroad* 209 (1959).

GI Dach, Joseph, and Nicholas Ujlaki, "Tax Aspects of Foreign Confiscations," 21 *Geo. Wash. L. Rev.* 445 (1953).

CD Daniel, James, ed., *Private Investment: The Key to International Industrial Development.* New York, 1958.

B Delaume, Georges R., "International Machinery for Financing Economic Development," 38 *Geo. Wash. L. Rev.* 533 (1960).

HI Delson, Robert, "Nationalization of the Suez Canal Company: Issues of Public and Private International Law," 57 *Colum. L. Rev.* 755 (1957).

N Develle, Philippe, *La concession en droit international.* Paris, 1936.

H DeVries, Henry P., and Berthold H. Hoeniger, "Post-Liberation Nationalizations in France," 50 *Colum. L. Rev.* 629 (1950).

CD Diamond, William, "Economic Problems in Foreign Trade and Investment in Underdeveloped Countries," 17 *Ohio St. L.J.* 254 (1956).

I Dietze, Gottfried, "The Disregard for Property in International Law," 56 *Nw. U. L. Rev.* 87 (1961).

C Dillon, C. Douglas, "United States Foreign Trade and Investment Policies," in P. O. Proehl, ed., *Legal Problems of International Trade* 107 (Urbana, Ill., 1959).

HI Doman, Nicholas, "Compensation for Nationalized Property in Post-War Europe," 3 *Int'l & Comp. L. Qu.* 323 (1950).

HI —— "Postwar Nationalization of Foreign Property in Europe," 48 *Colum. L. Rev.* 1125 (1948).

I Domke, Martin, "American Protection Against Foreign Expropriation in the Light of the Suez Canal Crisis," 105 *U. Pa. L. Rev.* 1033 (1957).

I —— "Foreign Nationalizations—Some Aspects of Contemporary International Law," 55 *Am. J. Int'l L.* 585 (1961).

HI —— "Indonesian Nationalization Measures before Foreign Courts," 54 *Am. J. Int'l L.* 305 (1960).

N —— "International Arbitration of Commercial Disputes," in Southwestern Legal Foundation, *Proceedings of the 1960 Institute on Private Investments Abroad* 131 (New York, 1960).

I —— "On the Nationalization of Foreign Shareholders' Interests," 4 *New York Law Forum* 46 (1958).

N —— "The Settlement of International Investment Disputes," in 1 American Society of International Law, *Investment Law Conference* 22 (mimeo., 1956).

N Domke, Martin, ed., *International Trade Arbitration: A Road to World-Wide Cooperation.* New York, 1958.

J "Draft Convention on Investments Abroad," 9 *J. Pub. L.* 116 (1960).

H Drucker, Alfred, "Compensation for Nationalized Property: The British Practice," 49 *Am. J. Int'l L.* 477 (1955).

H —— "Compensation Treaties between Communist States," 10 *Int'l & Comp. L. Qu.* 238 (1961).

I —— "Edmund Burke's View on Expropriation," 228 *Law Times* 85 (1959).

H —— "The Nationalization of United Nations Property in Europe," 36 *Grotius Soc. Transactions* 75 (1950).

H —— "On Compensation Treaties between Communist States," 229 *Law Times* 279, 293 (1960).

I Dunn, Frederick S., "International Law and Private Property Rights," 28 *Colum. L. Rev.* 166 (1928).

I —— *The Protection of Nationals: A Study in the Application of International Law.* Baltimore, 1932.

N Durand, Claude, "L'imprévision dans les contrats internationaux de concession d'après la jurisprudence internationale," 19 *Travaux juridiques et économiques de l'Université de Rennes* 63 (1956).

IN Eagleton, Clyde, *The Responsibility of States in International Law.* New York, 1928.

E Eder, Phanor J., "Some Restrictions Abroad Affecting Corporations," 11 *Law & Contemp. Problems* 713 (1946).

G Einaudi, Luigi, "La coopération internationale en matière fiscale," 25 *Hague Recueil* 5 (1928).

H Einaudi, Mario, "Nationalization in France and Italy," 15 *Social Research* 22 (1948).

H Einaudi, Mario, Maurice Byé, and Ernesto Rossi, *Nationalization in France and Italy.* Ithaca, N.Y., 1955.

CD Elliot, W. Y., and associates, *The Political Economy of American Foreign Policy: Its Concepts, Strategy and Limits.* New York, 1955.

ABC Ellis, Howard S., ed., assisted by Henry C. Wallich, *Economic Development for Latin America.* New York, 1961.

J European League for Economic Cooperation, *Common Protection for Private International Investments.* Brussels, 1958.

I "Expropriation of Alien Property," 109 *U. Pa. L. Rev.* 245 (1960).

H Fabre, Robert, "Les houillères du Nord et du Pas de Calais avant la nationalisation," 8 *Droit Social* 138 (1945).

I Fachiri, Alexander P., "Expropriation and International Law," 6 *Brit. Yb. Int'l L.* 159 (1925).

I —— "International Law and the Property of Aliens," 27 *Brit. Yb. Int'l L.* 32 (1929).

N Farmanfarma, Abolbashar, "The Oil Agreement between Iran and the International Oil Consortium: the Law Controlling," 34 *Texas L. Rev.* 259 (1955).

J Fatouros, A. A., "An International Code to Protect Private Investment —Proposals and Perspectives," 14 *U. Toronto L.J.* 77 (1961).

D —— "Obstacles to Private Foreign Investment in Underdeveloped Countries," 2 *Current Law and Social Problems* 194 (1961).

N Fawcett, J. E. S., "The Legal Character of International Agreements," 30 *Brit. Yb. Int'l L.* 381 (1953).

I —— "Some Foreign Effects of Nationalization of Property," 27 *Brit. Yb. Int'l L.* 355 (1950).

D Fayerweather, John, "Lawyers, Foreign Governments and Business Abroad," 44 *Va. L. Rev.* 185 (1958).

I Foighel, Isi, *Nationalization: A Study in the Protection of Alien Property in International Law.* Copenhagen, 1957.

J Folsom, Victor, "The Code of Fair Treatment for Foreign Investors," in 2 American Society of International Law, *Investment Law Conference* (mimeo., 1958).

HI Ford, Alan W., *The Anglo-Iranian Oil Dispute of 1951–52: A Study of the Role of Law in the Relations of States*. Berkeley and Los Angeles, 1954.

I "Foreign Seizure of Investments: Remedies and Protection," 12 *Stanford L. Rev.* 606 (1960).

K Foster, Austin T., "Some Aspects of the Commercial Treaty Program of the United States—Past and Present," 11 *Law & Contemp. Problems* 647 (1946).

I Friedman, S., *L'expropriation en droit international public*. Cairo, 1950.

I —— *Expropriation in International Law*. London, 1953.

D Friedmann, Wolfgang G., "Legal Problems in Foreign Investments," 14 *The Business Lawyer* 746 (1959).

D —— "The Role of Government in Foreign Investment," in 2 American Society of International Law, *Investment Law Conference* (mimeo., 1958).

I —— "Some Impacts of Social Organization on International Law," 50 *Am. J. Int'l L.* 475 (1956).

CD Friedmann, Wolfgang G., and George Kalmanoff, eds., *Joint International Business Ventures*. New York, 1961.

D Friedmann, Wolfgang G., and Richard C. Pugh, eds., *Legal Aspects of Foreign Investment*. Boston, 1959.

J Fulton, J. G., Address, 52 *Am. Soc. Int'l L. Proc.* 200 (1958).

A Furtado, Celso, "Capital Formation and Economic Development," 4 *International Economic Papers* 124 (1954).

H Gaither, Roscoe B., *Expropriation in Mexico: The Facts and the Law*. New York, 1940.

AD Galbraith, John Kenneth, "Conditions for Economic Change in Underdeveloped Countries," 33 *J. Farm Econ.* 689 (1951).

AD —— "Developed Economic Attitudes and the Underdeveloped Economy," 9 *Public Policy* 73 (1959).

DMN Galvin, Charles O., "Comments on the Oil and Gas Entrepreneur and Mineral Concessions in Latin America," 52 *Am. Soc. Int'l L. Proc.* 217 (1958).

IN Garcia Amador, Francisco V., "Responsibility of the State for Injuries Caused in Its Territory to the Person or Property of Aliens: Measures Affecting Acquired Rights" (Fourth Report to the International Law Commission), 1959-II *Yearbook of the International Law Commission* 1 (1960).

I —— "State Responsibility: Some New Problems," 94 *Hague Recueil* 365 (1958).

J Gardner, Richard N., "International Measures for the Promotion and

Protection of Foreign Investment," 53 *Am. Soc. Int'l L. Proc.* 255 (1959), 9 *J. Pub. L.* 176 (1960).

D Gaston, J. Frank, ed., *Obstacles to Direct Foreign Investment.* National Industrial Conference Board, New York, 1951.

HI Ghosh, S. K., *The Anglo-Iranian Oil Dispute. A Study of Problems of Nationalization of Foreign Investment and Their Impact on International Law.* Calcutta, 1960.

HI Gihl, Torsten, "Two Cases Concerning Confiscation of Foreign Property," in *Liber Amicorum of Congratulations to Alcot Bagge* 56 (Stockholm, 1956).

F Goldstein, Mortimer D., "Progress in Currency Convertibility and Its Significance for Trade and Investment," in Southwestern Legal Foundation, *Proceedings of the 1959 Institute on Private Investments Abroad* 165 (New York, 1959).

G Gordon, Nathan N., "Some Aspects of United States Policy in the Taxation of Foreign Income," in P. O. Proehl, ed., *Legal Problems of International Trade* 222 (Urbana, Ill., 1959).

H Gordon, Wendell C., *The Expropriation of Foreign-Owned Property in Mexico.* Washington, D.C., 1941.

L "Government Guaranties of Foreign Investment," 66 *Harv. L. Rev.* 514 (1953).

G Griziotti, Benvenuto, "L'imposition fiscale des étrangers," 13 *Hague Recueil* 5 (1926).

N Guldberg, Tatiana, "International Concessions, A Problem of International Economic Law," 15 *Acta Scandinavica Juris Gentium* 47 (1944); 25 *idem* 18 (1955).

H Gutteridge, Joyce A. C., "Expropriation and Nationalization in Hungary, Bulgaria and Roumania," 1 *Int'l & Comp. L. Qu.* 14 (1952).

N Haight, George W., "American Foreign Trade and Investment Disputes," 14 *Arbitr. J.* 73 (1959).

H Hamel, Joseph, "Le nouveau statut professionnel des banques françaises," 9 *Droit Social* 310, 349 (1946).

F Hamel, J., A. Bertrand, and R. Roblot, *Le contrôle des changes: ses répercussions sur les institutions juridiques.* Paris, 1955.

IN Harvard Law School, "Draft Convention on the International Responsibility of States for Injuries to Aliens," 55 *Am. J. Int'l L.* 548 (1961).

IN Harvard Law School, Research in International Law, "Draft Convention on Responsibility of States," 23 *Am. J. Int'l L. Sp. Supp.* 131 (1929).

G Harvard Law School, World Tax Series, *Taxation in Brazil.* Boston, 1957.

G —— *Taxation in India.* Boston, 1960.

G   —— *Taxation in Mexico*. Boston, 1957.

K   Hawkins, Harry C., *Commercial Treaties and Agreements: Principles and Practice*. New York, 1951.

A   Hazlewood, Arthur, compiler, *The Economics of "Under-Developed" Areas: An Annotated Reading List of Books, Articles and Official Publications*. 2d rev. ed., London, 1959.

H   Herman, S., "War Damage and Nationalization in Eastern Europe," 16 *Law & Contemp. Problems* 498 (1951).

I   Herz, John H., "Expropriation of Foreign Property," 35 *Am. J. Int'l L.* 243 (1941).

ABCD   Higgins, Benjamin H., *Economic Development: Principles, Problems and Policies*. New York, 1959.

I   Hornsey, G., "Foreign Investment and International Law," 3 *Int'l L. Qu.* 552 (1950).

A   Hoselitz, Bert F., ed., *The Progress of Underdeveloped Areas*. Chicago, 1952.

HI   Hoveyda, Fereydoun, "Les aspects juridiques de la nationalisation des industries pétrolières en Iran," 1 *Rev. Dr. Int'l Moyen-Orient* 127 (1951–1952).

HI   Huang, Thomas T. F., "Some International and Legal Aspects of the Suez Canal Question," 51 *Am. J. Int'l L.* 277 (1957).

F   Hug, Walther, "The Law of International Payments," 79 *Hague Recueil* 511 (1951).

BD   Hutcheson, Harold H., "Government and Capital in Point Four," 25 *Foreign Policy Reports* 66 (1949).

I   Hyde, James N., "The Exportation of Private Capital and Some Observations About Nationalization," in International Bar Association, *Fifth International Conference of the Legal Profession, Monte Carlo, 1954* (mimeo.).

IN   —— "Permanent Sovereignty over Natural Wealth and Resources," 50 *Am. J. Int'l L.* 854 (1956).

J   International Chamber of Commerce, *Fair Treatment for Foreign Investments: International Code* (ICC Brochure 129). Paris, 1949.

I   International Law Association, American Branch, Committee on the Study of Nationalization, "Nationalization of the Property of Aliens," 13 *Record of N.Y.C. Bar Ass'n* 367 (1958).

I   International Law Association, Netherlands Branch, "The Legal Effects of Nationalizations Enacted by Foreign States," in International Law Association, *Forty-Eighth Conference Report* 213 (London, 1959).

EK   "International Law—Reservations to Commercial Treaties Dealing with Aliens' Rights to Engage in the Professions," 52 *Mich. L. Rev.* 1184 (1954).

N   Jessup, Philip C., *Transnational Law*. New Haven, 1956.

I Jones, J. Mervyn, "Claims on Behalf of Nationals who Are Share-holders in Foreign Companies," 26 *Brit. Yb. Int'l L.* 225 (1949).

I Joseph, Franz Martin, "International Aspects of Nationalization—An Outline," in International Bar Association, *Fifth International Conference of the Legal Profession, Monte Carlo, 1954* 1 (The Hague, 1954) (separate print).

H Julliot de la Morandière, L., and Maurice Byé, eds. *Les nationalisations en France et à l'étranger. I: Les nationalisations en France.* Paris, 1948.

I Kaeckenbeeck, Georges, "La protection internationale des droits acquis," 59 *Hague Recueil* 317 (1937).

I —— "The Protection of Vested Rights in International Law," 17 *Brit. Yb. Int'l L.* 1 (1936).

D Katz, Milton, and Kingman Brewster, *The Law of International Transactions and Relations: Cases and Materials.* Brooklyn, 1960.

I Katzarov, Konstantin, "L'ordre public international et les nationalisations," 22 *Revue Internationale Française du Droit des Gens* 13 (1957).

I —— "Private Property and Public International Law," 84 *J. Droit Int'l* (Clunet) 6 (1957).

I —— *Théorie de la Nationalisation.* Neuchatel, 1960.

I —— "The Validity of the Act of Nationalisation in International Law," 22 *Modern Law Review* 639 (1959).

H Kazemi, Parviz, "Nationalization of the Oil Industry in Iran," in International Bar Association, *Fifth International Conference of the Legal Profession, Monte Carlo, 1954* 79 (The Hague, 1954) (separate print).

D Kelso, R. Charles, "Check List of Legal Problems in Considering Foreign Investment," in P. O. Proehl, ed., *Legal Problems of International Trade* 416 (Urbana, Ill., 1959).

A Kindleberger, Charles P., *Economic Development.* New York, 1958.

IN Kissam, Leo T., and Edmond K. Leach, "Sovereign Expropriation of Property and Abrogation of Concession Contracts," 28 *Fordham L. Rev* 177 (1959).

I Kollewijn, R. D., " 'Nationalization' Without Compensation and the Transfer of Property," 6 *Ned. Tijdschrift voor Int. Recht* 140 (1959).

H Kraus, Alfred, "La nationalisation de l'industrie en Pologne," 10 *Droit Social* 131 (1947).

I Kuhn, Arthur K., "Nationalization of Foreign-Owned Property in Its Impact on International Law," 45 *Am. J. Int'l L.* 709 (1951).

HI Kunz, Josef, "The Mexican Expropriations," 17 *N.Y.U.L. Qu. Rev.* 327 (1940).

G Kust, Matthew J., "United States Tax Concessions for American

Private Enterprise Abroad," in Southwestern Legal Foundation, *Proceedings of the 1959 Institute on Private Investments Abroad* 145 (New York, 1959).

AD Lacoste, Yves, *Les pays sous-développés.* Paris, 1959.

M Lambadarios, Constantine E., "Protection accordée par le décret 2687/1953 aux investissements à longue échéance de capitaux venant de l'étranger," 7 *Rev. Hell. Dr. Int'l* 219 (1954).

J Larson, Arthur, "Recipients' Rights under an International Investment Code," 9 *J. Pub. L.* 172 (1960).

I LaPradelle, A. de, "Les effets internationaux des nationalisations," in 43-I *Annuaire de l'Institut de Droit International* 42 (1950).

H Lauterpacht, Eli, ed., *The Suez Canal Settlement.* London, 1960.

D League of Nations, Special Joint Committee on Private Foreign Investment, *Conditions of Private Foreign Investment.* Princeton, 1946.

J Lee, Edward G., "Proposal for the Alleviation of the Effects of Foreign Expropriatory Decrees upon International Investments," 36 *Can. Bar Rev.* 351 (1958).

CD Lewis, Cleona, *The United States and Foreign Investment Problems.* Washington, D.C., 1948.

HI Lissitzyn, Oliver J., "Iranian Oil, Foreign Investments and the Law," 2 *Foreign Affairs Reports* (Delhi) 17 (1953).

I —— "The Meaning of the Term Denial of Justice in International Law," 30 *Am. J. Int'l L.* 632 (1936).

DM Littell, Norman M., "Encouragement and Obstruction to Private Investment in Foreign Investment Laws," 52 *Am. Soc. Int'l L. Proc.* 209 (1958).

DM —— "Improvements in Legal Climate for Investments Abroad," 38 *Va. L. Rev.* 729 (1952).

DEM —— "The International Investment of Private Capital—Opportunities and Problems: Legal Incentives for Private Investment Abroad," 40 *Va. L. Rev.* 977 (1954).

DEM —— "Obstructions to Private Investment Abroad," 36 *Va. L. Rev.* 873 (1950).

H Loiseau, P., *L'indemnisation des entreprises électriques et gazières nationalisées.* Paris, 1950.

H Lyon-Caen, Gérard, "Les diverses formules de nationalisation," 8 *Droit Social* 41 (1945).

H —— "Les nationalisations en Grande-Bretagne," 9 *Droit Social* 403 (1946).

N McNair, Arnold D., "The General Principles of Law Recognized by Civilized Nations," 33 *Brit. Yb. Int'l L.* 1 (1957).

I —— "The Seizure of Property and Enterprises in Indonesia," 6 *Ned. Tijdschrift voor Int. Recht* 218 (1959).

I Malik, Ch., "The New International Law: Nationalization and Partnership," 45 *Am. Bar Ass'n J.* 458 (1959).

N Mann, F. A., "The Law Governing State Contracts," 21 *Brit. Yb. Int'l L.* 11 (1944).

HI —— "Outlines of a History of Expropriation," 75 *L. Qu. Rev.* 188 (1959).

N —— "The Proper Law of Contracts Concluded by International Persons," 35 *Brit. Yb. Int'l L.* 34 (1959).

N —— "Reflections on a Commercial Law of Nations," 33 *Brit. Yb. Int'l L.* 20 (1957).

N —— "State Contracts and State Responsibility," 54 *Am. J. Int'l L.* 572 (1960).

F Marshall, Jorge, "Exchange Controls and Economic Development," in H. S. Ellis and H. C. Wallich, eds., *Economic Development for Latin America* 430 (New York, 1961).

ABC Meier, Gerald M., and Robert E. Baldwin, *Economic Development: Theory, History, Policy.* New York, 1957.

N Meron, Theodor, "Repudiation of *Ultra Vires* State Contracts and the International Responsibility of States," 6 *Int'l & Comp. L. Qu.* 273 (1957).

J Metzger, Stanley D., Comment, 10 *J. Pub. L.* 110 (1961).

K —— "Commercial Treaties of the United States and Private Foreign Investment," 19 *Fed. Bar J.* 367 (1959).

F —— "Exchange Controls and International Law," in P. O. Proehl, ed., *Legal Problems of International Trade* 311 (Urbana, Ill., 1959).

J —— "Multilateral Conventions for the Protection of Private Foreign Investment," 9 *J. Pub. L.* 133 (1960).

B —— "The New International Development Association," 49 *Georgetown L.J.* 23 (1960).

F Mikesell, Raymond F., *Foreign Exchange in the Postwar World.* New York, 1954.

C —— *Foreign Investments in Latin America.* Washington, D.C., 1955.

CD —— *Promoting United States Private Investment Abroad.* Washington, D.C., 1957.

BC —— *United States Economic Policy and International Relations,* New York, 1952.

N Miller, Arthur S., "The Corporation as a Private Government in the World Community," 46 *Va. L. Rev.* 1959 (1960).

J —— "Protection of Private Foreign Investment by Multilateral Convention," 53 *Am. J. Int'l L.* 371 (1959).

L Miller, J. T., "The ECA Guaranties and the Protection and Stimulation of Private Foreign Investment," 39 *Georgetown L.J.* 1 (1950).

AB Millikan, Max F., and Donald L. M. Blackmer, eds., *The Emerging*

Nations: Their Growth and United States Policy. Boston, 1961.

B   Millikan, Max F., and Walt Whitman Rostow, *A Proposal: Key to an Effective Foreign Policy.* New York, 1957.

H   Moodie, A. E., "Agrarian Reform in East Central Europe," 8 *Yb. World Affairs* 242 (1954).

H   Myers, Margaret G., "The Nationalization of Banks in France," 64 *Pol. Sc. Qu.* 189 (1949).

A   Myrdal, Gunnar, *Beyond the Welfare State: Economic Planning and Its International Implications.* New Haven, 1960.

A   —— *Economic Theory and Underdeveloped Regions.* London, 1957. United States edition under the title *Rich Lands and Poor: The Road to World Prosperity.* New York, 1958.

A   —— *An International Economy: Problems and Prospects.* New York, 1956.

C   Nakasian, Samuel, "The Security of Foreign Petroleum Resources," 68 *Pol. Sc. Qu.* 181 (1953).

G   National Council of Applied Economic Research, *Taxation and Foreign Investment.* 2d rev. ed., Bombay, 1958.

H   "La nationalisation des houillères du Nord et du Pas de Calais," 8 *Droit Social* 121 (1945).

H   "La nationalisation des usines Gnôme-et-Rhône et des transports aériens," 8 *Droit Social* 168 (1945).

HI   "Nationalization of the Suez Canal Company," 70 *Harv. L. Rev.* 480 (1957).

H   Newman, Andrew M. de, "Some Economic Aspects of Nationalization," 16 *Law & Contemp. Problems* 702 (1951).

CD   Nichols, Jeannette P., "Hazards of American Private Investment in Underdeveloped Countries," 4 *Orbis* 174 (1960).

M   Norberg, Charles R., "Industrial Incentive Legislation in Latin America," in Washington Foreign Law Society, *A Symposium on the Law of Latin America* 47 (Washington, D.C., 1959).

C   Nurkse, Ragnar, "International Investment To-Day in the Light of Nineteenth-Century Experience," 64 *Econ. J.* 744 (1954).

AC   —— *Problems of Capital Formation in Underdeveloped Countries.* Oxford, 1953.

A   —— "Some International Aspects of the Problems of Economic Development," 42 *Am. Econ. Rev. Proc.* 571 (1952).

N   Nussbaum, Arthur, "The Arbitration between the Lena Goldfields, Ltd., and the Soviet Government," 36 *Cornell L. Qu.* 31 (1950).

I   O'Connell, D. P., "A Critique of the Iranian Oil Litigation," 4 *Int'l & Comp. L. Qu.* 267 (1955).

N   —— "Economic Concessions in the Law of State Succession," 27 *Brit. Yb. Int'l L.* 93 (1950).

HI —— "Legal Issues in the Persian Oil Dispute," 28 *New Zealand L.J.* 57 (1952).

DEF Oliver, Covey T., "Impediments to American Investment in France. A Case Study of Another Aspect of the Restrictive Practices Problem," 2 *Am. J. Comp. L.* 474 (1953).

B Olmstead, Cecil J., "Economic Development Loan Agreements. Part I: Public Economic Development Loan Agreements; Choice of Law and Remedy," 48 *Calif. L. Rev.* 424 (1960).

N —— "Economic Development Agreements. Part II: Agreements between States and Aliens; Choice of Law and Remedy," 49 *Calif. L. Rev.* 504 (1961).

IN —— "Nationalization of Foreign Property Interests, Particularly Those Subject to Agreements with the State," 32 *N.Y.U.L. Rev.* 1122 (1957).

CD Organization for European Economic Co-operation, *Private United States Investment in Europe and the Overseas Territories.* Paris, 1954.

J Parliamentary Group for World Government, *A World Investment Convention?* London, 1959.

BC Pazos, Felipe, "Private versus Public Foreign Investment in Underdeveloped Areas," in H. S. Ellis and H. C. Wallich, eds., *Economic Development for Latin America* 201 (New York, 1961).

N Penrose, E. T., "Profit Sharing Between Producing Countries and Oil Companies in the Middle East," 69 *Econ. J.* 238 (1959).

A Perroux, François, *La coexistence pacifique.* 3 vols., Paris, 1958.

H Person, H. S., *Mexican Oil, Symbol of Recent Trends in International Relations.* New York, 1942.

HI Philonenko, M., "Une des affaires de l'Anglo-Iranian," 81 *J. Droit Int'l* (Clunet) 380 (1954).

K Phleger, Herman, "United States Treaties: Recent Developments," 35 *Dep't State Bull.* 11 (1956).

H Pinkney, David H., "Nationalization of Key Industries and Credit in France after the Liberation," 62 *Pol. Sc. Qu.* 368 (1947).

I Pinney, Harvey, "Property and the International Order," in H. P. Jordan, ed., *Problems of Post-War Reconstruction* 255 (Washington, D.C., 1942).

HI Pinto, Roger, "L'affaire de Suez: Problèmes juridiques," 2 *Annuaire Français Dr. Int'l* 20 (1956).

C Pizer, Samuel, and Frederick Cutler, *U.S. Business Investments in Foreign Countries.* U.S. Department of Commerce, Washington, D.C., 1960.

C —— *U.S. Investments in the Latin American Economy.* U.S. Department of Commerce, Washington, D.C., 1957.

D   "Point Four: A Re-examination of Ends and Means," 59 *Yale L.J.* 1277 (1950).

D   Pomeranz, Morton, "Legal Aspects of the Investment Climate in Latin America," in Washington Foreign Law Society, *A Symposium on the Law of Latin America* 36 (Washington, D.C., 1959).

G   —— "Taxation of United States Investments in Latin America," 44 *Va. L. Rev.* 205 (1958).

J   Porter, Paul R., "Multilateral Protection of Foreign Investment: A Pragmatic Approach," 3 *Int'l Development Rev.* No. 1, 23 (1961).

D   Proehl, Paul O., ed., *Legal Problems of International Trade*. Urbana, Ill., 1959.

J   Proehl, Paul O., "Private Investments Abroad," 9 *J. Pub. L.* 362 (1960).

H   Puget, Henri, ed., *Les nationalisations en France et à l'étranger. II: Les nationalisations à l'étranger*. Paris, 1958.

H   Rado, Alan R., "Czechoslovak Nationalization Decrees: Some International Aspects," 41 *Am. J. Int'l L.* 795 (1947).

N   Ray, G. W., "Law Governing Contracts Between States and Foreign Nationals," in Southwestern Legal Foundation, *Proceedings of the 1960 Institute on Private Investments Abroad* 5 (New York, 1960).

I   Re, Edward D., "The Nationalization of Foreign-Owned Property," 36 *Minn. L. Rev.* 323 (1952).

I   —— "Nationalization and the Investment of Capital Abroad," 42 *Georgetown L.J.* 44 (1953).

C   Reeves, William H., and Paul D. Dickens, "Private Foreign Investments: A Means of World Economic Development," 64 *Pol. Sc. Qu.* 211 (1949).

L   Rivkin, Arnold, "Investment Guaranties and Private Investment," 19 *Fed. Bar J.* 357 (1959).

H   Roblot, René, "La nationalisation du gaz et de l'électricité," 9 *Droit Social* 179 (1946).

HI   —— "La politique des nationalisations et le droit international privé," 12 *Droit Social* 43 (1949).

H   Rode, Zvonko R., "The American-Polish Claims Agreement of 1960," 55 *Am. J. Int'l L.* 452 (1961).

H   —— "The International Claims Commission of the United States," 47 *Am. J. Int'l L.* 615 (1953).

J   Rodriguez Sastre, Antonio, *Organizaciones internationales de cooperacion economica y proteccion de las inversiones extranjeras: situacion de los paises importadores de capital*. Madrid, 1958.

HI   Rolin, Henri, "Avis sur la validité des mesures de nationalisation décrétées par le gouvernement indonésien," 6 *Ned. Tijdschrift voor Int. Recht* 260 (1959).

BC   Rosenstein-Rodan, Paul N., "Les besoins de capitaux dans les pays sous-développés," 7 *Economie Appliquée* 77 (1954).

B   —— "International Aid for Underdeveloped Countries," 53 *Rev. Econ. & Stat.* 107 (1961).

GM   Ross, Stanford G., "Foreign Governments' Tax Incentives for Investment," in Southwestern Legal Foundation, *Proceedings of the 1959 Institute on Private Investments Abroad* 285 (New York, 1959).

A   Rostow, Walt Whitman, *The Stages of Economic Growth: A Non-Communist Manifesto.* Cambridge, 1960.

I   Roth, Andreas H., *The Minimum Standard of International Law Applied to Aliens.* Leiden, 1949.

C   Royal Institute of International Affairs, *The Problem of International Investment.* London, 1937.

I   Rubin, Seymour J., "Nationalization and Compensation: A Comparative Approach," 17 *U. Chi. L. Rev.* 458 (1950).

I   —— "Nationalization and Private Foreign Investment: The Role of Government," 2 *World Politics* 482 (1950).

J   —— "Private Foreign Investment—the ITO Charter and the Bogota Economic Agreement," American Foreign Law Association, *Proceedings* No. 31, November, 1948.

CI   —— *Private Foreign Investment—Legal and Economic Realities.* Baltimore, 1956.

C   Salter, Arthur, *Foreign Investment* (Princeton Essays in International Finance No. 12). Princeton, 1951.

I   Sarraute, R., and P. Tager, "Les effets en France des nationalisations étrangères," 79 *J. Droit Int'l* (Clunet) 496, 1138 (1952).

N   Sarre, D. A. Godwin, and Ayhan Unler, "Modern Oil Laws," 1960 *J. Bus. L.* 181.

H   Scammell, E. H., "Nationalization in Legal Perspective," 5 *Current Legal Problems* 30 (1952).

HI   Scelle, Georges, "La nationalisation du canal de Suez et le droit international," 2 *Annuaire Français Dr. Int'l* 3 (1956).

BC   Schachter, Oscar, "Private Foreign Investment and International Organization," 45 *Cornell L. Qu.* 415 (1960).

H   Schmitthoff, Clive M., "The Nationalization of Basic Industries in Great Britain," 16 *Law & Contemp. Problems* 557 (1951).

J   Schwarzenberger, Georg, "The Abs-Shawcross Draft Convention on Investments Abroad: A Critical Commentary," 9 *J. Pub. L.* 147 (1960).

J   —— "The Abs-Shawcross Draft Convention on Investments Abroad: A Critical Commentary," 14 *Current Legal Problems* 213 (1961).

I   —— "The Protection of British Property Abroad," 5 *Current Legal Problems* 295 (1952).

N   Schwebel, Stephen M., "The Alsing Case," 8 *Int'l & Comp. L. Qu.* 320 (1959).

IN   —— "International Protection of Contractual Arrangements," 53 *Am. Soc. Int'l L. Proc.* 266 (1959).

J   Seidl-Hohenveldern, Ignaz, "The Abs-Shawcross Convention to Protect Private Foreign Investment: Comments on the Round Table," 10 *J. Pub. L.* 100 (1961).

I   —— "Communist Theories on Confiscation and Expropriation: Critical Comments," 7 *Am. J. Comp. L.* 451 (1958).

I   —— "Confiscation et expropriation en droit international," 83 *J. Droit Int'l* (Clunet) 380 (1956).

I   —— *Internationales Konfiskations-und Enteignungsrecht.* Berlin and Tübingen, 1952.

J   Shawcross, Hartley, "The Promotion of International Investment," 8 *NATO Letter* No. 2, 19 (1960).

I   —— "Some Problems of Nationalization in International Law," in International Bar Association, *Fifth International Conference of the Legal Profession, Monte Carlo, 1954* 14 (The Hague, 1954) (separate print).

H   Sharp, S. L., *Nationalization of Key Industries in Eastern Europe.* New York, 1946.

ABC   Simonet, Henri, *La formation du capital dans les pays sous-développés et l'assistance financière étrangère.* Brussels, 1959.

C   Singer, Hans W., "The Distribution of Gains between Investing and Borrowing Countries," 40 *Am. Econ. Rev. Proc.* 473 (1950).

AD   —— "Obstacles to Economic Development," 20 *Social Research* 19 (1953).

G   Singer, Marcel, "Some American Discriminations Against Foreign Enterprises," 11 *Law & Contemp. Problems* 776 (1946).

H   Sipkov, Ivan, "Postwar Nationalizations and Alien Property in Bulgaria," 52 *Am. J. Int'l L.* 469 (1958).

I   Snyder, Earl, "Measure of Compensation for Nationalization of Private Property," 3 *Catholic U.L. Rev.* 107 (1953).

J   —— "Protection of Private Foreign Investment: Examination and Appraisal," 10 *Int'l & Comp. L. Qu.* 469 (1961).

H   Society of Comparative Legislation and International Law, *The Suez Canal: A Selection of Documents Relating to the International Status of the Suez Canal and the Position of the Suez Canal Company.* London, 1956.

J   Society to Advance the Protection of Foreign Investment, *International Convention for the Mutual Protection of Private Property Rights.* Cologne, 1957.

JN   Sohn, Louis B., "Proposals for the Establishment of a System of International Tribunals," in M. Domke, ed., *International Trade Arbitration 63* (New York, 1958).

IN Sohn, Louis B., and R. R. Baxter, "Responsibility of States for Injuries to the Economic Interests of Aliens," 55 *Am. J. Int'l L.* 545 (1961).

A Spengler, Joseph J., "Economic Development: Political Preconditions and Political Consequences," 22 *J. of Politics* 387 (1960).

A Staley, Eugene, *The Future of Underdeveloped Countries: Political Implications of Economic Development.* New York, 1954.

F Stanger, Roland L., "Exchange Control," 17 *Ohio St. L.J.* 302 (1956).

C Stassen, Harold E., "The Case for Private Investment Abroad," 32 *Foreign Affairs* 402 (1954).

N Stephenson, J. F. E., "Persian Gulf Oil Concessions," 4 *Int'l L. Qu.* 503 (1951).

G Sugarman, Norman A., "Current Issues in Taxation of Business Investment Abroad," 17 *Ohio St. L.J.* 277 (1956).

G Surrey, Stanley S., "Current Issues in the Taxation of Corporate Foreign Investment," 56 *Colum. L. Rev.* 815 (1956).

G —— "The United States Taxation of Foreign Income," 1 *J. Law & Econ.* 72 (1958).

G "Tax Incentives to Investment Abroad," 8 *Stanford L. Rev.* 77 (1955).

K Thibodeaux, B., "United States Government Assistance to American Business Abroad," 34 *Dep't State Bull.* 22 (1956).

I Thomas, A. J., "Protection of Property of Citizens Abroad," in Southwestern Legal Foundation, *Proceedings of the 1959 Institute on Private Investments Abroad* 417 (1959).

BC Thorp, Willard, *Trade, Aid or What?* Baltimore, 1954.

IL Tidd, J. Thomas, "The Investment Guaranty Program and the Problem of Expropriation," 26 *Geo. Wash. L. Rev.* 710 (1958).

H Trnec, Miloslav, "Le problème de la nationalisation de l'industrie en Tchecoslovaquie," 9 *Droit Social* 144 (1946).

G Udina, Manlio, *Il Diritto Internazionale Tributario.* Padua, 1949.

H Ujlaki, Nicholas, "Compensation for Nationalization of American Owned Property in Bulgaria, Hungary and Rumania," 1 *New York Law Forum* 265 (1955).

A United Nations, Department of Economic Affairs, *Domestic Financing of Economic Development.* New York, 1950.

G —— *The Effects of Taxation on Foreign Trade and Investment.* New York, 1950.

M —— *Foreign Investment Laws and Regulations of the Countries of Asia and the Far East.* New York, 1951.

BC —— *International Capital Movements During the Inter-War Period.* New York, 1949.

c —— *The International Flow of Private Capital 1946–1952.* New York, 1954.

A —— *Measures for the Economic Development of Underdeveloped Countries* (Report by a Group of Experts). New York, 1951.

ABC —— *Methods of Financing Economic Development in Underdeveloped Countries.* New York, 1949.

G —— *United States Income Taxation of Private United States Investment in Latin America.* New York, 1953.

c United Nations, Department of Economic and Social Affairs, *Foreign Capital in Latin America.* New York, 1955.

B —— *International Economic Assistance to the Less Developed Countries.* New York, 1961.

c —— *The International Flow of Private Capital 1956–1958.* New York, 1959.

M United Nations, Economic Commission for Asia and the Far East, "Laws and Regulations Affecting Foreign Investment in Asia and the Far East," UN Document ECAFE/L. 122, 12 March 1957 (mimeo.).

M United Nations, Office of Legal Affairs, *Survey of Mining Legislation with Special Reference to Asia and the Far East.* Bangkok, 1957.

c United Nations Secretariat, "The International Flow of Private Capital 1953–1955," UN Document E/2901, 21 June 1956 (mimeo.).

c —— "The International Flow of Private Capital 1956," UN Document E/3021, 21 June 1957 (mimeo.).

c —— "The International Flow of Private Capital 1957," UN Document E/3128, 4 June 1958 (mimeo.).

c —— "The International Flow of Private Capital 1958–1959," UN Document E/3369, 13 May 1960 (mimeo.).

c —— "The International Flow of Private Capital 1959–1960," UN Document E/3513, 14 June 1961 (mimeo.).

DJM —— "The Promotion of the International Flow of Private Capital," UN Document E/3325, 26 February 1960 (mimeo.).

D —— "The Promotion of the International Flow of Private Capital," UN Document E/3492, 18 May 1961 (mimeo.).

DM —— "Recent Government Measures Affecting the International Flow of Private Capital," UN Document E/2766, 2 June 1955 (mimeo.).

D —— "The Status of Permanent Sovereignty Over Natural Wealth and Resources," UN Document A/AC. 97/5/Rev. 1, 27 December 1960 (mimeo.).

B U.S. Congress, House of Representatives, Committee on Foreign Affairs, *Staff Memorandum on International Lending Agencies.* Washington, D.C., 1960.

K U.S. Congress, House of Representatives, *Private Foreign Investment.*

Hearings before the Subcommittee on Foreign Trade Policy of the Committee on Ways and Means, 85th Cong., 2d sess. Washington, D.C., 1958.

K   U.S. Congress, Senate, *Commercial Treaties Hearing before a Subcommittee of the Committee on Foreign Relations,* 82d Cong., 2d sess., May 1952. Washington, D.C., 1952.

K   —— *Commercial Treaties Hearing before a Subcommittee of the Committee on Foreign Relations,* 83d Cong., 1st sess., July 13, 1953. Washington, D.C., 1953.

D   U.S. Department of Commerce, *Factors Limiting U.S. Investment Abroad.* Part I: Survey of Factors in Foreign Countries. Part II: Business Views on the U.S. Government's Role. Washington, D.C., 1953, 1954.

DM   —— *Investment in Central America: Conditions and Outlook for United States Investors.* Washington, D.C., 1956.

DM   —— *Investment in Colombia: Conditions and Outlook for United States Investors.* Washington, D.C., 1953.

DM   —— *Investment in India: Conditions and Outlook for United States Investors.* Washington, D.C., 1953.

DM   —— *Investment in Indonesia: Conditions and Outlook for United States Investors.* Washington, D.C., 1956.

DM   —— *Investment in Japan: Conditions and Outlook for United States Investors.* Washington, D.C., 1956.

DM   —— *Investment in Mexico: Conditions and Outlook for United States Investors.* Washington, D.C., 1955.

DM   —— *Investment in Pakistan: Conditions and Outlook for United States Investors.* Washington, D.C., 1954.

DM   —— *Investment in Paraguay: Conditions and Outlook for United States Investors.* Washington, D.C., 1954.

DM   —— *Investment in the Philippines: Conditions and Outlook for United States Investors.* Washington, D.C., 1955.

DM   —— *Investment in Turkey: Conditions and Outlook for United States Investors.* Washington, D.C., 1956.

K   U.S. Department of State, *Commercial Treaty Program of the United States* (Department of State Publication 6565). Washington, D.C., 1958.

L   U.S. Department of State, International Cooperation Administration, *Investment Guaranty Handbook.* Rev. ed., Washington, D.C., 1960.

BL   "United States Agencies and International Organizations Which Foster Private American Investment Abroad," 71 *Harv. L. Rev.* 1102 (1958).

H   Vedel, Georges, "La technique des nationalisations," 9 *Droit Social* 49, 93 (1946).

N Verdross, Alfred, "Protection of Private Property under Quasi-International Agreements," in *Varia Juris Gentium: Liber Amicorum Presented to J. P. A. François* 355 (Leiden, 1959).

I Verzijl, J. H. W., "The Relevance of Public and Private International Law Respectively for the Solution of Problems Arising from Nationalization of Enterprises," 19 *Zeitschrift für ausländisches öffentliches Recht und Völkerrecht* (Festgabe für A. N. Makarov) 531 (1958).

HI Viénot, G., *Nationalisations étrangères et interêts français.* Paris, 1953.

HI Visscher, Paul de, "Les aspects juridiques fondamentaux de la question de Suez," 62 *Rev. Gén. Dr. Int'l Public* 406 (1958).

N Wadmond, Lowell, "The Sanctity of Contract between a Sovereign and a Foreign National," Address at the London meeting of the American Bar Association (mimeo., 1957).

H Waline, Marcel, "Les nationalisations," 8 *Droit Social* 84 (1945).

K Walker, Herman, "Commercial Arbitration in United States Treaties," 11 *Arbitr. J.* 68 (1956).

K —— "Modern Treaties of Friendship, Commerce and Navigation," 42 *Minn. L. Rev.* 805 (1958).

K —— "The Post-War Commercial Treaty Program of the United States," 73 *Pol. Sc. Qu.* 57 (1958).

K —— "Provisions on Companies in United States Commercial Treaties," 50 *Am. J. Int'l L.* 372 (1956).

K —— "Treaties for the Encouragement and Protection of Foreign Investment: Present United States Practice," 5 *Am. J. Comp. L.* 229 (1956).

K —— "United States Treaty Policy on Commercial Arbitration—1946–1957," in M. Domke, ed., *International Trade Arbitration* 49 (New York, 1958).

N Wall, E. H., "The Iranian-Italian Oil Agreement of 1957," 7 *Int'l & Comp. L. Qu.* 736 (1958).

A Wallich, Henry C., "Some Notes Towards a Theory of Derived Development," in A. N. Agarwala and S. P. Singh, eds., *The Economics of Underdevelopment* 189 (Bombay, 1958).

N Wengler, Wilhelm, "Agreements of States with Other Parties than States in International Relations," 8 *Rev. Hell. Dr. Int'l* 113 (1955).

HI White, Gillian, *Nationalisation of Foreign Property.* London, 1961.

L Whitman, Marina von Neumann, *The United States Investment Guaranty Program and Private Foreign Investment* (Princeton Studies in International Finance No. 9). Princeton, 1959.

J Whitney Debevoise, Eli, "Treatment of Private Property of Foreign Nationals in Peace and War—Is a Code Desirable?" in International

Bar Association, *Sixth International Conference of the Legal Profession, Oslo, 1956* (mimeo.).

J   Wilcox, Clair, *A Charter for World Trade*. New York, 1949.

I   Williams, John Fischer, "International Law and the Property of Aliens," 9 *Brit. Yb. Int'l L.* 1 (1928), reprinted in *Chapters in Current International Law and the League of Nations* 147 (London, 1929).

IN   —— "Some Legal Aspects of International Financial Problems," in *Chapters in Current International Law and the League of Nations* 257 (London, 1929).

K   Wilson, Robert R., "Access-to-Court Provisions in U.S. Commercial Treaties," 47 *Am. J. Int'l L.* 20 (1953).

K   —— "A Decade of New Commercial Treaties," 50 *Am. J. Int'l L.* 927 (1956).

I   —— "International Law and Some Contemporary Problems," 52 *Am. Soc. Int'l L. Proc.* 26 (1958).

K   —— *The International Law Standard in Treaties of the United States*. Cambridge, Mass., 1953.

K   —— "Natural-Resources Provisions in U.S. Commercial Treaties," 48 *Am. J. Int'l L.* 355 (1954).

K   —— "Postwar Commercial Treaties of the United States," 42 *Am. J. Int'l L.* 262 (1949).

K   —— "Property-Protection Provisions in United States Commercial Treaties," 45 *Am. J. Int'l L.* 83 (1951).

K   —— " 'Treaty Investor' Clauses in Commercial Treaties of the United States," 49 *Am. J. Int'l L.* 366 (1955).

K   —— " 'Treaty Merchant' Clauses in Commercial Treaties of the United States," 44 *Am. J. Int'l L.* 145 (1950).

K   —— *United States Commercial Treaties and International Law*. New Orleans, 1960.

ACD   Wolf, Charles, and Sidney C. Sufrin, *Capital Formation and Foreign Investment in Underdeveloped Areas*. Rev. ed., Syracuse, N.Y., 1958.

CD   Woolsey, Lester H., "The Problem of Foreign Investment," 42 *Am. J. Int'l L.* 121 (1948).

H   —— "The United States Mexican Settlement," 36 *Am. J. Int'l L.* 117 (1942).

J   Wortley, B. A., "Examination of Draft of International Chamber of Commerce Code of Fair Treatment for Foreign Investments," in International Bar Association, *Third International Conference of the Legal Profession, London, 1950* 241 (The Hague, 1952).

I   —— "Expropriation in International Law," 33 *Grotius Soc. Transactions* 25 (1947).

I — *Expropriation in Public International Law.* Cambridge, Eng., 1959.

HI — "Indonesian Nationalization Measures—An Intervention," 55 *Am. J. Int'l L.* 680 (1961).

H — "The Mexican Oil Dispute 1938–1946," 43 *Grotius Soc. Transactions* 15 (1957).

I — "Observations on the Public and Private International Law Relating to Expropriation," 5 *Am. J. Comp. L.* 577 (1956).

I — "Les problèmes soulevés en droit international privé par la législation sur l'expropriation," 67 *Hague Recueil* 345 (1939).

I — "The Protection of Property Situated Abroad," 35 *Tul. L. Rev.* 739 (1961).

L   Wu, Yuan-li, "Government Guarantees and Private Foreign Investment," 40 *Am. Econ. Rev.* 61 (1950).

Table of Cases

Table of Statutes

INCLUDING DECREES AND STATEMENTS OF GOVERNMENT
POLICY RELATING TO FOREIGN INVESTMENT

Note: Where two dates are given, the second date is that of publication or final promulgation of the instrument

Index of Names

The names in this index appear in notes on the pages cited.

Index of Subjects

Abs-Shawcross Draft Convention, 82-83, 132, 137, 140, 144, 146, 166-67, 174, 230; on arbritration, 182-84; on expropriation, 166-67

Abuse of Rights, 282*n*, 296 *ff*; as misuse of power, 226, 298-301; Harvard Draft Convention on, 282*n*, 300-1; as a general principle, 296-97

Adjudication, 86, 180-89, 228, 351-55; in concessions, 127, 187-89, 291; in FCN treaties, 184-85; in investment codes, 77, 180-84; in investment guarantees, 185-86; in investment laws, 186-87

Afghanistan, 101, 140-41, 159, 163

Africa, 17, 74, 76-77, 115

Aliens, 131-32, 137, 167-68, 214-15; business activities of, 41 *ff*, 141-48, 215-17; *see also* Employment of aliens; Expropriation; Most-favored-nation treatment; National treatment; Standards of treatment; State Contracts

Arbitration, *see* Adjudication

Asia, 17, 32

Australia, 2

Austria, 335

Balance-of-payments, 38, 47-48, 135

Belgium, 97 (*table*), 332

Bogota Economic Agreement, 72-73, 91, 130, 153, 174, 180; on exchange restrictions, 72, 153; on expropriation, 72, 164

Bolivia, 160, 163, 306

Bottlenecks, in economic development, 12 *ff*, 31 *ff*

Brazil, 43, 46*n*, 188

Burma, 2, 42, 46, 101, 163, 171-72

Cambodia, 172

Canada, 2, 25-26

Capital, domestic: in economic development, 12-16; need for foreign, 11, 16; role in economic development, 11 *ff*; *see also* Investment

Capital-exporting countries, 2-3, 75, 88-91, 225, 306; proposals for coalition of, 81, 83, 88

Capital-importing countries, 3 *ff*, 71, 75, 100, 102, 110, 120-28, 133, 173, 231, 306; attitude to proposed codes, 72, 87-92

Chile, 43, 46*n*, 193; guarantees on exchange control, 162; guarantees on taxation, 176-77

China, Republic of, 94*n*, 173

Colombia, 42, 97 (*table*)

Compensation, 72, 79-80, 86, 154, 164 *ff*, 224-25, 273-74, 302-38, 345-47; adequate, 168-69, 325-31, 333; assessment of, 315-25; effective, 325, 332-33; prompt, 169, 325, 331; recent state practice on, 272-73, 302-7; restitution and pecuniary compensation, 310-14, 347

Concessions, 84, 125-28, 187-89, 194-95, 233; distinguished from other contracts, 125-26; legal character, 125, 192 *ff*, 205-8; *see also* State contracts

Confiscation, *see* Expropriation

Conseil d'Etat, 198